Perspectives in Special Education
Personal Orientations

Burton Blatt
Syracuse University

Richard J. Morris
The University of Arizona

Scott, Foresman and Company
Glenview, Illinois

Dallas, Texas
Oakland, New Jersey
Palo Alto, California
Tucker, Georgia
London

To Ethel and Vinnie

Scott, Foresman Series in Special Education
Series Editor
Richard J. Morris, The University of Arizona

Library of Congress Cataloging in Publication Data
Main entry under title:

Perspectives in special education.

  Includes bibliographies and indexes.
  Contents: [1] Personal orientations.
  1. Mentally handicapped children—Education—United
States. 2. Exceptional children—Education—United
States. 3. Teachers of mentally handicapped children—
United States—Biography. 4. Teachers of exceptional
children—United States—Biography. I. Blatt, Burton,
1927-   II. Morris, Richard J.
LC4631.P47   1984   371.9   83-20243
ISBN 0-673-16566-3 (v. 1)

1 2 3 4 5 6 - KPF - 89 88 87 86 85 84

Preface

Embedded in the purpose and substance of *Perspectives in Special Education: Personal Orientations* is the belief that professionals in the field of special education should learn about our scholars and activists as well as about their scholarship and accomplishments. Of course, over the years we do pick up information about our leaders. When we were students, we enjoyed direct contacts with professors, and we learned about the personal lives and interests of those individuals who devote themselves to ideas and their implementation. As teachers, administrators, and other professionals in the various fields which contribute to special education, we have met and sometimes know intimately those people who have "labored in the vineyards" and made remarkable contributions to the thinking and practice of our professional lives. But, useful as those interactions have been, the resulting impressions of the scholar's or activist's life are fragmentary; they seldom include an appreciation of these individuals as flesh-and-bones human beings. Partly, this is because learning about the leader is almost always incidental to the work in which a student or professional is engaged. Moreover, even if intentionally sought, information about pioneers in our field is not readily available in the ordinary course of university study or professional activities.

Of course, the people invited to write chapters for this book have published many books and articles themselves, but these works almost always present the *results* of scholarly activity rather than ideas of what the activity itself is like. Indeed, it can be said that the more elegant and powerful a published work is, the more likely it is to conceal rather than reveal the person who created it. In this book, we have endeavored to present the scholar himself as well as what he has done, the activities of the activist as well as the accomplishments.

Specifically, we have asked these ten professionals and friends in the field of special education to explore their own understanding of how they came to enjoy and embrace the intellectual life, how their ideas were and are articulated and refined, and to share with us their lives as teachers, as shakers and movers, and simply as people. We wanted them to uncover for our readers how gifted scholars and activists think. We are convinced that the intellectual territory in which one lives is never confined to a narrow academic or administrative niche and that the "greater" the scholar or administrator the more extensive his or her territory is likely to be. While specialized study represents a sharpness of focus, it need not represent a narrowness of vision. Each contributor to this volume has come to identify his specialty as the fulcrum of his life—related to all other aspects of his existence, from the interests of his job to his obligations to civilization. It is a major purpose of this book to understand how this happens.

In order to understand *what* and *how* a leader thinks, it is important to study his or her *intellectual* history. The question of how a person becomes a *leader*, although enormously instructive, deviates from our central concern with how leaders think and act. Therefore, while we have invited these contributors to be as personal as they care—and dare—to be, the most significant question for us will always be what goes on in the mind of the leader.

Why the study of these particular leaders, these personal orientations? Because we think that the most important gains in understanding are made at the boundaries and limits of phenomena: illness teaches us about health, revolution about government, stress about endurance, and tragedy about the value of life. By definition, intellectual and administrative achievements occur at the boundaries. By their nature, inventions and discoveries exist well away from the mode; they are new, unfamiliar, strange, and difficult to grasp. Therefore, we have consciously sought out original thinkers who are also accomplished scholars, policy makers, and program leaders. We have sought out people who "see" connections and implications that go beyond conventional ideas. We have attempted to invite contributors who have the vision to sustain ideas which others do not see. We have looked for people who have concern for the future—particularly as education can influence our society, particularly as special education can heal wounds rather than inflict them. We have tried to interest colleagues who desire to make the world a better place for all people. We have tried to interest authors who are the kinds of individuals who we will not only want to learn from but who live lives we want to understand. Lastly, we have invited these people not only because they have a willingness to share their lives with us but because they seem to have mastered that paradox between what is known and what can be accomplished, the paradox which drives many people to lower their aspiration and ideals. That is, we seem to have attracted authors who are both awed with the world yet serene about their place in it.

Simply, we have asked each of the contributors to this book to reflect on these questions: What have you learned from your years as teacher, administrator, and/or scholar in the broad field of special education? Who influenced you and your writings? What accomplishments do you most value? What still remains as an enigma to you? What directions should the field take in the next five years, ten years, fifty years? In retrospect, what mistakes have we made—what mistakes have you made—what embarrassments have we suffered, what joys and successes can we claim as a field? If we could "do it all over again," what should *we* now do differently? What would *you* now do differently? What still puzzles you about the field? What are your unanswered questions? What are you doing now? Where are you going?

As editors, we wish to express sincerest gratitude to our distinguished contributors and to Chris Jennison, Molly Gardiner, and the superb Scott, Foresman editorial staff. We also want to thank our many colleagues in Arizona and Syracuse who help make the writing of books a joy as well as a responsibility. We hope you enjoy the work nearly as much as we enjoyed and were inspired by the effort in putting it together for you.

Burton Blatt

Richard J. Morris

Contents

Overview

Seymour Sarason, author of the first chapter, was introduced to the field of mental retardation in the 1930s, and has been making significant contributions to it ever since. One need only peruse the bibliography at the end of his chapter to realize the contribution that he has made to mental retardation and the education of special needs children. Dr. Sarason's discussion of those factors that contributed to the shaping of his career makes for fascinating reading, beginning with his undergraduate experiences at the University of Newark, continuing through his doctoral studies at Clark University, into his early work at the Southbury (Connecticut) State Training School, and, finally, his four exciting decades of teaching at Yale. In his chapter, Dr. Sarason also provides the reader with the insights into the people and events which led him to write by himself (and with others) some of the most influential books in the field of mental retardation.

Chapter 2 is written by an individual whom many professionals in the field have called the father of modern day special education, namely, **Samuel Kirk.** Not only did Dr. Kirk establish at the University of Illinois one of the first university-based graduate programs on research and teacher preparation in special education (in the early 1950s)[1], it was he who suggested the term *learning disabilities* in 1963 to a conference of parent organizations concerned with brain injured, dyslexic, and perceptually handicapped children and who, in turn, contributed substantially to the formation in that same year of the Association for Children with Learning Disabilities. Finally, it was Dr. Kirk who was invited to Washington in 1954 to help the Office of Education develop what later became the Bureau of Education for the Handicapped (with Dr. Kirk as its first director in the early 1960s). He also influenced markedly the careers of a number of scholars in special education, two of whom, James Gallagher and Herbert Goldstein, are contributors to this volume. Dr. Kirk traces his career from his early days at the University of Chicago, through his experiences at the Institute for Juvenile Research in Chicago and Wayne County (Michigan) Training School, to his doctoral studies at the University of Michigan, and his later teaching experiences at Milwaukee State Teachers College and nearly two decades of work at the University of Illinois as Director of the Institute for Research on Exceptional Children. Dr. Kirk's professional career and scholarly works span more than a half of a century, and his account of his life and contributions to special education is fascinating.

The third chapter is by **Herbert Goldstein,** a person who has made major

---

[1] Two other university-based graduate programs in research and teacher preparation in special education were established during these years by William Cruickshank at Syracuse University and Lloyd Dunn at Peabody College.

contributions to special education in the area of curriculum development and to our understanding of people labeled mentally retarded. Dr. Goldstein first discusses his undergraduate education at San Francisco State College as an elementary education major, his subsequent disenchantment with this area, and his later change to special education. He then addresses issues regarding curriculum development and teacher preparation, offers a candid view of his teaching internship experiences at Sonoma (California) State School, and reviews his first teaching job in special education with educable mentally handicapped children. Deftly and even humorously described by Dr. Goldstein, these experiences provide the reader with a penetrating analysis of a budding teacher's perspective on educating (handicapped) children. Dr. Goldstein then discusses his doctoral studies at the University of Illinois with Samuel Kirk, a period during which he was able to pursue his scholarly interests in societal factors relating to mental retardation, as well as his research on curriculum development. We are also introduced to the influence on his professional life of his Fulbright research scholarship in Norway, his subsequent move to New York City to build a special education department at Yeshiva University, and his thirteen-year research project on the Social Learning Curriculum. Dr. Goldstein closes his masterful chapter with a series of thought-provoking commentaries and reflections on the field of special education.

Chapter 4 is written by **William Morse,** one of the foremost leaders in the education of emotionally handicapped children. Dr. Morse writes skillfully about his undergraduate experiences at the University of Pittsburgh and University of Michigan, where he was first oriented toward the field of law but switched later to English drama and literature. He then discusses his graduate studies at Michigan in educational psychology, noting that his work with disturbed youth and delinquents during these early years at a summer camp, the Fresh Air Camp, led to his emphasis on clinical teaching. He also mentions that his approach to teaching emotionally disturbed children was influenced by Fritz Redl, by some of the children at camp, and by Bill Rhodes, who extended Redl's concept of milieu and became the "clarifier of the ecological position" regarding emotional disturbance in children. Dr. Morse then addresses a number of issues in education and discusses some of the factors that he believes are related to effective teaching. He also offers a thought-provoking commentary on scientific research as it is applied to the educational setting—stating that too often we examine variables rather than the person(s) who exhibits the variables—and then closes his chapter with a lively discussion of the future, as well as a look at the progress we have made in special education.

In Chapter 5, **Robert B. Edgerton** reflects on his fascinating study of mentally retarded persons from an anthropological perspective. Dr. Edgerton explains that he was introduced to the field of mental retardation following a job at Pacific State Hospital (outside of Los Angeles). Although he only intended to keep this job for a short time before a trip to East Africa to conduct anthropological research on culture and ecology, his experiences at Pacific were so positive that they led him to channel much of his subsequent research efforts into the study of mentally retarded persons. Dr. Edgerton recounts that many staff and consultants at Pacific confirmed his view that mental retardation is a social and cultural phenomenon, not just psychological and biological. Dr. Edgerton also describes the people, events, and insights that led to the publication in 1967 of his well-received book, *The Cloak of Competence,* and to his interest in the IQ controversy and labeling theory. He ends his chapter with a detailed discussion of his current research efforts and concerns regarding the field of mental retardation.

Chapter 6 is written by **Robert Guthrie,** the physician and microbiologist who developed screening tests to detect such rare metabolic conditions in infants as phenylketonuria (PKU). Medical research has shown that if this disease is detected and treated early enough in an infant's life, mental retardation can be avoided. Dr. Guthrie reviews his career from his under-graduate days at the University of Minnesota, to his medical school work at Minnesota, his masters work in microbiology at the University of Maine, and his doctoral work at Minnesota. He then discusses his research work in the mid-1940s to early 1950s at the National Institutes of Health (NIH) in Washington, D.C., his research at the Sloan-Kettering Institute for Cancer Research in New York City, and his positions at the Roswell Park Memorial Institute in Buffalo, New York, and the Buffalo Children's Hospital—leading to his fascinating discovery of the PKU screening test. Following this discussion, Dr. Guthrie briefly describes some of his recent research and presents a compelling commentary on the importance of directing our emphasis as professionals toward preventing mental retardation.

The next chapter (Chapter 7) is by **James Gallagher,** a leading researcher in the fields of special education and early childhood education and one of our foremost experts on gifted education. Dr. Gallagher traces his life from his undergraduate work at the University of Pittsburgh to his early work with retarded persons at Southbury (Connecticut) State Training School—where he met Seymour Sarason—to his doctoral studies at the Pennsylvania State University, and his experiences on the faculties of Michigan State University, University of Illinois, and the University of North Carolina at Chapel Hill. Dr. Gallagher devotes a good deal of space to the influence that Samuel Kirk had on his career and discusses how the Illinois experience helped shape the research and scholarly work that he did. He also reviews his research and writings on gifted children and gifted education, discusses his work in Washington, D.C., as director of the Bureau of Education for the Handi-capped, and ends his chapter by addressing some of the unresolved issues that he feels we still face in special education.

Chapter 8 is written by a leading scholar in the field of mental retardation and child development, **Edward Zigler.** In this chapter he first recounts his early experiences working with retarded children while he was a graduate student at the University of Texas at Austin and then places into captivating perspective the quarter of a century research that he and his colleagues have conducted in mental retardation. Dr. Zigler reflects critically on this discussion and offers some of his own beliefs on the meaning of this research. This is followed by a discussion of some of the critical issues in the field of mental retardation. Although he states that "the field of mental retardation is nearly unrecognizable from the time I happened into it some 25 years ago," it is largely because of Dr. Zigler's own research and scholarly writings, as well as those of his colleagues and students, that the field "is nearly unrecognizable" today. His work at Yale, as well as his leadership in Washington, D.C., at the National Institute for Child and Human Development, has proven Dr. Zigler to be one of the most distinguished scholars in the field of mental retardation.

In Chapter 9, **Richard L. Schiefelbusch** discusses his many years of noted research and service as a speech clinician and director of the Bureau of Child Research at the University of Kansas; he also reviews the various events, people, and activities that contributed to the shaping of his distinguished professional career. One such event was his two-year experience as a German prisoner of war during World War II in the Luftwaffe camp at Sagan, which directed him later to seek training in one of the helping professions. After the war, he enrolled in graduate school at the University of Kansas and decided to enter the fields of clinical psychology and speech pathology, completing his doctoral work at Northwestern University. Before receiving his doctoral degree, however, he returned to the University of Kansas to start a speech and hearing clinic which he directed for seven years. In 1955, Dr. Schiefelbusch was appointed director of the university's Bureau of Child Research (BCR), a position he has held for the past twenty-seven years. He describes in detail the early beginnings of and the people associated with BCR and traces the growth of its research projects over the subsequent years to the international renown of its present activities. Dr. Schiefelbusch then offers an excellent discussion of the variations in the meaning of the term "research," and provides some personal reflections on applied behavior analysis and its applications to various types of handicapping conditions. He closes his chapter with a brief account of some of the remaining puzzles that he perceives in special education and related fields.

The last chapter (Chapter 10) is written by one of the two editors, Burton Blatt. Dr. Blatt's contributions to special education cover nearly every aspect of the field. In his chapter he reviews his professional career, starting with a discussion of his first professional position as a public school teacher in 1949, followed by his doctoral studies at The Pennsylvania State University and his subsequent experiences as a faculty member at Southern Connecticut State College, Boston University, and Syracuse University. In his summary of each of these experiences, Dr. Blatt describes some of the people who helped shape his professional life, such as Richard Hungerford, Margaret Neuber, Seymour Sarason, and Fred Finn. He also discusses the people, events, and circumstances underlying his scholarly work and activities as an activist, his appointment as director of mental retardation for the Commonwealth of Massachusetts, and his years at Boston University and Syracuse University.

Burton Blatt

Richard J. Morris

1

Unlearning and Learning

Seymour B. Sarason

Seymour B. Sarason, born 1919 in Brooklyn, New York, received his B.A. in psychology from the University of Newark (1939) and his M.A. (1940) and Ph.D. (1942) in psychology from Clark University.

From 1942 to 1946 Dr. Sarason held the position of chief psychologist at the Southbury (Connecticut) Training School. He is currently professor of psychology at Yale University (1955–   ), where he has also served as assistant professor of psychology (1946–49), associate professor of psychology (1949–55), director of the graduate program in Clinical Psychology (1948–56), and director of the Yale Psycho-Educational Clinic (1963–70).

A past president of the Division of Clinical Psychology of the American Psychological Association, he has received Distinguished Contributions Awards from the divisions of Clinical and Community Psychology, and from the American Association on Mental Deficiency. He was awarded an honorary degree of Doctor of Humane Letters by Syracuse University in 1983.

My introduction to the field of mental retardation came in courses I took from Dr. Fred Gaudet at the University of Newark (now a Rutgers campus) between 1935–39. More important than the contents of these courses was my identification with Dr. Gaudet's questioning, critical attitude toward conventional wisdom: political, sexual, economic, and almost everything else. He was not a nihilist but rather someone who looked at the world through a comic/tragic lens. There was a "compliance factor" within me: as a political radical in a Trotskyite sect, I was quite responsive to a professor who seemed to turn any answer to a problem on its head. He was a superb classroom teacher and a gracious, helping counselor. In almost every one of his courses he taught some aspect of the nature-nurture controversy and, needless to say, conveyed to us the dangers of oversimplification and premature closure. As important to me as his attitudes was the simple fact that I was exposed to a broad spectrum of reading on mental retardation. It says a good deal about Dr. Gaudet that in the fall of 1939 he arranged for Dr. Lloyd Yepsen, a psychologist from the central office of New Jersey's Department of Institutions and Agencies, to teach a course in mental subnormality. Dr. Yepsen was a well-known figure in the field, less for his writings than for his leadership role in the American Association on Mental Deficiency. (Several years later he and Cianci did some important work helping families with severely retarded children.) His course was a fascinating but very "different" experience because, unlike Dr. Gaudet, he obviously believed that nature was far more powerful than nurture. In fact, when I and others disagreed with his position, he was taken aback and undoubtedly wondered what on earth Dr. Gaudet had been teaching us. There is no doubt that my emphasis on the power of nurture derived more from passion and political belief than it did from cold reason. But it is also true that Dr. Yepsen was less than skeptical about the nature of the evidence (he talked rather favorably about Goddard's Kallikak studies). His course was what a college seminar should be: give and take relatively uncontaminated by differences in status. One topic that Dr. Yepsen took up that several years later had fateful consequences for my life and career: the psychological assessment of the nature and consequences of brain injury. But more about that later.

I was fortunate to have gone to the University of Newark—formerly Dana College and housed in the former Feiganspan Brewery. A college for commuters, always struggling for survival, it was for all practical purposes unknown. I learned this when I applied to fifteen graduate schools, at least one of which said that, in the unlikely event I should be admitted, it would be on a probationary basis. I was rejected by all schools except Clark University; only later did I learn that Clark, most of whose distinguished faculty had left as a result of controversy with its president, could not be fussy about choosing graduate students. How could these schools have known that at Newark I had been exposed to an amazing number of stimulating, conscientious, even charismatic faculty? In economics, psychology, Shakespeare, anthropology (taught by Dr. Robert Watson, a psychologist), geology, the history of science—new worlds had been opened to me. What I did not fully comprehend at the time was how important it would be for me to be in the world of ideas and intellectual give and take. The thought had never occurred to me that I might be, or even want to be, in a university. Whatever thoughts I had about my future were directed to settings outside the university. In fact, up until the fall of my senior year I thought I would apply to law school, although my family had absolutely no funds to send me anywhere. Either I would get a scholarship (an unrealistic possibility) or work part-time and go to school at night. It was Dr. Gaudet who counseled me to apply to graduate school in psychology.

Why did the possibility of a university career never occur to me during my college years? One part of the answer is that nobody in my extended family had ever held a position in a university. There were, as one might expect in a Jewish family, a cousin who was a physician, a cousin who was a high school teacher, and an uncle by marriage who was a lawyer. Learning and achievement were treasured pursuits in my milieu, but never did I hear a word about a university career. That possibility was as foreign as becoming an airplane pilot. Neither my mother nor father, both born in Russia, were worldly. Quite the contrary: they were poor, struggling people who wanted "the best" for their children; that meant some kind of white-collar position that would give us some economic stability. The Great Depression was a horrendous experience for us. I knew times when there was no food in the house. To add injury to insult, I was crippled by polio. In fact, if it were not for the support I received from a state agency for "crippled children" (the euphemism "handicapped" was not yet in vogue), I would not have been able to go to the University of Newark.

Another part of the answer is more subtle and something of which I was not aware until I began to think about writing this chapter: with one exception, none of my college instructors was Jewish. (That was also the case in graduate school.) Today we talk about role models and how important they are for minority individuals. If you belong to a racial, or ethnic, or religious minority, to be taught by people with whom you share kinship can make a difference. For example, during my high school years many of my teachers were Jewish, as was the principal. At the very least, that said to me that being a high school teacher was a possibility. Such was not the case in college and graduate school. The university was intellectually entrancing and enthralling, but vocationally it was off limits for me. It was not that anybody said it was off limits but that nothing I experienced in college and graduate school allowed me to say to myself, "Why not seek to become a member of a university faculty?" The situation changed remarkably after World War II, and what had been off limits to me became on limits to succeeding generations of different minority students. When, with increasing frequency, undergraduate and graduate minority students would tell me they were headed for a career in the university, it all seemed natural. The explanation is complex but one of the factors is the change in the ethnic, religious, gender, racial composition of college and university faculties in the post-World War II era.

In my first year at Clark I took a social psychology course from Dr. Raymond Cattell, a British psychologist who later achieved some eminence in the field. This was the first time I had sustained interaction with an authority who believed that although nature may not explain everything, it comes very close to doing so. I will never forget a discussion during which Dr. Cattell asserted that salesmen were born "that way." He introduced us to the British and American literature on the nature-nurture problem which, from my standpoint, he interpreted in a most one-sided way. Dr. Cattell took his position very seriously, and that meant he favored public policies sanctioning sterilization and supporting the eugenics movement. It may be true (I doubt it) that I was no less one-sided in the opposite direction, but it is also true that I believed the future would show that the problem was far more complex than either of us thought. Although I did a lot of reading and thinking, I learned little or nothing about mentally retarded *individuals* and the myriad contexts in which they live. I learned a great deal about the IQ (its ups and downs and measurement) and about theories of intelligence. But what I learned was essentially "bookish" and had no basis in the observation of and interaction with individuals labeled either subnormal or mentally retarded. Then, as now, it was a cliché to say that each individual is unique, but apparently that truth did not hold for mentally retarded people. They were not considered interesting (let alone important) as individuals, but only as a class of unfortunate people—unfortunate, that is, for a society that had to tolerate them. That these individuals were born and reared into families with consequences ranging from disaster to unrivaled heroism; that responses to them ranged from outright rejection to unqualified love and devotion; that there were intellectual, social, and behavioral differences among those with the same label or diagnosis—about these facts I learned nothing.

I received my doctorate in 1942, six months after the beginning of our involvement in World War II. In the winter of my last year, I and two fellow student-friends (Jorma Niven and Harry Older) prepared vitae that we would send to colleges and universities, making sure that no two of us would apply to the same institution. In all my years at Yale I have always written introductory letters for my students to friends around the country telling them that I had a student tailor-made for them. If there was interest, I then told the student to submit his or her formal credentials. It makes a difference if the first letter comes from a faculty member rather than from a student. At Clark the faculty gave us no help whatsoever. One reason may have been that with our involvement in the war it appeared that colleges and universities would be denuded of students and that some institutions might even disappear. In any event, I remember discussing with my friends whether I should put on my vita that I was Jewish. In graduate school I had learned that placing Jewish

Ph.D.'s in universities was no easy matter. I was aware that there were Jewish psychologists at the Worcester State Hospital who had not been able to find teaching jobs. David Shakow, Saul Rosenzweig, Eliot Rodnick, Julian Rotter—all were at the state hospital and all became well-known academic psychologists in the post-World War II era. And they came from the "best" universities, including Yale and Harvard. Why should I, coming from Clark, expect to do better than they? Why not put on my vita the fact that I was Jewish and save myself and others from embarrassing situations? The fact is that my friends received offers and I did not. Since I viewed preparing and sending my vita as an empty ritual I was spared *any* feelings of disappointment. How could I feel disappointed when my level of expectation was zero?

At about the same time I learned that there was to be a civil service examination in Connecticut for clinical psychologists. *That* was a possibility that interested me and was within the compass of my expectations. There were three openings: one in a state hospital and two in institutions for the retarded. I took the exam, and therein lies the story I alluded to earlier when I talked about Dr. Lloyd Yepsen. The exam consisted of three essay questions. I do not remember the first two, but the last question was on the psychological diagnosis of brain injury, so I regurgitated everything Dr. Yepsen had taught us about it. I must have regurgitated rather well because I came out first on the written exam. A number of those who took the exam had far more clinical experience than I, had had their doctorates for a year or more, and had published (most of them were Jewish, *of course*). You have to be lucky, and I was.

And where was the oral exam held? First let me tell you that whenever I went home from Worcester to Newark, the bus would make a stop in New Haven within sight of Yale. The bus would stop near the Taft Hotel and then maneuver past Yale's Institute of Human Relations which, I knew, housed the Department of Psychology. I always felt awe when I saw Gothic Yale. It was a world I would never know. And so when I was told that the oral exam would be in the Institute of Human Relations, it was exciting and unsettling. When I walked into the room—the seminar room in which for decades I would conduct my classes—and was introduced to the examining committee, I felt I had no right to be there. The committee consisted of Donald Marquis and Robert Sears of Yale, and Richard Wendt of Wesleyan. I knew these people as "names" in American psychology, and had also been required to read their research publications. I have no memory about what went on in my orals except Don Marquis' Socratic manner, Bob Sears' sensitive probings, and Dick Wendt's serious, hard-nosed interpersonal style. Beyond that I only remember thinking to myself, "What in hell am I doing at Yale trying to answer the questions of these luminaries?" Apparently I did OK—which means that I did not make a damned fool of myself.

When I learned I had come out first on the examinations, I felt a sense of relief because I knew that I would have some kind of job. It also meant that I did not have to sit and wait for replies to my inquiries to a couple of score of colleges and universities. I arranged for interviews at the Norwich State Hospital and the Mansfield and Southbury State Training Schools.

I first visited Southbury, which had been open only a few months. That Southbury quickly became an international showcase was due in part to its architectural features. It looked like a new college campus nestled at the foot of and spreading upward to the surrounding hills. There was a score of red brick, residential cottages, some housing as few as twenty people and others double that number. Each cottage had a (married) "mother and father" and a cook. It was as homelike as possible and the opposite of any public institution I (or anyone else) had ever seen. The school building was spacious and extraordinarily well equipped—including a barber shop, a beauty shop, and a "clothing store" to which residents would come to be outfitted. It lacked nothing. The living quarters and dining rooms for employees were aesthetically delightful.

Aside from its architecture, Southbury, I was told, was an *educational* and not a *medical* institution. The major educational aim was to prepare its residents for return to home and community, and that meant that residents should experience a homelike atmosphere in which education and training would go on. This was called the "revolving door" policy: Southbury was not going to be a custodial institution. Residents would come in and go out.

Three things stood out in that first visit. First, the sincerity and seriousness with which everyone talked about the importance of the needs of the residents. Second, the director of the medical department, a pediatric researcher (Dr. Herman Yannet), was interested only in medical problems, which did not include what happened in the educational and cottage-life departments; notwithstanding, Southbury was *not* a medically-dominated institution. And if there was any doubt about that, it was erased by the third factor—*Mr.* Ernest Roselle, Superintendent. Mr. Roselle was one of the most remarkable individuals I had ever met. If Mr. Roselle had not been the moral person he was, he could have sold the Brooklyn Bridge at least ten times a day. He was not only a salesman-entrepreneur but a frustrated architect and engineer. Frustrated, that is, until he became consultant to the board of trustees who had been given the responsibility to plan and build Southbury. Mr. Roselle, who had a masters degree in education and had been Superintendent of Mooseheart (run for troubled youth by the Loyal Order of Moose), knew very little about mental retardation, but no one could teach him anything about what constituted a gracious, humane environment. To Mr. Roselle, the Training School (a private facility) at Vineland, was Mecca, and Dr. Edgar Doll was prophet. Roselle's knowledge of the field may have been superficial, but he knew what a quality place and person was. I was mightily impressed by Southbury (= Mr. Roselle).

Then I visited the Mansfield Training School, which for decades had been the only residential facility for mentally retarded people. In fact, Southbury was built because Mansfield had a very long waiting list and, in addition, pressure had been put on state officials to plan and build a facility for the southern half of the state. It was Governor Wilbur Cross, former dean of the Yale Graduate School, who appointed the commission in the mid-thirties to plan for a new institution that later became Southbury. Mansfield was a typical looking and typically run state institution. It looked old and in all other respects was old. The Superintendent was a physician—and not a subtle man. He began the interview by asking me about the origins of my last name. Within thirty seconds he knew I was Jewish and my parents had come from Russia. And in thirty seconds I decided that if I had to choose between Southbury and Mansfield, it was no contest. He informed me that he wanted "his" psychologist to use the 1917 Binet (not the 1937 revision) because that was the test that had long been used at Mansfield.

My last visit was to the state hospital, and I shall say no more about it except that as a consequence of my externship at Worcester State Hospital I wanted no part of a psychiatrically dominated institution. If that had been the only position available to me, I would have accepted it, but only as a last resort. I should add that the Department of Psychology in that hospital had very good people, but I was also aware that I would be one of a group and would have to adjust to its ways. Vaguely I knew that I would do best where I could, for all practical purposes, go my own way. What "my own way" meant I could not have defined in clear terms. I knew that I would be largely involved in psychological testing wherever I worked, but I also knew that I wanted and *needed* more than that. I was ambitious. I had and have as rich a fantasy life as anyone. I wanted to make a difference, to become well known, even famous, but I had no idea how or when that would happen. It is clearer to me now than it was then that part of me has always been very skeptical about tradition, received knowledge, and authority. That clearly was the case in my political attitudes and affiliations, but it was no less true in other spheres. I do not, I think, have a markedly oppositional character. I have always wanted to make a difference, and that motivation powered and directed my thinking. That type of motivation is dangerous—a double-edged sword which the possessor should regard with ambivalence and even fear.

THE SOUTHBURY EXPERIENCE

I could write a book about my Southbury experience, and some day I may. What I learned and unlearned there has influenced *everything* I subsequently thought and did. This is not hyperbole but phenomenologically a true statement. Over the decades I have written a fair number of books, some of which appear to bear no relationship to mental retardation. A close reading, however, reveals that Southbury is either explicitly in them or they implicitly reflect ideas and experiences from those years. Southbury not only *shaped* me but provided *substance*, an intellectual capital, from which I still draw interest and stimulation. Southbury was geographically in the middle of nowhere (a rustic, beautiful nowhere), but to me it was and is a microcosm of the whole social world. Because of what Southbury meant to me and because of the purposes of this chapter, I shall only briefly describe what I think that experience contributed to my professional development.

1. It took very little time for me to learn, as I never had before, what a vast separation there can be between a "real" person and clinical descriptions of him or her. I would read the case folder of an individual, then would meet and interact with him or her, and would see few points in common. It was not only that these descriptions tended to be incomplete, or wrong, or misleading because even when they contained valid facts they rarely communicated the "truth" about the individual. What these reports also contained were labels, or categories, or technical descriptions that served administrative-legal needs at the expense of the individual's distinctiveness. At best, language is an imperfect medium for describing human behavior and, at worst, it creates caricature, or myth, or outright but unwitting distortion. The imperfections of written language are ordinarily tolerable except when they serve as a basis for decisions fateful for the lives of people. And, as I learned every day, psychological reports were used by others, many of whom had never seen the subject, to make important decisions. I should hasten to add that my reservations about written reports were about my own as well as those of others. The more concerned I became about these reports, the longer became the reports I wrote—and the less others read them through. The problem became even more frustrating as I came to see that you could not write a report about an individual without writing about his or her social contexts: the present one and the one to which the individual might be sent. I was struggling to see and write about the "whole" context whereas most of my colleagues wanted to know about the IQ, problem behavior, and cottage placement. It was and is a bedeviling problem, and it forever made me skeptical about the nature and uses of written clinical reports. It is one thing to make decisions about people that are legally and administratively mandated; it is quite another thing to make those decisions taking into account the psychological, social complexities, and needs of people. I have never argued for perfection in this matter, but I have always argued against a decision-making process based on impersonal knowledge of the individual concerned. I would like to believe that whatever contribution I may have made to the field of mental retardation derived from the fact that I came to know in a truly affectively interpersonal way individuals who were seen by others through the lens of labels and categories. I am a gregarious person, and so at Southbury I spent a lot of time in the cottages with the residents and staff. As a consequence, I was sought out by them, enjoyed them, and knew them as few other staff members did. What these people were in "real life" and what they were in their case folders were entirely different. Things that reports said an individual did not do or could not learn to do were frequently being done by that individual outside of the testing situation.

2. Southbury taught me what it meant to work in a large, bureaucratic

organization. I was unprepared, conceptually and interpersonally, for such involvement. What is important here is not only how this milieu affected me, but how it inevitably, and usually adversely, affected the residents. It is a fact—obvious but nonetheless ignored—that in such an environment the factors that drive employees to distraction—factors that engender frustration, foster competitiveness, provoke anger, weaken curiosity and motivation, reinforce passivity, and reward either mindless or guilt-producing conformity—also affect the lives of the residents. I learned the hard way that one's overt and covert behavior is *never* devoid of the characteristics of the milieu. We like to think that our thoughts and acts are willed by us, that the traditions and structures of our milieu play only a minimal role. That view may protect our sense of autonomy, but it screens us from a realistic appraisal of how embedded we are in contexts. Slowly but inexorably Southbury changed from a setting in which the needs of residents were primary to one in which the needs of the staff and the place of the institution in the state apparatus became primary. That change had enormous effects on me and the residents. Southbury's innovative thrust was transformed into a rigid protection of the *status quo*. That experience and theme have been central to almost all books I have written. How are new settings created? Why do they so frequently fail or become deformations of the original intent? What does leadership contribute to this process? Can leadership prevent or dilute this transformation? If so, for how long? Why is it that we do not know how to manage organizational growth? The questions are many, and they all stem from the Southbury experience. I have as few answers today as I had then.

3. "If it cannot be done, it probably can be. If it should not be done, it probably should be." Those statements, simple but dangerous, became axiomatic for me at Southbury. Again and again I would be told that John or Jane cannot do this or that, or if you allow John or Jane to do this or that, terrible things would happen. Do psychotherapy with retarded people? Place them in the community after only a short period of institutionalization (e.g., a year or two)? Refuse to admit individuals who had a low IQ (below 70) but who could with a little help remain in the community? Invite cottage staff to case conferences when decisions will be made about residents in their care? Send residents for home visits as often as possible? Try to do *something* to prevent the need for institutionalization? Stop underestimating the role of affective factors in the lives of retarded people? The answer to each of these questions was either *no* or "that is not our responsibility." These answers were not given by stupid or insensitive people. Their moral sensitivities and sense of obligation were no better or worse than mine. But they were, from my perspective, averse to change and risk taking because they were prisoners of a narrow tradition and world outlook. I had less experience in the field than any other professional at Southbury; consequently, I had less to unlearn and less of a tradition to contend with. And, as I indicated earlier, I was not one to genuflect before authority or the establishment. I was sufficiently ignorant to ask simple questions and sufficiently questioning or curious or self-confident

to act on new ideas. Southbury reinforced my belief in myself and my ideas. Fortunately, my colleagues seemed to distinguish between my ideas and me as a person. I felt liked as a person even though I was somewhat controversial in my role as psychologist. It says something very positive about Southbury in its earliest years that despite controversy I might have engendered or took part in, I was able to do much of what I wanted to do. Helpful in this regard was Mr. Roselle whose interests were elsewhere and who did not interfere with what staff did unless it was morally or ethically gross. I was directly responsible to him, not to anyone else. In those days, and perhaps today, that was a most unusual arrangement for a psychologist.

4. There is a saying in psychotherapeutic circles that people do not get better *within* the therapeutic hour but as a result of altered thinking and action that takes place *between* hours. Analogously, the ability of institutionalized people to adjust successfully to community living depends on the relationship between *institutional* and *community* living. That is to say, if the institutional program does not provide for community experiences—the opportunities to act appropriately on what is learned in the institution—why should one expect "transfer of training"? The fact is that Southbury's stated educational objective (the revolving door metaphor) in no way provided opportunities for community living. Southbury, as I said earlier, was in the middle of nowhere. What Southbury provided was an unusually humane institutional atmosphere and a program to which most of its residents were successfully socialized. To the extent that the socialization was successful, it was an obstacle to learning to live and work in the community. The longer the period of socialization, the more problematic the later adjustment to the community. You get "better" in the institution, but that could mean that you were "worse off" when you were returned to the community. I did not understand these issues until near the end of my stay in Southbury. I was so impressed with what the institution was trying to do *in* Southbury that I missed seeing the trees for the forest. Southbury was impressive, and we were devoted to it, and we were myopic. It took the building up of a new waiting list and the knowledge that the state would not support another Southbury to force the policy makers to question what they were doing. The result was the regional center concept, another instance where Connecticut pioneered.

5. Henry Schaefer-Simmern: a political refugee from Nazi Germany; an art historian, theorist, and educator; a believer in the idea that every individual possesses some capacity for ordered artistic expression; a vehement critic of requiring individuals to copy what other people thought was a work of art. Schaefer, who was twenty years older than I, came to Southbury on a Russell Sage Fellowship to demonstrate that his ideas were as appropriate to the mentally retarded as to any other group. What he did—and I observed it all in the "studio" Mr. Roselle *enthusiastically* provided him—was a real eye opener. It is described and illustrated in his book *The Unfolding of Artistic Activity* (1948). What was remarkable was his insistence that the individual should not draw what he or she thought reality looked like, because one

cannot reproduce the complexity of reality. Rather one should start with what one could visually grasp on the paper, however simple or primitive, and build up from that. Read and *look* at his book. Describing works of art with words inevitably falls far short of the mark. At the very least, you will *see* that what his pupils (residents *and* staff), did was distinctive and *theirs*. In any event, Schaefer was the single most important intellectual influence in my development. He demonstrated what you can get people to do if you believe that they have the spark, however flickering and weak, for ordered, creative activity. It was not an act of blind faith because Schaefer had devoted his life to demonstrating that people tend to avoid artistic activity because they are required to make things look like what others say they look like. As important as the works the residents executed was the way they were transformed as people. "You mean that Sophie made that design?" "That scene came from Helen's head?" "Professor Schaefer-Simmern didn't tell them to draw or make that?"—these were frequent reactions reflecting disbelief and amazement. These works of art had a "primitive" quality, but they arrested the eye and compelled respect. Two rugs, designed and woven by one of the residents, still hang on my office walls. In any event, Schaefer opened up new vistas for me. He took me on teaching tours of the Metropolitan Museum of Art, the Philadelphia museum, and various galleries. His knowledge of art *and* human history was astounding, and whenever I was with him I felt like an intellectual pygmy. Although we differed markedly in age (he died in 1979 at the age of eighty-one, background, and personal style (intellectually he was a democrat; stylistically, a Prussian), we both shared the belief that people were capable of much more than the nature of our culture and the structure of our society permitted. It says a great deal about Schaefer that John Dewey wrote the preface to his book. It was one of the last pieces Dewey wrote, and why he agreed to write it will only be clear to those who have read one of the greatest books ever written: Dewey's *Art as Experience* (1934). I shall be eternally grateful to Schaefer for forcing me to take Dewey's writings seriously. Among the many things for which I am indebted to Southbury, my relationship to Professor Henry Schaefer-Simmern is at the top of the list.

THE YALE EXPERIENCE (PART I, 1946–1961)

How can I write briefly about almost four decades at a place like Yale? On the one hand, how can I convey an intellectual atmosphere, traditions, practices, and a style of professional living and, on the other hand, the diverse ways in which I was involved in mental retardation? It always surprises me (it should not, but it does) how many psychologists know me as someone who "once" was involved in the field of mental retardation. As I hope to show in the following pages, my identification with that field was constant and deep.

Yale is populated by assertive, ambitious, productive, extraordinarily bright people. You may not like all of them, you may not agree with what they say and write, you might not appreciate their judgments about who is or is not worthy to be in the Yale community, and you may derogate what may be termed their fierce and socially isolating individualism. But over time you come to respect their devotion to the life of the mind and to academic freedom. As an institution, Yale takes seriously the idea that if you want to attract and keep scholars and researchers, you have to create the appropriate conditions. By appropriate conditions I mean relatively low teaching loads, comfortable living space, and frequent leaves. If you like to be involved in the administration of Yale (i.e., academic politics), you can be very busy. If you want nothing to do with such affairs, your wishes are respected. What is required of everyone is to take teaching (i.e., classroom teaching, research supervision, dissertation sponsorship, advising) seriously. Teaching time outside the classroom can be great, but it usually involves matters of central interest to you.

So I became part of a setting that gave me freedom to think and act, surrounded me with intellectual stimulation and challenge, confronted me daily with the criteria by which my work would be and should be judged, and played into my own ambitiousness. Yale is inhospitable soil for shrinking violets or sterile acorns! Not long after I came to Yale I decided to write a book on mental deficiency. If I had stayed on at Southbury I do not think I would have written a book. I had published journal articles and would have continued to do so. The idea of writing a book had occurred to me at Southbury, but there was nothing in that atmosphere that made writing books natural. At Yale it was a different story. Fortunately, writing has never held any terror for me. On the contrary, I enjoy it. More correctly, I can tolerate and surmount the tortures of writing because of the feelings of joy, satisfaction, and relief I experience when I finish writing. And when I finish, it is always with the knowledge that a part of me has been ordered and excised and put "out there." Behind the decision to write that first book was the intuition that for me books were a better vehicle for intellectual *and* personal expression than journal articles. But there was another factor: I am the kind of person who after the close of a particular segment of my life has to make sense out of what I have experienced. I cannot permit the experience to remain purely internal. I have to prove to myself and the world that what I thought and did was worthwhile. Some would call that arrogance; others might call it self-confidence. It is both. Yes, I have always wanted to make a difference in this world. No, I have *never* assumed that my chances for achieving such a goal were much above zero. I live in hope, but I never underestimate my capacity (or that of others) to delude myself. The quest for immortality springs eternal! I resent the fact of mortality, but I accept it. There are certain windmills against which I will tilt, but only up to a point.

In those days there were very few books on psychological aspects of mental retardation, and none of them spoke to my experiences at Southbury. The paucity of books validly reflected the degree of interest the different disciplines took in that field. In fact, Harper agreed to publish *Psychological Problems in Mental Deficiency* (1949) only if I took reduced royalties on the first 2500 copies. They did not expect to sell that many, but at that time publishers (because of the financial bonanza provided them by the GI Bill of Rights) were looking for books that were worth publishing but would lose money. The book was well received and went through several editions. Projective techniques, psychotherapy, parent counseling—these and other topics had not been given the play they received in this book. I think that people in the field were ready for a broader conception of psychological factors in mental retardation. And those who read the book but were not in the field probably learned that mental retardation was a more interesting and important field than they had thought. Almost overnight, so to speak, I became known. I had become an expert, God help me! In the land of the blind the one-eyed astigmatic man is king. It was the right book at the right time, which is not to say that it was as good as it should have been.

I finished that book in 1948 and started research on test anxiety; its measurement, the conditions under which it could have negative and positive consequences, and its origins. That research was a direct outgrowth of the Southbury experience because I had become very sensitive to how frequently and with what adverse consequences residents experienced anxiety in the testing situation. Could test anxiety be simply, reliably, and validly measured? We began by studying the ever present college sophomore and then switched to elementary school children. The research project went on over a dozen or more years and from it came at least a score of journal articles, culminating in the book *Anxiety in Elementary School Children. A Report of Research* (Sarason, Davidson, Lighthall, Ruebush, and Waite, 1960). Two monographs followed the book and marked the end of the research project. But before these final publications there was a book, *The Clinical Interaction* (1954). That is the most clinical book I have ever written, focusing as it does on factors that play a role in any interaction, clinical or otherwise. These factors, if not taken into account, can lead to erroneous conclusions or serve as a faulty basis for helping actions. Here, too, I was either replaying (and relying on) the Southbury experience or building on it to come to broader conclusions.

And now I must write about my colleague Thomas Gladwin. When Tom returned to Yale after completing his field work in the South Pacific for his Ph.D. in anthropology, I independently analyzed the projective test protocols he had collected. Our collaboration resulted in the monograph *Truk: Man in Paradise* (1953). I had read in anthropology, but I had never had a sustained relationship with an anthropologist. So when I began to work with Tom I was immediately struck by our different emphases. I was riveted to the individual, to his or her psyche. Tom, on the contrary, focused on the culture: its structure, traditions, socialization practices, and its physical-geographic characteristics. When I "looked" at an individual, I knew that he or she lived in and was a product of culture, but to me *culture* was like an inkblot: an ambiguous potpourri of factors that was important (but not terribly important) to a clinical psychologist like me. My job was to fathom the psyche of individuals, not the vagaries of the spongy concept of culture. Slowly I began to understand how from the moment of birth on we are assimilating and accommodating to social-cultural factors (what we do and what we think about, our conception of time, our judgment about what is right and wrong, etc.) that are not understandable by an individual psychology. To the extent that our socialization into a culture "takes," we have inordinate difficulty recognizing important features of that culture. That is a point I started to comprehend through my collaboration and continuing friendship with Tom. It was not until decades later in my book *Psychology Misdirected* (Sarason, 1981) that I was able to put together what I had learned in a way that satisfied me.

When I was asked in 1954 by the National Association for Retarded Children (later Citizens) to canvas what was going on in the field (to survey the literature, visit researchers, programs, and institutions), I said I would do it only if Tom Gladwin (who was then at NIMH) would be my collaborator. Tom had no knowledge of the field of mental retardation, which I regarded as a plus, for he had less to unlearn. More correctly, Tom knew a great deal which he had had no occasion to relate to the problems and issues in the field. Also, if the idea of collaboration in what for him would be new territory appealed to Tom, there was no question in my mind that what he would ultimately write would have an impact on the field. The possibility that an accomplished, creative anthropologist would look at the field of mental retardation fascinated me, and I was in seventh heaven when he said he would collaborate. The result was a report published in 1958 (Sarason and Gladwin, 1958). There were two major consequences: a friendship that became lifelong was forged, and the impact of the report was widespread, an impact that would have been considerably less if I had done the report by myself. That is not modesty on my part. I do not lack self-confidence, and I do not derogate what I do. I have a clear perception of my limitations and style; I know when someone else has knowledge and skills I would love to possess but do not. That may sadden me, and I might experience a tinge of envy, but it does not push me to try to do more than my inner self says I can do.

How does one judge impact? In the case of my first book and the one with Tom, we know they were widely read because over the years scores of people have told me that reading these books meant much to them. But what impact did these books have on the field qua field, on research, on public policy and action programs? When I ask that question, I cannot conclude that those books had as much impact as we would have liked. When I used to read seriously the research literature in mental retardation, I had to conclude that the bulk of researchers either did not read these books, or read and disagreed with them, or that we had done a very poor job of conceptualizing and writing. I have learned not to confuse becoming known with making an impact.

I raise these questions as prologue to writing about a person whom I treasure as a friend, and with whom I wrote a book that I regard as very important, a judgment that no one except the authors held. That person had and continues to be a pervasive influence on my thinking and living. So now let me tell you about Burton Blatt: the wisest, most compassionate, most courageous, most honest human being I have ever known.[1] He changed a field! He illuminated features of our society, the dilemmas and opportunities of the policy makers, the immorality of wasted lives, and the true purposes of education as few professionals have ever been able to do.

I do not remember the occasion in the mid-fifties when I first met Burt. All I remember is that he sought me out—and in a manner that put me off at first. I am not used to meeting someone ebulliently open and friendly, from whom sincerity oozes, and who makes it clear that he not only respects you but also wants your friendship. Paranoia is not one of my characteristics, but my personality reflects the fact that in our society, especially in the circles of higher education, one's antennae are directed to sensing people's hidden agendas. My antennae are neither high nor strong, which is why on meeting Burt I was surprised to find that I was asking myself, "Is he for real?" He was and is for real.

Burt had recently finished his doctorate at Pennsylvania State University and had accepted the chairmanship of special education at Southern Connecticut State College in New Haven. Special education had long been a strong area at SCSC (formerly New Haven Teachers College), and in choosing Burt the president was signalling his desire to build on tradition and strength. That president, Hilton Buley, was an institutional builder, and when he chose Burt, it was another instance of "it takes one to know one." And Burt built: the number of majors escalated, there were additions to the faculty, and demonstration classrooms with one-way mirrors were developed. As our friendship and intellectual collaborations flowered, I was spending as much time at SCSC as I was at Yale. I became fascinated with the challenge of preparing teachers, but that took second place to the sheer personal and intellectual joy we experienced together. I owe Burt for many things, and especially for keeping me involved in the real world. Aside from being a thinker-moralist, Burt is an activist. He is like a biblical prophet, asking people to recognize their sins, their obligations, their capacity to be like the God who created them. (It is worthy of mention that Burt is a *religious* Jew.) So if you are connected with Burt, he helps you see the world, not through the window of theory but through directed action intended to change the world. Chairman at SCSC, then at Boston University, then Commissioner for Mental Retardation in Massachusetts, then chairman and later dean at Syracuse—in all of those roles Burt enlarged the scope of the settings, making the boundaries between each of these settings and its social surround porous. No one understands or reveres academic tradition and freedom more than Burt.

[1]As one of the editors of this volume, and because of the kind of person he is, Burt Blatt asked me to tone down what he thought to be undeserved praise. The gist of what I say about Burt is in print elsewhere. Here I introduce nothing new, just an elaboration in a type of chapter that calls for self-revelation. Candor requires that I say that the *sole* reason I agreed to be a contributor was the opportunity it afforded me to record my personal and intellectual indebtedness to certain people, to write what I have truly experienced, thought, and felt.

But, as he has countless times pointed out, the academic tradition does not justify a retreat from the world but commerce with it, commerce for the sake of knowledge *and* the betterment of the society.

Through our joint teaching at SCSC Burt and I came to agree on three points. First, that the preparation of teachers needed a drastic conceptual overhaul. Second, that it made no sense to have special and "regular" teacher training programs, as if the psychology on which they were based were different, e.g., as if we needed one theory for the oxygen atom and a different one for the hydrogen atom. Third, that at the very beginning of their professional training, students had to be exposed to all of the realities of the classroom so that their knowledge should not be bookish. At SCSC, therefore, we had a special education class which students observed through a one-way mirror. Following each observation Burt and I would elicit responses and react to student observations and conclusions. We wrote these up as a book, *The Preparation of Teachers. An Unstudied Problem in Education* (Sarason, Blatt, and Davidson, 1962). If the field had taken that book seriously, it might have avoided some of the deservedly scathing criticism of subsequent decades. That is an opinion we share with others: every now and then I hear from someone who happened (the book went out of print *very* quickly) to read it and wonders why it received the silent treatment. Ideas and books are no stimuli for change unless changes in the larger society have prepared the way for a positive reception. Insofar as the message of that book is concerned, those societal changes have not yet occurred.

I think I have been associated, to some degree at least, with every research and action program for which Burt had responsibility. That association has been personally and intellectually a delight as well as a refuge from a more or less impersonal world.

THE YALE EXPERIENCE (PART II, 1961-70)

This period begins and ends with the Yale Psycho-Educational Clinic. But before continuing this indulgence of reminiscence, I have to say a few words about Esther Sarason. Esther joined me at Southbury in 1943. I cannot plead objectivity about her or our relationship, and I cannot talk about her with dispassion. Let me just say that Esther played an important role in everything I have ever done. It was she who stimulated my interest in applying projective and psychotherapeutic techniques to mentally retarded individuals. It was she who forced me to think of, and ultimately to help create, the Yale Psycho-Educational Clinic. And on and on. I shall say no more.

The Psycho-Educational Clinic was an undertaking in community psychology. Its activities ranged from intimate involvement with the community action program (which began before the federal programs) to helping create the New Haven Regional Center for the mentally retarded. From its very conception this clinic has had mental retardation as a major focus. Before the

New Haven Regional Center was opened, the clinic was the site for scores of planning meetings and provided temporary offices for some of the staff. Later, we went through the same experience in helping create the Central Connecticut Regional Center (Sarason, Levine, Goldenberg, Cherlin, and Bennett, 1966). It was at the clinic that Dr. Frances Kaplan (now Grossman) did the research on and implemented programs for siblings of retarded people.

For me, however, one of several reasons for starting the clinic came out of the Southbury experience. You will recall that I came to Southbury a few months after it opened, but, inevitably, I was told a great deal about its preopening phases. As its innovative thrust began to dissipate, I began to think, superficially and quite unsystematically, about why this was happening. Why was this new setting falling so short of the mark? Why was a revolutionary rationale turning into traditional rhetoric? I did not realize then that I was asking questions identical to those I had been asking about the most momentous event of this century: the Bolshevik revolution in Russia. It was only after I had left Southbury and was toying with the possibility of starting the clinic that I began to formulate the theory of "the creation of settings" and to ask why so many new settings fail. Could I create a setting that would not fail of its purposes? What was required to keep a setting consistent with its purposes? Compared to the Russian revolution and the Southbury Training School, the Psycho-Educational Clinic was a minuscule, trivial affair but, nonetheless, like them, it was an instance of the creation of settings, which occurs when two or more people join together over a sustained period of time to accomplish agreed-upon goals. Developing and directing the clinic was a self-conscious exploration of the creation of a setting, and I took advantage of any opportunity to participate in or observe the creation of other settings. Helping to create the New Haven and the Central Connecticut Regional Centers was of great help to me as the problem was evolving in my thinking. During the sixties the rate of creation of new settings was as phenomenal as their rate of failure was demoralizing. At the end of that decade I wrote *The Creation of Settings and the Future Societies* (1972), a book which some colleagues consider the most distinctive of my writings. A separate book, *The Creation of a Community Setting* (Sarason, Grossman, and Zitnay, 1972), was devoted to the creation of the Central Connecticut Regional Center, an effort that was mightily influenced by our experience with the New Haven Regional Center.

The sixties was the decade of community, "togetherness," and a host of other reactions to loneliness, isolation, and resentment toward a social order that seemed too readily to countenance suffering, segregation, and cruelty (witting and unwitting). Mea culpas were heard around the land, and however sincere the breastbeating, it seldom initiated a process of sustained, productive change. This was the decade that saw deinstitutionalization put on the social agenda. I was in the forefront of that movement, but I was not psychologically part of it because I felt that the participants knew what they were against but not what they were for. More correctly, they had little understanding of what a complex problem it would be to keep retarded individuals in the community in ways that would do justice to their needs and rights as well as lead to social acceptance and integration. I knew that there was no way to accomplish this without conflict and controversy. Rhetoric aside, when push came to shove, there would be battles, not between virtuous and sinful people but between the passionate and the puzzled, between those who did not see themselves as goring the oxen of others and those who felt that their oxen were indeed being gored. I did not know the answers, but I was certain that most of those pressuring for deinstitutionalization had fearfully oversimple conceptions of how they would accomplish their goals. The first group home in Connecticut for adult females was developed by two Yale seniors, Frances Brody and Susan Waisbren, in my community psychology course at the clinic. It was an inspiring but sobering experience: inspiring because of what was accomplished and sobering because of the obstacle course it was. I am not being facetious when I say that what Frances and Susan accomplished was due largely to their ignorance: they had little to unlearn about what is supposed to be impossible in this world. They knew how to garner resources *free for nothing,* to a degree that I had not seen before (or since) in such ventures. I was and still am caught between two convictions: that deinstitutionalization is a morally justified, community-building, resource-conserving endeavor; and that those who are responsible for such an endeavor tend to have little or no conception of what is involved.

It was during the mid-sixties that I came to see that the 1954 desegregation decision could have (depending on how the courts interpreted and reinterpreted that decision) significance for special education, i.e., for the practice either of not admitting handicapped children to schools or of segregating them in special classes. I think I saw that possibility because I had already come to the conclusion that special classes were not necessary. That conclusion may strike most readers as foolish, or ridiculous, or just plain stupid. But the more I thought about it, the more convinced I became that special classes served the purposes of rationalizing prejudice and longstanding administrative practices and structures. It was not until the mid-seventies, when John Doris (more about him later) and I began the collaboration on *Educational Handicap, Public Policy, and Social History. A Broadened Perspective on Mental Retardation* (1979), that I thought through the problem to the point where I could write about it. My position is contained in the chapter "What Are Schools For?" No one (almost no one) has taken seriously what I have had to say. If I had been taken seriously, it would have required explanation, because what I was proposing was so foreign to what seemed natural, right, and proper. After all, during most of my stay there I had thought Southbury was the last word in the care and education of retarded people (we called them "children" then). Why should I expect others to be more responsive to change than I was? And the obstacles to change in the individual is as nothing compared to those that need to be overcome for institutional change.

Toward the end of my stay at the clinic I wrote *The Culture of the School and the Problem of Change* (1971). That book had a most favorable reception, but in one respect I felt it was incomplete as a record of what I had learned and believed. As I put it in the preface to the second edition in 1982:

> *I was quite aware when I completed the first edition that a set of problems with which I have long been associated, problems that later became important in the educational setting, were deliberately excluded by me. I refer to mental retardation in particular, and handicapped children in general. I excluded these problems for two related reasons. For one thing, I was very sensitive to the possibility that the book would be read as an unsympathetic criticism of schools, a reading that was quite the opposite of what I intended. But it was obvious that there was little in the book that could serve as a basis for an optimistic view of schools' future. Now, in regard to mental retardation I have always had strong feelings, i.e., I was a partisan for retarded people and their teachers, both of whom were segregated, second to third class citizens in the school culture. If I included this set of problems in the first edition, I was not sure that I could be dispassionate because I had long felt that these aspects of the school culture contained morally reprehensible features. Besides, when the book was written in 1969–70, I would have talked about special classes (which were on the rise) and their encapsulated, alien status in most schools. And then I would have gone into the legal-moral basis for special classes because I predicted then that the 1954 desegregation decision would some day serve as the basis for challenging special classes. But, I asked myself, would the reader understand? Would it appear as if I was critical and perhaps even nihilistic? Would the space I would have to devote to these problems appear as unexplainably disproportionate to their significance? So, I said little or nothing. A decade later it is a different ballgame and that is reflected in this second edition. Needless to say, I regret that early judgment because if that first edition had spoken to the issues of handicapped children, it might have been more edifying than it was.*

If I were the crusader that Burton Blatt was and is, the first edition of that book would have been more on target. It should have been. There are times when one holds one's fire, but the first edition was not one of them. People criticized Burt for *Christmas in Purgatory* (1966), but is there anyone today who can deny the desirable change in moral atmosphere that publication helped bring about?

THE YALE EXPERIENCE (PART III, 1970–   )

After the third edition of *Psychological Problems in Mental Deficiency* I had no inkling that there would be a fourth one. But I did not count on John Doris reappearing in my professional-intellectual life. Back in the fifties John had been one of my graduate students. That statement is literally true but very misleading. Not many years separate John and me. Because of a long physical illness John came to undergraduate and graduate school much later than is usually the case. He arrived at Yale a personally and intellectually mature person. In a formal sense we had a professor-student relationship but phenomenologically I always regarded him as my peer. The truth is that in terms of a knowledge and grasp of intellectual and social history, John was way beyond me. He not only had read widely, but he had organized what he had read. And he had a sense of problem: John always knew the difference between a trivial and an important problem. His appearance is deceptive: very tall, quiet spoken, introverted, sensitive; on the surface he seems somewhat passive in personal style. What I am trying to say is that John hides his light under a bushel. It did not take me very long to see that light. Here was a poor Irishman from the Bronx who had absorbed the best of the Jesuit traditions. Outwardly he tolerated fools gladly; inside he called fools fools but always with that sense of sadness that man is a most imperfect animal.

It was John's idea to do a fourth edition of *Psychological Problems* that would essentially be a new book. I at first resisted the idea, although I had to agree with his analysis of why the field needed the kind of book he was proposing. In descending order of importance here are the major reasons I agreed to the collaboration. First, I knew John was absolutely right—that the major problems of the field had to be put in a social-historical context. He not only was right, but I knew he was the only person who could do it extraordinarily well. Second, I knew that our contributions to the book would be different from and supplementary to each other. Third, each of the first three editions had consisted of new additions rather than of an integration of new material, and there was a need for me to reintegrate my past and present experiences. Fourth, I would learn a lot from what John would write. Besides, I knew that our friendship (like mine with Tom Gladwin and Burt Blatt) would withstand the travails of collaborations (in point of fact, in each of these collaborations the friendship deepened. There never was anything resembling a personal problem).

The fourth edition appeared in 1969. Although it was critically well received, it clearly had less impact than earlier editions. The first three editions had come at times when there were few texts in the field and while the book was never written as a text, it was used as one. By the time of the fourth edition there were texts that seemed more appropriate for people entering the field. I say "seemed" because I believe that an introductory course should not be a collection of facts but a presentation of issues in a social-historical context, a presentation that challenges and stimulates and does not avoid controversy or plays into the tendency to think that the past is not in the present and that the road to the future is taking us to "progress." I still think the fourth edition is a splendid book precisely because of the social-historical chapters written by John. In fact, if the participants in the nature-nurture controversy of the seventies (con *and* pro) had read John's chapters, the level of argument would have been considerably higher. At the very least, it might have made the participants more self-conscious about how much of the past was going unrecognized in the present. The nature-nurture controversy comes in cycles, but each time it reemerges—always in response to a perceived problem in the larger society—it is as if its past appearances have been left in the museum of intellectual relics.

Frankly, as a result of John's contribution, I was, relatively speaking, indifferent to the nature-nurture controversy sparked by Arthur Jensen's publications. How could I write something that essentially said: "Hey, you guys, why don't you read what John Doris wrote"? But when in 1973 I had to give an address accepting an award from the American Association on Mental Deficiency, I felt I should say something about the controversy that would reflect our orientation in a personal, nontechnical way. The result was "Jewishness, Blackishness, and the Nature-Nurture Controversy" (Sarason, 1973). The theme of that paper is very simple to state: group characteristics that have been honed over the decades, and even centuries, will not be significantly altered according to expectations reflecting a narrow time perspective.

There is a point I discuss in the fourth edition (it is mentioned in the third) that I regard as distinctive, important, and for some reason hardly discussed in the literature. It goes back, as everything else seems to, to the Southbury experience. The point is summarized in a review I wrote (Sarason, 1980) of Jensen's (1979) book.

> *The Achilles heel in Jensen's position, as well as in those of his critics, is the significance they all attach to standardized tests and testing conditions. The question I wish to discuss is: what is the relation between problem solving in test situations and in non-contrived, naturally occurring situations? I came to ask myself that question shortly after I took my first professional job testing individuals in a new institution for mentally retarded, a very innovative institution in the middle of nowhere. There was a certain problem with runaways. Although people ran away infrequently, there was always the fear when they did so that they would get lost in the woods and get hurt. Although I do not know how many of these runaways succeeded in not getting caught at all or only being found days later in their homes miles away, I did become aware that some of them had exhibited a kind and quality of problem-solving behavior that was simply not predictable from my testing of them. For example, I routinely administered the Porteus Mazes, which are scaled in difficulty from simple to complex. Some of the runaways who had done poorly on these mazes had managed to plan and execute their flights successfully, i.e., they demonstrated a level of planning and foresight quite at variance with their test performance. Part of my job was to make recommendations, on the basis of tests, for job placement within the institution. I began to learn that in a fair number of instances there was little relationship between the problem-solving behavior of an individual in testing and nontesting situations. I do not want to exaggerate the number of these*

instances; but their occurrence was frequent enough, and the discrepancies often dramatic enough, to make me wary of predicting from testing situations. This wariness received further support from the literature on what happened to mentally retarded individuals after they left special classes in the schools. They became part of the community in ways and at levels of competence that were at variance with their problem-solving test behavior.

A great deal happened in the seventies to John, me, and the field of mental retardation. John had begun to dig into the origins of the educational system, the impact of the different waves of immigration, the growth of the system, the origins of special education, and the fateful role of universal, compulsory education. And when John digs, he digs. I had become aware, for reasons that I discussed in the previous section, that indeed the spirit of the 1954 desegregation decision was percolating into attitudes toward mental retardation—and into the courts. Mainstreaming was not only in the air but also in the statutes of Massachusetts. And then there was that congeries of events, people, and processes that culminated in Public Law 94-142. As in the case of deinstitutionalization I had very mixed feelings about 94-142. Of course, I was heartily in favor of it. At the same time, however, I was certain that neither the proponents of that legislation nor school officials understood the resource problem. The problem and its amelioration were being defined in a way that was unrealistic and was setting the stage for a backlash. Also, the fact that the word or concept of *mainstreaming* did not appear in the legislation said to me that the special class was in no way threatened—indeed it was implicitly receiving further legitimization. Finally, and very important, in my travels around the country I learned that the bulk of school officials had no idea of what PL 94-142 really said. Indeed, many of them thought that loads of federal money would come pouring into their communities. The icing on this cake of ignorance and good intentions was that when they seriously began to confront the implications of the legislation, they could only come up with slight modifications of traditional rationales and practices. In any event, John and I decided to write a new book. *Educational Handicap, Public Policy, and Social History: A Broadened Perspective on Mental Retardation* was published in 1979. It continues to surprise me how little overlap there is between this and our previous book. it is not a book that confuses change with progress. Neither John nor I are temperamentally wet blankets; neither are we easily enthused about what will come from good intentions. Both of us are, I think, old and wise enough to know that, regarding societal and institutional change, the odds favor the status quo—"the more things change the more they remain the same." This is what Burt Blatt's follow-up of *Christmas in Purgatory* showed (Blatt, Ozolins, & McNally, 1979). The institutions were clean, there was more equipment, and they had a patina of humaneness—except that they continued to be the unstimulating, isolating, sleep-producing places they had always been. Today we have the boob tube, but the boobs are not the residents.

EPILOGUE

I have been, thank God, a willing prisoner of the place where my professional career started. I learned and unlearned a lot at Southbury. I had freedom there, although what true freedom meant I did not comprehend until I came to Yale. I have been amazingly fortunate in the collaborator-friends I have had (almost as fortunate as in the woman I married). This, I know *now*, was not happenstance but rather the result of my fairly realistic appraisal of my assets and limitations. That is to say, these collaborator-friends (including my wife) have had knowledge, skills, or outlooks that compensated for my lacks. I have been able to capitalize on these limitations by connecting with individuals who provided me, in a way easy to learn, what I needed but did not possess. I never walk into a library without becoming depressed because I will not be able to read every book in it before I die. Through my collaborator-friends that feeling has been somewhat diluted. Through and with them my horizons have been expanded. In a very real sense they have helped me in the most important of all processes: unlearning.

If I had to do it all over again, I would. There have been disappointments in my life, the death of loved ones, the ever present feeling of personal mortality, and the ever growing conviction that our passion for technology has been, and will be, ultimately, our Achilles' heel. Much of our history over the past few centuries is understandable in terms of an implicit axiom: if something can be done, it will be done, it should be done. Despite these dysphoric events and thoughts, I have managed to gain a great deal of satisfaction and pleasure from thinking and writing about the one theme that powers everything I have done: how do I understand where I and my society have come from? How do I unlearn what my society said I should learn and be? Those are the questions I take up in my most recent book *Psychology Misdirected* (Sarason, 1981). If I have learned a lot, it is because I unlearned a lot. If I have not learned as much as I should have, it is in large part because unlearning the substance and consequences of one's socialization into a society is, at best, something we can only partially do. Frankly, I am more impressed with what man has not done than with what he has done. Or, perhaps, with what he can or will do. That conclusion does not really depress me or in any way weaken my grandiose desire to save the world. That desire, in light of what I said before, may seem to some readers as inconsistent or even contradictory. So what else is new?

REFERENCES

Dewey, J. (1934). *Art as experience.* New York: Minton, Balch & Co.

Blatt, B., & Kaplan, F. (1966). *Christmas in purgatory: A photographic essay on mental retardation* (2nd ed.). Boston: Allyn & Bacon.

Blatt, B., Ozolins, A., & McNally, J. (1979). *The family papers: A return to purgatory.* New York: Longman, Inc.

Gladwin, T., & Sarason, S. B. (1953). *Truk: Man in paradise.* New York: Viking Fund Publications in Anthropology.

Jensen, A. R. (1979). *Bias in mental testing.* New York: The Free Press (Macmillan).

Sarason, S. B. (First edition, 1949; Fourth edition, 1969). *Psychological problems in mental deficiency.* New York: Harper & Row.

Sarason, S. B. (1954). *The clinical interaction.* New York: Harper & Bros.

Sarason, S. B. (1972). *The creation of settings and the future societies.* San Francisco: Jossey-Bass.

Sarason, S. B. (1980). [Book review of *Bias in mental testing* by A. Jensen]. *Society, 18* (1), 86-88.

Sarason, S. B. (1981). *Psychology misdirected.* New York: Free Press (Macmillan).

Sarason, S. B. (1982). *The culture of the school and the problem of change* (2nd ed.). Boston: Allyn & Bacon.

Sarason, S. B., Blatt, B., & Davidson, K. (1962). *The preparation of teachers: An unstudied problem in education.* New York: John Wiley.

Sarason, S. B., Davidson, K., Waite, R., Lighthall, F., & Ruebush, B. (1960). *Anxiety in elementary school children: A report of research.* New York: John Wiley.

Sarason, S. B., & Doris, J. (1979). *Educational handicap, public policy, and social history: A broadened perspective on mental retardation.* New York: Free Press (Macmillan).

Sarason, S. B., & Gladwin, T. (1958). Psychological and cultural problems in mental subnormality: A review of research. *Genetic Psychology Monographs, 57,* 3-290.

Sarason, S. B., Grossman, F. K., & Zitnay, G. (1972). *The creation of a community setting.* Syracuse, NY: Syracuse University Press.

Sarason, S. B., Levine, M., Goldenberg, J., Cherlin, D., & Bennett, E. (1966). *Psychology in community settings.* New York: John Wiley.

Schaefer-Simmern, H. (1948). *The unfolding of artistic activity.* Berkeley, CA: University of California Press.

2

Introspection
and Prophecy

Samuel A. Kirk

Samuel A. Kirk, born 1904 in Rugby, North Dakota, earned his B.A. in psychology (1929) and his M.A. in experimental psychology (1931) from the University of Chicago, and his Ph.D. in physiological and clinical psychology from the University of Michigan (1935).

Dr. Kirk is professor of special education at the University of Arizona (1968-   ) and is also professor emeritus at the University of Illinois, where he was director of the Institute for Research on Exceptional Children and professor of special education and psychology (1952-67). In 1963-64, Dr. Kirk served as director of the Division of Handicapped Children and Youth in the United States Office of Education. He was director of the Division of Education for Exceptional Children (1935-47) and also chairman of the Graduate School at the Milwaukee State Teachers College (1946-47). He has been a consultant and advisor in Germany (1950 and 1951), a lecturer over the National Broadcasting Corporation (NHK) in Japan (1965), and a consultant to the government of Brazil (1979).

Former president of the International Council for Exceptional Children (1940-42) and vice-president of the American Association on Mental Deficiency, Dr. Kirk is a diplomate in clinical psychology and a fellow of the American Psychological Association, the American Association on Mental Deficiency, and the American Academy for the Advancement of Science.

In 1962, Dr. Kirk became honorary vice-president of the British Association of Special Education, and in the same year, received the First International Award in Mental Retardation from the Joseph P. Kennedy, Jr. Foundation. He is also the recipient of the J. E. Wallace Wallin Award from the Council for Exceptional Children (1966), the International Milestone Award from the International Federation of Learning Disabilities (1975), the Distinguished Service Award from the American

Speech and Hearing Association (1976), an Award of Merit from the Division of School Psychology of the American Psychological Association (1979), the Award of Recognition from the Division of Early Childhood of the Council for Exceptional Children (1981), and the Edgar H. Doll Award from the Division of Mental Retardation of the American Psychological Association (1981).

He received the honorary degree of Doctor of Humane Letters from Lesley College in 1969 and the honorary degree of Doctor of Letters from the University of Illinois in 1983.

The request to write a paper on "personal orientations"—on what influenced my career and in what direction we are headed—has become a task in introspection and in prophecy. At an earlier date, a similar request was made to which I replied that a better title would be "A Confession of My Sins." In that paper, I continued:

> *My first sin is accepting the reputed posture of an expert in mental retardation and learning disabilities. In this field, such a posture today is usually reserved for those who can show that they have taken a sequence of courses in a field and can obtain a certificate from agencies such as the State Department of Public Instruction. I must confess to you that the two areas in Special Education in which I have never had a college course are "mental retardation" and "learning disabilities." In these two areas, according to our present certification criteria for trained professional personnel, I must admit that I do not qualify. (Kirk, 1970, p. 199)*

EARLY EDUCATION

When I first enrolled at the University of Chicago in 1925, after graduating from a small-town high school, I was unaware of the international reputation of that great university. I had not anticipated how much intellectual and scientific stimulation such an institution could offer a Midwest country boy suddenly exposed to a new world of thought.

At that time the University of Chicago gave a great deal of freedom to individual initiative in course selection. They awarded a Bachelor of Philosophy degree (Ph.B.) for only three requirements: 1) 9 quarter units constituting one full year of work in an academic major, 2) 3 quarter units in a foreign language, and 3) a total of 4 years of course work. The student was then free to explore many fields of study and concentrate wherever he or she saw fit. It was also possible to shop around during the first three days of each quarter. If one did not like the professor or the subject matter, it was possible to change to a different section or a different course.

It was through this course selection process that I came in contact with the great minds of the world. The internationally known physiologist Anton

Carlson taught an introductory course in physiology; the outstanding anthropologist Fay Cooper Cole taught the introductory course in anthropology; the famous sociologist Ernest Burgess taught the introductory course in sociology; and Harvey Carr, the head of the department of psychology, taught the introductory course in psychology. I mention these facts because today few internationally known professors teach undergraduate courses since their load of graduates and Ph.D. candidates is very heavy compared to that of professors in the 1920s. Few at that time scrambled for research funds, but they still conducted profound research on their own and with their students even without large grants.

Upon graduation I enrolled for a master's degree in psychology at the University of Chicago while working in a school for subnormal delinquent boys. At that time the functional school of psychology offered courses emphasizing experimental psychology. The requirements for a master's degree consisted of two or three thoroughly experimental courses in the psychology of learning and in work and fatigue. All students were required to take at least two courses in statistics from the father of factor analysis, Leon Thurstone, and a course in neurology from Judson Herrick, a famous neurologist of his day.

It was also a tradition of the University of Chicago to invite famous professors from other universities to teach during the summer quarter. We considered it a privilege to take advantage of this tradition. The university invited one of the few psychologists in special education in the U.S. in the late 1920s, Dr. J. E. Wallace Wallin, to teach during the summer quarter. In 1924 he had published a scholarly and authoritative book, *The Education of Handicapped Children,* one of the earliest books in the field of special education. This book and Dr. Wallin's lectures were inspiring and very helpful. Actually, it was the only course in handicapped children that I had during my undergraduate or graduate work.

I also enrolled in a very inspiring course taught by Dr. Stevenson Smith, the director of the child development laboratories at the University of Washington in Seattle. He scoffed at psychoanalysis, saying that you don't psychoanalyze a child who is biting his nails; you consider fingernail biting a habit which needs breaking by symptomatic training. He stated in class that if you file the nails short so that they will not be rough, you will aid the child in overcoming the fingernail-biting habit. Five years later at the Wayne County Training School I did just that—filed the nails of forty fingernail biters and assisted most of them in breaking the habit.

In addition to taking several courses relating to children and deviations, I enrolled in one offered by Visiting Professor Charles Spearman of England, the first theorist to describe intelligence as consisting of a general factor and many specific factors. He used as a text his 1927 book, *The Nature of Intelligence and the Principles of Cognition.*

EARLY EXPERIENCES

My professional interest in the field of deviating children began when I took a course in mental testing from Andrew Brown at the Institute for Juvenile Research (IJR) in Chicago. Here I was initiated into mental testing and became acquainted with behavioral problem children by attending case conferences for mentally retarded and delinquent children at the institute. Through this contact I applied for a position in an experimental school for delinquent, mentally retarded boys aged eight to sixteen near Chicago. The Oaks School had been designed by Dr. Paul Schroeder, a psychiatrist and director of IJR, as an experiment to determine whether freedom of choice would ameliorate behavior problems and help resolve mental retardation.

It was in 1929, at the beginning of the Depression, that I was happy to be offered the position of "resident instructor" even though at that time I had had no experience or training in education. Fortunately, they did not require teacher certificates in this area. My job was to manage fifty delinquent, mentally retarded boys, providing recreation in the late afternoons and evenings and on Saturdays and Sundays. In the evenings I helped the nurses in the dormitory put the boys to bed and see to it that they stayed in bed. In the morning I attended graduate classes at the University of Chicago toward a master's degree and in the afternoon I drove to Oak Forest, Illinois in a fifty-dollar Model T Ford to work with these boys.

After several days at this residential school, two of the sixteen-year-olds came to me after a football game and wanted to wrestle. I avoided this personal contact for a day or two. On Saturday, however, it was raining, and the fifty boys were forced to retreat to the gym. The two boys again met me in a corner of the room and insisted on wrestling. By this time I knew that my predecessor had been forced to quit because these boys had wrestled and successfully fought with him. I quickly scanned my psychology courses to find a psychological technique for avoiding this confrontation, to no avail. I decided to bluff by saying to them, "I don't want to wrestle two of you; I'll wrestle the whole group." They were delighted at this offer, calling the other boys and informing them that Mr. Kirk would wrestle all of them.

I explained the rules of the game as I had previously explained other games. The rule was that when any one boy was down, he was out of the game. When I went down, the game was over. The two boys rushed at me. I tripped the first one and threw down the second. The other forty-eight ran to the other end of the room. I was the winner. If the reverse had happened, I might have been forced to seek another career.

In reading the clinical folders of these children I noticed that one boy was labeled *word blind,* a term I had never heard before in my psychology courses. He was a nonreader, ten years old, and had a recorded IQ of 82. The clinical folder referred to Marion Monroe's monograph on reading disabilities, Hinshelwood's book on congenital word blindness, and Fernald's kinesthetic method. After reading these references at the university the next day, I arranged to tutor the boy at nine o'clock in the evening, after the boys were supposed to be asleep. This boy, who was eager to learn, sneaked quietly out of bed at the appointed time each night and met me in a small space between the two dormitory rooms—actually, in the doorway of the boys' toilet. We both knew we were violating a regulation by making this arrangement since the head nurse had directed me not to allow the boys out of bed after nine o'clock. When she came down from the third floor, the boy and I went into the boys' toilet so she did not catch us violating that sacred rule. I often state that *my first experience in tutoring a case of reading disability was not in a school, was not in a clinic, was not in an experimental laboratory, but in a boys' lavatory.*

This boy was very anxious to learn to read and within a period of seven months was reading at the second- to third-grade level. An examination at the Institute for Juvenile Research indicated that he was now reading at beginning third-grade level. The Institute, following the recommendation of Dr. Marion Monroe, who examined him, obtained a parole from a juvenile court judge, returned him to his home, and had him enrolled in a fourth grade. I hypothesized at that time that remedial reading might alleviate delinquency in some children.

The Institute for Juvenile Research had been organized in Chicago as a service and research institute and housed research psychiatrists, sociologists, and psychologists. Among the early researchers were William Healy and Augusta Bronner, who made major contributions to the study of delinquency; Clifford Shaw, the sociologist who studied the delinquency areas in Chicago; L. Hewett and R. Jenkins, who made a lasting contribution in their studies of patterns of maladjustment; Carl Lashley, who in a rat and monkey laboratory conducted research on neuropsychology; Chester Darrow, one of the first psychologists to research the E.E.G.; and Andrew Brown, who headed the clinical psychology section and conducted research on mental testing.

It was in this research environment that Dr. Marion Monroe, a former affiliate of Dr. Samuel T. Orton, was conducting relevant research on reading-disabled children. In her office I received individual tutoring and guidance in the diagnosis and remediation of reading disabilities. Many years later, unbeknown to me, Dr. Monroe was asked to review my first book *(Teaching Reading to Slow Learning Children,* 1940) and to write a foreword to it.

It was at the Oaks School that I conducted my first published experimental project using single-subject research. It dealt with the Fernald kinesthetic method. I used six boys at the school, teaching them to read five words one day using the look-and-say method, and five words the next day using the Fernald manual tracing method. The third day they relearned the words to determine how many fewer trials they took (retention savings score), and then learned another five words. This experiment continued for thirty days. In contrasting the Fernald method with the look-and-say method I found that the number of trials for learning was the same for both methods but that retention over twenty-four hours was greater when the manual tracing (kinesthetic) method was used (Kirk, 1933).

In 1931 the Great Depression hit the United States. The banks were closed and Cook County, Illinois, in its attempt to retrench, closed the Oaks School. I became unemployed and applied for job after job, in most instances receiving no answer. At about this time, the Wayne County Training School at Northville, Michigan, was looking for a psychologist with a master's degree who was trained and experienced in reading disabilities of the mentally retarded. Dr. Marion Monroe recommended me for the position in spite of my meager experience which consisted of tutoring approximately three children with reading disabilities. There seemed to be a shortage of people who had done research in the remediation of mentally retarded reading cases. For this reason, I was offered the position.

My work at the Wayne County Training School consisted of half-time teaching and half-time research. At this residential training school the children had many disabilities—reading, language, perceptual, and behavioral. I was fortunate to have this great opportunity to teach and conduct research on children with a variety of problems.

In the early 1930s great emphasis was placed on brain theory and its relationship to aberrations of behavior, such as mirror reading, mixed eyedness and handedness, and strephosymbolia. Brain dysfunction was proposed by Samuel T. Orton, Lee Edward Travis, and others to explain many of these aberrations. At that time cerebral dominance and strephosymbolia were the most prominent theories held to account for stuttering, disorders of reading, and language. Since the children with whom we worked had reading, language, and perceptual problems, it was necessary for us to understand the workings of the brain. I consequently enrolled in a doctorate program at the University of Michigan. The emphasis of the Department of Psychology was on physiological and experimental psychology and on neurology. Dr. Normal Maier, who did his postdoctoral work in Berlin in Gestalt psychology and studied with Carl Lashley for two years, was my advisor.

My doctoral research consisted of testing the handedness of rats and training them to discriminate between an *F* and a mirrored *F* on a Lashley jumping apparatus. It resulted in a monograph entitled "Hemispheric Cerebral Dominance and Hemispheric Equipotentiality" (Kirk, 1935). Studying physiological psychology and neurology and conducting experiments with the brains of rats bore little relationship to what I did then, to what I have done since, or to what I do now for children with learning disabilities. It did teach me, however, that the study of the brain and behavior is important and that eventually scientists may bridge the gap between neurology and psychology, and between psychology and education. When this occurs we may have an integrated discipline entitled "neuropsychologicaleducation."

At the Wayne County Training School I had the rare opportunity to spend half-time teaching mentally retarded children, supervising graduate students from the University of Michigan who were interning in the research department, and doing research, while also studying at the University of

Michigan for a Ph.D. in psychology. This opportunity was afforded me by an unusual superintendent, Dr. Robert Haskell, a psychiatrist who had ambitions in research and science. He established a department of research in this children's institution and treated it as a "sacred cow." He insisted that an institution was responsible for conducting research and advancing knowledge.

Dr. Haskell knew that the Vineland Training School had become famous through the research contributions of Dr. Henry Goddard and Dr. Edgar Doll. He wanted the Wayne County Training School to become as famous as Vineland through research. He appointed Dr. Thorleif Hegge as director of research and asked him to develop research related to the academic abilities of mentally retarded children. Dr. Hegge, a native of Norway, had obtained his Ph.D. in psychology from Göttingen, Germany, and had spent a year in the research department at Vineland with Dr. Edgar Doll.

The research department was manned primarily by psychologists and graduate students in psychology, speech pathology, and social work from the University of Michigan. The list of the scientists who worked in the research department at the Wayne County Training School testifies to the insight of the superintendent and Dr. Hegge. Among them are Alfred Strauss, Heinz Werner, Sidney Bijou, Newell Kephart, Boyd McCandles, William Cruickshank, Bluma Weiner, and many others. It is interesting to note that these people developed their own ideas in an institution for the mentally retarded rather than in a university. After World War II many of them accepted positions in universities when their contributions from this institution became known. Unfortunately, today few residential schools offer such outstanding opportunities. Few serve as centers of research, and few feel that among their obligations is the advancement of knowledge.

MAJOR INFLUENCES

It is difficult to list in order the many contacts and experiences that influence one's thinking and one's career. In most instances there is a combination of influences and, sometimes, the accident of the environment. Nevertheless, I shall try to list in retrospect some of the people and conditions that may have directed my thinking.

The first influence, of course, was the contact with great thinkers at the University of Chicago. Harvey Carr's functional school of psychology had a profound impact. It was a precursor of Skinner's behaviorism, which Calfee (1981) states had its roots in American functionalism. The application of the principles of learning to education and teaching was dominant. The names of Watson, Thorndike, and Judd were in the forefront of psychology.

The second major influence (in the 1930s) was Dr. Marion Monroe and her research. Her many years of research at IJR resulted in a book entitled *Children Who Cannot Read* (1932), which was, for a while, my bible. Her work was an outgrowth of her association with Dr. Samuel T. Orton at the University of Iowa. Her system of diagnosing errors in reading (repetitions, reversals, omission of sounds and words, etc.) is still used today. Through standardization of these errors for each grade from one to four, she was able to draw a profile of the kinds of errors each child made. Her hypothesis was that if we are able to eliminate the symptoms of poor reading through the correction of reading errors, the reading level will improve. Many years later I used the same approach in profiling the abilities and disabilities revealed by the Illinois Test of Psycholinguistic Abilities (Kirk, McCarthy, and Kirk, 1968).

The remedial methods which we later developed were influenced by Marion Monroe and the Fernald kinesthetic method. Fernald and Keller had published an article which was impressive (1921). The Hegge, Kirk and Kirk Remedial Reading Drills (1936) evolved from trial-and-error teaching of children with reading disabilities. This phonic system evolved independently at about the same time as the Gillingham method, both influenced by Samuel T. Orton and Marion Monroe. The Hegge, Kirk and Kirk Remedial Reading Drills were developed in 1933 and 1934. They emphasized the principles of learning from the Chicago school of functional psychology in a way similar to the emphasis in programmed instruction promoted more recently by the behavior analysts.

The third influence was my experience at the Wayne County Training School. This experience exposed me to several personalities who influenced my future. One was Dr. Thorleif G. Hegge, who took a personal interest in developing in me the same accuracy and careful interpretation of data he had acquired in his German university training. Another was my wife, Winifred Day Kirk, also a graduate of the University of Chicago functional school of psychology and a team member in the research department at the Wayne County Training School. We have been professional as well as family partners ever since.

Dr. Robert Haskell, the forward-looking superintendent, taught me much about techniques of interviewing youngsters. As a lowly psychologist, I screened boys in the psychiatric office for his evaluation. In this position I learned a great deal about the practical application of psychoanalysis, milieu therapy, and behavior modification. I also learned from Dr. Haskell the value of holding on to the goal of research and scientific approaches even in the face of financial and political opposition. Dr. Haskell maintained our research department against much opposition throughout the Great Depression of the 1930s.

The experience at the Wayne County Training School pointed out to me that much more could be done with handicapped children than most people believed. The case histories and diagnoses by clinics and schools in the Detroit area and by the staff of the Wayne County Training School were an education in case analysis and procedure. Case conferences added to the belief that many children considered hopeless in behavior or learning could be rehabilitated.

One boy, with whom we worked for three years, had an IQ of 56 on the Binet, was declared delinquent, could not read two words. The only thing he could write was his name, and that he wrote backwards. This boy was trained by me one hour a day, five days a week, outside of his classroom. After two years of tutoring he was reading at the beginning fourth-grade level. He could score at a seventh-grade level on the Gray's Oral Reading Test because of his decoding abilities, but his comprehension was at the beginning of the fourth grade. He was tutored for a third year in an attempt to increase his comprehension. At the end of the year he was testing at the middle fourth-grade level in comprehension. On a repeated psychometric test at the age of 15 he now showed an IQ of 70 and was consequently paroled to his grandmother. In a follow-up study it was found that he not only had become a self-supporting citizen but was also supporting his grandmother and his sister while working for a fair salary at the Ford Motor Company.

The fifth major influence was my education after I acquired the Ph.D. While attending the University of Chicago we had discovered that Leon Thurstone was taking advanced courses in mathematics because he was trying to develop factor analysis. This activity demonstrated to us that the Ph.D. degree does not complete one's education and that it is necessary to continue studying. With this in mind, I registered for a two-semester laboratory course in speech pathology at the University of Michigan. In addition, I learned a great deal from working with the speech clinicians. While at the Milwaukee State Teachers College and after that, I attended courses in the education of the deaf and in cerebral palsy and took a workshop in the visually handicapped. I make these statements because I do not wish to leave the impression that one can make progress in teaching and research in special education without study or experience in the field beyond courses in experimental and physiological psychology. Special education knowledge and skills had to be acquired through experience and through related course work after the Ph.D.

TEACHER EDUCATION

My first appointment in college teaching was a fortunate one. In 1935, fresh out of direct work with children and with a brand new Ph.D., I was offered a position as Director of the Division of Exceptional Children at the Milwaukee State Teachers College. This was an unusually fine institution which later became the University of Wisconsin, Milwaukee branch. With Frank Baker as a socially minded, flexible president, this institution had initiated many innovative ideas. Geared primarily to kindergarten/primary, elementary, and secondary education, the college also offered degrees in special areas such as music education, art education, and the education of exceptional children.

Students in this state college were offered free tuition and free textbooks. Because of the small size of the building and faculty, the college restricted its enrollment to 1200 students. Out of several thousand applications each year, it admitted 500 freshmen who ranked at the top of their high school graduating classes. This selection process tended to elevate the caliber of instruction offered.

One outstanding feature of the program was that the students completed their liberal arts courses and studies in related areas during the first three years of college and devoted the senior year to concentrated practicums in teaching and small-group instruction. During this fourth year, students were enrolled in practice teaching for three hours each morning for nine months, with practice in several grades. Each faculty member was assigned twelve students to supervise in the morning; they taught them methods, theory, and curriculum in the afternoon.

This College served as a postdoctoral training center for me since teacher education was relatively new to me, especially at the kindergarten/primary level. It thrust upon me new responsibilities: directing the Division for Exceptional Children; training teachers of the mentally retarded; chairing the Counseling Department; chairing the freshmen selection committee; and giving preservice training to kindergarten/primary and elementary students in the management and teaching of handicapped children in the regular grades.

This intensive teacher education program was successful because it provided a low student/faculty ratio and extensive and varied practice teaching. What teacher training program today assigns students for practice teaching in different settings for a full year? What teacher training center today assigns one faculty member to twelve undergraduate students with no other course requirement except to supervise them, show them how to teach, and give them didactic experiences on what to teach, how to teach, and why?

Since few people know everything, each one of the instructors at this teachers college invited others to help them with their students. My involvement was the result of a trade-off with instructors in the elementary and kindergarten/primary divisions. They supervised and instructed the students majoring in the deaf and the mentally retarded, and in elementary education, while I reciprocated by instructing their students in handling children with minor handicaps found in the regular classes. This required that I visit classes for normal children, study school curricula, observe techniques of instruction, and apply what theoretical knowledge I had in learning, reading, and child development to the program for primary and elementary grade students. By combining my theoretical training in psychology and observing teaching techniques, I obtained postdoctoral training in the education of normal children from the professionals in the field. It was necessary for me to observe how elementary teachers managed a class, taught the children, and handled problems. These observations helped me diagnose children who had problems in the classroom and show the student teachers how to adapt instruction to minor handicaps in the regular grades.

This experience is related to the current trend toward mainstreaming in which elementary teachers are asked to manage minor handicaps in children in regular classes. This was the system in the 1930s, since special classes at that time only served children who were definitely handicapped.

INTEREST IN PRESCHOOL EDUCATION

The contact with the kindergarten/primary division at the Milwaukee State Teachers College aroused my interest in the programs for preschool children of normal intelligence. In supervising and assisting student teachers in the correction of minor problems in children in nursery school and kindergarten I obtained some experience in teaching and in the programs for so-called average children.

In 1939 I attended a lecture at one of the social welfare meetings in which Harold Skeels told about early training of the mentally retarded. He described his experience in rehabilitating young mentally retarded children in a state institution for the mentally deficient. He described how he had placed two young retarded girls from an orphanage on separate wards of an institution for mental defectives and asked the retarded women in the wards to play with them and to teach them to talk and to walk. Several years later these two girls were nearly normal and were paroled to foster homes. Skeels proceeded to take twelve other children from the orphanage who tested low in intelligence tests and left thirteen similar children in the orphanage. Two years later the IQs of the children placed in the wards of the state institution with the older mentally retarded women had increased by 27 points, while those of the 13 children left in the orphanage dropped 27 points.

When I questioned Skeels about these results that evening, he showed me a manuscript by Alfred Binet published in 1911, *Modern Ideas About Children*. In the chapter "The Educability of Intelligence" Binet presented a curriculum to develop memory, attention, reasoning, language, and other vectors of intelligence. In other words, Binet was not obsessed with the constancy of the IQ, but believed that it can be changed through educational intervention. (See a reprint in Kirk and Lord, 1974.)

That article and the work of Skeels had a profound effect on my future interests and activities. My experience at the Wayne County Training School also biased me toward a belief in the power of intervention.

While teaching at the teachers college and shortly after the contact with Skeels, I began an experiment with six- and seven-year-old mentally retarded children in Milwaukee in an attempt to improve their behavior and their intelligence. The public school had organized a special class of young retarded children who were causing great difficulties in the classrooms. These children were not as young as I wanted, but they had IQs in the 50s and 60s and histories of behavior problems in school in addition to the inability to learn. The curriculum was organized around Thurstone's primary mental abilities which isolated seven factors in intelligence. These seven factors would be related to ordinary readiness activities such as language training, quantitative thinking, space relations, and so forth. The teacher selected for this class had minored in arts and crafts and was interested in organizing games for the development of such functions in children (Kirk and Stevens, 1943). She devised a great number of educational games of interest for these children, all designed to develop the primary mental functions.

Formal evaluation of this class was never accomplished, since with the incursion of World War II I was commissioned in the Army and had to drop the program. The principal of the school believed, however, that it was the best-behaved class in his school since these children were happily working whenever he came to their class.

SPECIAL EDUCATION DURING WORLD WAR II

During World War II the Army discovered that it could not reject all the illiterates that were drafted. They decided to accept 10 percent of the illiterates going through the induction stations each day. As a consequence, it became necessary to organize special training units in various camps to teach these inductees how to read and write. These soldiers were required to attend special training classes for eight weeks, eight hours a day.

To organize these programs and to develop appropriate tests and training materials, the Army commissioned Dr. Paul Witty and me as the reading experts and stationed us in the Pentagon. Our duties were to (1) develop tests for screening illiterates, (2) develop training materials and books, and (3) conduct workshops for officers in charge of special training units in the various camps. These special training units enrolled 385,000 illiterate soldiers during World War II.

Later in the war, I was assigned to Walter Reed Hospital in Washington to rehabilitate wounded soldiers and to organize appropriate training programs for the disabled soldiers. These two experiences served to remind me that we cannot wait for a war to recognize such problems. It is necessary to expand education for all children as an important function for national defense.

RESEARCH

Following World War II, the state of Illinois developed an extensive program in special education but was extremely short of professionally prepared personnel. Through the urging of the State Department of Public Instruction and Mr. Ray Graham, the Director of Special Education, the University of Illinois decided to employ one person to launch a program in special education. Having been asked to fill that position, I soon discovered that a large university of that type was not equipped to prepare teachers. Instead, it seemed wiser to concentrate on research and graduate programs. Therefore, we minimized undergraduate teacher training and attempted to develop a research and graduate program leading to a Ph.D. in special education.

To continue my previous research I applied for a grant from the Institute for Mental Health, in spite of the fact that at that time the institute was not allotting money for educational research. The project for which I sought funding was a study of the effects of preschool education on the social and mental development of young mentally retarded children. It was also supported partly by the Illinois State Department of Social Welfare and the State Department of Public Instruction. This experiment was conducted for approximately five years both in an institution and in the community. The results of the study were published in book form in 1958 under the title *Early Education of the Mentally Retarded* (Kirk, 1958). Together with the Skeels study, it had an effect in stimulating research on disadvantaged children, in influencing the development of Head Start, and in persuading Congress to enact the Early Education Assistance Act in 1968 (Kirk, 1968). By way of comment, it is interesting to note the extensive lag that exists between social science research results and the response of society. The Skeels study was reported in 1939. It was not widely accepted at that time. The Kirk study was reported in 1958. Not until 1968 did Congress enact legislation to promote preschool education for the handicapped, ten years after the Kirk study and thirty years after the Skeels study.

Besides the experimental results that have been reported for the preschool children, there are a number of observations that may be even more important. To organize a program for mentally retarded children it was necessary for us to observe their behavior and to organize programs for each child's particular needs. For each child we asked the questions: "What abilities does this child have? What deficits exist? What do we do about these particular deficits?"

The analysis of the preschool children—to find out what they could do and what they had difficulty doing—alerted us, in the early 1950s, to the fallacy of classification. Their classification as mentally retarded had little relevance for the training of these children. Each child needed a diagnosis, and each child needed a different program.

One child with marked nystagmus as a result of rubella was diagnosed as legally blind and severely mentally retarded (an IQ of below 50). She was recommended for commitment to a state institution for the mentally retarded. We found that she could learn to respond to and label pictures if we waited long enough. It appeared that this child's nystagmus and visual problems resulted in a deficit in speed of perception. Through the use of a tachistoscope this central dysfunction improved over a six-month training period until she could respond to pictures at 1/25th of a second. This improvement transferred to a life situation where she was able to decode and describe pictures. At the age of ten, in a followup study, she was doing adequate third-grade work in the regular classes. Through intensive training, this child, diagnosed as severely mentally retarded and legally blind at the age of four to five, was at the age of ten considered within the average range educationally and intellectually.

Another child in the same school labeled "mentally retarded" had a recorded IQ of 37. She could not talk. She did not even understand language, but used gestures. With this child we organized a different remedial program, namely, auditory training, auditory discrimination, and teaching her to listen and decode auditory stimuli. Within nine months this girl was talking; at the age of eight her psychological tests ranged between 80 and 90, and her progress in the regular grades was slightly below average.

After finding a number of children with functional deficits of auditory reception, verbal expression, speed of perception, memory, and other problems, we began to look for tests to confirm our clinical diagnoses. At that time (1950) there were very few tests of specific functions. We began in 1950 to develop tests of abilities to aid us in diagnosing the specific problems of these children.

After ten years of work with these concepts we were able to organize an experimental edition of the Illinois Test of Psycholinguistic Abilities. After it was used for approximately six or seven years, it was revised and published in 1968 (Kirk, McCarthy, and Kirk). The ITPA was popular from the beginning because it is an intraindividual test, comparing a child's own abilities and disabilities for the purpose of organizing remediation for deficits. The times were apparently right for working with individual children instead of classifying them into groups for instructional purposes. The ITPA has been translated and standardized in seven other languages. Unfortunately, this test has also spawned many illusions and false hopes. Some people have taken the ITPA as the instrument for the diagnosis of all ills and educational problems. In spite of our numerous warnings, it is being used for junior high students even though it was intended for young children. This problem, of course, is common in many areas of assessment and remediation. We misuse tests and other materials by taking remedial methods developed for one type of child and using them for children for whom they are not suitable. The ITPA, like many other instruments, is only an aid to clinical judgment for children with language and related disorders (see Kirk and Kirk, 1971, 1978).

THE RESPONSIBILITY OF A MAJOR UNIVERSITY FOR RESEARCH DEVELOPMENT

The experiment on preschool education at the University of Illinois was a joint venture of the university, the state Department of Public Instruction, and the state Department of Welfare, which operated the state institutions for the mentally retarded. This experiment demonstrated the advantages of research conducted as a joint venture of several state agencies.

The effectiveness of this cooperation stimulated the participating agencies to establish a research institute that would utilize their resources. With the help of the forward looking Director of Special Education in the state of Illinois, Ray Graham, and the enthusiasm of Dean Willard Spalding and President George Stoddard of the University of Illinois an Institute for Research on Exceptional Children was organized and approved by the two operating agencies and the trustees of the University of Illinois. (For a description of the institute, see Kirk and Spalding, 1953).

The faculty of the institute consisted of professors who held joint appointments with other university departments, plus research associates from the state Department of Public Welfare and the state Department of Public Instruction.

The initial university faculty, James A. Gallagher, Bernard Farber, Oliver Kolstoe, Lawrence D. Stolurow, Herbert Goldstein, Merle Karnes, Clifford Howe, and Samuel Kirk, served between 1952 and 1967. This small but high quality faculty produced volumes of research in many areas of exceptionality (see Kirk and Bateman, 1964).

The state departments were happy to have a research team based at the university to assist in answering some of their practical problems. One project that was dominant in the early 1950s was the problem of trainable children: are they the responsibility of the Department of Public Welfare or of the schools? This became a national problem. At a meeting of the institute, the state Department of Public Instruction, and the school boards (who were opposed to admitting trainable children to public schools) it was decided to ask the legislature for funds to conduct pilot projects and to evaluate the programs after two years. The legislature accepted the report and appropriated funds for the project. The organization of twenty-four classes was arranged and financed by the state Department of Public Instruction, while the institute coordinated the evaluation. This project led the way to the organization of programs for trainable mentally retarded children in many other states (Nickel, 1954).

Another practical problem at this time was how children with high IQs were adjusting or progressing in the regular grades. The problem of gifted children had been worked on sporadically in a number of places, but the state was interested in a practical answer. These problems were partially solved from the pooling of resources, physical and financial, of the university and the state Department of Public Instruction. Again the legislature accepted the reports of research and appropriated funds to extend these services in the public schools in Illinois.

THE PARENTS' MOVEMENT

In the late 1940s and early 1950s parents of retarded children became frustrated by the schools' refusal to admit children with IQs below 50. The institutions were so overcrowded that they were unable to admit them. The parents were taxpayers like everyone else; they paid school taxes, and also paid taxes for the support of the institutions. They were being refused services from both these state agencies.

The parents consequently began to organize locally and to operate schools for their trainable children. These organizations finally founded The National Association for Retarded Children. This movement became a political force and, in the middle 1950s, obtained legal and financial support from state and federal sources.

Later, in the early 1960s, another group of parents whose children were not mentally retarded, or blind, or deaf, or crippled, became concerned for their children who were not learning for other reasons. A. A. Strauss had postulated that these children were brain-injured. They had relatively normal intelligence, often had no obvious overt difficulties, unlike children with cerebral palsy, or the deaf, blind, or crippled. Following Strauss' impact and his book in 1947, parents began to organize under such names as The Society for Brain-Injured Children, or the Society for the Perceptually Handicapped. After many such state and local organizations were formed, the groups decided to hold a national conference. This Conference on Exploration into Problems of the Perceptually Handicapped Child was convened in Chicago in April, 1963. Professional people active in the field (including Myklebust, Kephart, Lehtinen, and I) were invited by this organization to present their points of view concerning children who did not fall into the traditional categories of exceptional children but who nevertheless appeared to be handicapped in learning. Since many names were used for this group, the parents were seeking an inclusive name for their national organization.

In my address to them I stated

> *Recently I have used the term "learning disabilities" to describe a group of children who have disorders in development, in language, speech, reading, and associated communication skills needed for social interaction. In this group I do not include children who have sensory handicaps such as blindness or deafness, because we have methods of managing and treating the deaf and the blind. I also exclude from this group children who have generalized mental retardation. (Kirk, 1963. See Kirk and Lord, 1974, p. 78)*

After much debate on terminology the groups decided that *The Association for Children with Learning Disabilities (ACLD)* was an appropriate designation. Since that date the term *learning disabilities* has become the general term for a heterogeneous group of disabilities of varying degrees of severity which are, however, similar in that they seem to stem from intrinsic cognitive or perceptual difficulties interfering with a child's learning.

This commendable initiative and activity on the part of parent groups stimulated me to give what assistance I could. I had earlier been shocked, saddened, and embarrassed by conditions I had seen in state institutions with indifferent, underpaid, untrained caretakers in understaffed, dilapidated buildings. Tearful parents had come to me time and time again seeking counsel. Often their children had been labeled *feebleminded.*

At that time (the 1930s), I tried to appeal to state senators for better services for these children. I tried to explain the plight of the parents. I remember the following dialogue from that period:

> *Senator: (looking down at me over the rim of his glasses) Do you have a handicapped child?*
> *SAK: No, I don't.*
> *Senator: Then why are you interested?*
> *SAK: My interest is professional, not personal.*
> *Senator: Oh, you are trying to make your profession important.*

Another traumatic experience occurred when I presented a technical report to welfare workers. I had prepared a document with slides of statistics and trends showing wherein the state was lacking in services for the handicapped. Commenting on my speech, the state director of special education said, "These statistics remind me of the statistic which showed that the male graduates of Yale and Harvard had 2.3 children and the female graduates of Vassar and Smith had 1.8 children, thus proving that men have more children than women." With that joke he wiped out my three weeks of research on the status of handicapped children in Wisconsin. I knew then and thereafter that I was completely ineffective as a political advocate for handicapped children and that the dormant political power of parents had to be aroused.

It has been a source of satisfaction to participate and help the parent movements—first, for children with cerebral palsy, then for the mentally retarded, and lastly, for the learning disabled. I found a satisfaction in associating with many intelligent and knowledgeable parents in these organizations. I found that through association with other parents they learned what the best programs were for their children. If I were to give credit to one group in this country for the advancements that have been made in the education of exceptional children, I would place the parent organizations and parent movement in the forefront as the leading force. I am happy to see that now parents, under Public Law 94–142, are partners in the educative process.

THE FEDERAL IMPACT

Shortly after World War II the country found itself with understaffed and overcrowded institutions for the handicapped. Many state institutions refused to admit more children and placed them on three- and four-year waiting lists. Although some states subsidized public school programs for children with physical and sensory handicaps, it was not until the late 1940s and early 1950s that state legislatures appropriated funds for local public school programs for the mentally retarded, emotionally disturbed, and speech impaired. These subsidies were provided before there was an adequate supply of appropriately trained teachers, creating a major shortage of well-prepared teachers of special education. In addition, the financial disproportion among states resulted in a situation in which rich states were stealing experienced teachers from poorer states through higher salaries.

It has been rumored that a prominent parent of a mentally retarded child obtained an interview with President Eisenhower and informed him of the plight of the mentally retarded. The president then requested Congress through the Department of Health, Education and Welfare to do something about the problem. At that time (1954) I was invited to Washington to help the Office of Education formulate plans for programs for the mentally retarded. The same two obstacles to the development of programs for exceptional children that existed at the state level also existed at the federal level: ignorance of what should be done with these children, and a paucity of highly trained, professional personnel. In attempting to solve these problems, the US Office of Education accepted my two proposals.

The first recommendation was for educational research funds. It was pointed out that little research in the education of the mentally retarded was being conducted due to a lack of research funds specifically for education. A second recommendation was for the federal government to support the preparation of professional personnel. Only a few colleges at that time were preparing teachers of the mentally retarded, and many of the classes in the public schools were being manned by partially trained teachers. Furthermore, universities were reluctant to support a training program for minorities like the mentally retarded.

These recommendations resulted in the appropriation of funds for the cooperative research bill PL 83–531 in 1954. The commissioner of education was interested in obtaining research funds for all of education and believed that the prevailing interest of the Congress in the mentally retarded would help support research for education in general. It did.

One million dollars for educational research was appropriated in 1955–56, but Congressman John Fogarty amended the bill to allot $675,000 of the total appropriation to research in the education of the mentally retarded. This amendment made many people unhappy since only one-third of a million dollars was left for all education including other exceptional children. This distribution of funds appeared unfair to them. Two years later the categorical funding of research for the mentally retarded was removed.

In analyzing the grants made for the mentally retarded, I found (as shown in the following figure) that when the categorical appropriations of funds were removed, the Federal grants to researchers decreased from year to year. In 1957, 61 percent of one million dollars appropriated went to research on the mentally retarded. In 1959, when categorical funding was removed, the grants were 36 percent. Funds decreased gradually until in 1963 only five percent of the appropriation was allotted to research in mental retardation and *that* five percent was for the continuation of previously granted research. Actually, *no* new grants for research were made in 1963. These results were presented to Congress in 1966 to convince them that a categorical bureau for the handicapped was needed.

Figure 2.1

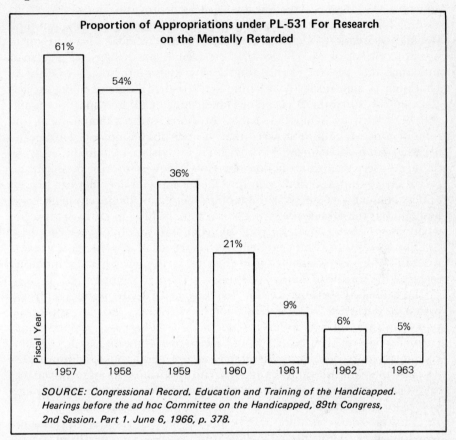

Proportion of Appropriations under PL-531 For Research on the Mentally Retarded

SOURCE: *Congressional Record. Education and Training of the Handicapped. Hearings before the ad hoc Committee on the Handicapped, 89th Congress, 2nd Session. Part 1. June 6, 1966, p. 378.*

Congress had enacted the cooperative research bill in 1954 and appropriated funds in 1956. They were reluctant, however, to accept the recommendation for the preparation of personnel. Some congressmen argued that federal aid for education would result in federal control of education. However, in 1958 Congress passed PL 85–926 with an appropriation of one million dollars for the preparation of personnel in the field of the mentally retarded and in 1960 provided an appropriation for the education of teachers of the deaf.

The cooperative research bill and the appropriations for the preparation of professional personnel under the Eisenhower administration was a beginning. The major impetus to the education of exceptional children, however, was launched during the short period that John Kennedy was president.

In 1962 President Kennedy sent a six-man task force to the Soviet Union to study their programs for mentally retarded children. As members of this scientific commission Lloyd Dunn and I made a report on the status of work for the retarded in Russia (1962). Shortly thereafter, President Kennedy presented to Congress a request for legislation providing for research and training for mentally handicapped children. In signing the ensuing bill, The Mental Retardation Facilities and Community Mental Health Centers Construction Act of 1963 (PL 88–164), President Kennedy stated, "I am glad to announce that we are establishing a new division in the US Office of Education to administer the teaching and research programs under the act. This will be called the Division of Handicapped Children and Youth, and will be headed by Samuel A. Kirk." Previous to the announcement, the commissioner of education asked that "in the public interest" I suffer the necessary cut in salary in order to start this new division. I was informed by the president's secretaries that one does not refuse a request from the president and that if the country can draft men into the military service, they can request professionals to serve in Washington and help run the government. I was hesitant, but the president's earlier words were ringing in my ears: "Ask not what your country can do for you; ask what you can do for your country."

Three weeks after President Kennedy had signed PL 88–164, the world was wounded by his assassination. On my first day on the new job in Washington I attended the sorrowful funeral of President John F. Kennedy.

As indicated the Division for Handicapped Children and Youth was organized in the US Office of Education in November, 1963. The appropriation of fourteen million dollars was not made until February, and the money had to be committed by the following June, the end of the fiscal year. In a short six months it was necessary to develop rules and regulations to administer the Act; distribute the rules and regulations with application forms to universities and state departments; appoint seventeen committees to survey the application blanks; and have the fourteen million committed by June.

This program could not have been completed in six months had it not been for a great public interest and the volunteer help I received from all parts of the United States. We received a large number of applications from state departments, school districts, and universities for research and training, and particularly for the training of professional personnel. We allowed six weeks from the deadline of the applications to the awarding of grants which were all completed by June 1, 1964. Two days after I submitted a report indicating how many grants were received for research and how much money was requested for teacher preparation, Congressman Fogarty introduced the data in the *Congressional Record* with the statement:

> At a meeting of the New England Educators held on May 22 at Rhode Island College in Providence, Samuel Kirk made a progress report on the adminis-tration of the Act by the Office of Education. In view of the great significance of the Act for education and the extent to which it will help the nation's schools fill a critical gap in teachers for handicapped children, I wish to call the report to the attention of all members of Congress. . . . Requests for aid that have been submitted amount to three times the funds now authorized in the Act. (Congressional Record, *June 1964*)

As a result of Congressman Fogarty's effort, Congress doubled the appropriation the following year.

Every ten years the president of the United States awards a Presidential Merit Award to the most efficient department of the US government. That year, shortly after Dr. Maury Wirtz took over as Director of the Division of Handicapped Children and Youth, the Presidential Merit Award went to the Division of Handicapped Children and Youth.

It is ironic to note that, in the face of the Presidential Merit Award and other accolades, the division was abolished eighteen months after its creation when the Office of Education was reorganized by the White House into four bureaus. This action caused great concern in Congress and interested groups throughout the United States. As a result, Congressman Hugh Carey, later Governor of New York, requested that Congress create a Committee for the Handicapped. My testimony at the committee hearings recommended two actions: (1) the creation of a Bureau for the Education of the Handicapped, and (2) the creation of an advisory committee of citizens to advise the bureau and to protect it against itself and against onslaughts by others (*Congressional Record* testimony, 1966).

Congress created the Bureau for the Education of Handicapped Children in 1967 with Dr. James Gallagher as director and Dr. Edwin Martin as assistant director. Following this development, the work for handicapped children moved into a progressive phase. After a period of eight years the work of the bureau culminated in Public Law 94-142, the Education of All Handicapped Children Act.

REFLECTIONS

For over half of a century I have been privileged to study and to work in the field of special education. During this period I have seen many changes and much progress. Service programs, teacher preparation, and research have been the major areas of our professional development.

Service Programs for Handicapped Children

Many changes, of course, have taken place in the philosophy, funding, and organization of programs for handicapped children.

Residential Institutions Our first thrust for services for handicapped children in the US was the organization and development of state and private residential institutions. This was an improvement over leaving to the family all of the responsibility for the care and support of these children. The enthusiasm for these residential schools between 1850 and 1900 resulted in the creation of numerous state schools for the blind, the deaf, the mentally retarded, delinquents, and orphans. After fifty years of expansion of residential schools, the enthusiasm for them began to wane. Instead of habilitation and return to the community, the children stayed in these schools, which became bigger, overcrowded, and poorly supported.

Special Classes   Not until the turn of the century were special classes for the mildly handicapped initiated in an attempt to integrate these children into the community. The special class movement progressed slowly between 1900 and 1950. A few states encouraged the expansion of special classes by providing state subsidies. However, the public school special class movement did not make marked progress until after World War II when it was found that states could not build institutions fast enough for the number of handicapped identified. Enthusiasts for this movement, including myself, alleged that segregation in institutions was not working and was inhuman and expensive. Instead these children should be integrated with the family, the neighborhood, and the public school by way of special classes.

Following World War II, state after state began to appropriate funds for the organization of local special classes for the educable mentally retarded and the emotionally disturbed, as well as continuing earlier established programs for the hearing, visually, and orthopedically impaired.

As usual in many such situations, our society goes too far in one direction and then throws the baby out with the bath water. So it was with the overenthusiasm for special classes, especially classes for the mildly mentally retarded. Wisconsin, for example, in 1927 had defined the mentally retarded psychometrically as those having an IQ below 70. When funds became available for such special classes in the 1950s, school systems began to raise the IQ eligibility requirement to 75, 78, and higher.

In 1962 the American Association on Mental Deficiency defined as mildly retarded those children testing below minus one standard deviation or having an IQ of 84 or 85 and below. This eligibility criterion caused a great increase in enrollment in these classes, especially among minority groups. In addition, special education personnel readily accepted the slow and problem children referred to the special classes. They didn't exactly say, "Give me your tired, your poor,/Your huddled masses . . . .", but they did say, "Give us your slow learners, your behavior problems, your misfits . . . ." Dr. Lloyd Dunn called this "The Sheltering Arms" philosophy. During this period elementary teachers supported the expansion of special classes because this removed from their classes children who were causing them some problems.

The overenthusiasm for classes for the mentally retarded resulted in their becoming dumping grounds for all unwanted children in the regular grades, including behavior problems, bilingual children, Blacks, Mexican-Americans, and native Americans whose IQs were low, often because of language or cultural differences. Ethnic groups took special educators to court, and, fortunately, won. A reform was brewing. New ideas were needed. The concept of special classes in public schools which kept the children out of institutions, at home, and in the community was now called segregation. The new movement was mainstreaming.

Mainstreaming The enthusiastic advocates for mainstreaming tended to disregard certain facts. (1) Mainstreaming is not new. It has been practiced since 1913 when so-called "sight saving" classes were established in subjects requiring close eye work. "Special" students attended regular classes for other studies. (2) Speech-impaired children have always been placed in regular classrooms but given itinerant therapy. (3) Hard-of-hearing children, since the advent of the vacuum tube hearing aid, have attended regular grades but are given short periods of instruction in speech, lip reading, and the use of hearing aids. (4) Resource rooms for the mentally retarded had been used by well-trained teachers of the mentally retarded for many years without being called "resource rooms." Godfrey Stevens, one of my first graduates at the Milwaukee State Teachers College, organized a resource room in south Milwaukee in 1936.

Although mainstreaming is philosophically a sound idea, our enthusiasm for it is gradually waning because we have failed to train regular teachers to teach and manage these children. The grants to deans of colleges of education, referred to as Deans Grants, which were made by the US Department of Education to educate teachers to deal with minor handicaps are, as usual, a drop in the bucket for such a task. Teachers will not be prepared for their duties by attending conferences or being harangued by their superiors or college professors about their duty to teach all the children of all the people. Taking the children out of the classes for short periods in resource rooms for tutoring in the academic subjects may not tilt the scales. Today, many regular educators are dissatisfied because they feel they have been given additional responsibilities without adequate support. Although the philosophy calls for consultation and support, adequate professional support is lacking in many school systems.

Our mistake, as usual, was to launch a program without adequate preparation and without really training the classroom teacher. I recommended to an advocate of mainstreaming many years ago that he teach a second- or third-grade of thirty children, accept into that class three or four mentally retarded, learning-disabled, and emotionally disturbed children, and study exactly how mainstreaming could be accomplished adequately. He did not accept my suggestion. As everyone knows, it is easy to tell someone else what to do, but it is more difficult to accomplish the task adequately and to describe exactly how it is done. We, as yet, have no detailed description of how mainstreaming is accomplished nor an exact distribution of responsibilities of both regular and resource teachers. Until and unless this is done, mainstreaming for the mentally retarded may falter or fail. Mainstreaming for other handicapped children is more readily accepted.

Community Services for the Severely Handicapped   Another major development for service has been the organization of community services for the
severely retarded. Community centers for the severely retarded are now well-
established organizations. State institutions for the mentally retarded have
been gradually replaced by community services. Although Samuel Gridley
Howe, who organized the first institution, warned against their continuance
saying they may be "created needlessly, sometimes even in violation of
political economy . . ." (p. 4), he considered institutions as temporary and
advocated boarding with families in private homes (Howe, 1857).

In 1955 Kirk, Karnes, and Kirk advocated a total community program for
the retarded to be supported and managed by an intermediate governmental
unit such as a county. It was proposed that this total community program
include (1) a diagnostic center, (2) a family counseling center, (3) a temporary
residential unit, (4) a day care unit, and (5) a sheltered workshop (Kirk, Karnes
and Kirk, 1955, Chapter 12). Approximately 12 to 15 years later, community
programs were organized in the United States after Denmark demonstrated
their feasibility. This is another example that shows the lag between an idea
and its implementation in social movements. How to decrease this lag is a
problem for future generations.

Services for the Learning Disabled   The field of learning disabilities is
experiencing the same types of expansion and difficulties encountered in
programs for the educable mentally retarded. Originally we conceived of a
child with a learning disability as one who had a major psychological or
neurological impediment to the learning of reading, spelling, writing, or
arithmetic. These are relatively rare cases, probably only one or two percent of
school children. Today, however, the term *learning disability* applies to
nearly every kind of learning problem a child may encounter.

That heterogeneous part of the population now labeled learning disabled
for funding purposes appears to consist of any child not achieving up to grade
level in the academic subjects, plus children with minor language problems.
Whereas in 1969, 120,000 learning disabled children were reported to be
enrolled in public school services, in 1982–83 over one and two-thirds million
are enrolled in these services. This probably means that many slow-learning
children formerly classified as mentally retarded and many children with
minor reading difficulties are being assigned to learning disability services.

Before our overenthusiasm and expansion of services generates a backlash, it is necessary to find a resolution since nonlearning-disabled children
with learning problems (slow learners and those with minor reading
difficulties) also need services. I should like to propose two types of service
delivery systems:

1. One service would include only the severely learning-disabled children
who need intensive remediation, probably one hour a day, five days a week.
Such children have a marked academic disability associated with a significant
psychological or developmental learning disability of attention, memory,

language, and so forth. The remedial program would be designed to ameliorate both the developmental learning disability and the academic disability. Such a child can attend the regular grade when not in intensive remediation. One special teacher will be able to serve only six or seven such children each day.

2. The second service would assist children who are educationally retarded as a result of lack of motivation, lack of school attendance, inadequate instruction, and other environmental conditions. Such children can be educated in the regular grades supplemented by resource rooms for part of the day or through consultation and help of the regular teacher. One remedial teacher may serve twenty to thirty such children since they will learn by methods of teaching used for regular children.

Teacher Education

Having had experience in the preparation of teachers in both a teachers college and in a university, I regret that teachers colleges have tried to upgrade themselves by becoming universities instead of upgrading teacher education. By becoming universities they have tended to minimize the importance of teacher preparation, and begun to emphasize research and publication as their major function.

I was shocked when I went to a university from a teachers college to find that students studied theoretical courses but only had nine weeks of practice teaching in one elementary class. The supervisor was usually a professor who had not been in a classroom for many years (if at all) and for supervision depended mainly upon the critic teacher to teach the students how to teach. At another university two professors taught the courses in mental retardation and supposedly supervised 70 students a year who had a half-day practicum throughout one semester.

Professors of education in universities and colleges of education are forced to become split personalities because their promotion in rank and pay is dependent upon their scholarly research and publications. Teacher training for those desiring quick promotion becomes a secondary duty.

It may be advisable in the future to establish centers, either as separate teacher colleges or within universities, that would require a master teacher faculty to devote 100 percent of their time to the preparation of teachers. Their promotion in rank and pay would be contingent upon their performance as experts in the preparation of teachers. They would not be required to publish for their advancement.

University faculties of education can then concentrate on graduate teaching and research and need not be encumbered with teacher training. Our current system of teacher training in universities with pressure on the faculty to "publish or perish" is not always accomplishing our objective of graduating master teachers or even producing many research-trained and -motivated personnel. In other words, we need a two-track system for faculties, one group of faculty to devote 100 percent of their time to the preparation of teachers and another who would give 100 percent of their time to the advancement of knowledge and graduate teaching.

Graduate Programs in Special Education

In 1947, when I accepted a position at the University of Illinois, I tried desperately to find Ph.D.'s who had some specialization in special education. The two or three Ph.D.'s in existence at that time were directing programs and were unavailable. Since then, and with federal fellowships for graduate training, we now have a supply of individuals with doctorates in special education. The programs that have evolved have become varied, some stressing research with a heavy minor in psychology and some stressing service, teacher training, and administration. There appears to be little differentiation in course content and experience for a Ph.D. and an Ed.D.

It is my belief that there should be a difference between a Ph.D. and Ed.D. A Ph.D. should be offered to those who desire a career in research in one or more of the areas of special education. These individuals should have had training and experience in at least one area of special education and should, at the graduate level, obtain a cognate or minor in psychology (for the areas of mental retardation, the emotionally disturbed, or learning disabilities) and in linguistics, or speech and language, or speech pathology (for the area of the hearing impaired). Such an individual will then know the major problems needing investigation and the research methodology to investigate them. The dissertation would be of an experimental nature.

An Ed.D. should require a different course of study. Since it is a professional degree, the dissertation need not be required. In its stead, the student should take an extra year to intern in supervision, administration, or teacher training. The Ph.D. degree would require a minimum of two years of course work and a substantive experimental dissertation, while the Ed.D. degree would require four years of graduate work to cover all areas of handicapped children, to intern or to conduct survey studies on problems encountered in teacher education and administration.

A two-track system for doctoral students would allow them to concentrate either on theory and scientific methodology or on the applied and technological areas needed for quality services to handicapped children.

Research and Research Training

It was indicated that the earlier research efforts in special education were conducted in state and private residential schools; the Vineland Training School, the Wayne County Training School, and the Central Institute for the Deaf are examples. In these institutions researchers with ideas had subjects upon which research could be conducted. After World War II and with the expansion of universities, many of them moved to universities. The availability of subjects became a problem unless arrangements were made with the schools or institutions.

Currently, few residential institutions employ research personnel and few university faculties have readily available subjects for research. The problem of clearing a research project with a number of committees in a university, and then clearing it with a school board, school or institutional superintendent, and finally with parents has created a bureaucratic climate not conducive to research.

Federal funding for research has been quite useful in many instances, but the major problem here has been the short-term nature of grants. Good research is developed gradually with programmatic research. Federal grants with yearly reports and varying funding has tended to produce short-term or incomplete research projects, whose reports conclude with the traditional remark that "more research is needed." One wonders sometimes in reading some of the data-based research reports how much the results are objective and how much they are stretched to obtain further research grants.

Research production needs continuous and stable funding. It needs to be conducted in schools and other facilities which serve handicapped children. It needs a cooperative arrangement on a permanent basis between the service agencies and a university. An example is the former Institute for Research on Exceptional Children at the University of Illinois which produced a great deal of research in a ten-year period and offered a research climate for doctoral students. This organization, a cooperative effort of the Department of Welfare in charge of institutions, the state Department of Public Instruction, and the state university, has not been repeated or continued on a permanent basis.

One of the difficulties encountered by this institute was that it became too large. When it operated with four and five highly dedicated research professors and a small group of selected doctoral students, research was accomplished. Generous private and federal funding increased the projects and personnel. Unfortunately, at that time there was a shortage of research personnel, and less competent individuals were employed to conduct these projects. This expansion of research with partly inadequate personnel tended to decrease the quality of research.

The lesson to be learned from the institute venture is that big is not better. If I were to do it over again, it would remain small with only four or five productive professors and a small group of highly selected doctoral students. The desire to bring more money into the university and to expand and expand may not be in the best interests of research and development.

The Federal Roles

Education has traditionally been the responsibility of local and state governments. During the last two and one half decades the federal government has entered the scene, first in research, second in the training of professional personnel, and last in services to equalize education for handicapped and minority children. Under the Reagan administration, an attempt is being made to decrease federal funding for all three programs—research, teacher training, and service.

It is not the purpose of this essay to discuss the pros and cons of the federal budget, but rather to present a personal opinion about our past, and possibly, our future. These opinions are naturally biased and based on my own experience. As indicated, it has been my privilege to help in forming policies, first under the Eisenhower administration when support for research for the mentally retarded was initiated and second, when funds for the preparation of professional personnel for the mentally retarded and for the deaf were appropriated. In addition, I served for a short period as a bureaucrat administering the Kennedy bill, PL 85–926 in 1963 and 1964. I also served as chairman of the Advisory Committee for the Handicapped for two years after the creation of the Bureau for the Education of the Handicapped and also as chairman of the Psychosocial Research Committee for Vocational Rehabilitation. Consequently, I have intimate knowledge of the role of the federal government in special education from its first intervention until now.

My comments about these developments are as follows:

First, special education would probably still be in its primitive stages if it were not for the federal leadership in research and in the preparation of professional personnel. These two support systems have made special education an important segment of education in general. Although some states, like California and Illinois, were making rapid strides for a number of years without the support of the federal government, the other states were moving very slowly.

Secondly, one concern about federal aid is that the funds allotted tend to determine the direction of programs. When research funds became available, universities training doctoral students emphasized the training of research personnel. When teacher training subsidies were appropriated, departments of special education tended to direct their programs toward the preparation of administrators and teacher trainees. There is no question that financial support influences the direction of programs. If the federal government continues in the support of research (as I think it should since research results are of national importance), some system should be developed to support the best researchers without harassment or pressure or political influence.

Thirdly, when BEH was organized, an Advisory Committee for the Handicapped was formed which was to be composed of professionals and citizens from the field. I was privileged to be chairman of this committee during the first two years. This advisory committee reviewed the work of the bureau, helped protect it from unreasonable demands of outside special interest groups, and protected it from itself. It also recommended new legislation to Congress. The advisory committee assisted the development of the bureau for the first few years but was later abolished because the appointees to the committee were selected primarily on the basis of political affiliation and their support of the administration. An advisory committee should be reinstated, but its members should be recommended for appointment by some objective group outside the federal government.

Where Do We Go from Here?

The history of special education has indicated that we tend to move enthusiastically in one direction, become disillusioned with that program, and then become enthusiastic in another direction. We first thought that residential schools would solve the problems of the care and education of the handicapped. After fifty years of building institutions, we found this procedure was not the answer. We then became enthusiastic about day schools and self-contained special classes in public schools. After fifty or more years, we decided that these classes were not the answer. We then became enthusiastic over mainstreaming. Today, some feel that mainstreaming is not the answer, especially for the mentally retarded. Many are raising questions about our future in special education.

It would be pretentious of me to predict the direction that special education will or should pursue in the next two decades. In spite of the significant progress that has been made since the end of World War II, many controversies and questionable practices still exist.

To solve many of these problems, I suggest that we create a National Center for the Study of Policies, Practices, and Issues in Special Education. This center should not be under governmental auspices but should be privately endowed with sufficient funds to guarantee its independent existence for many years. It should be apolitical and free of pressures from private interest groups. Its function would be 1) to study periodically practices in universities and colleges in the preparation of professional personnel and make recommendations for improvement, 2) to evaluate the practices in service delivery by local and state agencies and make recommendations for improvement, 3) to study current research productions and recommend directions for research, and 4) to investigate the current responsibilities of local, state, and federal agencies and make recommendations for the adequate division of responsibility.

This center could be staffed by a small group of the most objective and knowledgeable scholars in the field, who would be free to publish the results of their studies and deliberations and call a spade a spade without fear of political or financial recriminations. The independence of the center should be clearly delineated in the charter for its existence.

REFERENCES

Binet, A. (1974). The educability of intelligence. In S. A. Kirk & F. Lord (Eds.), *Exceptional children: Educational resources and perspectives.* Boston: Houghton Mifflin Co.

Calfee, R. (1982). Cognitive psychology and educational practice. In *Review of research in education* (pp. 3–74). Educational Research Association.

Dunn, L. M., & Kirk, S. A. (1963, March). Impressions of Soviet psycho-educational service and research in mental retardation. *Exceptional Children, 29*(7), 299–303, 305–311.

Fernald, G. M., & Keller, H. (1921, December). The effects of kinesthetic factors in the development of word recognition in the case of non-readers. *Journal of Educational Research, 4,* 355–377.

Hegge, T. G., Kirk, S. A., and Kirk, W. D. (1936). *Remedial reading drills.* Ann Arbor, MI: George Wahr.

Howe, S. G. (1974). Letter to the Governor of Massachusetts, 1857. In S. A. Kirk & F. Lord (Eds.). *Exceptional children: Educational resources and perspectives.* Boston: Houghton Mifflin Co.

Kirk, S. A. (1933, October). The influence of manual tracing on the learning of simple words in the case of subnormal boys. *Journal of Educational Psychology, 24,* 525–535.

Kirk, S. A. (1935). Hemispheric cerebral dominance and hemispheric equipotentiality. *Comparative Psychology Monographs, 11.* Baltimore: Johns Hopkins Press.

Kirk, S. A. (1940). *Teaching reading to slow learning children.* Boston: Houghton Mifflin Co.

Kirk, S. A. (1958). *Early education of the mentally retarded: An experimental study.* Urbana, IL: University of Illinois Press.

Kirk, S. A. (1964, June). Organization and implementation of programs for handicapped children and youth, Public Law 88–164, Title III, and Public Law 87–276. In *Administration of education programs for handicapped children. Congressional Record.* 88th Cong., 2nd sess.

Kirk, S. A. (1968, July). Statement before the Select Subcommittee on Education of the House Committee on Education and Labor on *H.R. 17829.* 90th Cong., 2nd sess.

Kirk, S. A. (1970). Reflections on learning disabilities. *Seventh Annual International Conference of the Association of Children with Learning Disabilities.* San Rafael, CA: Academic Therapy.

Kirk, S. A. (1978). The federal role in special education: Historical perspectives. *UCLA Educator,* Spring/Summer *20*(2), 5–11.

Kirk, S. A., & Bateman, B. (1964). *Ten years of research at the Institute for Research on Exceptional Children.* Urbana, IL: University of Illinois Press.

Kirk, S. A., & Gallagher, J. (1979). *Educating exceptional children* (3rd ed.). Boston: Houghton Mifflin Co.

Kirk, S. A., Karnes, M. B., & Kirk, W. D. (1955). *You and your retarded child: A manual for parents of retarded children.* New York: Macmillan & Co.

Kirk, S. A., & Kirk, W. D. (1971). *Psycholinguistic learning disabilities: Diagnosis and remediation.* Urbana, IL: University of Illinois Press.

Kirk, S. A., & Kirk, W. D. (1978, March). The uses and abuses of the ITPA. *American Journal of Speech and Hearing Disorders, 43,* 58–75.

Kirk, S. A., & Lord, F. (1974). *Exceptional children: Educational resources and perspectives.* Boston: Houghton Mifflin Co.

Kirk, S. A., McCarthy, J. J., & Kirk, W. D. (1968). *The Illinois test of psycholinguistic abilities* (rev. ed.). Urbana, IL: University of Illinois Press.

Kirk, S. A., & Spalding, W. B. (1953, May). The Institute for Research on Exceptional Children at the University of Illinois. *The Educational Forum,* pp. 413–422.

Kirk, S. A., & Stevens, I. (1943, April). A pre-academic curriculum for slow learning children. *American Journal of Mental Deficiency, 47*(4), 396–406.

Monroe, M. (1932). *Children who cannot read.* Chicago: University of Chicago Press.

National Advisory Committee on Handicapped Children. (1968). *First annual report, Subcommittee on Education of the Committee on Labor and Public Welfare, U.S. Senate.* Washington, D.C.: U.S. Government Printing Office.

National Advisory Committee on Handicapped Children. (1969). *Second annual report, Subcommittee on Education of the Committee on Labor and Public Welfare, U.S. Senate.* Washington, D.C.: U.S. Government Printing Office.

National Advisory Committee on Handicapped Children. (1970). *Third annual report, Subcommittee on Education of the Committee on Labor and Public Welfare, U.S. Senate.* Washington, D.C.: U.S. Government Printing Office.

Nickel, V. L. (1954). *Report on study projects for trainable mentally handicapped children.* Springfield, IL: Department of Public Instruction.

Spearman, C. (1927). *The nature of intelligence and the principles of cognition.* London: Macmillan & Co., Ltd.

Strauss, A. A., & Lehtinen, L. (1947). *Psychopathology of the brain-injured child.* New York: Grune & Stratton.

Wallin, J. E. Wallace. (1924). *The education of handicapped children.* Boston: Houghton Mifflin Co.

3

A Search for Understanding

Herbert Goldstein

Herbert Goldstein, born 1916 in Hamilton, Ontario, holds a B.S. and M.S. in special education from San Francisco State College (1949) and an Ed.D. from the University of Illinois (1957).

Dr. Goldstein was research associate at the Institute for Research on Exceptional Children and associate professor in the College of Education at the University of Illinois (1957–62). In 1962, Dr. Goldstein was made chairman of the Department of Special Education at Yeshiva University, where in 1966 he established the Curriculum Research and Development Center to develop the Social Learning Curriculum. He was professor in the Educational Psychology Program in Special Education at New York University from 1978 until his retirement.

He is now professor emeritus in educational psychology and special education. He has received the Citation for Outstanding Service from the American Academy of Pediatrics and was awarded the Fulbright Research Scholarship to the University of Oslo (1962).

Sooner or later, most doctoral students fall prey to an insidious and contagious ailment I call "fulminating pomposity." The symptoms are readily discernible: an obsessive drive to uncover clay feet and a compulsion to split hairs into infinite filaments. In the final stage, the student becomes encrusted with an impermeable layer of clichés that prevents forevermore the penetration of the ideas and opinions of others.

Sam Kirk has an effective remedy for "fulminating pomposity." When he saw the obsessive behavior taking hold, he would inject an immunizing factor in the form of the question, What is special about special education? The first reaction by the group was predictable—first, incredulity: Who doesn't know the answer to that simple question?—and then, discomfort: Are we witnessing the onset of senility? But Sam would ignore the reaction and press on with the question.

From the cacophony of responses, there soon emerged the students' biases. Those with a psychological orientation talked about psychometry, characteristics of handicapped children, and ways of coping with learning handicaps and deficits; students with administrative experience detailed organizational factors and how services are brought to bear, while former teachers stressed curriculum, teaching methods, and classroom management.

It soon became evident to most that Sam had thrown us one of his many Kirkian curves. His objective was more to shake complacency than to find an answer—and he succeeded. In fact, his question has remained important to me to the present. From time to time I arrive at an answer that seems comfortable and complete only to come upon a scholarly work such as Hobbs' *The Futures of Children* (1975), Sarason, Davidson, and Blatt's *The Preparation of Teachers* (1962) and, just recently, Ysseldyke and Algozzine's *Critical Issues in Special and Remedial Education* (1982) and the question is revived.

In an important sense, this chapter is a kind of reification of the question. After many years, I have come to the realization that there is no conclusive answer—only the need to keep asking the question.

INTRODUCTION TO EXCEPTIONAL CHILDREN

For at least a decade following World War II, special education was one of the better kept secrets in the education establishment. In fact, in the late 1940s, when I enrolled at San Francisco State College as an elementary education major, I was totally unaware of any educational provisions for the handicapped as was the Veterans Administration counselor who "sold" me on a career in education.

But for a spate of propaganda from San Francisco State's Department of Special Education, I would have probably changed my career goal because

My thanks to Marjorie Goldstein for comments, helpful criticism, and much patience.

elementary education courses were difficult to endure. Many descriptions come to mind, such as soft, dogmatic, uninspiring, and unchallenging. With few exceptions, the faculty preached (e.g., "If you don't love children, you don't belong in this profession"). Faculty saw questions as to premise, theory, or philosophy as apostasy. Too many questions, and one earned the reputation of dissident, obstructionist, and all-around nuisance from faculty and students alike.

Bearing the heavy load of the frustrated seeker of the truth, I came across an array of posters, heroic in proportion but depressing in message. Each depicted the same handsome, albeit mournful, little boy. "I need you to teach me" was the plea emblazoned in huge letters at the top of each poster. At the lad's feet was a separate legend: "I am blind." "I am mentally retarded." "I am deaf."

In disbelief that such a wholesome-appearing child could be so drastically afflicted, I entered the nearby office and inquired of the secretary the meaning of the posters. Before she could reply, I was confronted by a faculty member who responded to my questions with clarity and enthusiasm. In less than fifteen minutes, I was given a minicourse in what special education was all about, an overview of the teacher preparation program, and the range of career opportunities. This was my first association with Jerome Rothstein and the beginning of a long and productive professional relationship.

When I departed the office, I was enrolled in the special education program with a minor in elementary education so that I could have dual certification. Some thirty years later, I look back on my rapid indoctrination into special education without an iota of regret. From the outset, courses in the program were stimulating. While they were mainly didactic, faculty was open to questions and did not look upon requests for substantiation as a challenge to their integrity or a violation of the caste system. While there was breadth to the program, specialization along with a sharing of interests characterized the faculty approach. Most important, each in his or her own way presented a solid empirical base to course work. While I opted for specialization in mental retardation and therefore worked closely with Dr. Rothstein, I had extensive and direct experiences with Dr. Leo Cain (giftedness and administration), Priscilla Pittinger (auditory handicaps), and Leon Lassers (speech pathology).

Apart from the intellectual vigor provided by its faculty and many of its students, the guidance in the literature of special education was most stimulating. The text for the ubiquitous survey course was Baker's *Introduction to Exceptional Children* (1945), a text that served as a model for many that followed. Beyond Baker's text, there was little contemporary work available except in journals and pamphlets. The richest sources were the *Vineland Training School Bulletin* and the American Journal on Mental Deficiency. The *Training School Bulletin* was the source of important information. Most noteworthy were the articles by Edgar Doll and Henry Goddard. In a more educational vein, publications from the US Office of Education by Elise

Martens and articles in the *Journal of Exceptional Children* described local programs for the mentally retarded and often detailed classroom activities appropriate to the education of these students.

The nature of the articles and texts available in the late '40s and for some time thereafter clearly depicted the state of the art of educational programs for mildly retarded (EMR) students. There were no foundational programs, no curriculum areas in any way comparable with the reading, arithmetic, science, social studies, humanities, and aesthetics typical of regular education. Whereas programs in regular education represented a continuum with a common base for all grade levels within a school district, teachers in special education were left to their own devices to cobble up whatever programs they could.

Lacking a substantive frame of reference, teachers became adaptors and scroungers of regular class materials and whatever special class procedures they could glean from their professional journals and other publications. Inevitably, then, special education became and, to a considerable degree, continues to be a cottage industry with relatively little continuity over the twelve to twenty years of schooling guaranteed most children.

This is not to say that there was no concern for the effects of discontinuity in the education of retarded children. Ingram (1935) refined and then extended the unit form of instruction and helped teachers organize subject matter around an array of psycho-social themes considered relevant to educational programs. The popularity of Ingram's contribution was manifest in its adoption as a basic element in teacher preparation. For a long time, candidates for certification in the education of the mentally retarded could not expect to graduate unless they fulfilled the curriculum-and-methods course requirement to construct a unit.

Somehow, our teacher educators felt that the key to their students' success was the unit they carried with them into their first teaching job. The notion that the unit might have little or no relevance to the children was not at issue. Most of us, leaving the halls of ivy with a multi-page unit on the post office or the supermarket, complete with motivating activities and lists of audiovisual aids, felt somewhat secure. At least, we agreed, we had something to get things rolling once we had inscribed our names on the chalkboard. The concern that our so-called motivating activities might not inspire our students or that our school district might not have a film projector, let alone the films on our list, was not an issue.

Probably more important, the mental set for a pragmatic approach to educating children was not an important part of our orientation to teaching. We learned a great deal about the characteristics of mentally retarded children in the abstract, e.g., that mentally retarded students cannot manage concepts and have low tolerance for frustration. The issue of individual differences and their implications for characteristics and manifest behavior was rarely the focus of lectures or the literature.

As I look back, I can see the unintended paradox in our preparation for teaching, a paradox that persists, I believe, to the present. On the one hand, the social psychology of the classroom requires that the teacher be a thinking person if he or she is to fulfill the role of teacher effectively. Decision making is the most significant teaching behavior: deciding what to teach to whom, when, and under what conditions; how to gain and sustain interest, attention, and involvement; and a myriad of other issues with implications for productive teaching. On the other hand, much, if not most, of teacher preparation is didactic. Opportunities to practice decision making—to analyze critical information, evolve a plan, activate the plan, and evaluate results—is a rare college classroom activity. Instead, students are involved with *how-to* and *if-then* gambits based on research findings, discursive articles, and interpolations of the experiences of others.

These condition students to believe that the behavioral sciences consist of a sizeable array of immutable facts and concepts that need to be memorized and recalled when an eliciting stimulus is presented. It is little wonder that students come to their key professional courses ready and eager to be spoon-fed a bag of tricks, with few if any questions as to the rationality of a static approach to a dynamic setting. A carefully constructed, elaborate unit designed for use with a phantom class is a logical by-product of this approach to training teachers. While some bridle at the use of the term *training* (and all of the highly over-simplified S-R transactions that it connotes) it nevertheless is a more accurate description than the term teacher-education.

Despite common goals and interests, regular teacher preparation and special education training are more likely to stress differences in customs and mores than similarities. This was very clear to me even as an undergraduate. One of the major differences that has persisted to the present is the investment in the content of instruction. In regular education, I found, content is an integral part of teacher preparation. It is more often than not viewed as a continuum; the term *series* is common and indicates that the content is organized developmentally, particularly in academic areas. In my special education courses, however, the emphasis was almost exclusively on processes for managing the so-called characteristic behavior of mentally retarded children. We spent a lot of time evolving tactics for coping with short attention span, poor retention, and a sizeable array of behavior disorders. Our preoccupation with these abstractions did not leave us much time to be concerned about curriculum. We did have the Elise Martens pamphlets and Ingram's text and a handful of articles from professional journals describing programs, and that was about all. While the curriculum library was well-stocked with elementary and secondary education curricula, the special education section had a few text books and a small number of curriculum guides which were little more than subject matter outlines.

As I look back, I can see and understand why process was a high focus topic. By the time I entered the profession, special education and particularly the area of mental retardation was heavily influenced by psychologists. The leading people in psycho-educational research and in teacher preparation programs were psychologists. The most notable in our readings included Cyril Burt, William Featherstone, Samuel Kirk, Edgar Doll, Henry Goddard, Seymour Sarason, J. Wallace Wallin, William Sloan, William Cruickshank, Heinz Werner, Thorlief Hegge, and others who have undeservedly faded from memory. In contrast, comparatively little time was spent on the content of instruction. Influential people such as Seguin, Duncan, Itard, and Decroly were mentioned briefly in lectures but were not on the required reading list.

In retrospect, I can appreciate the influence faculty have on their students' value systems. We sometimes underestimate our ability to indoctrinate students and to infuse them with our values and often our biases. The things we do not say or omit from required reading have, by default, as much impact as what we verbalize. Since the faculty hammered away at process while underplaying content, we came away with the belief that the key to successful teaching of mentally retarded children lay in counteracting their learning and behavioral deficits. It must have been assumed that if we were successful, the children would somehow learn to read and reckon as well as master the subject matter of science and social studies. Further, we were somehow expected to select the proper reading and arithmetic materials. The futility of this expectation can be found in the frequency with which teachers persisted in confronting hulking teenagers with Dick-and-Jane preprimers and other demeaning materials. The argument that regular class preprimers were all that was available begs the question. The role of teachers in the modification, adaptation and in-class development of instructional materials must always be an important feature in teacher education if appropriate matches between childrens' characteristics and content are to be effected.

THE SONOMA EXPERIENCE

Having completed my course work, I was eligible, if not ready, for student teaching. I opted to fulfill my elementary education requirement in the fall semester and devote the spring to special education. I only mention this conventional experience because it brought on my first confrontation with a school bureaucracy. Since we were given our choice of grade level, I chose the first grade. My reason was, in effect, to get a sense of how mental age is manifested in an educational setting. We had dealt with MA in the abstract in our course work and had accepted intellectually that an MA of 6 in a nine-year-old was not the same qualitatively as an MA of 6 in a six-year-old. Here was a chance to see the latter so that I would have a referent when I began to teach retarded children. Little did I realize that so worthy an objective could arouse the passions of an otherwise phlegmatic group of middle managers. My request first met resistance from the student teaching office on the grounds that there was no precedent for a male teacher in the first grade. Undaunted, I insisted that my rationale was sound and that the request be carried forward to the authorities in the San Francisco schools. The response from the school system was quick and negative. The reason: first graders need a mother figure. Refusing to accept such an oversimplification, I stood my ground, arguing that a father figure was equally appropriate. My message to the school people that it was either the first grade or nothing settled the issue. They capitulated, and I began one of my more productive experiences. The first graders were homogeneous only in age and in their honest approach to learning and classroom activities. Equally important, I saw firsthand the effects of all-around good teaching and classroom management. Most important, I learned how diverse an MA of 6 can be.

While I was involved with the first graders, Dr. Rothstein was arranging a teaching internship for me at Sonoma State School. The internship was to extend through the spring semester to the end of summer session. My time was to be divided equally between the psychology department and the education unit. Thirty years ago, institutions for the mentally retarded were not as prominent as they have been for the past decade. Sonoma was no exception. Distant from population centers, major travel routes, Sonoma had taken on a life and culture all its own. Physically, it was far from the present stereotype of the institution for the mentally retarded. Set in Jack London country, the Valley of the Moon, its well-tended lawns, flower beds, and groves and red-brick buildings conjured up the image of an ivy league college. The buildings, not at all overcrowded, were clean and well maintained. Not far from the central grounds were the institutional farm, orchards, and a prize herd of milk cows.

All of this was possible because Sonoma, like other institutions, could deploy a competent work force of considerable size. Since special classes in the public schools were not numerous then, Sonoma's population was predominantly the mildly retarded. Thus, a small staff of artisans, craftsmen, and ward personnel, augmented by platoons of so-called "high grades," was able to maintain buildings and grounds at a very high level inside and out. Every day was like the first day of spring cleaning in the cottages, including the few housing severely and profoundly handicapped teenagers and adults. At the time, the admission policy did not accommodate infants. If memory serves, the youngest children at Sonoma were of school age. The elite of the institution were the elderly men who shared rooms in a comfortably furnished cottage. They were the "first assistants" to the craftsmen and artisans and did the routine work in administrative offices. Elderly women also lived relatively comfortably but had less glamorous work. They headed the work crews in the laundry and the kitchen and assisted in the management of the cottages for girls.

I have dwelt on the physical attributes of the institution because they presented to the passerby and the visitor a picture of care and comfort more in keeping with a luxury rest home than a state operated institution. There were even entertainers on hand to amuse visitors: a group of Down's syndrome children who were trotted out to sing and dance and otherwise reinforce the notion that "mongoloids" were invariably happy and tractable.

All state institutions in California at that time were administered by psychiatrists. Mild mental retardation was seen as a behavior disorder, while more severe retardation was attributed to central nervous system damage as a function of disease, accident, or heredity. The mildly retarded residents were theoretically treatable psychotherapeutically. The individualized nature of psychotherapy suggests a sizeable staff of psychiatric and psychologic therapists. This was not the case nor could it possibly have been at Sonoma, given the constraints of state support. In a sense, then, professional staff was tacitly freed from any compulsion to achieve other than self-made goals. And since the vast majority of the mildly retarded residents were committed with lengthy histories of social transgressions, goals were almost invariably long range. This is not to say that the therapeutic orientation of the administration was endorsed by other professionals. The psychology staff, for the most part, disagreed with the policy as did the social work staff, while education and recreation tended to side with the administration. The attitudes of the dissidents had evidently been expressed, rebuffed, and then contained by the time I started my internship. Professional workers had fallen in line, and work went on.

One of the more obvious results of the institution's policies was the encapsulation of services. With my background it did not take me long to realize that here psychology and education worked independently of each other. As it turned out, this was typical of all services except social work. The social work staff saw themselves as the residents' bridge to the community, and they worked at this role assiduously despite considerable heckling and harrassment.

Recreation and education served two purposes. First, these services had a humane quality; they provided diversion from the boredom of cottage life, and they offered avenues for growth consistent with a therapeutic milieu. Second, they were powerful means for controlling behavior. Since these services were seriously understaffed, they could only accommodate a limited number. All other criteria being equal, the best behaved were selected for these services. Similarly, retention in the service depended on good behavior. A cottage staff member, for example, could bar a resident from school, the hobby and crafts classes, attendance at movies, weekly dances, and the like. Banishment from an activity often meant termination from the service. One can understand, then, the terror of residents when teacher or recreation worker threatened to send the resident to his or her cottage.

My work in psychology was to go through the files to identify residents who hadn't been retested in many years. This was a pet project of the staff but one they couldn't tackle because of ongoing testing and their membership on the cottage therapy teams. I found an alarmingly large number of residents with long tenure who either had never been tested or who had not been retested since their admission some two or three decades earlier. My job was to bring their files up to date by administering either the Binet or WAIS and the Vineland Social Maturity Scales. Many of my clients were long-term residents of the back wards. This was not a population addressed in my mental measurement courses. The psychology staff, however, gave me a thorough tutorial, and I was able to make some inroads into the moribund files.

As interesting and stimulating as my work with the psychology staff was, my work in the school was even more invigorating. Half my time was devoted to an intermediate-level class in the school building, and half to a secondary-level class on one of the locked wards. The locked wards were cottages surrounded by tall, chain-link fences topped by loops of barbed wire. All doors to the cottages were locked and guarded. The residents were mainly youngsters of junior and senior high school age whose criminal records qualified them for state prison. Since they tested in the slow-learner range and below, they were packed off to Sonoma where they could be locked up indefinitely.

Somehow, I got along so well with my class of fifteen dedicated felons that I was offered their accolade of acceptance—the services of the ward whore. Those of you who have worked closely with dedicated delinquents will recognize that the offer was far from a casual gesture; it was tantamount, in their value system, to an invitation to membership in their society. Fortunately, I realized the sensitivity of the situation and, with a little fancy footwork, came up with an acceptable reason for not availing myself of the proffered recreation. With obvious regret, I thanked them for the honor and went on to say that, since I was being treated for a social disease, I was reluctant to infect the membership. To this moment, I cannot think of a way of rejecting the offer that would have been more face-saving for both sides. The fact is, I lost no ground with my students and may, indeed, have gained a few points in their estimation.

The school principal wanted me to focus on occupations in the event that any one of my students should return to the community. Clearly, my well-prepared unit on the post office was not going to be of much help here. I reverted to my own work experiences spanning the decade between high school graduation and college entrance. I quickly found that their interests were far from conventional. They dismissed such key matters as how to get a job, what is entailed in different lines of work, and the like. What excited them was the shady side of an occupation—how to short change customers, how to get away with stealing, fraud, malingering, and other acts looked upon by most of us as counterproductive. Accepting that my few months with them would have little impact on their moral development but being unwilling to assume the role of Fagin, I compromised by including in the lessons the constructive aspects of the world of work along with the machinations and scams of dishonest customers, clients, and employers.

My half day in the institution school was far less colorful. The most outstanding characteristic of the school was its pervasive quietness. The student body, selected on the basis of compliant behavior, lived up to its reputation. The so-called teachers (none certified, few more than high school graduates) focused on reading, writing, and arithmetic with interludes of arts and crafts. Children labored almost exclusively in workbooks. In an important sense, the school was a testimonial to the drudgery and boredom of life in the cottages.

Lest I leave the impression that my experiences at Sonoma were exclusively negative, I must point out that many good things were happening and there were many able and productive people as well. Comparing later experiences in institutions, I would judge that the psychiatric influence in the administration sustained the plantation atmosphere and inhibited more productive approaches to habilitating the residents. The psychiatric concept was the framework within which the institution operated and to which all services were designed to conform. The two key services, psychology and social work, were staffed by learned and energetic people who struggled mightily to accommodate themselves to the policy without surrendering their professional integrity. Some were able to bootleg their theories into the daily effort; a few succumbed and went through the prescribed motions while finding their intellectual and professional stimulation outside of the institution; others struggled as long as they could and then departed quietly. All were most generous to interns with their time and attention. Questions got thorough, and detailed responses and informal seminars were invigorating and productive.

Cottage staff were, for the most part, responsible local people. I found most of them cooperative and concerned for their clients. Though they did not have much to do except to supervise the cleaning and maintenance efforts of their residents, most were willing to do more. They were candid in their observations that there was too much sitting around and random activity. They deplored the fact that only a few of the children attended school, and many volunteered to teach reading and arithmetic if the school would provide the materials. When I carried this message to the principal, it was rejected on the grounds that cottage staff lacked the competence to be effective and might, indeed, undo the work of the teachers. Clearly, territoriality was operating at the expense of the residents. This is doubly ironic when one considers the limited competence of the untrained teaching staff and their phlegmatic approach to their jobs.

Interestingly, the cottage staff was the only group willing to talk about the rampant homosexuality in the cottages. The issue came to light when I mentioned to a cottage attendant the offer of the services of the ward whore on the locked ward. He convinced me that I had chanced upon one of the most serious problems in the institution: the widespread nature of homosexual acts and, in particular, the exploitation of the younger and more helpless boys and girls. He complained that cottage staff was never able to impress the professionals with the pervasiveness of the problem, even though many residents were reinstitutionalized after community work placement because of homosexual incidents.

Not long after I completed my internship, changes in policy and therefore in activities developed. Leadership in the education service, for example, was taken over by a well-prepared energetic person who was able to overcome the inertia by upgrading the teaching and supportive staff.

Not long afterward, radical changes in Sonoma and other state institutions came about because of the expansion of provisions for mildly retarded children in the public schools and the reduced death rate of severely handicapped infants. The change from plantation to human warehouse swept through state institutions. The disappearance of large work gangs and the incapacities of an essentially helpless population, along with the reluctance of state legislators to underwrite the costs of care and maintenance, accelerated the physical, social, and psychological deterioration of state institutions. This historical fact became known some years after my departure from Sonoma, so I will leave the details of this transition until later.

In retrospect, my most positive experience at Sonoma came during the last two months of my internship. It was then that I came upon a section in the institution's small, professional library devoted to old journals and texts. There I learned for the first time of the *Journal of Psycho-Aesthenics* and the precursor of the *American Journal on Mental Deficiency*, the *Proceedings of the American Association on Mental Deficiency.* While many volumes were missing, there were enough to provoke my interest in the history of the movement on behalf of the mentally retarded. Along with the journals, I found medically oriented texts devoted to mental retardation. Like the journals, these provided a view of early concepts and theories and described procedures for habilitation. Among those that left a lasting impression were Barr's (1904) history of the treatment and training of mental defectives. I was impressed by his category, the morally retarded, and how apt his description was to many of the residents, particularly in the locked cottages.

Of course, the old standby, Tredgold's (1937) text on mental deficiency was there, and it was an education in itself. His discussion of the work of the Royal Commission on the Care and Control of the Feebleminded (1908) was provocative and led me to an in-depth study of this voluminous report soon after I enrolled at the University of Illinois. Beyond the detail incorporated in his text, I was taken by Tredgold's distinction between mental retardation, amentia, and mental illness, dementia, and the prominence he gave to social adaptation as a distinguishing criterion. On the same shelf I found Binet and Simon's article in the Vineland Training School Bulletin which contained an allusion to the social aspects of mental retardation that is worth quoting here: "a peasant, normal in ordinary surroundings of the fields, may be considered a moron in the city" (1916, pp. 266–67).

To the reader, who is undoubtedly more sophisticated than I was in the late 1940s, these discoveries may seem of little moment. One should remember, however, that my orientation to mental retardation was essentially psychometric; the faculty at San Francisco State and the Psychology Department at Sonoma, both heavily psychological, stressed the measurable aspects of intelligence as the criteria for diagnosis. While my first inclination was to dismiss the social aspects underscored in the early literature as an aberration of the times, my experiences with the residents at Sonoma provoked questions. For example, while they shared the same IQ range, they differed notably in the reasons for their commitment to the institution. Their records showed that social adaptation or, more accurately, maladaptation, played a powerful role in their placement. When I raised this issue in our informal seminars in the Psychology Department, the staff agreed that social factors were important. However, their position was that tests of intelligence are samplings of important social behaviors and therefore implicitly measure social adaptation. Later, I found this concept the source of much controversy. In particular, Jastak (1949), Sarason (1949), Wallin (1949), and McCulloch (1947) wrote extensively on the question of the role of social adaptation as a criterion in the diagnosis of mental retardation but without much resolution. In essence, then, while social adaption was accepted as respectable and an important factor in placement decisions, it was not considered as reliable or generalizable as the results of intelligence tests. In my own experience, I found that it was common practice to assign children to special classes solely on the basis of intelligence test scores. The psychological reports accompanying children to my class rarely included information about their social skills apart from the mention of obnoxious behavior in the regular class that had provoked their referral in the first place.

The pioneering texts and journals were provocative. Certainly for one whose preparation to teach the mentally retarded was mainly psychological in orientation, they raised many questions about the messages of history. Since I had exhausted the few publications available, I looked forward to studying the early literature in greater depth. The opportunity to do so did not emerge until I engaged in graduate study at the University of Illinois.

TEACHING EDUCABLE MENTALLY
RETARDED CHILDREN

The interval between Sonoma and the University of Illinois was crowded with the efforts and energies demanded by my students in the special class assignment I accepted in San Anselmo, California. This class for educable mentally retarded (EMR) children was remarkably different from the classes at Sonoma, physically and in its constituency, though not philosophically. The physical facilities were inferior. My intermediate-level class shared a condemned school building with another class for primary-level children. All of the regular classes were across the playground in a beautiful new building. My classroom contained vintage student desks, a pox-pitted blackboard, and a teacher's desk that was undoubtedly rejected by the second-hand dealer who had carted all the other furniture away. The floor boards had long since parted company, leaving open spaces into which disappeared anything smaller than a half inch in diameter. A sizeable portion of my salary went to replace my students' milk and lunch money that persisted in rolling into the spaces.

Teaching materials consisted of a few boxes of worn crayons, a stack of dog-eared first- and second-grade workbooks, a companion series to children's classics (popularly known as high interest-low vocabulary texts), some odd scraps of blank paper, and a modest stack of primers, preprimers, and pre-preprimers. I immediately drew up a list of supplies and teaching materials which disappeared into the bureaucracy never to be heard from again. The principal saved the day by providing me with materials to help me get started.

My students were a mixed bag, mainly boys, who were rejects from three or more regular classes. They ranged in type from a hemiplegic youngster to familial retarded children, with all kinds of neurological and emotional disorders in between. They ranged in age from ten to fourteen. At the upper limit were two young ladies of the bovine persuasion who, while placid in most ways, actively affected the classroom atmosphere. One didn't have to look up to realize that Zita or Joanne was approaching. They were preceded by an aroma that caught one's attention quickly. Respecting the delicate psyches of my students, I tried to solve the air pollution problem by a series of lessons on hygiene and health, but to little avail. Zita and Joanne participated in the lessons enthusiastically, and there were a few days when my eyes stopped watering, but these were rare and infrequent. The school nurse finally provided the explanation for the impasse. The young ladies, she told me, were flowering into womanhood, and their physical changes accounted for the atmospheric conditions. Assistance in correcting the situation was not forthcoming; the school nurse was preoccupied with other duties.

When I approached the girls' families, I was informed through clenched teeth that decent people do not talk about such things. In desperation, I responded to an advertisement by the Kotex Company offering teaching materials and persuaded the young ladies to engage in the prescribed activities. The problem was solved but, more important, I had further confirmation of the critical role maladaptive behaviors play in conceptualizing mental retardation. This experience also confirmed my feelings of isolation from the larger educational establishment.

While many experiences reinforced my notion of the lonely teacher, the one that almost had fatal results is most illustrative. Eddie, my hemiplegic boy, was a quiet and docile child. His psychological report was the only document I had. A paragon of brevity, it told me that his condition was due to birth trauma, that his IQ was within the educable range, and that I should generate a warm, accepting environment for him.

Since I had found the preprimers to be anachronisms, I taught reading by way of experience charts. To evolve subject matter, I often took the class on walks where we observed certain neighborhood phenomena such as homes, flora and fauna, shops and the like. Because of his physical disability, Eddie would gradually fall behind, and I would urge him to keep up. I soon noticed that his otherwise pale visage would gradually take on a bluish tinge as he exerted himself to keep up with the class. I had no realization of the meaning of the changes in Eddie until I chanced to mention my observations to our family pediatrician, who gave me a short course on "blue babies" and the results of overexertion. While this is an extreme case, it nevertheless illustrates the distinction between what teachers need to know about their students and the kinds of information they may receive. I am still shaken by the recollection of how close I came to forcing a fatal accident.

My experiences as a classroom teacher were, at first, positive and constructive. My college preparation was helpful up to the point of actual teaching confrontations. From that point on, any increments in knowledge were a function of on-the-job training. What to teach, when to teach it, how to teach, and what to teach with I learned as I went along. Since I had no supervision or coordination of any kind, I felt free to experiment and to manage the class as I saw fit. I can see how this isolation can breed contentment and, at the same time, a reluctance to change once one has struggled to evolve a program that seems to work. Teachers are often chastised for being unwilling to implement innovations in content and/or process. In many cases, such resistance is nothing more than their adherence to the first rule of wing walking: "don't let go of what you have a firm grip on until you have an equally strong grip on something else."

GRADUATE STUDY AT THE UNIVERSITY OF ILLINOIS

My on-the-job training was productive but not to the degree that it reduced anxiety. More and more I realized that each increment in knowledge engendered its own mysteries: Why was a procedure successful with one student but not with another? How could I be sure that my results derived from what I thought was the correct procedure? These questions increased to the point that teaching became wearing.

The only way to recapture the fun of teaching, I believed, was to enter a graduate program where I could find the answers not forthcoming in the classroom. Since there were no doctoral programs in special education in the San Francisco area, I applied to the University of California's Department of Educational Psychology. My rationale was that this was as close as I could get to appropriate theories and principles of learning which I would then apply experimentally to mentally retarded children for my dissertation. Shortly after I was notified of acceptance, I happened across a publication containing an article by Samuel A. Kirk which described the Institute for Research on Exceptional Children at the University of Illinois. The article ended with the statement that there was financial assitance for qualified graduate students. This started a chain of events that culminated in my acceptance into the doctoral program and as a research assistant in the Department of Special Education at the University of Illinois.

I never returned to the public schools as a teacher, but have always maintained a keen interest in their purposes and functions. Early on, I learned a lesson that has been reinforced over time, namely, that the value of all educational and supportive services is determined by the extent to which these contribute to the classroom teacher's work with students within the context of the goals of education. I know from experience that a teacher can get along without school psychologists, social workers, and other support staff. The opposite is not true. The best condition (one we have yet to approximate) is a well-prepared, pragmatic teacher supported by well-prepared, educationally sophisticated ancillary staff whose work is facilitated and supported by a knowledgeable administration.

To contribute to this professional complex became my goal when I joined the institute in 1953. My plan was to become an administrator and thereby infiltrate the ranks of the decision makers. My first meeting with Sam Kirk changed this goal. He urged me to delay commitment to a career pending my experiences as a graduate student. The rigors of coursework and my assistantship at the institute took precedence, and I fell into the flow of activities.

It early became evident that while the doctoral program was rich and stimulating, it paled alongside the work and associations at the institute. The mid-morning coffee klatch that usually included Sam Kirk, James Gallagher, Bernard Farber, T. Ernest Newland, and Lawrence Stolurow was invariably the most stimulating, enriching, and yet casual experience on the campus. Fellow students like Bluma Weiner, Herb Boyd, Lloyd Wolf, Sam Ashcroft, Dorothy Sievers, Jim McCarthy, and Roger Frey rounded out the informal sessions. Topics ranged from current or projected research problems to legislative and organizational matters. Since most of the faculty were immediately involved in policy-making activities on a national level, we were privy to prospective trends in the field.

The doctoral program brought us into direct contact with many members of the outstanding faculty in the College of Education and in the Psychology Department. Among them, Lee Cronbach, Nate Gage, B. Othanel Smith, David Krathwohl, and David Ausubel are most memorable for their excellence as teachers and as informal sources of guidance and advice.

All these invaluable sources of knowledge were supported and often matched by an outstanding university library. Recalling my invigorating experiences in the small library at Sonoma. I began a search for and quickly found a far more extensive collection.

Rarely do we give credit to a library and its staff for important aspects of our educations. The library at the University of Illinois was a scholar's dream. Its holdings far exceeded my expectations. When I was unable to locate a volume, a staff member would join in the search. If a desired publication was not part of the holdings, the acquisition department quickly located it and arranged for an interlibrary loan.

Accessibility to a literature of such scope made the study of mental retardation more nearly recreation than work. Early on, I decided to deal with primary sources whenever possible. With such an extensive library and so much help from interlibrary loans, the vast majority of primary sources became available despite the backtracking it took to locate them. It is worth noting the frequency with which I found that familiar quotations were either cited out of context, extracted from a larger statement, or both. Thus, having the primary source at hand gave a more reliable and complete view of the writer's position.

Random rummaging through the literature turned up many interesting tidbits but very little that held together. The most logical procedure seemed to be to select a point of departure and to work backward in time, with the hope that a reasonably acceptable base would materialize.

I began with the popular notion that the education of the mentally retarded started with Itard's (1801/1932) work with Victor. In my course work and readings, this work was mentioned briefly, and then abandoned in favor of more contemporary issues. Itard was more often than not described as a physician engaged at a school for deaf children who somehow became interested in a feral child captured in the forests of Aveyron. In an attempt to socialize Victor, Dr. Itard tried to teach him the basic elements of self-care and interpersonal relationships. Itard achieved, in his view, little success after four years of training and so discontinued his efforts. Having thus disposed of our heritage, we leaped over time to Binet and Simon and their contribution to the mental measurement movement. This was meatier stuff. Unlike social factors, intelligence was something tangible because it was measurable. There were tests and articles and texts about testing that one could hold in one's hands and dissect. There were issues of standardization, validity, reliability, standard error, and the like to stimulate thinking and discussion.

As I found, however, Itard's work was far more than a springboard to the twentieth century. It soon became evident that his efforts represented the convergence of ideology and technology. The concept of the perfectability of man, as explicated in the essays of Montaigne, Bacon, Descartes, Locke, Hume, and in the poetry of John Donne, was the ideologic center of the humanist movement. The technology is found in the psychology implicit in the theories of Condillac (1930) and Rousseau (1896), who proposed that knowledge was acquired through experience, with the senses being the avenues of learning. Rousseau stressed the correlation of experience and the growth and development of the individual. Most will quickly recognize that this is contrary to the homuncular theory of human development and in harmony with Locke's theory that individuals are born without preexistent mind or soul. (It will also be evident to the historically sophisticated that the foregoing is a gross oversimplification of the complexity and dynamism of the humanist and sensationalist movements.)

Since Itard's work was unquestionably linked to social change, I looked for the source of that change. It seemed to me that the precipitating factors were the Enclosure system, the beginnings of the Industrial Revolution, and the accompanying move to the cities (Jernegan, 1931). As Jennings (1930) points out, the growth of industry as well as the separation of people from the land resulted in an army of beggars. To put it in a way that has meaning for the present and future, when agriculture and cottage industries were the dominant economic pattern, mental retardation and other handicapping conditions did not emerge as serious social problems. The severely handicapped as we know them rarely survived. Work could be found in the fields and in the home workshops for handicapped individuals. For those seriously incapacitated, the family looked after its own. We see this today in cultures where the family is a strong and unified institution. Even in such cultures, as technology rises and workplaces become centralized, handicapped individuals become more and more of a problem to society. Then legislative acts and the involvement of governmental and voluntary agencies respond to families' needs for assistance. In England, for example, laws to control and reduce the number of wanderers appeared as early as 1388. By the seventeenth century, the first of the Poor Laws were passed which divided the poor into three classes, the able-bodied, the incapacitated, and children.

Of greater interest to behavioral scientists is the fact that mental retardation and other limiting conditions did not become a social problem in Western societies until the conditions associated with the Industrial Revolution materialized. Social change at that time reduced the stability of life on the farm and the security of the home industry. It ended the protection by the landowner who was responsible, in important ways, for the welfare of those who worked his lands and maintained his property and his person. It put people out on the byways to fend for themselves, to find work in cities, to find shelter, and to provide for themselves. To put it another way, people had to attain autonomy in order to survive. The ultimate test of autonomy was the competition for jobs, housing, and other elements of survival. As is the case today, the standards for survival and for success, however these are defined, become the criteria leading to classifications of people. The literature suggests that when the behaviors of individuals threaten the autonomy of the larger group or society in important ways, the larger group pursues actions— sometimes benign, sometimes hostile—that it believes will preserve its strength and well-being.

Sociologists tell us that the evidence of a social problem is found in the uncodified and codified actions of the society—the legislative actions, the formation of special purpose groups and organizations, the generation of labels and attitudes, and, in many cases, the institutionalizing of the problem in the form of procedures and physical accommodations. In Western societies we can see all of these actions emerging with the Enclosure system and the Industrial Revolution and continuing to the present as technology and societal complexity flourish.

As is usually the case, the implementation of laws and regulations inevitably raised issues of definition and classification. These problems persist to the present. In the years since John Locke proposed a distinction between mental illness and mental retardation, the literature on definitions, classification, and, of course, mental measurement has assumed huge proportions. The concept of intelligence as it relates to the attainment of autonomy appeared early. John Locke's definition is worth quoting here because of its trend-setting content: "Herein seems to lie the difference between idiots and madmen, that madmen put wrong ideas together, and so make wrong propositions, but argue and reason right from them; but idiots make very few or no propositions, and reason scarce at all" (1801). While some may focus on the intellectual factors implicit in this definition, i.e., making propositions and reasoning, they run the risk of overlooking the larger social context and the effects on this context of faulty or impoverished reasoning. I have the uncomfortable feeling that the mental measurement movement went off on a tangent when it attempted to isolate purely intellectual factors.

Not being convinced of the infallibility of intelligence testing, I had little difficulty in accepting the concept of autonomy in society. I pursued this phenomenon with an eye primarily on the substance of social interactions and the reasoning process and secondarily, on the qualitative and quantitative aspects of measured intelligence. My heresy was rewarded when I searched the Human Relations Area File, a systematic cataloging of known societies and cultures, at the University of Chicago. Anthropologic data on the conventional categories of social structures, e.g., division of labor, political forms, child rearing, mental health and the like, were available, and I searched thoroughly for codified and uncodified measures to accommodate mental retardation. In the course of work too extensive to report here, certain facts emerged that took on an inescapable consistency: (1) all societies irrespective of size, nature, and location, had deviants and ways of coping with them—sometimes cruel by our standards, sometimes benign; (2) mental retardation was not a form of deviance common to all societies; (3) where mental retardation was listed, the extent to which it constituted a problem to the society was clearly correlated with levels of technologic complexity. Thus, data on technologically simple societies, those that fished and/or farmed in relatively primitive styles, rarely included mental retardation, while those that boasted of mechanization in their enterprises and had large population centers always listed mental retardation along with complex legal structures to accommodate the problem. Not surprisingly, the most elaborate rules and regulations were subsumed under education. Next came some form of vocational rehabilitation and/or placement with social service provisions a distant third.

The vast amount of detail in the Human Relations Area File suggested that the anthropological literature might be a productive source of more useful information. After much exploration, the relationship between mental retardation as a social problem and the dynamics of society began to take shape. Most notable were texts and articles by Malinowski (1944), Hebb (1949), Linton (1947), Mead (1937), and Eaton and Weil (1955). In particular, Malinowski's theory of culture provided a framework for the contemplation of definitions, the effects of social change, the strain toward individual and societal autonomy, the role of education in the growth and development of mentally retarded individuals, the role of mental measurement and, most important, a basis for understanding how and why mental retardation becomes a social problem. To summarize his theory briefly, and with no intention to oversimplify, Malinowski states that a society is characterized by the seven cultural responses it makes to the needs of its members. The cultural responses are:

1. Commissariat: functions satisfying the metabolic needs of the membership, e.g., means for procuring food and disposing of wastes.
2. Kinship: functions satisfying reproductive needs, e.g., provisions for marriage or union.
3. Shelter: functions satisfying needs for comfort, e.g., house construction, weaving, and heating.
4. Protection: functions satisfying needs for security, e.g., protection from animal and human predators, ways for anticipating future security needs such as insurance.
5. Activities: functions satisfying needs for interactions and participation, e.g., games, gatherings, and excursions.
6. Training: functions for satisfying the needs for continuance of the group lore, e.g., education and indoctrination.
7. Hygiene: functions satisfying the needs for physical and mental health, e.g., medical and psychological provisions. (Malinowski, 1944)

By using Malinowski's theory as a framework within which to consider Linton's position on achieved and ascribed status and role, the relationship between cultural responses and the competencies of individuals fell into place. Looking at our own society as representative of complex society, we can identify statuses and roles associated with each cultural response. For example, under *commissariat* we can identify farmers, herders, cooks, foodstore employees, sanitation workers, and many others. In less complex societies such as the Trobriand Islanders or the people of Ifalik, we find that people are assigned to act on the same cultural responses but the statuses are notably fewer and the roles less complex.

As I began to list the statuses and roles associated with each cultural response, I found that I was also placing them in hierarchies ranging from statuses that demanded considerable schooling, knowledge, and skills, to those requiring minimal preparation. Thus, under *protection*, for example, the status of police commissioner would rank high in the hierarchy while that of the patrol officer would rank much lower. This is not to say that a patrol officer is necessarily less intelligent or less skillful than his or her superiors. It is only that the demands of the role associated with his or her status do not require an analogous fund of facts, concepts, and skills.

When I considered the qualitative definitions suggested by Locke and others, it became clear that one important way an individual could find himself at odds with society was to occupy a status whose role demands exceeded his ability to meet the expectations set by society. Without intending to oversimplify the conflict, I concluded that if one is deprived of his or her status because of incompetence due to intellectual inadequacy, he or she is then assigned the status of mentally retarded. Of course, in a complex society such as ours, individuals occupy several achieved statuses simultaneously. For example, one can be the wage earner who, among other things, supplies the wherewithal to shelter and feed his family. He may be, at the same time, a husband who helps plan the activities of the family, raises children, belongs to the PTA, and monitors the health and behavior of his children. If he is incompetent in one or two of these statuses, he may become unemployed or be seen as an abusive parent and possibly earn an undesirable reputation in his neighborhood or community, but he would not necessarily be assigned a status associated with deviancy. On the other hand, an individual who is a failure across a number of statuses—who can't get or hold a job, does not maintain an adequate residence and household, does not manage personal affairs with appropriate prudence, and falls short of acceptable interpersonal and social relationships would more probably achieve one of the statuses subsumed under deviancy such as mentally retarded, mentally ill, or criminal. The index, in most cases, would be the extent to which social institutions such as welfare, law enforcement, and/or community counseling or, in the case of children, education, provide support or control at public expense. In practical terms, the distinction between people occupying statuses in the social structure and those assigned the status of mental retardation and the like lies in the extent to which they have achieved autonomy in the management of their lives.

I could see that the notion of mental retardation as an achieved status fits nicely into the educational scene. When a child comes to school he or she achieves the status of student. The role of a student is influenced by his or her age and grade placement and, in some instances, the ascribed status of sex. Thus, boys and girls in the third grade are expected to behave similarly in some ways, most notably in academic achievement, but differently in others such as comportment and interests. (Some of the latter distinctions will probably be blurred as stereotypes in sex roles lose their mystique.) At the same time, the role expectations of boys and girls in the third grade are different from those of students in the sixth grade insofar as academic achievement and certain behaviors are concerned. To put it another way, an important role for a third grader is to be able to read and reckon within an acceptable range for his or her grade. Behavior may be somewhat odd, but so long as it does not threaten the autonomy of the classroom, the student will maintain the status of third grader. If academic achievement is not up to expectations but behavior is, services will be provided to bolster achievement. When both academic achievement and behavior fall below the norms for the grade to the degree that autonomy is threatened, the status of the student may be changed. In such instances, the student may achieve the status of mentally retarded, for example, if procedures reveal that lack of academic achievement and other behaviors are associated with intellectual deficit. Convention suggests that once achieved, the status of mentally retarded is difficult if not impossible to change. This view is contradictory to the very concept of an achieved status because, by their nature, achieved statuses can be "un-achieved." In the case of mental retardation, an improvement in either intellectual status or in the maladaptive behavior should qualify the individual for a change of status. It seemed to me that if, as it has been claimed, mentally retarded children rarely, if ever, are reassigned to regular classes, it was because the programs in the special education setting tended to contain rather than change behavior. This line of thought turned out to be the first of a long series of events that led to the development of the Social Learning Curriculum (Goldstein, 1974, 1975).

I found that the concept of mental retardation as a status was far from the prevailing thought of the 1950s. Psychometric tests were almost the only way of diagnosing mental retardation. In the academic world, definitions were relatively broad. There was much discussion of the developmental, social, and psychometric aspects of definitions and their implications for the quality of intelligence. Beyond this, much attention was given to the stability and the immutability of the IQ. At the public school level, the result of an intelligence test was the major decision-making criterion.

While the Institute for Research on Exceptional Children provided a rich psychological environment, I remained invested heavily in the educational aspects of mental retardation. Thus, while I was in tune academically with the prevailing views of the psychometric approach to mental retardation, I was equally interested in the classroom and how teachers interact with their students.

CURRICULUM DEVELOPMENT—THE FIRST EXPERIENCE

In 1956, my hewing to the pedagogic line paid off. When Ray Graham, then state director of special education, decided that Illinois needed a statewide curriculum guide for teachers of EMR children, he approached Sam Kirk for advice and assistance. Sam suggested that Dorothy Siegle, then the lone state consultant in mental retardation, and I chair the development effort. I accepted the appointment because of my interest in classroom operations though I had no idea of how much work was entailed or how we would go about completing the task. I admired and respected Dorothy Siegle's competence and felt that we would find our way. Parenthetically, I had no idea that the work on the proposed guide would influence my career as markedly as it did, nor did I dream that it would be the key to my involvement in special education at an international level. The pressures inherent in getting the curriculum guide underway, in maintaining course work, and raising a family required that I put further study of mental retardation as a social status on hold.

Having had no prior experience in curriculum development, Dorothy and I had to lay the groundwork as best we could. Since I was surrounded by bright, learned people, I polled staff and students for their recommendations as to how to start and how to proceed. Briefly, the consensus was that we should scour the state for the best teacher in each subject-matter area, observe how the teacher worked and what content he or she favored, and then transcribe our observations into manuals that other teachers could follow. Being respectful of the wisdom of my colleagues and, at the same time, lacking the time to do justice to a statewide search, I asked a representative sample of directors of special education to list their best teachers in each area of instruction. At the same time, I asked my colleagues to list the attributes of an outstanding teacher so that I would know one if I saw one. This exercise in futility taught me two facts. First, I learned that everyone knows the attributes of the superior teacher but no two people, lay or professional, agree as to what they are. Second, I learned that educators' and psychologists' criteria for superior teachers differed according to their own functions in the education establishment. For example, process-oriented people, mainly psychologists, described superior teachers as those who know and implement principles of learning, are aware of affective qualities of their children, generate a warm accepting classroom environment, and the like. Administrators, we found, described superior teachers as those who "ran" orderly yet attractive class-rooms, who did not need or ask for administrator's help, who somehow managed to keep their classrooms supplied without unusual demands on the school's budget, and who had no obvious problems with parents or, if they did, took care of matters themselves. Of course, we work in a more enlightened era presently, and the probability of such differences in perceptions are accordingly reduced—but don't bet on it. In any case, it was clear that we were not going to find our design by following this line of guidance.

Our collection of available curriculum guides was equally unhelpful. In many cases, these were the same basic curriculum guides cut and pasted into constrasting formats but built on the same array of heartfelt educational clichés. Despite the implications for special education, clearly stated in the many follow-up studies of mentally retarded school leavers, curriculum guides adhered vigorously to the academic line with secondary emphasis on arts and crafts. As far as prosocial learning was concerned, there was little apart from recommendations to teachers to stress such behaviors as sharing, politeness, and other aspects of good manners. It is worth noting that curriculum guides have not changed much over the years.

Because of my experiences at the University of Illinois and particularly my exposure to the lectures and writing of B. Othanel Smith and Archibald Anderson, I felt that a curriculum guide needed a conceptual base if the content was to be consistent with the goals of education. About this time I learned that Godfrey Stevens, one of Sam Kirk's first students at Milwaukee State College, was well into a similar project in the Cincinnati, Ohio, schools, where he was director of special education. Godfrey steered us to Florence Stratemeyer's work at Teachers College and her view that curricula in general should be organized along the lines of universal persisting life problems. Like John Dewey, Stratemeyer stressed the extrinsic value of school learning and organized conventional content within the context of such familiar issues as maintaining a family, managing personal affairs, and understanding and appreciating the aesthetic qualities of life.

With the results of follow-up studies in mind and our own experiences as guidelines, we drew up a format for the Illinois guide and organized sixteen committees across the state to work on the identified elements of the guide: ten persisting life problems and six academic and aesthetic areas. The committees met frequently and regularly, and Dorothy and I made the rounds to provide consistency in effort and content. In two years' time, the task was completed and published.

In the course of the committee meetings, the fallibility of the committee approach to curriculum development became evident. As one would expect, the committees differed considerably in competence and motivation and particularly in their consideration of what special education for the mentally retarded should be. Dynamically, the committees ranged from anarchic to autocratic. The former milled around for many sessions changing decisions with each meeting; the latter were whipped into shape by someone with self-claimed authority who marched the group off in the direction he or she decided was best. Only rarely was this within the framework of the proposed plan. In the final analysis, the work of the curriculum committees can best be described as compromises. The best ideas were not understood by the less competent members and were watered down in order to achieve consensus. Similarly, the more hackneyed ideas were dressed up rather than discarded so that sensibilities could be preserved. As is frequently the case, the weaker ideas and formulations far outnumbered the solid innovative efforts so that the trend toward mediocrity was always present. In the course of editing the committee's work, I upgraded materials and, in some cases, had to redo an entire section, thereby salvaging some of the better ideas lost in the committee's deliberations.

In the late 1960s, when the Social Learning Curriculum was initiated, I remembered the lessons learned in developing the Illinois Guide and opted for an employed, full-time staff. This is not to say that the committee system is necessarily a total failure. To the contrary, Ed Meyen (1969) in the SECDC project demonstrated that teacher committees can work, if participants are carefully selected and provided with immediate and ongoing leadership. The leadership needs to have the authority to discard ineffective members. Dorothy Siegle and I did not have such authority.

INTRODUCTION TO SPECIAL EDUCATION—EUROPEAN STYLE

Shortly after the guide's distribution to Illinois teachers, Ray Graham was deluged with requests for copies. Since he lacked the means to accept payment, he offered the Illinois Association for the Mentally Retarded, a parents group, the opportunity to sell the curriculum guide to out-of-state people. Their income from it was such that when I was invited by the Guild of Teachers of Backward Children in England to present a paper on curriculum development at their International Congress in 1960, the association was able to cover the expenses.

Among the congress participants was the Norwegian delegation, Oddvar Vormeland, Hans-Jorgen Gjessing, and Trygve Lie (not the former UN Secretary General). The first two were lecturers at the Institute for Educational Research at the University of Oslo. Trygve was head of special education in the Norwegian Ministry of Church and Education. Our evenings together and our long walks from the hotel to the meeting hall were more nearly stimulating seminars than the usual casual comparing of notes. Their interest in American special education was profound. The outcome of these exchanges was an invitation to accept a Fulbright research scholarship to work half-time with the university and half-time with the ministry. Nineteen sixty-two was therefore one of the most fruitful years of my professional and personal life. Beyond receiving a thorough education in the Scandinavian approach to handicapped children and adults (I visited extensively in Denmark and Sweden, as well), I spent profitable time in England where I met and formed personal and professional relationships with Alan and Anne Clarke, Neal O'Connor, Ron Gulliford, Herbert Gunzberg, and the late Jack Tizard.

In 1962, the contrast among the American, British, and Scandinavian approaches to education and services to mentally retarded individuals was marked. Quantitatively and in some ways qualitatively, we were far ahead of the others. We were spending more, had more extensive staffs, and offered a broader array of services for mildly handicapped children. Most notably, we were more advanced in the basics of public education. Whereas both the British and the Scandinavians were strongly influenced by the European heritage of academic proficiency, American public education was more diffuse and, along with emphasis on reading and arithmetic, offered a more balanced curriculum. One notable exception was the Norwegian emphasis on folk crafts and music. While special classes were commonplace in American public schools, the British and Scandinavians had separate schools. Trygve Lie in Norway was leading a movement to include special classes in the public schools and was making some headway, but special schools were the rule.

While we were still in an emergent state in getting *moderately* retarded children into the public schools by 1962 but making rapid progress, the British had already established a separate system of special schools for these children. In Norway, educational provisions for moderately and severely retarded children were provided by voluntary agencies who received most of their financial support from the central government.

Most important, I was introduced to the concept of *normalization*, particularly in Denmark and Sweden, not as an abstraction or philosophy but as policy that was being implemented. Compared with American and British institutions for the mentally retarded, the Danish and Swedish institutions and community residences were more like well-kept, comfortable, and pleasant homes.

While the Scandinavians were making excellent and, by conventional standards, radical progress in the care and treatment of mentally retarded people, our British colleagues were taking huge strides in areas of training. British facilities were for the most part ancient and depressing: Moneyhull, where Gunzburg was activating a revolutionary program in the social development of moderately retarded youth, was older than most institutions in the US and showing the wear and tear of time; Mauldsley Hospital, where Tizard and O'Connor conducted some of the seminal research of our time, and Epsom Downs Hospital, where Alan and Anne Clarke applied principles of learning in training studies with moderately retarded adults, were equally antiquated and run down. Nevertheless, their work continued and, in a relatively short time, their treatment procedures spread throughout Great Britain. The Junior Training Centers (schools for school-age moderately retarded children) and Senior Training Centers (essentially sheltered work-shops) became stimulating, productive environments. I saw work accomplished there that far exceeded in complexity the tasks typical of our sheltered workshops. True, some workers were engaged in relatively low-level tasks such as stuffing envelopes and packaging manufactured products. Most, however, were performing complex tasks involving power tools, machinery, and extremely sensitive assembly of electronic equipment.

In all fairness, it should be recognized that in England the complex work was there to be done. That is, the Senior Training Centers were not restricted, as many of our sheltered workshops are, by labor agreements or local regulations. Much of their work was done for other institutional systems in England: cribs, toys, and other equipment for foundling homes; wrought iron materials, metal cots, and office equipment for prisons and hospitals. In addition, Senior Training Centers had contracts with large electronics firms and air frame manufacturers, at one extreme, and local businesses and small manufacturers at the other. The important fact was that the moderately retarded people acquired the skills that made fulfillment of these tasks possible. They owed their skills to the training programs so carefully thought out and constructed by our colleagues. Later, in this country, their counter-parts, most notably Marc Gold, demonstrated the value of rational training programs.

A STUDY OF THE EFFICACY OF SPECIAL CLASSES FOR RETARDED STUDENTS

With the Illinois Guide completed, I was greeted by Sam Kirk with the prospects of directing a study of the efficacy of special classes for mildly retarded students (Goldstein, Moss, & Jordon, 1965). The issue of the effectiveness of educational programs for these children was under continuous examination at the institute. Sam and other faculty continually took the role of devil's advocates, while students searched assiduously for data that would support the continuation of these programs. Arguments supporting special classes based on opinion, morality, decency, and logic were quickly devastated by the simple question: Where is the evidence? This sent everyone digging for studies and analyzing their results. Among these studies were the pioneering works of Pertsch (1936), Bennett (1932), Blatt (1958), and Cassidy and Stanton (1959). Initially, the evidence was overwhelmingly in favor of dropping special classes until we dissected the research design. Then it became clear that serious flaws in the research methods rendered these studies little more than intellectual exercises.

A step ahead of us, Sam Kirk had laid the groundwork for an efficacy study to be supported by the US Office of Education. He asked me to put my new-found standards for such a study to work. To avoid the errors of earlier studies, it was decided to establish special classes where they did not exist. This would control for the contaminating experiences of teachers, students, and administrative practices already in place. To control further for experiences of students, it was decided to look at all newcomers to the first grade and to randomly assign the eligible children to special and regular classes. There were additional remedies to earlier design problems but I will not detail them here. They are available in the final report and the many reviews the study has received.

Finding communities with no special education provisions in 1958 was not difficult. Persuading district superintendents to let us establish these classes was quite another matter. I approached the county superintendent's office by first orienting him to the study and its objectives and asking him to assemble the district superintendents so that I could present my case. Suspecting that some lacked special classes because they could not recruit qualified teachers, I offered to staff the classes if they would provide salaries. I had already recruited four of my best graduating seniors. The meetings with district superintendents were rife with suspicion and reservation. I sensed that most were reluctant to do anything to threaten the status quo. This attitude surfaced with statements to the effect that since parents of mentally retarded children were not troublesome, it would be hazardous to do anything that might arouse them to action. This experience gave me a firsthand view of conditions that led to Public Law 94–142 and judicial mandates that required equal protection for handicapped children.

After many meetings, four classes were negotiated. The actual carrying out of the study is now a matter of record so I will discuss only some behind-the-scenes facts and events which do not appear in the final reports. For one, the management team, Dr. James W. Moss, Laura Jordan, and I, represented a well-balanced educational-psychological approach to the study. Jim Moss managed the psychological aspects, including data collection, testing, and test construction, while Laura supervised and coordinated the work of the experimental teachers. We were backed up by a cadre of able and dedicated graduate students and always had access to the faculty of the institute and the College of Education for counsel.

The teachers, who went directly from caps and gowns into experimental classes, suffered greater anxiety than was usual. They felt pressure to be productive so that the study would not fail on their account. While they were familiar with the Illinois Guide, the keystone of the program, they had little experience with its implementation and even less in generating teaching materials and aids to complement the curriculum. To reduce anxiety and instill confidence, I put them to work under Laura's guidance, developing teaching materials during the summer preceding the start of the study. Indications were that an intensive readiness program would benefit students and teachers alike. Using the Primary Mental Abilities Test (Thurstone and Thurstone, 1953) as a matrix, we proceeded to develop reams of activities, seat work, and teaching aids in each area covered by the P.M.A.T. Just knowing that they had the wherewithall to get started in September boosted morale tremendously. This, combined with Laura's almost daily supervision, got them off to a positive start. Three of the teachers, Jane Page Ferguson and Pete and Evy Torchia, served the full term of the study and became outstanding teachers. The communities that had employed them originally benefited since they stayed on long after the study was completed.

The results of the efficacy study were equivocal, as has been pointed out many times in many places, but not as equivocal as the final report would suggest. In 1962 when the final report was written, the rules of the research game limited one to discussing collected data. And the only data we had was quantitative. Observations by teachers, parents, administrators, or members of the research staff had no place in a report in those days. Thus, some important changes are not a matter of record. In particular, the return of children to the regular grades has gone unrecognized. The children made the transition quickly and smoothly and so well that their earlier labels faded quickly. Similarly, the remarkably low attrition rate for students and teachers attests to the dynamic nature of the program and teachers. The teachers noted an attitude toward school life in their students that led them to assume some responsibility for their own learning activities, a kind of creativity not usually associated with mildly retarded students. They became risk takers in the more positive sense of the concept. As compared with other children in their schools, they showed fewer behavior problems and were, in time, well accepted as part of the student body.

There is always a temptation to set the record straight, so to speak, in a forum such as this, but I will forego the temptation by turning, instead, to a retrospective view of the study tempered by twenty years of experiences for which it was an important point of departure. The 1950s was a decade of rapid and, sometimes, disorderly change. There was an upsurge of interest in the education of mentally retarded children with the close of World War II.

Although the schools had previously rejected all but mildly retarded children, parents, having organized into a powerful and active national association, now demanded acceptance of a broader spectrum of children. They pressured public education at every level and their state legislatures as well. As more special classes were opened, demand for teachers and related staff increased. At the same time, major universities expanded their research capabilities to include handicapped children. With the availability of financial support from government agencies in the mid-1960s, research momentum accelerated, some might say, beyond the rate at which funds could be used wisely and effectively.

Emerging from this turbulent context, the efficacy study stimulated a healthy interest. Whereas most research came out of laboratories, here was a study taking place in the real world. Similarly, while most studies explored the characteristics of mentally retarded learners in clearly defined, often simulated learning situations, this one included most of the things that teachers and children do in the classroom. I see it now as a courageous, albeit foolhardy and somewhat naive enterprise whose contribution has been two-fold. First, it made for long and lively exchanges in graduate seminars focusing on research design, policy formulations, and measurement without requiring that anyone come to a conclusion or commitment. Second, I believe that it sensitized many to the vicissitudes of in situ research. It may have driven some otherwise viking-spirited people back to the laboratory while, at the same time, encouraging others to go out into the real world to take a hard look at life in the raw.

Some say that the efficacy study is the last of its kind. Actually it should be, but not for the reasons usually proposed. It is often stated that efficacy studies should not be done until more precise controls can be executed and better systems for measurement are devised. I would agree that efficacy studies are futile, but I feel strongly that the only people who should do these studies are those who are accountable for educational provisions and programs—the local school districts. Realistically, it is impossible to design a single study of this type from which one can generalize results to the field as a whole or even in part. In our case, for example, the teachers were unique in that they were all newly graduated from an undergraduate special education program—hardly the background of the typical teacher. Our teachers were supervised for a full day at least once a week by a most competent person who thought nothing of taking over the class to demonstrate to the teacher how to improve his or her work—hardly the amount and kind of supervision provided for most teachers. The children were homogeneous in age and their IQ range was unusually limited—not quite what one finds in the typical class where a four-year age span or more is often the case.

With these conditions in mind, let us take the best-case situation—or worst, depending on one's attitude toward special education. Suppose the results of the efficacy study showed that the experimental class children were superior in every aspect. Would this justify any school district administration going before its board of education with claims that its special education program is worth all of the funds and effort the community is expending? Or conversely, if the results were clearly negative, would this justify the dissolution of the special education programs? It is probable that unequivocal results in one direction or the other would have provided people with unjustified leverage and educational programs for mentally retarded children would have suffered. So it is probably just as well that ambiguity reigned in our study.

Thus, whether or not this efficacy study or any other, for that matter, produces equivocal or unequivocal results is begging the question. The crucial question is: Is *our* special class providing an education that is superior to other delivery systems? To the degree that anyone is interested in validating administrative decisions and policies, the question needs to be asked by the local school board and/or the school administration.

ON TO NEW YORK AND A CAREER TRANSITION

As stimulating as the academic environment of Illinois was, the social and cultural atmosphere was stultifying. To underscore matters, the experiences in Norway along with travel to many of the principal cities in Europe reminded me of the excitement of life in the big city.

The urge for a change of scenery was stimulated by more than the bucolic way of life. There was also the fact of living and working in the shadow of the likes of Sam Kirk. This man is of such professional and personal stature that, in effect, he was the institute. While this was not a problem because of the humane and democratic nature of his leadership, it did circumscribe areas of interest. When an invitation to start a department of special education came from Yeshiva University, I accepted. The fact that the Graduate School of Humanities and Social Sciences was in mid-Manhattan added spice to the challenge.

At Yeshiva University, Dean Joshua Fishman assured me of his support in developing a department, asking only that it be of an academic stature commensurate with a graduate school already boasting a leading department of psychology. This was consonant with my own goals. I envisioned a department that would limit its concentration to intellectually handicapped learners and would focus its research on studies that had direct implications for educational practice. I limited the scope of the department to the intellectually handicapped because New York City and environs was well stocked with good teacher preparation programs for sensory and physically handicapped children.

In a period of two years, I was able to attract Drs. Bluma Weiner, James Moss, Martin Miller, Paul Graubard, Morton Bortner, Dorothy Sievers, and Oliver Hurley as a faculty core. Dr. Weiner immediately designed and activated the masters-level teacher preparation program in mental retardation while Dr. Graubard did the same in the program for the emotionally disturbed. Jim Moss was with us long enough to secure a doctoral program from the National Institute for Mental Health to provide special training in research methodologies. This program was the counterpart to one at Peabody College for Teachers led by Dr. Gordon Cantor. While ours was pledged to students with educational backgrounds, the Peabody program accepted students majoring in psychology. A year later, Jim Moss was recruited by Sam Kirk to help lay the groundwork in the US Office of Education for the nascent Bureau for the Education of the Handicapped. Marty Miller assumed the leadership of the doctoral program and provided keen leadership; it was more than coincidence that both Jim Moss and Marty Miller were graduates of the Peabody program.

With the doctoral fellowship provisions of PL 85–926, we were able to attract a formidable array of doctoral students, many of whom have contributed significantly to special education in leadership and research roles. The more outstanding among them are Warren Heiss, Esther Minskoff, George Mischio, Gary Siperstein, Gerald Minskoff, and Jay Gottleib.

With such able faculty, I was free to continue my research interest. The efficacy study together with my experiences as a teacher of the educable mentally retarded continued to stimulate me. As I said earlier, the design of the study and the way it was reported masked some important findings and neglected others. In all but the Cassidy and Stanton study (1959), academic achievement was the standard for success. Social and psychological growth was all but ignored even though Tisdall's study (1962) showed that the children in our experimental classes were significantly superior to the comparison children in academic tasks involving conceptual ability such as arithmetic problem solving and in productive thinking (Tisdall, 1962).

The limitations of generalizability were also a source of concern. The three most ignored aspects of the study were teacher characteristics, curriculum, and teaching methods. To cast more light on these variables, I designed an approximation of the efficacy study that would, this time, take place in already existing classes but where the Illinois Guide and the inductive teaching method were not in use (Goldstein, Mischio, and Minskoff, 1969). With the financial support of the Bureau for the Education of the Handicapped (USOE) and the assistance of George Mischio and Esther Minskoff, then graduate students, classes were located in New Jersey that were typical of special classes in all important ways; teachers represented the usual variability in preparation, kinds of experience, years in special education, and age. The students were pretty much what one would find in randomly selected classes in urban, suburban, and rural settings. Having received permission to use a number of special classes in the same school districts as comparison groups, we set about to train the teachers in the use of the Illinois Guide and the inductive methods. They were given a year of in-service training consisting of fourteen after-school sessions and four half-day workshops. These were intense and included demonstrations and the use of teaching aids and audiovisual materials. I soon noted that teachers were having difficulty in achieving a common interpretation of the Illinois Guide in the classroom. Like other curriculum guides, it confronts teachers with, at best, an outline of ways to achieve objectives. The burden is on the teacher to provide the substance that fleshes out the bare-bones outline. Such limited guidance made for a broad range of teacher assumptions about what was called for in any given activity. Clearly, consistency and continuity in educational programming for mentally retarded students was going to be hard to come by even when all of the teachers used the same guide. At the conclusion of the study, our data substantiated earlier concerns. Less than one-third of the teachers achieved high ratings in the proper use of the curriculum guide although all felt they were on the right track. In contrast, most had been able to learn how to teach inductively.

The failure of the curriculum guide to provide the framework for consistency and continuity in educational programming was disturbing. I have always felt that mentally retarded students, more so than nonhandicapped students, need, beyond a relevant program, one that is continuous over the school years and consistent with the growth and development patterns of children on their way to maturity. While this concern has not been widespread in special education, it strikes me as being basic to good, effective programming. We take for granted the fact that a child in a regular class can move to another school across town or across the country and, having made adjustment to a new teacher, new classmates, and different customs and mores in the school itself, can nevertheless continue with his education.

Mentally retarded students, however, may remain with the same teacher for as long as four years. When they move to the next level, they stand a good chance of having to begin a new career in special education. Much of this is due to the fact that special education is still a cottage industry; teachers generally receive little immediate supervision and certainly little program coordination. Their dispersal through the school system reduces communication between teachers. Each teacher is left to design, activate, and evaluate his or her own best estimate of an appropriate education. Because so many teachers of handicapped children receive sketchy, part-time preparation, they fall back on earlier experiences in the regular grades as a means of survival.

I found all of this to be the case in our New Jersey study. Despite the social orientation of the Illinois Guide (life functions) and intensive preparation in its use and in its coordination with academic content, George Mischio and Esther Minskoff nevertheless recorded observational data that revealed not only lack of consistency in programming but also a tendency to give priority and emphasis to reading and arithmetic.

The basis for this paradox was found in the teachers' statements. On the one hand, they expressed a clear-cut awareness of the need to provide prosocial learning as intensively as they provide academic learning. On the other, they pointed out that they had the texts and tools to accomplish the academic teaching, but were left to their own devices to provide the prosocial learning content.

The results of the study, while definitely favorable for the experimental classes, nevertheless convinced me that special education for the mentally retarded was functioning somewhere below its potential. At this point, I will deal with two issues directly related to the New Jersey study. The first, in-service training, I will discuss briefly. The second, curriculum guides, led to a refocusing of my career and to work that I will shortly detail.

The concern about in-service training arose because it was plain that efforts to train the teacher in matters closely associated with their day-to-day operations yielded results that fell short of the expectations. If our teachers had been reluctant to participate, if the trainers had been marginally competent, or if the subject matter of the training sessions had been obscure or abstract, we would not have given the disparity in results a second thought. Quite the opposite was true in each instance. The merits of in-service training as a means for changing teaching behavior remains questionable.

The widespread faith in curriculum guides as the instruments for organizing and presenting the content of classroom instruction was also placed in a dubious light. From the time that the Illinois Guide had been developed and distributed, I was aware that curriculum guides were, more often than not, discarded shortly after they were distributed. This I attributed to teachers' obtuseness and to their lack of preparation to use guides. Since assumptions of this type were not supported by our experiences in the New Jersey study, I had to conclude that the curriculum guide simply did not fulfill teachers' requirements. Some other form for organizing content was needed. Interviews with teachers illuminated the problem. While the teachers felt comfortable with the academic elements of their program, they were confused by the content related to the development of prosocial learning. Outlines of the content of each of the ten life functions did not provide them with enough guidance to translate such abstract principles into classroom activities. This explained why fewer than a third of the teachers applied the guide in the ways that the developers intended. To the teachers, the content outlines made sense intellectually but made for confusion and anxiety when used pedagogically. It is worth noting that teachers did not reject the notion of teaching prosocial learning.

After a period of rumination and discussions with colleagues and graduate students, the solution became obvious: if a curriculum guide is not seen by teachers as a useable instrument, we needed to provide them with a curriculum that would guide without confusing or locking them into a rigid formulation that might repress their creativity. The most reasonable middle ground seemed to be to organize curriculum content in the form of model lessons. Since each lesson would be linked to a behavioral objective, it would be seen as *a* way rather than *the* way for attaining the objective.

It was immediately clear that the method by which curriculum guides are usually developed would not work: teacher committees armed with paste pots, scissors and curriculum guides developed elsewhere. Instead, we needed a procedure that would provide immediate supervision and control of the development of model lessons, a means for making sure that the lessons were relevant to the education of mentally retarded children, and a test for the utility of the lessons in the classroom; at the same time, it was necessary to capitalize on the knowledge and creativity of teachers.

The alternative to a part-time volunteer development committee was a full-time development staff and ultimately a field-testing procedure that would be responsive to formative evaluation. Though a costly and time-consuming enterprise, time has confirmed that it is an effective way to evolve a curriculum (Mayer, 1975).

A full-time staff embarking on the uncharted waters of curriculum development requires a common frame of reference if there is to be consistency in their efforts. Experience told me that the laissez-faire attitude toward the committee's plan, a trade-off for their participation, would open the door to the usual compromises that mark committee efforts. To develop a common frame of reference, we turned to a more evident behavioral base. An extensive survey was made of the problems of mentally retarded adults. Vocational rehabilitation counselors in state agencies, United States Employment Service counselors, and family service agencies were asked to list the behaviors that got their clients into the kinds of trouble that required service. The response was more than generous, and we were able to catalog hundreds of maladaptive behaviors of which the vast majority were common-place, e.g., personal offensiveness, irresponsibility and unreliability, poor management of personal affairs, and inability to get along with co-workers. While most researchers use work behaviors as a standard for success, we found that other areas were also critical in the over-all adaptation of the individual. These included use of leisure time, the ability to communicate, and the ability to maintain physical and mental health. Further examination of the data revealed that problems did not emerge from single-incident events as much as they did from repeated behavior. That is, clients would be dismissed from job after job for the same reason. This suggested to us that clients had limited repertoires of responses to social situations. Counselors readily admitted that they had not, in most cases, found a way to extinguish these defeating behaviors; that it was too late in the game to re-educate most of their clients.

To provide a theoretical basis for understanding these problems and to guide the development of the curriculum, we fell back on psychological theory. After much exploration and help from the Psychology Department, we found that a modified form of need theory (Maslow, 1962) made the most sense. Our hypothesis was that there was something in or about the social situation that was in conflict with the client's need and that the client did not have a socially acceptable way of meeting the need. Thus, we conjectured, the client who was fired time after time for absenteeism and tardiness was bored by the dull, repetitive work; needing change or variation that the job did not provide, he or she was attracted to other activities. Further, while most of us, when faced with a boring situation, can find a number of socially acceptable ways for fleeing the scene, these agency clients had only one way for meeting their need and that was to turn to something more pleasurable regardless of the penalties.

We were able to agree on an array of needs extending beyond the basics postulated by Maslow to use for categorizing negative behaviors and identifying their socially acceptable counterparts. This array of needs and the development model by which we organized the content of instruction from birth to maturity appears elsewhere for those interested in a more complete treatment (Goldstein, 1969; Meyen et al., 1972).

Having laid the necessary foundation, I then applied to the Bureau for the Education of the Handicapped for support. The proposal was approved but not before my impressions about the lowly status of curriculum in the educational scheme of things were confirmed. In 1966, when I submitted the proposal, the peer review system was in its formative state. After the proposal had been reviewed and found controversial, I was asked to appear and reply to questions. I found myself before a prominent member of the special education community, a bureau staff member, and a representative of a different but related discipline, Dr. Robert Glaser. His well-earned reputation had preceded him, and while I was somewhat concerned about his sophistication in matters curricular or in special education, I did not question his scholarship. I answered their questions and was then asked to wait in the corridor for their decision. Unbeknownst to me or them, the wall in the corridor was being repaired, and a thin, temporary sheet of wallboard was all that separated me from the committee. I realized that I could hear their every word clearly. My superego decreed that I absent myself, but my id reminded me that they said "Wait", not "Don't listen." In the midst of this conflict, I could hear the prominent member say scornfully, "This is utter nonsense. All that needs to be done in curriculum has already been done. All teachers need is the Kirk and Johnson book and their problems are solved" (Kirk & Johnson 1951). Bob Glaser (may his research prosper) commented to the effect that while he was unfamiliar with the field of special education he could, nevertheless, not believe that any one problem was completely and irrevocably solved. He took the position that the concepts highlighted in the proposal were novel but of sound basis and then suggested that the history of the proposer warranted positive consideration. I can recall the long, breathless pause and could see my aspirations poised on a razor's edge. And then Bob said, "I'd recommend an approval as a matter of principle." This evidently influenced the bureau member and, after some bluster on the part of the prominent member, the vote was unanimous in favor of the proposal. By that point, my superego won the argument, and I removed myself to the end of the corridor where the bureau member brought me the good news.

Thus began a thirteen-year project culminating in the Social Learning Curriculum which covered a continuum from neonate to school leaver and which has relevance to the full range of handicapped individuals from the profoundly disabled on. In the course of the project, we field-tested in thirty-three states and Canada in order to accommodate to the demographic variables that generalization requires. We involved over six hundred teachers and some nine thousand children representing all handicapping conditions except blindness and some serious physical handicaps.

With its completion, the Ministry of Education in Taiwan supported a project to adapt and translate the curriculum into Chinese and has distributed it to some five hundred teachers (Lin, Chen, & Kuo, 1982). An adaptation for deaf, mentally retarded children has been completed (Naiman, 1982) and a Norwegian translation is in process. Of all of the accomplishments, however, I am most proud of those of the project staff. A dozen pursued doctoral studies in the course of their work on the curriculum, received their Ph.D.'s, and now contribute in their own ways to special education and related areas.

Beyond the satisfaction that comes from reaching a career goal, the curriculum project provided me with an education unobtainable under ordinary circumstances. Most who are familiar with the classroom level of special education are limited to a particular geographical area. Because our field testing ranged from Saskatchewan to the southern US borders and from coast to coast, I was able to spend valuable time with teachers in representative communities throughout the country. This came about because of the field-test model designed and implemented by Marjorie Goldstein, the project field-test coordinator. Her field-test model, one that worked effectively from the start, is detailed in another publication (M. T. Goldstein, 1981).

With the help of the evaluation staff, we identified nine demographic variables that needed to be incorporated into the field-test operation. These included urban, suburban, rural, and remote areas with all of the conditions affected by socioeconomic factors. In selected states, State Directors were contacted for permission to work within their boundaries. Protocol being what it is, it was incumbent upon the project director to meet with state directors and then local directors and finally their teachers to orient them to field testing and to then recruit volunteers. The fact that volunteerism created a selection factor was secondary to our need for teachers who would use and evaluate the teaching materials and teaching aids. As soon as teachers and directors stated a willingness to participate, Marjorie would organize the group and designate a local supervisory person as the Field-Test Advisor. Henceforth, all communication would be through that person. My role thereafter was assistant troubleshooter and reinforcer of lagging spirits. This brought me into frequent contact with teachers, supervisors, and local directors and provided experiences at the educational front often denied to academicians.

My view of teachers as the heart and head of special education was confirmed. It was plain that without a good teacher in the classroom there was no special education program, regardless of how elaborate the administrative, diagnostic, and ancillary services might be. Within the administrative structure, the most influential person insofar as the quality of education was concerned was the supervisor of special education. If this person was educationally sound and sensitive to teachers' needs for coordination, the local program was, for the most part, vital and productive. I learned quickly that competent teachers and supervisors were to be found everywhere and that the stereotypes associated with isolated communities and the large cities did not hold up. Parenthetically, our view of the competent teacher was one who provided students with a balanced program of academic, prosocial, aesthetic, and humanistic content and who applied, consciously or not, sound principles of teaching and learning. To repeat, we found such teachers in remote areas of Iowa, Mississippi, and Utah, among others, as well as in New York City, Tampa, and Miami.

The picture would not be complete if I did not confirm that we had our share of mediocre and less competent teachers. In a few cases, we found teachers who while well-motivated were nevertheless only a shade brighter than their students. Lest anyone conclude that those who did not volunteer for field testing were different from their participating colleagues, let me assure you that this was not the case. Since I visited as many classrooms as possible, I had the opportunity to learn why they were reluctant. Some were reluctant to alter a program they had worked long and hard to get in place, no matter its quality, while others needed to get a firm hold on their classes—these, more often than not, were new teachers. Many of them volunteered to field-test the curriculum once they had taken control of their classes.

My experiences in the field left me with a number of lasting impressions. I saw teachers working under terrible support conditions, low-quality leadership, and ineffective ancillary staff, who nevertheless pressed on to provide their students with sound programs. Where leadership and support were of high quality, teachers were more effective, but the differences in support systems were almost always greater than the differences among teachers.

I came away from the field experience convinced that getting an innovation accepted in the education establishment is a Herculean task. This was later born out in a dissertation by a staff member (M. T. Goldstein, 1979).

THE PARC CASE

I learned more about the strengths and weaknesses of special education from teachers than from any other source. More than anything else, they showed by what they did and did not do how actions by others affect the range and quality of their contributions. This served me well when I was appointed Master in *PARC v. the Commonwealth of Pennsylvania* (1972), a class action suit brought by parents of handicapped children who had been denied access to public schools. This suit, initiated four years before the passage of PL 94-142, provided the leverage that opened public school doors to severely and profoundly handicapped children in the community and in public institutions. This case has been prominent in the legal and educational literature (Turnbull & Turnbull, 1978). While these articles describe the visible legal and administrative aspects of the case, they do not discuss the behind-the-scenes maneuvers designed to confound the consent decree and to delay its implementation. I am still reluctant to discuss these aspects of the case. A detailing of experiences would portray many of the state staff as villains because they were the visible, albeit reluctant, implementors of undocumented policies they did not endorse. Suffice it to say that these policies were ultimately frustrated with the help of the state attorney general's office and the counsel for the plaintiffs.

No one should be surprised to learn that sentiment in the legislature and in the local school districts ran against accepting the plaintiffs in the public schools. In the face of the Fourteenth Amendment to the Constitution and democratic principles basic to public education, their key argument was that benefits were seriously out of line with costs. It was plain that their concept of benefits was limited to proficiency in academic areas. Their arguments bore no weight and were unacceptable reasons for noncompliance. Because the court maintained an active interest in the case, the threat of a contempt citation was real and a powerful impetus to compliance.

The substantive issues in the case were far more onerous than the legal issues because the professional community was unprepared to comply with the broad array of requirements in the consent decree. In almost every way this was a repeat of the experiences of the late 1950s when parents of moderately retarded children were able to promote legislation admitting their children to public schools. Once again, attention was given to the logistical aspects of the problem such as finding children and arranging for classroom space and transportation. The need for curricula, competent teachers and teacher support, and assessment procedures was overlooked. Children were being located and tested for classification purposes but no one knew toward what end. Having called this to the attention of the state staff, we all set about filling the gaps. Fortunately, we were able to bring to the state scholars whose work had assessed the educational needs of severely and profoundly handicapped children. Most noteworthy of these was Dr. Lou Brown of the University of Wisconsin, who almost singlehandedly laid a workable foundation for teachers in those locales with enough insight to avail themselves of his help. While most college and university people in Pennsylvania were notably absent from the scene, the special education people at Temple University were exceptions. They quickly designed teacher preparation plans and activated them in time to provide a small cadre of teachers who were able to get the school year started.

The spring and summer of 1973 were chaos as local school districts scrambled for teachers and psychologists waded through crowded testing schedules. There were no standards for teachers so each district had to use whatever criteria it could live with. The earthiness of these standards was best described by the director of a wealthy, active district during a Master's hearing on compliance. Boasting of the rate at which his district's program was taking shape, he claimed that his program was blessed by the best teachers in the state. Sensing a source for criteria for teacher selection, I asked him to state for the record the standards he applied. He fell silent as he pondered the question and after a long delay said, "It comes down to this. If they're willing to wipe the kids' asses, they've got a job." In his brief expletive-undeleted statement, he described the state of affairs succinctly and accurately.

During my tenure as Master in the PARC case, I began to get indications of similar suits being prepared in other states. Since there was no reason to believe that the plaintiffs would not be upheld or that educators in other states would be any better prepared to deal with the requirements of impending consent decrees or judgments, I could foresee spreading chaos. It seemed to me that a national effort was called for to formulate teacher selection standards and teacher preparation, to design curriculum alternatives, and to evolve assessment procedures, methods for classification, and even some models of classroom organization. Made available through the network of instructional material centers and regional resource centers, these guidelines and models would provide, at the very least, a point of departure for emerging programs and a foundation upon which indigenous programs could then be built.

I met with the full leadership of the Bureau of the Education for the Handicapped to present my case and recommendations. It was a stimulating meeting, and I was reasonably confident that my recommendations were well received. Unfortunately, however, little came of it because, as I was later informed, the authority of the bureau did not include funding to accommodate children who, because of age and/or category, were not yet part of the public school scene. I also learned that there were ways the bureau could support such projects if the initiative came from state departments and/or local districts.

We would be ignoring a basic fact of life if we overlooked the role of state and local education authorities in planning for the future. While the Bureau of the Education for the Handicapped was national in its visibility and operations, nevertheless, the legal responsibility for education was and still is the responsibility of state and local governments. Active and impending lawsuits brought by parents' associations and other advocates were far from unheard of. Despite this, little preparation was made at the state level, and there ensued the usual actions based on expediency and compromise soon to be repeated with advent of PL 94–142 and related legislation.

A SOCIAL SYSTEMS MODEL

There have been great and dramatic changes in the thirty years since I became a teacher of educable mentally retarded children. Our political, social, economic, and technological world is remarkably different from that of the early 1950s, but what teachers of the mentally retarded do and how they get things done are still, with small exceptions, what they were then. The case can be made that there has been more progress in areas related to the classroom than in the classroom itself.

I can hear indignant rebuttals to the foregoing. The claim is that we are mainstreaming mentally retarded children and they have individual educational plans. The fact is, children have always been mainstreamed where the conditions permitted, and competent teachers have always planned for each of their students. That we now have more mentally retarded children in regular classes and that file cabinets are stuffed with IEP's does not mean that the students are receiving a better or more relevant education. In fact, recent data suggest that moving children about and occupying committees and teachers' time to cobble up IEP's are reducing students' and teachers' effectiveness. Certainly, administrative changes have made little difference in the growth and development of mentally retarded children. There are no convincing data to indicate that changing the designation of a classroom from "educable mentally retarded" to "learning disabled II" or "emotionally handicapped" makes any difference educationally.

As I look to the future, conditions in the educational setting for mildly mentally retarded students provide the criteria by which change is measured. More than ever, I am convinced that the standard for all decisions and actions in education and related areas is the effectiveness of teacher-student transactions. And further, that these transactions only have meaning to the degree that they move students toward the attainment of the goals of education.

Applying this standard, I can see that cosmetic change has far outweighed substantive change over the past thirty years. On the perimeter of the classroom, systems and technologies for ascertaining childrens' intellectual and learning characteristics have improved over the years. But data gained from improved procedures fall short of what teachers need to refine their teaching. Administrative procedures are far more systematized and scientific than in the past. However, there is little coordination or substantive guidance of teachers' efforts. Placement procedures have become elaborate. Data on students' histories are collected from all sides, and children are placed with the least restrictive setting as the goal. There is little agreement, however, as to what criteria should be employed to stabilize placement decisions. Standards for admission to teacher preparation programs have not changed since I was a student nor has the preparation itself. Some concepts and jargon have been updated, but the lecture system and the short, often random, practicum still prevail. Research and development have proliferated dramatically, but one sees relatively little impact on classroom operations. While it is popular to lay the blame for this on teachers' inabilities to understand and capitalize on research, the fact still remains that relatively little research has notable bearing on classroom operations. Research that does so is designed and reported in a way which all too often defies generalization.

As I see special education in operation, I am more impressed by the discontinuities than by the coherence of the programs. Teachers are not sure what a well-balanced program should be, so they fall back on what they know best and put most of their time and effort into teaching reading and arithmetic. School psychologists and other support staff have no better notion of the goals of education than teachers, so they do what they do best and collect data on intelligence and affect and some on academic achievement. Administrators have had to become business managers and to oversee compliance with federal, state, and local regulations and, in many communities, with court orders. These activities limit them insofar as the formulation and implementation of educational policies and practices are concerned.

How can we reverse the ever-expanding universe of special education for the mentally retarded and arrest the flight from its center, the classroom? Is there a concept or principle around which our actions can coalesce? There was and there still is. From Itard onward, the goal of education has been implicitly the same for exceptional students as it was for nonhandicapped children, namely, to engender in them the skills and proficiencies that would help them attain autonomy in accord with society's expectations. Seguin (1841/1866) was remarkably explicit in this goal, and his curriculum and methods of instruction are clearly instruments to this end. In this country, Howe (1848) and his colleagues articulated the same goal, and their educational programs reflected this philosophy. When we study the theories of Descoeudres (1928), Anderson (1917), and others, we find differences in the ways and means for attaining the goals of education but not in the goals themselves.

As one reviews the literature on the education of the mentally retarded, it becomes evident that, as public school commitments to these students increased, there was a discernable drop-off in the number of texts and articles on educational thought and practice. At the same time, there was an increase in the number of texts and articles dealing with factors important to diagnosis and differentiation. The pivotal years were the 1930s and 1940s. From the 1950s on, the only exception to this abandonment of educational thought is found in the work of DeProspo and Hungerford (1946) and Hungerford and his colleagues (1948, 1957). By this time, however, momentum in education issues other than substantive was such that the work of the Hungerford group was pretty much ignored. This was unfortunate because it could have provided the leverage that could have helped the education establishment revitalize its goals and regain its position as a social institution.

Since the 1950s, the instrinsic values of education have far transcended the extrinsic. This change in educational outlook is manifested in the overriding emphasis on childrens' acquisition of literacy skills. It has materialized in the form of the competency test movement which by 1980 was in place in some 34 states (Jaeger & Tittle, 1980).

In its early stages, I predicted that the competency test movement and its punishing effects on handicapped students would bring the special education community roaring to its feet protesting vehemently the impoverished concept of competency inherent in the movement and its discriminatory effect on handicapped students. Quite the opposite happened. Apart from a few desultory articles that missed the point, special education did not react except to suggest that handicapped students be excused from taking competency tests and that successful fulfillment of Individual Education Programs (IEPs) be recognized as qualification for a diploma. Where this procedure has been tested in the courts, it has been rejected. The result is that too many handicapped children are leaving school carrying the documentation of their second class citizenship—a certificate of completion or its equivalent.

A reinstatement of the educational aims for mentally retarded students is necessary before reforms can be effected. We need to recognize that the defectological approach to the education of these children has created more problems than it has solved. It has led us into creating a quasi-medical model that directs much of our attention and energies to diagnosing and remediating disabilities. In the process, we overlook many assets. The preoccupation of teachers and supportive staff with the teaching of academic subjects at the expense of content important to growth and development is a natural outgrowth of the quasi-medical model. Above all, the narrow focus in educational practices, research, and administration has almost assured that the achieved status of mentally retarded will evolve into an ascribed status with all of its fixed properties.

The alternative, a social systems model, is consistent with the origins of education for mentally retarded students. Above all, a social systems model preserves the idea that achieved statuses can be altered and replaces the pessimism inherent in the notion of mental retardation as a fixed state with the optimism consistent with an achieved status. Many follow-up studies, along with the experiences of school people, show clearly that a sizeable proportion of students who have achieved the status of mental retardate leave school and gain the autonomy society requires and, in the process, shed the status. This is not to suggest that school norms are as broad as those in the larger society. However, with the increasing pluralism in public education, we are justified in expecting that norms will broaden and become more inclusive.

In the past two years, the hysteria and fervor associated with the competency test movement is being supplanted by more sober and deliberate considerations. The pressures that have led special education to assume the proportions of minor-league regular education are fading as issues such as reductions in enrollment and in finances rise. Further, with the expansion of mainstreaming, the possibility for broadening norms, usually restricted to literacy skills, is increased.

The adoption of a social systems model broadens educational thought and substance. Instead of confining the concept of autonomy to the school environment, it reinstitutes the school and society as the matrix within which autonomy must be considered. Thus, the extrinsic value of schooling comes into focus, and content such as reading and arithmetic can be seen for what they are in life: the means toward the end of problem solving rather than skills and proficiencies with values all their own. Within the system, then, all of the behaviors that are congruent with autonomy gain equal attention and are weighted accordingly. This leads to reforms in many aspects of educational endeavors. Foremost, I can foresee important changes in curriculum and in methods of instruction. Content will become broadened and balanced. Instead of heavy emphasis on academic content and a random tailing off of prosocial learning, aesthetics and humanities, prosocial and related content will become formalized elements in the school day. Like reading and arithmetic, they will be developmental in organization and consistent with behavioral norms along the way to and at maturity. This reorganization of the total educational program need not raise the fear that academic content will be abolished or even vitiated. It will, instead, open up many opportunities to capitalize on reading and arithmetic skills in other areas of learning.

A return to a social systems approach does not entail radical or expensive changes in teacher preparation or graduate education. Nor does it require changes in administrative structures or certification procedures. The technologies for curriculum development are in place and can be readily integrated into course content (Goldstein, 1981). To put it in practical terms, for not much more than an ideological reform in special education, great change can be effected in the consequences of educational decisions and actions. As Mercer (1970) stated, "The social system view of mental retardation is quite different from the pathological perspective. It focuses attention on the 'definer' as well as the 'defined' and permits us to move away from the search for causes, cures, treatments, and true 'prevalence' rates in order to restructure the phenomenon of mental retardation from a different vantage point. It leads us not only to see the world differently, but to pose new and different kinds of questions."

Implicit in Mercer's statement is the position that, given the appropriate educational policies and practices, the prevalence of mental retardation in schools and society can be reduced as children who have achieved the status of mental retardate return to more conventional and less demeaning statuses as a function of their behavioral change. Further, with the expansion of preschool provisions, the involvement of at-risk children in a curriculum that includes prosocial learning increases the probability that a sizeable proportion will never achieve the status of mental retardate (Garber and Heber, 1982; Weikart, 1970). For those of you who are hard line defectologists, this can be read as cure and prevention.

Thirty years in special education have not blinded me to the inertia in educational operations. At the same time, the history of special education has been dotted with remarkable innovations. Our present doldrums are in great part due to our preoccupation with the procedural reforms imposed on us by the dramatic social change accompanying the civil rights movement. As we get our procedures in order, the need for substantive change will become more evident. Society will surely demand evidence that its investment in procedural reforms is productive. My optimism that substantive change will constitute our next major goal is unabated.

REFERENCES

Anderson, M. (1917). *Education of defectives in the public school.* New York: World.

Baker, H. (1945). *Introduction to exceptional children.* New York: Macmillan.

Barr, M. W. (1904). *Mental defectives: Their history, treatment, and training.* Philadelphia: P. Blakeston's Son & Co.

Bennett, A. (1932). *A comparative study of subnormal children in the elementary grades.* New York: Teachers College, Columbia University, Bureau of Publications.

Binet, A., & Simon, T. (1916). The development of intelligence in children. (E.S. Kite, Trans.). *Vineland Training School Bulletin,* No. 11.

Blatt, B. (1958). The physical, personality, and academic status of children who are mentally retarded attending special classes as compared with children who are mentally retarded attending regular classes. *American Journal on Mental Deficiency, 62,* 810–818.

Cassidy, V. M., & Stanton, J. E. (1959). *An investigation of factors involved in the educational placement of mentally retarded children* (Project No. 043). Washington, DC: US Office of Education.

Condillac. (1930). Condillac's treatise on the sensations. (Geraldine Carr, Trans.). Los Angeles: University of Southern California Press.

De Prospo, C. H., & Hungerford, R. H. (1946). A complete social program for the mentally retarded. *Occupational Education, 3,* 95–197.

Descoeudres, A. (1928). *Education of mentally defective children.* (E.F. Row, Trans.). Boston: Heath.

Eaton, J. W., & Weil, R. J. (1955). *Culture and mental disorder.* Glencoe, IL: Free Press.

Garber, H., & Heber, R. (1982). The efficacy of early intervention with family rehabilitation. In M. Begab, H. Garber, & H. C. Haywood (Eds.), *Psychological influence in retarded performance for improving competence: Vol. III.* Baltimore: University Park Press.

Goldstein, H. (1969). Construction of a Social Learning Curriculum. *Focus on Exceptional Children, 3,* 1–10.

Goldstein, H. (1974). *The Social Learning Curriculum, Level I.* Columbus, OH: Charles E. Merrill, Inc.

Goldstein, H. (1975). *The Social Learning Curriculum, Level II.* Columbus, OH: Charles E. Merrill, Inc.

Goldstein, H. (ed.). (1981). *Curriculum development for exceptional children.* San Francisco: Jossey-Bass.

Goldstein, H., Mischio, G. S., & Minskoff, E. (1969, October). *A demonstration-research project in curriculum and methods of instruction for elementary level mentally retarded children* (Grant #32–42–1700–1010). Washington, DC: Bureau of Education for the Handicapped.

Goldstein, H., Moss, J., & Jordan, L. J. (1965). *The efficacy of special class training in the development of mentally retarded children.* (Cooperative Research Project No. 169). Washington, DC: US Office of Education.

Goldstein, M. T. (1979). *Diffusion tactics influencing implementation of a curriculum innovation.* Unpublished doctoral dissertation, Yeshiva University, New York.

Goldstein, M. T. (1981). Implementing a curriculum field-test model. In H. Goldstein

(Ed.), *Curriculum development for exceptional children.* San Francisco: Jossey-Bass.

Hebb, D. O. (1949). *The organization of behavior: A neurophysiological theory.* New York: John Wiley.

Hobbs, N. (1975). *The futures of children.* San Francisco: Jossey-Bass.

Howe, S. H. G. (1848). *Report of Commission to Inquire into Conditions of Idiots of the Commonwealth of Massachusetts.* Boston: Senate Document No. 51.

Hungerford, R. H. (1948). Philosophy of occupational education. Reprint from *Occupational Education* (Publication of the Association for New York Teachers of Special Education, 224 E. 28th St., New York, NY).

Hungerford, R. H., De Prospo, C. J., & Rosenzweig, L. E. (1957, October). Education of the mentally handicapped in childhood and adolescence. *American Journal of Mental Deficiency,* pp. 214–28.

Ingram, C. P. (1935). *Education of the slow learning child.* New York: World Book.

Itard, J. M. G. (1932). *The wild boy of Aveyron.* (G. and M. Humphrey, Trans.). New York: Century. (Original work published 1801)

Jaeger, R. M., & Tittle, C. K. (Eds.). (1980). *Minimum competency achievement testing.* Berkeley, CA: McCutcheon Publishing.

Jastak, J. (1949). A rigorous criterion of feebleminded. *Journal of Abnormal Social Psychology, 44.*

Jennings, W. I. (1930). *The poor law code.* London: Charles Knight.

Jernegan, M. W. (1931). *Laboring and dependent classes in colonial America.* Chicago: University of Chicago Press.

Kirk, S. A., & Johnson, G. O. (1951). *Educating the retarded child.* Boston: Houghton-Mifflin.

Lin, K., Chen, Y., & Kuo, W. (1983). Chinese revision of the Social Learning Curriculum. *Education and Training of the Mentally Retarded, 18*(1), 29–33.

Linton, R. (1947). Concepts of role and status. In Newcomb and Hartley (Eds.), *Readings in social psychology.* New York: Henry Holt.

Locke, J. (1801). *An essay on human understanding.* London: Bye and Law.

McCulloch, T. L. (1947). Reformulation of the problem of mental deficiency. *American Journal on Mental Deficiency, 52,* 130–136.

Malinowski, B. (1944). *A scientific theory of culture.* Chapel Hill, NC: University of North Carolina Press.

Maslow, A. H. (1962). *Toward a psychology of being.* Princeton: Van Nostrand.

Mayer, W. V. (Ed.). (1975). *Planning curriculum development.* Boulder, CO: Biological Sciences Curriculum Study.

Mead, M. (1937). *Cooperation and competition among primitive people.* New York: McGraw-Hill.

Mercer, J. (1970). Sociological perspectives on mild mental retardation. In C. Haywood (Ed.), *Socio-cultural aspects of mental retardation.* New York: Appleton-Century-Crofts.

Meyen, E. L. (1969). Demonstration of dissemination practices on special class instruction for the mentally retarded: Utilizing Master teachers as in-service educators—Final Report. Washington, DC: Bureau of Education for the Handicapped.

Meyen, E. L., Vergason, G. A., & Whelan, R. J. (Eds.). (1972). *Strategies for teaching exceptional children.* Denver: Love Publishing Co.

Naiman, D. (in press). *The Social Learning Curriculum for deaf mentally retarded children.* Washington, DC: National Association for the Deaf.

Pennsylvania Association for Retarded Children (PARC) v. Pennsylvania, 334 F. Supp. 1257 (E.D. Pa. 1971) and 343 F. Supp. 279 (E.D. Pa. 1972).

Pertsch, C. F. (1936). *A comparative study of the progress of subnormal pupils in the grades and in special classes.* New York: Teachers College, Columbia University, Bureau of Publications.

Report of the royal commission on the care and control of the feebleminded, Vol. VIII. (1908). London: H.M. Stationery Office.

Rousseau, J. J. (1896). *Rousseau's Emile.* (Wm. H. Payne, Trans.). New York: Appleton. (Original work published 1762)

Sarason, S. B. (1949). *Psychological problems in mental deficiency.* New York: Harper & Brothers.

Sarason, S. B., Davidson, K., & Blatt, B. (1962). *The preparation of teachers: An unstudied problem in education.* New York: John Wiley.

Seguin, E. (1841). *Theory and practice of the education of idiots.* Paris: L'Hospice de Incurables.

Seguin, E. (1866). *Idiocy and its treatment by the physiological method.* New York: William Wood and Co.

Thurstone, L. L., & Thurstone, G. (1953). *SRA primary mental abilities.* Chicago: Science Research Associates.

Tisdall, W. (1962). Productive thinking in retarded children. *Exceptional Children, 29,* 36–41.

Tredgold, A. F. (1937). *Mental deficiency.* Baltimore: Wm. Wood & Co.

Turnbull, H. R., & Turnbull, A. (1978). *Free appropriate public education, law and implementation.* Denver: Love Publishing Co.

Wallin, J. E. W. (1949). *Children with mental and physical handicaps.* New York: Prentice-Hall.

Weikart, D. P., et al. (1970). *Longitudinal results of the Ypsilanti Perry pre-school project.* Ypsilanti, MI: High Scope Educational Research Foundation.

Ysseldyke, J. E., & Algozzine, B. (1982). *Critical issues in special and remedial education.* Boston: Houghton-Mifflin Co.

4

Personal
Perspective

William C. Morse

William C. Morse, born 1915 in Erie, Pennsylvania, received his B.A. and teaching certificate in English-education (1938), and M.A. (1939) and Ph.D. (1947) in educational psychology (1947) from the University of Michigan.

Dr. Morse is chairman of the Combined Program in Education and Psychology at the University of Michigan (1965–   ) where he has also served as professor of education and of psychology and director of the Fresh Air Camp (1945-61). The University of Michigan has honored Dr. Morse as the William Clark Trow Professor of Educational Psychology (1977–   ) and as the recipient of the 1970 Distinguished Teaching Award.

Past president of the Michigan Psychological Association and past vice-president of the American Orthopsychiatric Association, Dr. Morse received the J. E. Wallace Wallin Award from the Council for Exceptional Children (1978) and has served as a member of the National Commission on Mental Health of Children and Youth. He is a fellow of the Orthopsychiatric Association and of the American Psychological Association, and has published numerous books and articles.

The terminal stages of one's career do not always bring with them that last benign Eriksonian state where wisdom and perspective merge. Some professionals slip into a panic near the end and feel great pressure to record everything lest a lifetime of profound thoughts be lost; they hang on, wanted or not, until infirmity or retirement rules do them in. Others elect to fade away and extol their escape from creative effort; perhaps they never enjoyed it much anyway. But the greatest danger of these end games we all come to play lies in not recognizing that the golden years are really mostly brass. Retrospection becomes increasingly selective, with memories made over to suit present intentions. What passes for wisdom is usually hindsight revisited. As we fine hone essential beliefs and biases, they take on the character of mental statues— and we ignore the work of the birds.

Even sage examination of the past is severely limited as a guide for charting the future. Mindful of these caveats, I will proceed to be didactic without meaning to be arrogant. At my point in life matters can be discussed with the certainty of youth, although that certainty has in truth become hamstrung with the qualifications of age. Only those from Harvard can know they are right and still appear open-minded.

INFLUENCES—EARLY AND LATE

It has always been a puzzle how much professional life is premeditated and how much fortuitous. Is there continuity to life or is it ad hoc? If the events which look like turning points had not happened, what other ones might have taken their place and to what end? Though my parents were both teachers and vastly enjoyed their profession, that was not my direction. In those days one's duty was to seek a "better" profession. In my case, that meant the law or medicine: I began with law. Now I know that lawyers run the world; they not only make law, they also spend the rest of their lives deciding for us what they meant. But in those naive days I found law boring because it always looked to past precedent and not to new solutions. After struggling to translate the origins of our law from Latin, I made a career migration and obtained a certificate to teach English drama and literature. This change in direction was probably the result of working as an assistant for an English professor who took great pleasure in literature. I do know I admired his manner, which seemed urbane and sophisticated to an undergraduate. His "work" seemed delightful. Perhaps the change in career direction was really the start of a lifelong search concerning the nature of man, for drama is the personification of life's dilemmas.

When I finished in the Great Depression, (then as now) there were very few teaching positions. With a part-time assistantship and a wife with a job, we felt that a master's degree was a reasonable step. In those days Roosevelt had devised what was called NYA, the National Youth Authority. Somewhat like the current work-study, this program paid a student fifteen to twenty-five cents an hour for doing useful university work. It was one of a series of government efforts to provide work for artists and others without jobs. Today such efforts are disappearing; now the worse things get, the more help is cut.

In those days additional education was considered an asset in getting a job, not a handicap. The belief was that education was of intrinsic value. We had already fallen in love with Ann Arbor, the excitement of football, the music, and the drama. We roamed the streets freely then, never locked our doors. It was a wonderful place to be. I started my graduate work with a course from an old-style scholar whose standards and expectations scared the hell out of me. The course was touted as the key to unlock the nature of the self. While the key was not forthcoming, he did admonish me to pursue a Ph.D. in educational psychology, which became a new goal. This included a few courses in what passed as school psychology training. Since I was low man on the totem pole, a teaching assistant, the dean of the School of Education made the next professional decision for me. He needed a fill-in instructor for an oddball assignment—to teach graduate student counselors at the university Fresh Air Camp, a group-therapy operation for disturbed and delinquent boys. As a very junior person, I was picked to be it. The dean explained this as we drove through Hell (Michigan) on our way to my first site visit. He was highly amused about going through Hell with the dean. It was prophetic, for in truth I had never dealt with kids like these kids. Year after year they expanded my appreciation of human nature, this great mixture of delinquent, aggressive, and neurotic urchins with a sprinkling of psychotics to keep one guessing.

Working and teaching at the camp became the major force influencing my professional career; all others pale in comparison. It shaped my concepts of nature of humanity, of both children and adults, and made me eschew the ritualistic classical style of therapeutic intervention. Of course, I learned more about myself too, but haltingly and with pain. Finally, the camp enabled me to see the essence of effective teaching, even though the practice still eludes me. At first I was rightly anxious. My academic knowledge seemed esoteric and impractical. My predecessor had taught formal psychology to the counselor-graduate students up to their necks in pathological behavior which demanded a hundred decisions every day. He assigned them papers on Thrasher's book *The Gang* (1937), no matter that they were caught in the midst of ongoing gang life almost twenty-four hours a day. After teaching a few class sessions according to this model, I was too embarrassed to continue. Over the years and especially when I directed the camp, I became an advocate of clinical teaching. Its components are simple to state but hard to carry out. First, give students an active practical role with enough responsibility to tax them to the limit of their endurance. Second, involve the "instructors" equally in the reality of practice, making them the over-group members of the team when the going gets too tough. Third, base your teaching on the actual cases and situations which everyone recognizes in the environment. This will dissolve the artificial demarcation between theory and practice since theory is born of practice and must facilitate it. Seminars explicate what is going on and provide concepts for organizing experiences.

The winters between camp sessions were tame—teaching and graduate study—vacations really; or that is the way the regular modulated academic world seemed. Soon the university authorities began looking for a person of prestige and reputation to direct the camp. Anyone of that status knew better than to accept such a position. Who wanted to be tied up all summer with a bunch of crazy kids and distraught adults? Grubbing for money in those days before grants was an endless task too. So I got the job by default and our own children spent their summers from infancy through adolescence in, to say the least, a vigorous environment. My goal had been to find a position teaching educational psychology in a small teachers' college, far from the publish-and-perish rat race—a calm place where relationships between students and faculty were like an extended family. Many of my Ph.D.'s who graduate today have this same wish, and some little nostalgia remains. But I stayed at Michigan. So much for Mr. Chips.

The concepts of diagnosis and therapy I had previously learned were never the same after the Fresh Air Camp. Talking with kids might help and was necessary at times, but feeding them well, teaching them things they valued, working through problems with them as fellows in life's struggles (without pretending to be perfect)—these proved even more effective. The power of the family in socializing children comes from its many resources which cannot be duplicated elsewhere, really. But we tried.

There was one person who not only understood all of this but even explained it so that it made everyday sense. The ideas he used seemed so real, so simple, and so helpful that one could easily use them as cognitive tools. The person was Fritz Redl. First he taught me about being human, for he respected lowly graduate students as much as the well-known figures who were his associates. He also knew how to do business with kids since he understood them so well. His research was observational and clinical, always creative. The invention of life space interviewing (Morse, 1981) was a breakthrough and freed the educational profession from stupid simulation of classical interviewing techniques. Fritz's explanations cut to the dynamic core of both individual and group behavior. The other gift he had was the understanding of group and leadership dynamics and the concept of milieu. The latter was the forerunner of what is now called ecological psychology, which holds behavior is a product of *both* the person and the external stimuli, whether seductive or prophylactic. How we arrange the environment and what ingredients are in the milieu were keystones in Redl's thinking. But, to me, his most fascinating contribution was his unique appreciation of group behavior. He helped us see how a group interacted to become an organic whole even as he clarified adolescent and adult leadership roles. Few children are hermits: as he put it, most kids are so group oriented that, even when alone, they are surrounded by an invisible group of their own making. But mostly they operate in real groups.

It has always seemed to me that we seldom recognize that education is a milieu operation and that teachers are leaders of groups. It is one thing to deal with a series of individual child-adult interactions. But put those youngsters together, and they change their performances. Redl's discussion of these matters in *When We Deal With Children* (1962) and Newman's *Groups in Schools* (1974) are lifelines for teachers of both normal and special children. In these matters we still have not caught up with Redl in training teachers or school psychologists.

Returning to the theme of career, I have found that the course of shaping events hardly appears self-directed or of constant purpose. However, in my case, the direct involvement with these distraught youngsters and the dedicated graduate students trying to help them was a profound experience, miles away from academic educational psychology. This was the "growth of the self" in the trenches. There was a dualism in this work: one learned as much or more about one's self as about the youngsters. This process has persisted throughout my professional years. The effort to apply the camp knowledge to teaching led to my first book (educational psychology embedded in philosophy) with a colleague who was a scholar of Dewey (Morse & Wingo, 1955). A radical departure from the typical educational psychology of the time, it was based on teaching through simulated experience through cases, descriptions of actual classes, and school problems to foster a sense of reality. A book cannot adequately convey the sense of clinical teaching, so for years I ran a different style of teaching-training program. It was a field-based program in which, for a year, students worked in classrooms; seminars were held right at the school where we used the milieu as the basis and included the supervising teacher's participation. Two special education training programs were designed based on this strategy at Hawthorn Center for Disturbed Youngsters. The last training effort following this model was an open-ended combined Ph.D. program in education and psychology at the University of Michigan, which incorporated extensive field-based learning. Nothing, however, achieved the intensity of the learning experience at the Fresh Air Camp. I have come to understand that you cannot create a powerful training enterprise without also assuming responsibility for managing it. You must be totally committed to keeping it on track. Otherwise it dissipates and soon becomes perfunctory.

The retreat from the ivory towers to summers with twenty-four-hour-a-day living with over a hundred distraught and trying youngsters and half as many neophyte staff was certainly the decisive learning experience in my graduate training. But there were also many individuals who made specific contributions to my professional evolution. First and foremost was a youngster. First cases are often our most profound teachers, especially if they are there from childhood, through adolescence, and even into adulthood. Peter was a hard teacher and drove me to the end of my control many times. One could say we each drew blood, for he needed much more than I could give; yet neither of us ever gave up. He taught me that while the human dilemma is

the same for all of us, some have added handicaps of race, family disintegra-
tion, poverty, and adverse fate. He taught me that youngsters struggle, even as
adults do, to figure out what life is about, that they are desperate for hope and
help, and that they present layers, each concealing another beneath it. He
taught me attribution theory before the psychological concept had emerged,
but I missed a great deal of it. Either fate fingered him or Pete had a fine
personal talent for being in the wrong place at a given time: he seemed to be
disaster prone. He had figured out, in a fatalistic way, a dead-end life: no
matter how he tried, things went awry; by the time he reached adolescence, he
no longer even hoped except in thin wisps. Now they call it *learned
helplessness*, but it might better be termed *taught hopelessness*. Peter
demonstrated how, after a surge of seeming progress, one can slide into the
pits again. Our interactions ranged from profound discussions to physical
holding when he was in a fit of frustration. Therapy was never like this in the
books. His infrequent periods of happiness came from exploring of nature,
swimming, or participating reasonably in a group activity. The last I heard of
him, he was married and sort of making it marginally, in and out of "sync"
with a satisfying and satisfactory life. His legacy to me included an entirely
new concept of therapy with youngsters: the importance of support groups
and the restorative consequences of jobs for adolescents. Nothing was simple
after Pete. He taught me that massive human energy is necessary to change the
direction of a person who has been seriously damaged. There is no easy way,
no quick way, and no gimmick that will work. Bettelheim once stated that it
takes an ego to build an ego. So I marvel at the expectations for change in
children in special education. The Individual Education Plans (IEPs) have
generated a decade of professional deception—at least when it comes to
disturbed youngsters. We seldom have the resources or are willing to make the
investment necessary to make the significant difference. Our superficial
appreciation of our business is its most depressing condition. I do not blame
the teachers; their leadership has misled them.

The effort to understand the helping process has been an abiding search
throughout my professional life; it of course is blended with the more
narcissistic and essential quest to explain myself. It seems that there is more
nonsense written about helping than about anything else except consultation,
perhaps. Humankind is said to be engaged in the act of *helping* one another
by such diverse efforts as benign neglect or incarceration, whether the help is
aimed primarily at the helper's welfare and comfort or at the recipient's.
Bandura's (1974) masterful description of our ability at self-deception is a
cognitive explanation of the same processes that Freud explains using other
terms: we use mental tricks to disguise our self-serving aims and to maintain
high purposes while continuing our primitive behavior. It is a convenient
confusion. Everything works or nothing works depending upon how and for
whom one defines *work*. It is difficult enough to conceptualize helping an
adult: with children the process is vastly compounded by both their

developmental level and their individual natures. They are so much at our mercy. Conversely, our own adult counter-transferences and needs foul up our transactions with them. The problem of understanding another human being is always great. Even adults I know well surprise me often, as indeed I even surprise myself by my own behavior. With children, the gulf can be impassable for many adults. We were all children once, but we have lost our childhood and even most of our adolescence. The resonance of those times has either died out or we feign deafness. Those few books that tell it like it is from the other side of the age span need to be read and reread—books like *Life Among the Giants* (Young, 1966), for example.

When any human riddle becomes too complex for satisfactory comprehension, we reduce it to simplistic terms and superficial explanations. Our credulity dispels the actual ambiguity and produces psycho-religion. In Erikson's terms (1977), we have a ritual which becomes the explanation. It used to bother me to observe the gullibility of both lay and professional people. I could not believe that they really believed what they said they believed. Since I was less assured in my own psychological assertions about the nature of man and the course of development, others' incredible beliefs generated in me a tremendous need to enlighten them. It took me a long time to recognize the folly of this and to come to terms without trying to persuade others to abandon their tenuous hold on explanations for life and to join with me and increase my self-assurance. I came to realize that we are all, young and old, working on the same problems that Erich Fromm (1973) has summarized: whence do we come, what is it all about while we are here, and what, if anything, comes after? Children are particularly involved in these matters, trying to make sense of the conundrum. Our problem is to give some explanation of what is obviously the absurdity of life. We want to order life, to make reasonable that which defies reason. We need our myths to live by. I have come to respect the struggle people go through to get their myths in shape, even if their answers seem implausible to me. We wish there were explanations, and we need to believe, in the face of contrary evidence, that this is a just world. We create lay and professional psycho-religions to provide answers and then seek cohorts to increase our assurance. This is the guru syndrome, the sparkle of charisma. Those who are most uneasy about the ultimate truth of their own beliefs want to prevent the challenge of contrary ideas. We would censor opposing notions, political or psychological. We are so afraid, that we are willing to kill off our opposition lest they have evidence which will threaten or contaminate our beliefs. This restriction of the free concourse of ideas about what we should be able to read or what we select to teach is repression. I once walked into a special education program under a sign that said, "Stamp Out Dynamics." There are a lot of Jonesvilles in special education. It is a messy situation. On one hand, the various psycho-religious practices should be tolerated if they do not do direct harm; on the other hand, it is hard to take the long view and maintain that the truth will eventually be distilled out over time when you only live once and believe with the existentialists that this moment is important. We are back to everything works and nothing works.

Somehow, it is more difficult for me to accept oversimplifications produced by professional leaders who take a slice of the human being and project it as if it were a whole. Teaching a course in personality theory over the years has convinced me of the limited utility of the piecemeal theories, be they Skinner's or Freud's. Teachers have to start all over to put together a useful concept of the child's self-development, and academic courses offer little help. No wonder so many professionals end up with an atrophied set of guiding concepts to use in relating to children.

The simpler the theory, the better it seems. The more charismatic and authorative the advocate, the more wide the spread of the theory. Unthinking belief helps us avoid the difficulty of living an open-ended scientific life of continual doubt, evaluation, and decision making. No wonder teachers seek a method, any method. Special education is like a pop culture where one test or methodology after another comes along, each one designed to solve everything. Training is too often only indoctrination in a particular psychoreligion. It would take an extended experience with gifted collaborators to provide understanding of how diverse people are and of the many ways in which change can be induced. We are back again to the helping process.

There have been a few high points in this search for an understanding of the helping process. Four remain prominent. One came from observing a gifted child psychiatrist work with youngsters. He said he never talked with a youngster without first knowing, from the life history and diagnostics, what the child's life problem was; what he then did was to find out from the child how he or she perceived that problem, its nuances and nature. Whether or not he was to be the eventual helper, the youngster was always left with hope and an indication of a possible plan of help. His empathic resonance was broad, and he could be sensitive to the pain of the neurotic, the confusion of the psychotic, and the blatant exploitation driving the sociopathic delinquent. He at once represented both the impulsive and reality sides of life, calling the shots in strategic ways when appropriate. He believed in a nurturing milieu for assisting disturbed youngsters which was a replica of the best of the extended family in concern and control. In the terms of Eckstein & Motto (1969) helping, parenting, and teaching are the common impossible professions. They demand the constant vigilance to mediate the youngster's narcissistic motivations and the reality of social responsibility. (And you can expect to be damned for your mediation efforts even when done well.) From these forces arise the ambivalence youngsters feel for helpers, both love and anger. The upbringing of the next generation is not a pleasant romp: the rebalancing of a distorted young life is a racking excursion.

There was a time when students wanted to listen to nothing but their own gastrointestinal rumblings. Bill Rhodes and I were teaching several courses together, and we both found it well nigh impossible to practice our profession of "teaching." Working with Rhodes during this period (1972) constituted another formative experience. He was my cultural revolution. He would replace my conservative myths with the myths of the counterculture: out with the old rituals—in with the new.

The deep pervasiveness of the counterculture was also evident in Rogers (1977) and Holt (1968) where the cognitive processes were abandoned for worship of gut feelings. Everyone was a self-proclaimed king and socialization became a dirty word. The social contract by which a democratic society maintains itself was declared null and void. Perhaps we needed this decade of the id since, as Rhodes has put it, we progress in dialectic swings, never pausing around the golden mean. But the main thing Rhodes did for me was to extend Redl's concept of milieu. Rhodes was the clarifier of the ecological position: personal difficulties are the outcroppings of the social system as much as the individual. As he said, deviance is a system in pain and the system includes the person. As a consequence we must study the precipitating system every bit as thoroughly as we study the individual. We help as much by contravening the support system as by trying to change the individual. Over the years we were colleagues, this position of Rhodes probably has done as much as anything to change my whole stance toward special education for the socio-emotionally disturbed, although he might not recognize his influence or be pleased with my resolution.

Another milestone along the trail to understanding helping was Kopp's (1976) work. He drops sharp insights along the way throughout his rambling discourse. Among the most useful to me was his statement that you cannot help those you feel are alien to you. You must realize that all the "pathology" you work with out there also resides within you, and you must tune in on that empathic awareness. The helper and the recipient are in the same dilemma on the same journey. Helpers tend to act as if they have arrived at a superior point; yet they should harken to their own struggles. You can't help one if you are not one. Who has left all neurosis behind? Who does not have remnants of escape and autistic behavior, little replicas of a devastating psychotic mind break with reality? Who does not grapple with alienation at times? Who does not drop the veneer of socialization now and again and operate on a narcissistic basis? The contract of helping is also described by Kopp—the sets of expectations on both sides which often imply conditions that can't be met. One does not help someone: one interacts with another human being and part of the interaction may help that human being (as well as the helper) to find his or her way. The rituals we learn as a part of our formal training in therapy are, in a way, rules which protect us from an honest and completely conjoined experience. As a teenager once said to me, "I've told you about me, answered all the questions, listened to your explanations. Now, how about you?" Well, I must confess my life journey has not been exemplary. I must confess, too, that I was blessed with an unusually interactive and tolerant support system, a forbearing wife and offspring, who tutored me patiently over the years. This continues. And now there is a grandson who is my living link with the joys and pains of growing up. He is a better text on the emergence of the human self than anything I have read or written: he tells things to me like they are. I am reminded of how, when studying for prelims, I turned off my little neighborhood friends to hit the books. I passed the exams all right and delayed understanding children for years.

The idea of a contract in helping has been recently treated in a demanding paper by Brickman and his cohorts entitled *Models of Helping and Coping* (Brickman et al., 1982). It turns out that helpers often operate on one set of assumptions while institutions, parents, and kids may have another overt or covert set of assumptions about the process. Often these assumptions are unconscious and do not easily become subject to negotiation. Brickman's four paradigms have to do with our attribution theory, which asks two questions: (1) who is responsible for the predicament of a person who is in personal distress and/or is distressing to others? In brief, whose fault is it that I am in the fix I'm in? and (2) who is responsible for changes which will get me out of the fix? Assumptions about these two questions will determine how the helper behaves and the helpee responds. In the first paradigm, which Brickman calls the *moral*, one assumes that the individual in distress is responsible for his plight and responsible for the solution as well. Since helpers can't perform magic rescue missions, they resort to exhorting and blaming the person in trouble. "Try harder" is the adage. The person is seen as lazy, ineffective, and not trying hard enough. The moral stance allows the helper to be free of responsibility since the person has to solve his problem by himself. Currently the government is dominated by a political philosophy based on this premise: it's your fault if you are poor or having a hard time, and it's up to you to lift yourself out somehow by your own bootstraps. There is an implicit assumption that life is just and everyone gets what he or she deserves. Now what does the moral paradigm teach about coping? Those who are able to raise themselves increase their sense of power over their own destiny and become self-made. They learn they can cope and feel in control and strong. They are living proof of the validity of their own theory. But what of those who fail? Well, it is their fault, and this adds to their sense of inadequacy. They are made to feel guilty: others can do it; why not you? The theory breeds self-fulfilling failure and alienation. Bandura, who always deals with critical problems in refreshing new ways has discussed this condition, which he calls the perception of self-efficacy (1982). Self-efficacy is the key to a person's effort to engage in the work of self-change and a highly predictive measure of potential for success. Special education has been concerned with this in one way or another, and Bandura's experimental evidence clarifies a great deal for us.

Brickman calls the second paradigm the *medical-behaviorist model*. Here the person is seen as helpless and not responsible for his condition nor for getting out of it. External forces put him there, and external forces must get him out. There are pills to take or behavior modification to be arranged to produce change. The person remains a pawn of external forces. The therapist is in control and of course takes on grandiose power. The dependency of the "patient" is encouraged; cures are in the hands of helpers who are the masters; helping procedures are the key. Thus coping becomes a matter of getting help and following admonitions: take your medicine as directed. In a third paradigm called *compensatory*, the person is not at fault for his state and not to be blamed but is responsible for getting out of it. This view produces less guilt about the condition: life dealt you a bad hand and it's not your fault. Nonetheless, you must face the reality of your plight and do something about it. Getting out of the dilemma is up to you. Use willpower. You must learn to cope, to take advice, and to respond to exhortation. Some programs for black youngsters follow this paradigm—it's not your fault that society put you under, but don't count on anyone's help to get out except your own. You have to do it yourself. Work hard in school to get ahead. Be assertive. Energy is directed at solving the problem, not at removing the causes. The helper is really not at fault for failures. When this plan works, as in the moral model, success inflates the victim's ego and makes him or her strong, enhancing future effort and coping capacity. When the slightly assisted bootstrap self-help operation fails, it of course teaches and reinforces the "I-can't-cope" syndrome. In the last of the models, which Brickman calls the *enlightenment model*, you got yourself in but can't be expected to bail yourself out. After all, if you could do that, you could have avoided being in the fix in the first place. The therapist provides enlightenment about the true nature of the problem and especially solutions. To compensate for the personal inability to extricate one's self, the subject must listen to the helper or do as God says or follow some guru. The power is in the helper and given on loan. The person can't cope alone. Dependency on the program is advocated. The magician will wave the wand, but you must follow exactly. Programs to cure delinquents often follow this pattern and there are cures of the same genre for learning disabilities. Often if the pupil is not cured, the fault is his or hers, because the program is above reproach. People learn to cope by following its magic ways.

Now an IEP meeting is a good laboratory for seeing these contrasting paradigms acted out. Of course the Brickman helping-coping schemas are oversimplified. I find myself using different ones at different times for the same youngster, or fixating on a given pattern for those who irritate me. Parents often use these dimensions when they talk about their offspring: "he won't do anything for himself" or "I can't do anything with him." Younger children tend to be seen as helpless, as needing our expertise, hence the gratification that helpers of young children feel when things go well. Adolescents are often supposed to be as dependent on their own resources as adults are. How did you come to be this way? How can you change or get changed—or can you? Work with children involves a constant stream of decisions we make about whether a child can do what we request at this or that point in time. Most of us do not want to risk a series of failures for those we help: am I setting him up for failure by this expectation? The most difficult thing is to set up situations with a high probability of success which become generalized so that the child learns to cope and feels increasing control over his life. Can the specific successes be generalized or will they remain specific to a given class of events? Is Bandura's self-perceived efficacy a trait? Does it not have to be mediated by one's actual capabilities?

We who are protectors of the young often overprotect them to such an extent that they never find themselves. At the same time it is naive to believe that anyone operates as a truly independent organism. We operate in a social context and not on our own for most of what we do. We all need support systems and relationships. We do not learn to cope alone. Thus, while Brickman has caused me to think deeply about helping, there is more to it than how one got in and how he or she gets out.

Hobbs was another landmark influence for me, more in his seminal thinking than in the ReEd system. In his writing on the sources of therapeutic gain (1968) he speculates about whether or not insights have much of anything to do with therapeutic gain. He suggests that insight therapy has been based upon a limited concept, essentially the sequence of trauma, repression, insight, revelation, and relief. In the place of this he thinks through the whole problem of effecting and sustaining change. His first requirement for change is that the person needing to learn new behavior have a sustained, intimate experience with another human being under conditions where he or she can experiment without getting hurt. The second source of gain is in helping the client to divest his or her verbal and other symbolic sources of anxiety. Third is the understanding of the transference relationships which underlie the association between human beings. Fourth is practice at making decisions about one's own life. Hobbs indicates that all therapies have a conception of the nature of man, explicit or implicit, which fortifies the believer against the absurdity of the human condition. Such a conception enables a person to give explanations for his own and other's behavior. So I ask, do I provide the youngster with these opportunities which are the essence of helping? Do special education programs provide these elements? Could they?

In a more recent work, Hobbs has examined behavior change within a general but penetrating matrix of variables (1981). He asks, "What is it that causes substantial and predictable changes in human behavior?" He includes psychotherapy and other effective movements and searches for common characteristics in them which transform individuals. As I see it, each has a counterpart for helping disturbed children in schools.

First, Hobbs says, is a *belief system*. This could be behavior modification, Freudianism, Catholicism, or whatever. A system, in its own way, imposes order on experience, making a sense of it, so to speak. Belief systems vary, but it is necessary to have some set of beliefs. This helps me understand the issue of credulity and everything works and nothing works discussed previously. In my view, this belief system for special education for the disturbed should be an explicit and clear set of principles expressing the democratic ethic, how we live and work together, our rights, our goals, and our responsibilities. In effect, it is what Sarason (1971) called the constitution of the classroom and is best established in concert with the pupils. Second, says Hobbs, there must be *an interpreter of the belief system*—the guru, therapist, or teacher-counselor. This person helps the youngster see his own life in terms of the beliefs. The teacher lives the code of behavior and enhances identification with it through example. Now the power of the charismatic figures becomes evident. The effectiveness of iconoclastic teachers is explained. It has often been observed that the most effective special teachers operate outside of usual teacher roles. Hobbs' third aspect is *communication:* communication includes abreaction, confession, and group discussions in the case of youngsters. Verbal plans are made and shared, as in Alcoholics Anonymous. Next comes some *constructive action* in keeping with the belief system and representing the communicated plans. He points out how well the Moonies recognize this. After the indoctrination, the initiates take to the streets. In schools, this step can include constructive problem solving and reporting of actual behavior.

The last common element of effective change programs is in what Hobbs calls *community*—a sense of fellowship with a caring group. If we want to sustain change, we have to embed the new behavior in a social context. The struggle in special education is to make the class membership supporting, mutually facilitating, and helpful. To my mind this is the reason for attention to group process as well as to teacher support. Then attachment to the teacher is transferred to a more normal, natural support group outside of special education. If we do not aid this transfer, the youngster is left to find his own "caring group" and often it is of a delinquent character. Most often there is no support group to replace the teacher. This is where the ecological considerations of Rhodes must be brought in. The fact is, we do not cure kids, but we can start a process which needs support from a community. When I look at Hobbs' ideas, I find them perceptive and functional. He has charted the next revolution in helping for me. It is a wonder that we get anywhere at all with most of our special education efforts for the disturbed child. I can look back on a very few programs which did do these things. They were usually created by a dedicated leader, free of the conceptual constrictions of traditional special education. Hobbs describes the process in a general, value-free way. The same set of processes can be put to devastating use as well as guide positive designs. Outside of vague goals, we have not yet described the end product which will determine the substance and quality of the change programs we propose.

Somehow, we in special education for the disturbed seem far from incorporating into our practice the profound observations of Brickman, Hobbs, and others. We are still busy playing games. The credulity of professionals (and I certainly include myself) is a continual source of wonderment. As Bandura says, we are masters at self-deception. We project our beliefs on the past, and think our views represent the future. The period of credulity we are now going through demonstrates how thin our scientific dedication is, how superficial our commitment, as we attempt to handle a depressing lack of money. We are looking for a quick fix. When an otherwise sane, recent Ph.D. in special education tells me she has seen levitation and a special teacher diagnoses by horoscope, I wonder. There are twenty thousand astrologers in America to two thousand astronomers (Gardner, 1981). Perhaps, as has been suggested (Abell & Singer, 1981), people do not truly believe such things but use them as relief from the hard facts of life. They are the fairy tales of adults. In the *American Psychologist* one can read letters on a debate on the afterlife from reports of the nearly dead! And we learn that death is the last great creative experience! We redo the monkey trials to hear that the earth is only a few thousand years old! We are shocked to learn that some scientists fabricate data on occasion. I am well aware that what I personally believe will hardly stand the test of time and that I argue loudest when I am least sure—as if I must defend my beliefs since they lack their own integrity. This credulity business both in special education and in society in general has made me revise my concepts of human nature. We are great at self-deception and are too easily made captive of our internal convictions.

Apparently, power roles in "professing," administration, or government tend to foster self-deception and encourage intoxication with one's own utterances.

THE INTELLECTUAL QUEST: SCIENCE AND OTHER MATTERS

I am reminded now of the colleague who said that no important psychological discovery ever resulted from a strict reliance on the scientific method. But I didn't hear about this early enough in my professional life. At the same time as I was learning about helping at the Fresh Air Camp, I led a schizophrenic life, also being introduced to quantitative research. It took a long time to learn that the accepted formal model for scientific research is one thing, while scientific thinking and skepticism as a way of life is quite another.

Of course, all of graduate education was not science with a capital S. The humanistic teacher who meant the most to me had a unique way of personalizing a teacher-student relationship. Howard Y. McClusky was a global educational psychologist and holistic thinker, and we found him always moving across boundaries. He would not be constrained by the traditional barriers of a discipline. He read everything, or so it seemed, and absorbed it; then he resynthesized it in new combinations. He was a dreamer, activating hope. No matter where you sat in class, you felt he was really talking with you. Overcommitted, never a slave of precise time, he worked in an office that was a mass of reprints in piles, mimeographed articles, and, here and there, an odd paper which had strayed from its appointed place. Only he could find anything in this unfiling system. Once, on a picnic with him, two of us opened the car trunk to get out the food baskets and were shocked to find a pile of unmarked papers from the previous term—including our own! When you did get a paper back, it was covered with reactions. If he ever found even a tiny spark of original thinking, he would call you in to discuss your ideas. He was one of the few in those days who understood that even graduate students have to eat, and he managed various support systems which by now are the only way to have a vigorous advanced program. He was so warm and personal in his relationships that a class with him was an engaging experience. He believed that students were important and could even be friends. His teaching provided a great deal to imitate.

Fortunately for my training in scientific thinking, I had a Harvard-trained research professor, Irving Anderson, one of the few around at that time who was familiar with newer methodology and statistics. Taciturn, enigmatic, and lacking small talk, he had been trained as an English teacher before becoming a psychologist. This was before the advent of Edwin Newman, and I thought I could write. But every sentence in my thesis was tested for its ring, and most failed to produce the desired tone. This silent Finn, as we called him, would give endlessly of his time to work out a theory, experiment, or paper. He was something else again as a teacher, possessing a dramatic, expressive delivery and forever juxtaposing common sense with scientific evidence. It did not matter whether one was discussing an experiment or health or politics; everything was examined for alternative explanations and contrary evidence. His mind was open to iconoclastic thinking, but everything was subjected to excruciatingly careful scrutiny.

Since he was interested in reading, I became interested in reading and worked out a thesis under his direction. Hundreds of children had to be tested to find the proper groups, reading at grade level, normal in ability, and in the proper grade. Then reading passages had to be standardized. The opthalmograph was dragged around to schools in Detroit where the right students resided, and their eye movements were photographed as they read easy, grade-level, and difficult material. In analyzing their fixations and regressions, we found amazing variation. Some made more regressions in reading a passage than others made fixations, and the comprehension ranged from little to perfect. There were LD records, but the term had not been invented yet so I didn't realize what those atrocious eye-movement patterns signified. Also, by and large, each pupil read in his own particular style regardless of the difficulty of the passage; thus comprehension might be high or low, but the reader kept his rhythm. Two general consequences of the research affected my own professional learning. One was serendipitous: the huge variation in human performance among so-called normal youngsters. The other was an identification with the scientific method as a way of life. My mentor checked not only the experiment but everything else in life as if it were an experiment, giving cautious interpretations and possible alternative explanations. He always said that what we didn't know was much greater than any findings. But he believed in the building of knowledge through experimentation and generally took a behavioristic stance in his search for frugal explanations.

Over the years I have felt a disenchantment with classical research design. Part of this came from the Center for Group Dynamics at Michigan and especially from the work of Alvin Zander and Ronald Lippitt. They did what was called action research, in which they dealt with real situations. Some of the work was conducted at the Fresh Air Camp, where they examined the group behavior. The observers followed the groups, charting their behavior as if the group members didn't exist as human beings. In a camp for disturbed boys this "scientific neutrality" didn't work, and the whole project had to come to grips with the participant observation in action settings. It also taught us the difficulty of evaluative research when an investment has been made in certain goals. Subsequently I have found that few programs want to find out more about themselves once the evidence implies shortcomings. In an interdepartmental school research seminar in recent years we were eagerly invited into schools to do research until they found out that the results were often not encouraging. Ongoing operations prefer to live with their myths.

At any rate, after many years, it seemed more important to know a limited amount about the actual behavior of real children than to know a great deal about an abstract psychological construct. That aptitude x treatment (Cronbach & Snow, 1977) should be hailed as a new discovery shows how hung up psychology is over studying variables rather than people. We make assumptions about the meaning of a variable as if that phenomenon exists outside of the context of a person and place. We know about *anxiety*, but we don't know about *anxious people* as *persons*. Even the new path analysis, which deals with predictions instead of correlations, still is attached to variables and not to people.

My uneasiness about psychological research led to the study of persons rather than dimensions through *N of 1* studies, so to speak. The goal of my studies is to discipline the illusive case-study method, which suffers from excessive interpretation and minimal data from which to generalize. Personality theory was declared virtually dead in the last decade, and it is easy to see why. The classical style of research enabled us to write books about almost any variable—anxiety, locus of control, achievement motivation, what have you. But we still stumbled along as individual human beings and as helpers of human beings. Unfortunately we couldn't treat dissociated variables: the people owning the variables kept messing things up. The lack of a science of *persons* has caused us to spawn endless theories about how to bring up the next generation, how to teach, and especially how to be helpers of others; the theories never seem to reach a saturation point and never distill any definitive program.

It has been pointed out that we know more and more about less and less when it comes to human behavior. Bronfenbrenner (1977) has lamented this, as have others. We have also been cautioned not to use personality tests to try to predict the behavior of an individual case. What this means, to those of us in an applied field such as education, is that we are dealing with actuarial psychology. Out of one hundred high risk kids, a certain percentage will do poorly in school—on the average. Out of a given population we might know how many could be expected to be delinquent or drop out of school. But we would still not know *who* they would be. An experiment on a teaching method will provide statistical information and averages. It is obvious that such knowledge is important to social and institutional planning. But any social operation which requires predictions about *individuals* is in bad shape. Isn't it depressing to realize we don't know whom to let out of prison and whom to keep in to safeguard our welfare? Which person will commit another murder? Another holdup. There is, as we shall see, an additional variable— *who* will commit a murder *under what conditions*—but more of this later. The point is, we study variables and not people. We examine locus of control as if it existed as a construct apart from the person who has "it." We act as if traits were floating around inside us someplace doing their thing. This crowning of the characteristic as an entity matches the pronouncements of an earlier period when the abstractions of id or superego were supposedly conducting their private internal battles inside us. Gestalt theory—and I speak of the basic psychology and not current Gestalt therapy—held that the whole determined the meaning of the parts, and that the whole was greater than a mere addition of the parts. Meaning comes from relationships of the parts. We cannot rely on atomistic items.

Before we examine the concept of *N of 1*, as we now find it in the literature, it is important to recognize that the most famous paradigm of *1* is not the paradigm we are intent on explicating. Both of the rubrics which are entitled *N of 1* are as far apart as could be and are important. One is the behavioristic charting of the single case, in which a single dimension of individual performance is observed and graphed. For example, a baseline might be the number of times a pupil leaves his or her assigned seat over a given time interval. An intervention is then applied to change the behavior, i.e., the teacher does something. The graphing proceeds. The observed behavior changes, or may change. The added contingency may be applied in differing patterns or removed to test what happens to the behavior. There must be ten thousand such reports in the literature with new ones published every month. In this day and age when managing behavior is critical, when there is so little time to work with youngsters, and teachers are confronted with conditions they must change to survive, it is no mystery why this style *N of 1* has developed so rapidly. Whether you believe it is a sufficient paradigm or not, there is no question that this is what most people consider when speaking of *N of 1*.

From another tradition, the dynamic position, stems the other concept of *N of 1*. It evolves from the case study, the study of individual persons. It has been said that if you know the outcome, you can't miss explanations when you do a case study: you simply organize the material to fit the results. In the hands of a gifted clinician, who serves as the computer, it can be mighty convincing. But it is undisciplined and not replicable—but replication is necessary if we are to be able to understand and predict human behavior and develop a science of persons.

If we study a person's behavior, the goal is to know as much as we can about the individual. This does not mean collecting a mass of low-power demographic variables. It does mean collecting data on significant variables for the behavior in question. In effect, it is an experiment based upon theoretical relationships within a person. This *N of 1* is based upon the concept that individuals, even small children, have an internal consistency and functional pattern which should enable us to predict behavior rather than just relationships. In place of a simplistic correlation between intelligence and achievement, say a correlation of +.65, which accounts for a little over one-third of the variance, again on the average, the effort of *N of 1* is to put together a set of meaningful elements which should theoretically predict achievement. High ability plus low motivation plus poor teaching is one pattern. High ability plus low motivation plus good teaching is quite another pattern. High ability plus demanding teaching is still a third. An anxious person in a threatening environment should respond differently from an anxious person in a nonthreatening environment. Persons with high anxiety and low coping skills should perform differently from those with high anxiety and high coping, other things being equal. Predictions are made about all individuals with a given personal profile rather than about how psychological dimensions behave in the abstract. Mischel (1978) and Stephenson (1979) have demonstrated that consistency lies within the individual and not with isolated dimensions, if we wish to appreciate an individual's behavior. What we need to do in this type of research is to conceptualize the salient, relevant, and powerful psychological dimensions within the individual and how they would work differentially in patterns to produce given behavior. We have to predict. Then we should examine other children with similar internal organization since they should all perform the same way. Thus individual cases or individual classes of cases can be grouped and nonparametric statistics applied. Johnson (1981) has developed techniques for research on personal patterns of behavior.

Of course, it doesn't work very well, no better than classical models. There are two major reasons. One is that psychological measurement, even when you require consensus from several measures to ascertain a single psychological condition, falls short of being accurate. We can't measure personal attributes very well, which is why we resort to big N studies; then it doesn't matter that the knowledge we put into the computer is poor. The second problem of *N of 1* is that people are always reacting in settings which issue unique stimuli. I may be classified as having an internal locus of control, but, at times, I'll still be devastated by external criticism from people I hold important. The result is that the research model will be not only the *N of 1* person but also the *N of 1* person-setting configurations for study. Personal profiles and setting provocations have to be matched. Particular testing methods can kill off the effort of even highly motivated, able students. The vast personal variability and multitude of situations with which we are confronted are enough to make any of us long for nice, neat variables and nice, neat so-called control groups and experimental dimensions treated with large group statistics.

But it is not an either/or. All efforts to systematize observations about human behavior are needed. There are various ways to work back and forth. For example, one can examine the individuals in a classical experiment who were hidden by the mean change even though they were there, too, and behaved in reverse of the overall trend. The most upsetting current trend is the naive phenomenology where one's own declaration that it's so is enough to make it so. With no consensus and no check, there is no information to be shared, no science. The first signs of the emerging new science of persons are signaling a new vitality for special education (Salzinger, 1980). We might even become a science with robust knowledge, as the current saying goes!

WHAT OF THE FUTURE?

If retrospection has pitfalls, futurism is a quagmire. One thing about prediction is that nobody keeps book. The insatiable desire to know what is just around the bend keeps the futurists in business. We can't wait for the next pronouncement, even from the oracle who was dead wrong last time— perhaps he or she learned from old errors. Maybe we like to read predictions because it makes us feel superior: we can do as well as the next guy, or better. For young professionals it is a different matter. Where will the jobs be? How can I meet my obligations? What methods should I apply? At any rate, if I kept book on what I expected to happen, it would only serve to lower my self-regard.

One thing seems evident: things move in cycles. If one lives long enough there is déjà vu. In the old days we integrated the special kids and treated them, unfortunately, as we treated all pupils. Then we took them out and put them together—for their own good, of course. Then we put them back again—also, as we said, for their own good. There is already an indication that some of them are going to be taken out yet again—of course still for their own good. What else?

A basic problem in our decision making is its political rather than psychological basis. We do things en masse as a response to the tenor of the times regardless of the psychological significance to the consumer. We manipulate the youngster to suit our own convictions. It is good to be integrated; the social revolution said so. It is hard to believe the screaming and crying that actually took place in the early meetings of the Council of the Behavioral Disorders. We beat our chests and assuaged our guilt. We stereotyped program entities as ipso facto good or bad. Institutions were bad, and regular classes were good. In fact, there were obviously good and bad of both and appropriate and nonappropriate for both. Politically motivated name-calling took over for quality control. In this we lost our sense of a graduated and differential intervention sequence.

A useful exercise is to follow a child through the day (and night) to see, as Barker did (1968), the interactions which take place with the child and the environment. Are the interactions, psychologically speaking, in line with our best insight? The issue is the quality of the exchanges, not just the number and selections. Not *where*, but *what* was going on in the child's mind. Also, what is done about what happens? If unfortunate exchanges take place, is there mediation?

I do not think our present diagnostic schemas provide the cues for educational placement especially for disturbed pupils. Certainly the worship of the "least restrictive" was myopic: the goal should be to find the most productive setting to provide the maximum assistance for the child.

Since every such decision is a personal one, it is a matter of considerable effort, clinical effort. One tries to match needs and services. Since help given can be perceived by the recipient as anything but the help we think we have provided, we must be in close touch with the self-concept of the youngster. How does the situation seem to him or her? What does it do to self-esteem? What does he or she think will help? Any placement requires counseling to encourage commitment on the part of the youngster. To the best of his or her ability we want the child to understand the situation. This is why some of us have moved away from the typical diagnostic studies toward the study of the person. How does the world seem to these we hope to help? Rather than making arbitrary decisions in those great adult decision-making meetings, called IEP meetings, (Cruickshank, Morse & Grant, in preparation), we need to share our ideas with the pupil as well as with the family and work through the issues until there is a reasonable understanding. Generally speaking, our diagnostic process is inhumane, as anyone knows who has been diagnosed for any problem—psychological or medical. Children are in triple jeopardy, first from diagnostic processes, second from parent preferences, and third from the special education decision makers. We decide what the kids need, but more often we give them what we have available. My first wish for the new special education would be to humanize the placement process.

The second hope I have is for an expanded commitment to the special child. The IEP is one thing, but an LEP is another—a Life Educational Plan. Can we begin to see the complete youngster and his or her ecological setting? Speaking of the socio-emotionally disturbed selves, can we become serious about the observations Hobbs makes? Every child is in a milieu, but how therapeutic is it? If we are going to quit playing games in special education, we will have to take Hobbs' ideas seriously. This will mean a re-examination of current method-bound practices and of dependence on a particular theory and an attempt to gain knowledge about the self we are trying to help. One of the obvious implications is that we should export our best special education concepts rather than our special children. More and more our business requires the integration of special education with medical centers, since schools will be responsible for the follow-up plan. It is rare to find mental health and social welfare agencies and special education meeting in joint responsibility for children. As long as the school is naive enough to assume responsibility, the other agencies can be off the hook. Our next big effort should be to use our knowledge of milieu helping in community efforts. Otherwise we all waste money (what little we will have left). This is the ecological stance on intervention as I see it now. You don't refer—you integrate.

Perhaps we have reached the peak of the paranoid time we have been passing through in special education for the socio-emotionally disturbed. First we confessed our sins, reversed our field, and rejected the practices which had been special education. (And special education had been impaired by a great deal of inhumane treatment of both parents and children.) In the process we demonstrated that we were not to be trusted, since we didn't even trust ourselves. Instead of expressing change in terms of growth, we exercised repudiation. The pundits reversed fields and then expected their new dicta to be believed. Suspicion ran rampant. Then came advocacy and the lawyers to make us honest: since we did not have the welfare of our charges at heart, we would have to be watched to see that we were honest. Of course the same thing happened in other domains of education and in other professions such as mental health. The lawyers were augmented by a surveillance system of special education personnel, who were to ensure compliance from the local district, classroom, and specific pupil.

Can we turn the profession back to the teachers and other first line practitioners? Can we train people in the more profound skills which our work requires? Gadgets and gimmicks have their place, and they should be put in that place. The most taxing work is not consultation but the direct work with youngsters as teachers, but at present that role requires less training, is paid less, and given less status.

Not all teachers who seek to migrate to positions in administration, consultation, or higher education do so because they are burned out. The greater the distance from the child, the higher the pay. Anyway, it is not people who burn out; *systems* burn out with the people in them. Teachers often say if they could get rid of the paperwork and were free to do the things they knew would help, they would not want to leave teaching for less taxing positions. The next stage in special education may well be attention to the support system for the persons who do the really hard work on the line. The dog-and-pony shows which constitute much special education inservice need a transmigration, as Groesnick and Huntze (1980) have said.

Part of the stress of teaching the emotionally disturbed comes from unwarranted assumptions that we can cure our pupils. The field as a whole and IEPs in particular perpetuate these beliefs. We create expectations which are impossible to meet and make the teacher rather than the system accountable. We are guilty of oversell. Special education performs many miracles, but it promises still more and demands that the teacher perform the miracles.

It will be interesting to see what will happen as we meet more youngsters with multiple and more serious disabilities. As the medical profession saves more high-risk infants, a new liaison is emerging between pediatrics and special education. This may help us to make more sober prognoses without giving up on all that is really possible. This will be a very difficult task in a society which calls certain types of variability deviant and an anathema.

In a recent demonstration program, the need for generic special education was again brought home. The Intervention by Prescription Project (Rezmierski, 1980) revealed that many children (12 percent or so) were under stress and in need of attention. For various reasons, a great number did not fit the categories for special help. Teachers from the mainstream are saying they will take our special children if we will take theirs (children needing help but ignored by the special education system). At least for the socio-emotionally impaired we have made a great mistake in failing to blend the school mental health programs and special education. Sometimes they touch lightly, but often there is no school mental health effort at all. This means that no one is concerned about the overall school climate, about prevention or about the well-being of all the teachers and pupils. It is a tragic mistake to imply that special children are more worthy than other children. In Orwell's terms, all animals were to be equal but some more equal than others. Our preoccupation became prejudicial. There is no systematic screening or affective education. This is not to say that schools don't react to the consequences of deficiencies, for there are schools with emotional flack at every turn and primitive responses. It is assumed that repression is cheaper than efforts to improve the lives of those who spend the better part of their lives in the school. We neglected the pollution of the mainstream, and our special children are paying dearly for that neglect as we send them back to the mainstream.

In short, special education is for everyone. If individual planning is useful for our special children, why is it not for others? The same goes for parent involvement and IEPs. To repeat, we seem to be more interested in exporting our special children to the mainstream than in exporting our concepts. Superficial inservice education to teach regular teachers how to endure our special kids is certainly not an adequate answer.

HOW ABOUT PROGRESS?

We are certainly passing through a period which is distressing to professionals. Things we have spent our lives achieving are being jettisoned. There is a fear we will never again regain what is being lost, although some of the attrition may not be loss at all. When budgets are reduced and staffs are cut in half, it is very hard to be encouraged about the future. Especially if it is your job that was cut.

We seem to be entering a period of doing less, settling for weaker interventions while all the time the society is putting new hazards in the way of both normal and special children.

While it does not take away the pain of the moment, the only way to get a perspective is through the study of social history. If you were a special child, would you prefer to be born now, in the eighteenth century, or in the seventeenth century? Our current ideas may look as primitive in the future as the practices of decades and centuries past do now. We have a long way to go but we seem to be gradually moving toward greater concern for the welfare of children as well as adults—in spite of the present regression. Of course, we think we have the answers, only to realize it does not work out as expected. The social changes which were spawned by the Great Depression seemed to me at the time to be final solutions to vexing problems, but they have produced as many new difficulties as solutions. We seem to move ahead sidewise, fall back, and go ahead again. From our history, we can extrapolate progress only by taking the long view.

How can we continue to upgrade the lives of all children? The proper study of man is of mankind. What are we like? What are the variations? How can help be given? I am inclined to believe understanding will come more from direct interaction with youngsters, more openness, and more searching for meaning in behavior. There will be less didactic and more clinical teaching. Reciprocal learning, in which we learn about youngsters even as we learn about ourselves, may reduce the cul-de-sacs.

For me, the abiding questions about human nature and helping are, to this day, unsolved and more puzzling than they were at first. I cannot even say that my confusion is now on a higher level (the supposed outcome of scholarship). I keep searching and reading to see if there is someone who has a better key rather than just little bits or small pieces. Clearly, the psychology one really uses as a base of daily operations is the one that best explains life to the believer. This psychology makes sense because it explains things, and brings awareness to what we implicitly act upon in our daily behavior. To follow this path requires personal humility as well as a scientific skepticism. One is never sure. It is a way of life. But, as was said of democracy, there is no other choice. It is the worst system—except for all the others.

REFERENCES

Abell, G. O., & Singer, B. (Eds.). (1981). *Science and the paranormal: Probing the existence of the supernatural.* New York: Charles Scribner's Sons.

Bandura, A. (1974). Behavior theory and the models of man. *American Psychologist, 29*(12), 859-870.

Bandura, A. (1982, February). Self-efficacy mechanism in human agency. *American Psychologist, 37*(2), 122-147.

Barker, R. G. (1968). *Ecological psychology: Concepts and methods for studying the environment of human behavior.* Stanford, CA: Stanford University Press.

Brickman, P., Karuza, J., Cohn, E., Rabinovitz, V., Coates, D., & Kidder, L. (1982, April). Models of helping and coping. *American Psychologist, 37*(4), 368-384.

Bronfenbrenner, U. (1977, July). Toward an experimental ecology of human development. *American Psychologist, 32*(7), 513-531.

Cronbach, L. J., & Snow, R. E. (1977). *Aptitudes and instructional methods: A handbook for research on interactions.* New York: Irvington.

Cruickshank, W., Morse, W., & Grant, J. (in preparation). *The IEPC: A step in the history of special education.*

Ekstein, R., & Motto, R. C. (1969). *From learning for love to love of learning.* New York: Brunner-Mazel, Inc.

Erikson, E. H. (1977). *Toys and reasons: Stages in the ritualization of experience.* New York: W. W. Norton & Company, Inc.

Fromm, E. (1973). *The anatomy of human destructiveness.* New York: Holt, Rinehart & Winston, Inc.

Gardner, M. (1981). *Science: Good, Bad, and Bogus.* New York: Prometheus Press.

Groesnick, J. K., & Huntze, S. L. (1980). *National needs analysis in behavior disorders.* Columbia, MO: University of Missouri, Department of Special Education.

Hobbs, N. (1968). Sources of gain in psychotherapy. In E. Hammer (Ed.), *Use of interpretation in treatment.* New York: Grune & Stratton, Inc.

Hobbs, N. (1981, October). The role of insight in behavior change: A commentary. *American Journal of Orthopsychiatry, 51*(4), 632–635.

Holt, J. (1968). *How children fail.* New York: Pittman Publishing.

Johnson, M. C. (1981, May). Pattern analysis by an adaptive classifier. *The American Statistician, 35*(2), 110.

Kahle, L. R. (1979). *Methods for studying person-situation interactions.* San Francisco: Jossey-Bass, Inc.

Kopp, S. B. (1976). *If you meet the Buddha on the road, kill him.* Toronto, Canada: Bantam Books, Inc.

Mischel, W. (1978). Personality research: A look at the future. In H. London (Ed.), *Personality: A new look at metatheories.* New York: John Wiley & Sons, Inc.

Morse, W. C. (1981, Winter). LSI tomorrow. *Pointer,* pp. 67–70.

Morse, W. C., & Wingo, G. M. (1955). *Psychology and teaching.* Glenview, IL: Scott, Foresman and Company.

Newman, R. (1974). *Groups in schools.* New York: Simon & Schuster, Inc.

Redl, F. (1962). *When we deal with children.* New York: The Free Press.

Rezmierski, V. (1980). *Intervention by prescription project.* Dearborn, MI: University of Michigan Press.

Rhodes, W. C., & Tracy, M. L. (1972). *A study of child variance* (Vol. 2). Ann Arbor, MI: University of Michigan Press.

Rogers, C. (1977). *Carl Rogers on personal power: Inner strength and its revolutionary impact.* New York: Delacorte Press.

Salzinger, S., Antrobus, J., & Glick, J. (Eds.). (1980). *The ecosystem of the "sick" child.* New York: Academic Press.

Sarason, S. B. (1971). *The culture of the school and the problem of change.* Boston: Allyn & Bacon, Inc.

Stephenson, W. (1979). Q methodology and Newton's fifth rule. *American Psychologist, 34,* 354–357.

Thrasher, F. M. (1937). *The Gang.* Chicago: University of Chicago Press.

Young, L. (1966). *Life among the giants.* Hightstown, NJ: McGraw-Hill Book Company.

5

Mental Retardation: An Anthropologist's Changing View

Robert B. Edgerton

Robert B. Edgerton, born 1931 in Maywood, Illinois, earned his B.A. in Anthropology (1956) and his Ph.D. in Anthropology (1956–60) from the University of California at Los Angeles.

Dr. Edgerton is associate director of the Mental Retardation Research Center at the University of California at Los Angeles (1976–   ) where he was assistant professor to professor of Anthropology (1962–   ) and recipient of the Distinguished Teaching Award in 1974.

Past president of the Society for Medical Anthropology (1976–77), Dr. Edgerton received a Research Award from the American Association of Mental Deficiency in 1976. In 1981 he was a member of the Steering Committee for the Study of Health-Related Effects of Marijuana Use (Institute of Health, National Academy of Sciences), and in 1978 Governor Brown of California appointed him to the State Commission, Institutional Review Board. He was elected a fellow of the American Association for the Advancement of Science in 1982.

My first known encounter with a mentally retarded person took place at Pacific State Hospital,[1] late in 1959. I was within a few months of completing my Ph.D. dissertation in anthropology at UCLA and, sorely in need of a job, I was off to Pacific State Hospital to have a job interview with the late Harvey F. Dingman. As I walked from a parking lot toward Harvey's office located in a nearby Quonset hut, I was confronted by a man of thirty or so with Down's syndrome who was dressed as a cowboy, complete with boots, chaps, Stetson, and toy six-guns in holsters. As I approached him, he turned his back to me, then whirled, drew his guns, and said, "Bang! Bang!" Not knowing quite how to react, I smiled and walked past him. He called after me, "You're dead!" Taking this as an omen that I could have done without, I went on to Dingman's office nonetheless.

My ignorance of the phenomenon of mental retardation and of research in the field could hardly have been more obvious to Dingman. He hired me nevertheless, and I hope I did not give him too much cause for regret in the tragically few years of life that remained to him. I mention this otherwise unremarkable episode to emphasize my total ignorance of mental retardation when I entered the field. While I had everything to learn about the field—and there are those who will quickly enough say that I still do—I prefer to think that my innocence allowed me to avoid some of the errors inherent in the then-current orthodoxy. Sometimes it is possible to ask better questions and take more original lines of inquiry if one enters a field as a complete outsider, but one can also be intimidated by the discovery of a new conventional wisdom, particularly if it is backed by an imposing medical authority as was then the case in the field of mental retardation. Perhaps both cases were true for me, although it is difficult for me to judge. Whatever the judgment, I certainly came to the study of mental retardation in a state of ignorance that was very nearly total, if not blissful.

EARLY INFLUENCES

To the best of my recollection, before that trip to Pacific State Hospital I had never met anyone who was mentally retarded; I don't even recall hearing about any friends or neighbors who had a retarded child. I like to think that I was sympathetic to the handicapped people I met, trying to be protective and kind—and probably making a hash of it—but I was almost totally unaware of the presence in the world of mentally retarded people. And like the other children and adults I knew, I blithely referred to "idiots," "morons," and said other tasteless things. The only academic work about mental retardation that I can recall was a single chapter in the text on abnormal psychology. Most of it I quickly forgot.

I gratefully acknowledge research support from NICHD Grant No. HD 04612. The Mental Retardation Research Center, UCLA, NICHD Grant No. HD 09474-02, The Community Context of Normalization, and NICHD Grant No. HD 11944-02, The Community Adaptation of Mildly Retarded Persons.
[1]Now Lanterman State Hospital.

As a graduate student in anthropology, I concentrated on psychological issues and approaches; I was especially interested in deviant behavior and mental illness, but nowhere in my graduate training, which included several seminars in psychology, did I encounter anything about mental retardation. The anthropologist Thomas Gladwin had joined with Masland and Sarason to write *Mental Subnormality* in 1958, but I did not read the book until I went to Pacific State Hospital. Instead, I concentrated on anthropology, particularly psychological adaptation to varying cultural and environmental conditions. I received my Ph.D. in 1960, for a dissertation based on field research on the topic of values among the Menomini Indians of Wisconsin. When my major professor, Walter R. Goldschmidt, asked me to join him as a participant in a large-scale research project dealing with culture and ecology in East Africa, I jumped at the chance. It was a good research design, a fascinating part of the world, and my colleagues were good people and exciting scholars. The catch was that the project did not call for us to assemble in Kenya until July of 1961. That meant that I would have to find some sort of interim job for all of 1960 and half of 1961.

It was Wally Goldschmidt who told me of the opening at Pacific. He suggested that I apply, reminding me that I might be able to do some useful research there and learn something as well. I had never heard of the hospital and knew only that its patient population was "mentally retarded." It is often better to be lucky than knowledgeable. Unwittingly I had blundered into a field of research that has held my interest ever since, and I was privileged to discover that field alongside some of its most gifted and accomplished practitioners. Before I left Pacific for my research commitment in Africa, I was to be blessed with the opportunity to know and work with George Tarjan, Stan Wright, Harvey Dingman, Dick Eyman, Art Silverstein, Ed Meyers, Jane Mercer, Georges Sabagh, Lindsey Churchill, and many others.

The research ambiance at Pacific was simply extraordinary. This was so partly because all of us except Tarjan and Wright worked together in very small quarters. We shared all sorts of ideas, knew and cared about one another's work, and were truly joined together by a common sense of purpose. We would discuss research design, epidemiology, special education, demography, multivariate statistical procedures, and psychometrics, and then ask how any or all of this could be brought to bear on the problems of the mentally retarded. There were droves of consultants from many disciplines; from one day to the next, you never knew whom Harvey Dingman would bring through the door. I best remember the comments of Leonard Duhl, Morton Kramer, and Harold Garfinkel; but I was also impressed by Raymond Jessen, Robert Nisbet, Aaron Cicourel, and Joseph Gengerelli. In different ways each reinforced my conviction that mental retardation was a social and cultural phenomenon and not just a psychological or biomedical one. I also came quickly to believe that to center the study of mental retardation on hospitalized populations was surely the drunkard's solution—looking for the lost object where the light was best, not where it was dropped. The study of mentally retarded persons had to include all the environments in which they lived.

Yet it was important for me (and, I think, for any fledgling investigator) to come to know at firsthand the kind of patient population then cared for in a large state hospital like Pacific. There were those in need of continuous medical care, many of whom had no measurable IQ, no speech, and no mobility. They lived in cribs for thirty or forty years or more. There were all sorts of ambulatory persons, sometimes acrobatically so, who had IQs well below 20; there were also much more intelligent persons who lived their lives in beds, sometimes to be wheeled outside to sit with others in collective solitude. There were all manner of physically limited patients whose intellectual deficits were difficult to assess, and there were a good many patients, young and old, who looked and acted more or less like other people I had known. Were it not for their lack of uniforms, some could easily have passed for staff. I spent time with all these kinds of people. I went to see them on the wards at all hours, and I sometimes stayed for hours at a time. I knew many of them by name, and some knew me in turn. I also sometimes accompanied those who could leave their beds and wheelchairs to stroll about the hospital to attend recreational activities or were permitted to leave the hospital for special occasions.

From these many months of immersion in the lives of these people I learned invaluable lessons. First, I learned that there is no such thing as mental retardation; there are instead all kinds of quite different people who share that unflattering appellation. Next, I learned that their lives could be understood like those of anyone else: as boring, heroic, frustrating, trivial, or awful. They might have shared among themselves a sort of incompetence, but I could never be sure what, exactly, it was or, for many, whether it was even there. What I could tell without any effort was that they were all human, with pains, sorrows, hopes, and joys like the rest of us. I remain convinced that without this experience—one that was so often painful and almost always exhausting—I would never have understood the social and cultural character of mental retardation. And, I confess, I am sometimes skeptical about the conclusions of fellow investigators who have had no comparable opportunity to meet and know all the kinds of persons who were thought by appropriate authorities to be psychometrically mentally retarded.

My unlimited access to these people—these "patients" as they then were known—was made possible by George Tarjan. Tarjan was dedicated to patient welfare, as was the late Stan Wright. Long before human subject protection committees, patients' rights and especially their human dignity were paramount concerns at Pacific. I rarely saw anything there like the horrors that Blatt (1970) has so chillingly described in other institutions. Yet Tarjan was also dedicated to science, and he continually attempted to interest outstanding scientists in carrying out research on mental retardation at Pacific. From the start, he encouraged me to do ethnographic research at Pacific, saying that, as long as what I reported was true and my research respected the human dignity of patients and staff, he would support me. He always did, even when it could not have been easy for him. I sometimes offended the ward staff by becoming too inquisitive, too critical of some of their practices, or too close to patients.

Once I upset virtually everyone, including parents, community leaders, and even the superintendent of another state hospital, when I reported (Edgerton & Dingman, 1964) that some patients at Pacific were engaging in clandestine sexual activities on the hospital grounds. I documented my observations carefully, adding that the sexual conduct did not include sexual intercourse and suggesting that these opportunities for heterosexual interaction were highly adaptive since they taught the patients to internalize a moral code and to develop interpersonal skills that would be helpful when they returned to community settings. Tarjan withstood the considerable pressure created by those who witlessly accused him of running a large bordello at state expense, and he encouraged me to continue as before. Years later I came to suspect that George secretly enjoyed doing battle on this issue because he knew that his critics were wrong, but at the time the heat was considerable; I was threatened with litigation—whether for lying or telling the truth I could not determine—and I was terribly grateful for his support. Harvey Dingman supported me, too, but without the support and sincere encouragement of the medical director, no worthwhile behavioral research would have been possible. In fact, George Tarjan's warm enthusiasm combined with hardheaded "Hungarian" skepticism made it impossible for me *not* to do the best research I could.

When I wanted to study the lives of former patients released from Pacific, I continued to receive support and encouragement. My predecessor at Pacific, C. E. Windle, had already done major follow-up research (Windle, 1962), as had Tarjan, Georges Sabagh, Jack Brown, and others. Tarjan and Dingman were determined to develop a major community study, and they saw my more modest plans for a follow-up study as consistent with that larger goal. Harvey, ever driven and ever lovable, was a tremendous help to me in everything I did at Pacific. When I completed the data collection on the cohort of 110 former patients whose lives outside of Pacific would later be described in *The Cloak of Competence*, Harvey asked me to join with him and others at Pacific to discuss a research design for what we called "the Riverside Study." The ensuing discussions, frequently involving highly competent consultants, impressed me again and again with the need for ethnographic research to complement the standard procedures of enumeration and data collection used in social epidemiology and survey research. The planning was meticulous and exciting, and I wish that I could have played a larger role in it, but I was due to leave for Africa. When the Riverside project was funded, it was ably carried out under the primary guidance of Jane Mercer with the assistance of Edgar Butler (Mercer, 1973).

These were heady times for students of mental retardation. Not only was the research staff at Pacific exceptional, the sense of mission so strongly encouraged by the new Kennedy administration infused enthusiasm and financial support into the field. Thanks largely to George Tarjan's accomplishments, Pacific was in the national spotlight. Delegations of scientists, clinicians, parents, and politicians—some direct from the White House—become commonplace. The atmosphere at that time was often exhilarating. There was so much to learn and so much to do with the knowledge that was already available that we lived with a sense of urgency. Mental retardation had definitely moved out of the shadows of back-ward oblivion. No one could have entered a new field at a more propitious time nor could they have hoped for a finer set of colleagues or research opportunities. When I left for Africa, it was with painfully mixed feelings.

My experience in East Africa was every bit as formative as my time at Pacific had been. As an anthropologist, I learned a great deal from the opportunity to work and live among various tribal peoples during the time of political and social unrest just prior to independence in Uganda, Kenya, and Tanganyika (now Tanzania). Again, I had wonderful colleagues with whom I shared the joys and rigors of field research and from whom I learned unforgettable lessons about research methods. As planned, most of my research was not related to mental retardation as such (Edgerton, 1971), but I had the unusual opportunity of doing research on four tribal societies, in eight separate locations, from Mt. Elgon in Uganda to the southern province of Tanganyika, over a thousand miles away. The expressions of adaptive behavior and the cultural contexts of competence in these societies varied greatly, and my efforts to relate social and intellectual incompetence in these societies to comparable factors in our own society perplexed and puzzled me, as it still does. On the one hand, I found it almost impossible to predict how mentally retarded persons would be treated in any given society. Even when there were rather clear cultural norms about the treatment of severely retarded children, not every parent did what was prescribed (Edgerton, 1970). As a result, some dreadfully handicapped children, even microcephalics, were nurtured to adulthood. On the other hand, it was far easier to predict the response to mentally retarded persons by governmental agencies in these newly developing African nations. Government officials and physicians, not without regret, told me that concerns about the mentally retarded were a luxury that Third World states could not afford because there were not enough resources available to educate and provide health care for more than a small minority of even their most capable and potentially productive children. I was asked what Western nations would do if they faced a similar lack of resources. I protested that I could not say, but of course I could, and I knew they were right.

I had accepted a job in the Department of Psychiatry at UCLA before I left for Africa, and when I returned late in 1962, I became a beginning assistant professor and a research anthropologist. Although I was absorbed with my African material, some of which related to psychiatric issues, I reviewed my research on mental retardation. I visited Pacific often, sometimes with Craig

MacAndrew, whom I had met at UCLA and introduced to Pacific. We collaborated on several projects together, including ethnographic research on a ward of severely and profoundly retarded men (MacAndrew & Edgerton, 1964). I also worked on the data from my pre-Africa follow-up study, finishing the manuscript for *The Cloak of Competence* (1967) in 1965. At Carl Haywood's invitation, I also attempted a comprehensive review of what was known at that time about mental retardation in non-Western societies (Edgerton, 1970). I tried to debunk some widespread misconceptions about incompetence in smaller and technologically simpler societies, and point to some areas where research was needed. I should add in passing that what I concluded then still holds: the issues are still important, and the needed research is still needed.

The decade of the 1960s was enormously eventful. It began with the catalytic actions of the Kennedy presidency and ended with deinstitutionaliza-tion and "normalization" firmly established; mainstreaming was well underway. There was a growing concern for the apparent relationship between poverty and mental retardation and a realization that children of rural or inner-city poverty, especially if they came from ethnic minority backgrounds, were especially vulnerable. Sensitivity to cultural differences was dramatized by the concept of the "six-hour retarded child"—a child considered retarded only during school hours. The IQ test as the sovereign criterion of mental retardation came under fire. For the first time in our recent history, social and cultural considerations in the study of mental retardation became central. I was obviously influenced by all these currents and many others.

Of those that consciously vexed me the most, the effect of institutionaliza-tion was at the head of the list. Like most social scientists of that time I was influenced by Erving Goffman's (1961) formulation of the "total institution," and earlier I had thought a good deal about other accounts of life in hospital settings. I most readily recall Ivan Belknap's (1956) book about a mental hospital in Texas, and William Caudill's account of his experience as a pseudopatient (1958). At Pacific, despite some occasional departures from common decency and common sense, I thought that most of the ward staff had good intentions, as did most of the professional staff. I even wrote about ways in which the hospital unwittingly served the needs of its patients by affording them microcosmic examples of the outside world or opportunities to enhance their self-esteem by comparison with less capable patients (Edgerton & Sabagh, 1962), in other words, by performing a kind of latent function in Merton's terms.

Yet as someone who had a visceral hatred for institutional regimentation such as I had endured in military service, I had no difficulty understanding why patients wanted to be released. To be sure, a few patients could not be forced out of Pacific, however great the rewards or dire the threats, but almost all patients badly wanted to leave. That is a singular fact, greatly reinforced by the complementary fact that I cannot recall ever meeting anyone released from a large institution like Pacific who wanted to return. But it was not simply that large institutions alienated their inmates; they also failed to teach them the social skills necessary for successful community adaptation, and often they did not even provide entry-level job skills.

My concerns about the benefits of institutional placement were tempered by the realization that Pacific and other large hospitals that I visited in California and elsewhere offered essential medical care and a range of therapeutic and recreational services for patients who could not easily hope for anything comparable anywhere else. For many more severely handicapped patients, these services seemed to be indispensable. Yet I could not help being forced to the hardly original realization that the fate of mentally retarded persons is determined by broader societal factors, some cultural, others economic, some quite arbitrary, others less so.

One of the cultural factors has to do with the assessment of IQ and the belief in the prognostic power of the score the psychometrician produces. There is no point in rehashing here the history of the concept of intelligence, the belief in IQ as its index, or the astoundingly rapid rise of the IQ-industry in the United States. All these have been dealt with thoroughly elsewhere, for example, in Stephen Jay Gould's new book, *The Mismeasure of Man* (1981). Yet it is important to point out again and again, as psychologist John Garcia (1972) has done so incisively, that just as the IQ-test developers juggled test items so that males and females would score equally, so items or tasks could be juggled in order to ensure that racial or ethnic minority children would achieve the same mean IQ as children from upper middle-class white backgrounds.

My concern is not only with the arbitrary cultural character of the test itself, but for the political uses to which it has been put. The IQ controversy ignited by Jensen, Herrnstein, Eysenck, and others has received well-deserved attention; the ethnocentrism and cultural naiveté of those who propound such views is as amazing as it is appalling. But such ethnocentrism is hardly recent. Thanks to such writers as John Higham (1955) and later, Leon Kamin (1974), we are by now quite familiar with how the newly developed IQ technology, especially in the World War I testing of prospective soldiers, was used to demonstrate the inferiority of virtually every immigrant group that came to this country. What influenced me the most at that time was not that ethnocentrism has remained so pervasive a theme in our society; I already knew that. Nor was I surprised by the linkage of IQ with ethnocentrism; that had long been obvious, too. What continued to impress me, although hardly in a favorable way, was the apotheosis of IQ. From modest beginnings as Binet's tool for identifying marginal learners in French schools, it had achieved an almost sacred inviolability as the single sovereign measure of mental incompetence. Nothing that proponents of adaptive behavior as a complementary measure were able to accomplish was capable of shaking the true believers' faith in IQ. IQ seemed an arbitrary measure to me then, an almost absurd reflection of America's fascination with technology. And I must say that it still does.

I was also influenced by the realization that the well-being of mentally retarded persons was inescapably tied to fluctuating socioeconomic conditions. It was not simply that governmental contributions to the care of handicapped people varied with general socioeconomic conditions, as had been suggested to me by African leaders, but also that the ability of mentally retarded adults to sustain themselves outside of institutions was largely a function of economic opportunity. Release from an institution was often contingent on success in holding a job during "vocational leave," and remaining "out" called for continued vocational success. It may well be, as so many have reported (Kolstoe & Shafter, 1961; Cobb, 1972), that mentally retarded persons are consistently less successful members of the labor force than are persons of normal intelligence, and that far more mentally retarded persons are able to find and hold jobs during periods of peak employment such as World War II (McKeon, 1946) than can do so today.[2] If the availability of Supplementary Security Income were radically reduced tomorrow, community living would no longer be a viable option for many mentally retarded persons. When Bernard Farber (1968) observed that mentally retarded persons, like many other kinds of people in industrial societies, were "surplus," his choice of metaphor was hauntingly apt. Our society, like many others, continues to generate surplus populations, unwanted and unneeded, and the mentally retarded are among the least needed of our surplus.

The last major influence that I felt during the decade of the 1960s came from the newly emerging interest in "labeling" or "societal reaction" theory. Although the interest of social science in the consequences of labeling goes back at least as far as the 1930s when Frank Tannenbaum (1938) published *Crime and the Community*, it was during the 1960s that Howard Becker, Thomas Scheff, Thomas Szasz, and many others gave labeling a prominent place in social scientific thinking. Their basic contention that various categories of "handicapped," "deviant," or "stigmatized" people were socially created largely by the process of labeling was extended to the mentally retarded by L. A. Dexter (1964). This view, so consistent with the idea that surplus populations are the result of social processes, was soon to become highly controversial in the study of mental retardation. The extent to which labels such as *mental retardation* actually produce the incompetence that they name seems to me a vital and complex topic, one that I'll return to later in more detail.

The first thing that struck me about mental retardation as a label was not its power to create imcompetence—although I was convinced that it could

---

[2]In this regard, the recent work of Stephen A. Richardson (1978) is significant. Compared to normal controls, the young mentally retarded persons he studied in the United Kingdom found jobs almost as easily as the control group during this period of almost full employment, but their jobs involved less skill, required fewer dealings with people, and paid less.

have just this effect—but its power to stigmatize the individual, to devastate self-esteem. I learned early that our label—mentally retarded—was a self-shattering horror which people would do their utmost to reject and escape. It seemed to me then that no other label in our lexicon of pejorative terms for one another was so unacceptable. Surely the mildly retarded people I came to know preferred to think of themselves as *anything* else (Edgerton, 1967). I subsequently learned that, as the years went by, these same men and women devoted less of their time and energy to denying the truth of this label (Edgerton & Bercovici, 1976), while mentally retarded persons who were newly confronted with the label reacted with the same familiar horror and shame. More recently, our studies of mildly retarded black adults living in low-income, inner-city neighborhoods makes it quite clear that the label has the same power to destroy self-esteem as it does for more affluent white people, and their efforts to deny the label and to pass as normal are every bit as continuous and important (Koegel & Edgerton, 1982).

RECENT DIRECTIONS

In late 1970 I returned from an abbreviated sabbatical leave at the Social Science Research Institute at the University of Hawaii to take up the new challenge of developing a socio-behavioral research group within the Mental Retardation Research Center at UCLA.[3] I was given a free hand to organize the group and to direct its energies, at least in the early stages before the group developed goals and energies of its own. My first thought was to choose a research emphasis that would allow anthropological perspectives and methods to be most effective. The obvious choice was the study of community adjustment. As a consequence of "deinstitutionalization," rapidly growing numbers of the mentally retarded, most of them young adults, were entering community-based residential settings. The lives of these "surplus" persons were intrinsic to an understanding of human adaptation, but, more than that, they had great significance for social policy. If normalization were to be made possible, then deinstitutionalization required careful study.

Colleagues, graduate students, and postdoctoral scholars from several behavioral science disciplines joined the group, bringing with them their respective concepts, theories, and methods. This diversity still exists and has proven invaluable. Yet, from the beginning we were committed to a common problem and a shared approach. We focused our work on mildly mentally retarded persons in all of the community settings of their lives. We chose the mildly retarded because they constituted the overwhelming majority of those being deinstitutionalized and because their lives had the greatest potential for becoming normal or nearly so. Because many of these people lived, worked, and played more or less as other people in similar communities, we believed

[3] I was happily reunited with George Tarjan and Stan Wright and had the pleasure of beginning an association with Nat Buchwald.

that the most effective method for understanding them was one that had proven successful with other people in communities. We chose long-term, intensive participant-observation.

Participant-observation calls for an investigator to enter into the life of the community being studied so continuously and so naturally that members of that community will learn to take him or her for granted and to behave almost as though the researcher were not there; in time the investigator may learn how these people actually behave and why they do so. The use of this approach in anthropology goes back at least as far as the field research of Franz Boas before the turn of the century, and it has continued to serve anthropologists well. The method calls for prolonged, natural, and therefore increasingly unobtrusive participant-observation with the persons being studied. There are limits, of course, since we cannot observe everything nor participate in everything as a member of the community would. But we do our best. In applying this approach to mentally retarded persons, our field investigators visit mentally retarded persons in their residences, accompany them during their everyday activities, and join them on various special occasions. We eat together, bowl together, go visiting together, watch television together, and talk about anything that comes up. We also take them places they need to go, and sometimes we help them with problems in their lives. In many cases we have made lasting friendships, but we have also been used as resources; in a few cases we have never really been accepted.

We spend large amounts of time—not months, but years—and we proceed as humanely as we can, making it clear that we are concerned with the people we study as human beings, not simply as objects of scientific scrutiny. Needless to say, we do not pretend to be nonreactive. We are not sure that would be ethical in long-term research, and we know that it would not work. There can be no long-term research relationship without sensed reciprocity. So we offer concern, some companionship, and a certain amount of diversion for people who are so often lonely. If our approach sometimes alters the behavior we see, we take that for granted, attempt to compensate for it (Edgerton & Langness, 1978) and we continue. That is why participant-observation requires such long periods of time if it is to be effective. One's role in a reciprocal research relationship is one of the foci of study, and it takes time, as well as the perspective of one's less-involved colleagues, to see that role clearly.

Of course, we also use other data collection techniques. We interview parents and caretakers, systematically observe certain behaviors, collect documents, and even administer some psychological tests. Yet we rely most on participant-observation as our way of knowing. The ad-lib or subjective quality of the method has alienated many researchers who prefer the precision of more positivistic approaches such as tests, interviews, experiments, or systematic observation. Participant-observation has many weaknesses, certainly, but its strengths should not be overlooked or underestimated. Because of its reliance on prolonged face-to-face involvement in the lives of others, it offers a valuable means of comprehending the changing complexity of human behavior. No science uses only one method and none should. We use multiple methods, too, but the goal of all of them is to understand behavior as it naturally occurs, in various circumstances, over long stretches of time. This is a difficult and expensive approach. The resulting data are difficult to reduce. What we learn contains contradictions and uncertainties. We fret about all of this and continually search for better ways to employ qualitative research methods. Yet I still believe that the results produced by our approach are valuable and could have been achieved by no other means (Edgerton & Langness, 1978).

Although this is not the place to consider these findings in any detail, I would like to mention three rather striking phenomena in the lives of mentally retarded persons that have come to light through our long-term, ethnographic approach. The first of these has to do with concealment. The lives of mentally retarded people, like those of the rest of us, are never entirely open to the scrutiny of others. Mentally retarded adults present themselves in many roles, some of which are guises: sometimes to pass as normal, sometimes to claim false entitlement to some sort of accomplishment, sometimes to keep secret a potentially discrediting fact. Some of these people dedicate themselves to creating and maintaining more desirable selves, others do so less often, but all do so sometimes. Those who know them often join the concealment or misrepresentation, especially when they are close to them and share in their circumstances, their reputations, and their fates. Others, such as certain group home operators, conceal information because the truth might affect their licensing and their income.

I think it is accurate to say that in all of our research experience we have never encountered a mentally retarded person who had not succeeded in concealing something from us for at least one year, and many did so for two or three years. Most have no doubt managed to conceal something important for as long as we have known them. I don't want to suggest that all these people are masters of deception engaged in Machiavellian impression management. Some are quite inept, others hide trivial matters while letting important things slip out. But most of them conceal from others matters that are important for an accurate understanding of their lives. Even our approach, based on prolonged, frequent, and personal contact seldom sees behind all the deceptions and masks. But approaches that rely on infrequent and impersonal contact are certain to miss much that is important. Now I am not so naive as to suggest that it is ever possible to cut through *all* deception, to get to the bottom of another person's life, as it were, but I am suggesting that our methods get a good deal closer to the bottom than others do. I am also insisting that it is important to get as close to the bottom as possible.

Perhaps an example would help clarify this point: for more than a year a young, mildly retarded black mother was extremely convincing in her self-portrayal as a "normal" person capable of managing all the necessary tasks of life and not at all worried that anyone might think her slow or incompetent.

Not until the day she was required to spell her daughter's name on an application form did it become obvious to our researcher that she could not read or write. She was rattled, then embarrassed, and finally began a long revelation about her inability to read or spell, even something as important as her child's name. After this event she went on to confess the depth of her self-doubts about her intelligence and her fears about coping with what the future might bring. This sort of revelation, followed by a break-through into a more intimate expression of information, is commonplace in our research.

I think that this is a very important point, and I have chosen to emphasize it. But I must repeat my earlier cautionary note. It is important to realize that there is always more revelation to come. Several of my colleagues and I have been studying one man for twenty-one years now. He is a few years older than fifty with a recorded IQ to match, but he has lived more or less on his own for the entire twenty-one-year period. We know a great deal about his life and about his perceptions of himself, enough to be able to write biographical accounts about him with at least some confidence (Whittemore, 1983). But this man, who wants to be referred to by his real name, Ted Barrett,[4] is so complex and so changing that there remain many fundamental puzzles about him and his life. We now know that we will never know all that is worth knowing about Ted Barrett. This is partly because he is a complex man, partly because he hides some parts of himself from our scrutiny, and partly because he changes. And that is the next point.

The same aspects of our approach that allow us to see behind some of the images people construct also allow us to document the often dramatic changes that occur in their patterns of adaptation. The lives of the mentally retarded people who live in community settings are marked by dramatic changes. Or at least this is so in the case of those young men and women, white and black, whom we have studied. These changes are often abrupt and have dramatic consequences, but they occur irregularly. An individual or a couple living in a group home or their own apartment may have a highly stable pattern of life activities for a year or even longer before any significant change occurs, although change is usually more frequent than this. When change does take place it is often abrupt and traumatic, followed by a turbulent period of adjustment the outcome of which is difficult to predict. Jobs are lost, then regained. Friends or lovers leave, often to reappear or be replaced. Happiness is quickly replaced by despair and sometimes just as quickly by happiness again.

None of this in itself should be surprising. Contemporary life in our urban centers is anything but static. In her poignant book, *Worlds of Pain* (1976), Lillian Breslow Rubin graphically documents the unstable life patterns of working class families who have little job security in poor economic conditions. Most mildly retarded adults in community settings also live markedly unstable lives, unless they are closely supported by their parents

---

[4]See "Fred," (Edgerton, 1967, pp. 41–57).

or other devoted relatives. They face the ordinary vicissitudes of life plus some not-so-ordinary ones. They usually come to community life with little experience in managing everyday life, and they seldom have resources available to support them in times of stress. They not only lack job security, they lack credit, union support, insurance, savings, and, most important, they often lack friends or relatives who will support them. If personnel from the service delivery system do not intervene effectively, the result is turmoil. And, unfortunately, support from agencies is often slow in coming or is absent altogether (Edgerton, 1979; Bercovici, 1983). Sometimes, agency actions only produce more traumatic changes; the instability of these lives is often increased by the emotional lability or psychiatric disorders of many of these people (Koegel, 1981).

We have provided various examples of this pattern of change (Edgerton, 1975, 1979; Langness, 1983), so one additional example here should be all that is needed to make the point that change, both positive and undesirable, is a recurring fact of life for the mildly retarded people whom we study. It is quite common for us to document life patterns like those of a mildly retarded young woman who lived in a nice apartment, had a job and a boyfriend, and seemed happy and confident. Within a six-week period she lost her job, was evicted for nonpayment of her rent, found that she was almost three months pregnant, and saw her boyfriend abandon her, taking some of her few valuables as he went. She spent two nights homeless and penniless, became severely depressed, and attempted suicide. With help, she was hospitalized.

One might have expected her to become a "failure" in the process of community adaptation, one of those unfortunates who is shunted off the track toward more normal existence to a restricted life in a group home and tedious days in a sheltered workshop. Not so. A month later she had a new apartment, was receiving SSI, and did not regret the abortion that terminated her pregnancy. Two months later she was engaged to be married to an attractive man of normal intelligence. This vignette is pathetically incomplete, I know, but it is meant only to show how dramatic these life changes often are and how unpredictable their outcomes usually prove to be. These people very often live teeter-totter lives, swinging from despair to elation within short periods. It will come as no surprise, then, to learn that the life of the woman I have been describing has continued its pattern of unpredictable ups and downs.

Many mildly retarded people who live in community settings today have lives that are much less complex than ours. That is particularly true for those who live in group homes, go to sheltered workshops, seldom have visitors, or travel outside their residences. There are many such people—far too many. Their lives are relatively simple and regimented. We would not think of these lives or the people who live them as complex. Their lives may indeed be relatively simple, but the people who live them are not necessarily so (Bercovici, 1983). Many of them have complex fantasy lives, sometimes based on the television programs that provide so much of their entertainment, but often involving imaginary friends or complex ideational systems. And many

others develop extraordinarily rich fantasy lives, including dream interpretations, built around the people they know at their workshops (Turner, 1983).

However, increasing numbers of mentally retarded persons live more
independently and have more varied activities; they and their lives are
complex by any standards. They have friends and engage in varied recreational activities; they marry and some have children. They work, at least some
of the time, ride buses here and there, and sometimes drive their own cars. In
short, their life activities are very much like those of normal persons of low
socioeconomic status, and their relationships with others are every bit as
emotional as those of other people in our society. To study these lives it is
necessary to be with these people in many settings—home, work, play; to learn
what they feel and think it is equally necessary to listen to what they say when
they choose to say something. Direct questions evoke trivial answers or
outright deceptions, and they destroy rapport. Direct methods of interviewing
or obtrusive forms of observation may be effective in restricted settings, but
they will not work in multiple settings, public as well as private, especially
when the people involved are highly sensitive to being "studied." If there is
one generalization about research with mildly retarded adults that I believe
has been fully demonstrated, it is this: direct questions lead to misinformation
or no information.

I have dwelt on research procedures at such length because I am convinced
that our approach, costly and difficult as it is, allows an understanding of
human lives in all their contradictory complexity that can be achieved in no
other way. Nobel laureate Percy Bridgman once said that there is no single
scientific method, just "doing one's damnedest" to put common sense to
work. Our common sense tells us that Irwin Deutscher was right when he
said (1966):

> *There was a time earlier in this century when we had a choice to make, a*
> *choice on the one hand of undertaking neat, orderly studies of measurable*
> *phenomena. This alternative carried with it all of the gratifications of*
> *conforming to the prestigious methods of pursuing knowledge then in*
> *vogue, of having access to considerable sums of monies through the granting*
> *procedures of large foundations and governmental agencies, of a comfortable*
> *sense of satisfaction derived from dealing rigorously and precisely with small*
> *isolated problems which were cleanly defined, of moving for 30 years down*
> *one track in an increasingly rigorous, refined, and reliable manner, while*
> *simultaneously disposing of the problems of validity by the semantic trickery*
> *of operational definitions. On the other hand, we could have tackled the*
> *messy world as we knew it to exist, a world where the same people will make*
> *different utterances under different conditions and will behave differently in*
> *different situations and will say one thing while doing another. We could*
> *have tackled a world where control of relevant variables was impossible not*
> *only because we didn't know what they were but because we didn't know how*
> *they interacted with each other. We could have accepted the conclusion of*
> *almost every variant of contemporary philosophy of science, that the notion*
> *of cause and effect (and therefore of stimulus and response or of independent*

*and dependent variables) is untenable. We eschewed this formidable chal-
lenge. This was the hard way. We chose the easy way. (p. 244)*

Deutscher's lament was directed toward social science in general but it
applies just as well to research in mental retardation, as Michael Begab (1978)
has observed:

*Much of the past and current research in mental retardation has relied on
standard psychometric instruments, task performance tests, questionnaires,
interviews, adaptive behavior measures, and clinical judgments. Although of
unquestionable value for certain purposes, these approaches tell us little
about the process of adaptation or how the retarded individual applies his
learning, communicative, and interpersonal skills to real life situations.
Furthermore, they do not assess the setting-specific nature of most behavior
nor specify the environmental context in which behavior is shaped. (p. xii)*

IN RETROSPECT

I closed the last section on a note of challenge not because I wanted to discredit
other methods of inquiry or insist that all students of mental retardation adopt
participant-observation as a métier or face the Grand Inquisitor. Different
problems require different research methods. That, surely, is obvious. The
problems of research in classrooms, restricted residential settings, or parental
homes may call for other methods. Psychological research methods should
prosper, and so should those of epidemiology, etiology, and psychiatry. My
challenge came not from a lack of appreciation for other methods—most of
which I have used at one time or another and will use again as the occasion
arises (Edgerton & Langness, 1974)—but to call attention to what I believe has
been a reluctance on the part of many in the field to acknowledge participant-
observation, or any other qualitative approach, as a credible method in the
study of the naturally occurring behavior of mentally retarded persons.

Qualitative research, including ours, has been condemned or dismissed as
"subjective," "anecdotal," and even "political," this last presumably referring to its intent as well as its effect. It is not that such views have been
expressed in scientific conventions or other research colloquia where debates
about methods are proper and productive; such opinions are also at work
behind the scenes—in editorial decisions about what should be published and
in site visits and council deliberations about what research should be funded.
My own work has suffered on both counts, and so has the work of others
throughout the country. Very recently, there have been signs that the use of
qualitative research methods in "natural" ecologies is gaining some acceptance in mental retardation research (Haywood, 1976; Brooks & Baumeister,
1977). Whether funding agencies (so typically conservative, as Deutscher
noted) will soon reflect this change remains to be seen. Until the domination
of physicians and experimentalists in funding decisions about social research

into mental retardation declines, however, this may be too much to hope for.

Sectarian dispute about the correctness of methods is not confined to the field of mental retardation; nor is it the only or even most important form of sectarianism in the field. Nevertheless, sectarianism is counterproductive in a field that badly needs the contributions of many disciplines. But, instead of multidisciplinary cooperation, the field has been riven by territorial claims among disciplines and by a pervasive willingness to engage in name calling. Those who favor normalization are seen as scientifically naive and politically motivated; the motives and research skills of those who favor the retention of large institutions are impugned with equal vigor. Demons are seen everywhere, especially in special education and the service delivery system. Investigators who merely hope to find the truth in complex and muddled matters are assumed to have political motives or hidden factional loyalties.

To be sure, there is every good reason why such important social policy issues as normalization or mainstreaming should stimulate citizens to become advocates. Our values are vital, and they must inform social policy. I cannot see any reason why social scientists should not take sides based on their values. But to take sides based on the *evidence*—when the evidence is altogether equivocal, if not plainly absent—that is quite a different matter.

Social change in our society has often, and perhaps typically, been set in motion by underlying economic or political considerations and initiated by judicial or political bodies. This has certainly been the pattern in recent years with regard to human handicaps including mental retardation (Turnbull & Turnbull, 1975; MacMillan, 1977; Soskin, 1977). The courts and the various agencies that carry out policy make reference to existing research as the warrant for change, but it can rarely be shown that the research in question provides an adequate basis for the decisions taken. Research does not accumulate until it compels change (Haywood, Meyers, & Switzky, 1982); change occurs, and the agents of change then cast about for some research findings that appear to justify their position. This pattern of change may be positive; it is not always possible or desirable to wait for research to build up compelling evidence before social action can follow. But sometimes the consequences can be unfortunate. Let me take an example from California where my own research has been done. The underlying sociopolitical and economic factors that led to the rapid implementation of deinstitutionalization in California have been debated (Bradley, 1978; Scull, 1977), but one underlying premise was that the movement of mentally retarded persons from large state institutions to community residential facilities located in ordinary residential areas would provide "less restrictive environments" where, in the language of the courts, they would be able to live more nearly normal lives (Turnbull & Turnbull, 1975). Plausible in conception, commendable in intent, it may well have occurred as planned in some parts of the country (Vitello, 1977; Biklen, 1979), but California was not one of those parts.

As I reported some years ago (Edgerton, 1975), conditions in community residential facilities in Southern California were often abysmal. In 1972 when we made a survey of "board-and-care" facilities in Southern California, we found that some of these facilities were indeed "less restrictive," providing much more "normalized" living environments than anything available in the large state institutions of that time. The majority, however, were very restrictive indeed. I wrote that they were "closed, ghetto-like places, whose residents are walled off from any access to community life" (Edgerton, 1975, p. 130). Residents of those places were in every respect treated as if they were still locked in a closed ward of a state hospital. Indeed, many of these facilities were so "closed" that neither the residents' social workers nor representatives of the US General Accounting Office (1977) were able to get past the front door. That is closed. It goes without saying that residents were not allowed the freedom to come and go either. As Sylvia Bercovici (1983) has described so well, residents of some of these facilities were regularly subjected to outrageous abuse and illegal restriction. Conditions have improved some in recent years, although dreadful group homes continue to be licensed and occupied because no better alternatives exist. But the point is this: the agencies and institutions that set rapid deinstitutionalization into effect in California should have ascertained the quality of available alternative care facilities. They did not, nor did they adequately fund research by anyone else to do so. As a result, policy decisions were less and less informed by any knowledge of empirical reality. What Townsend & Mattson (1980, p. 1) wrote in reference to special education applies equally to deinstitutionalization in California: "During the past decade, the pursuit of courtroom victories for handicapped people has been accompanied by dichotomization of policy issues. Complex problems are no longer recognized, belief systems have hardened into ideological commitments, and a professional reward system has been established that discourages attempts to obtain critical feedback from front line personnel working in the field."

The rush to laissez-faire deinstitutionalization in California may have saved money for the tax-payers, although that remains to be demonstrated; it did create needless hardships for many mentally retarded people. It would appear that planners of social policy change not only do not base their decisions on existing research, they also do not undertake implementation research to determine the consequences of change (Throne, 1979; Townsend & Mattson, 1980). But the fault should not be laid entirely at the doorsteps of others. We have done a decidedly inadequate job of carrying out research relevant to the everyday realities of deinstitutionalization, and, worse yet, we have often rushed forth to interpret the available research findings with an enthusiasm that the data cannot possibly support. When social scientists are called upon to serve as expert witnesses, it is not uncommon for otherwise good scientists to throw cautious inferences based on probability out the courtroom window while they maintain a dogmatic insistence on the "facts" that would never do in the classroom (Schwartz, 1978).

IMPORTANT RESEARCH DIRECTIONS

We need better research on deinstitutionalization, and we also need better interpretation of that research. To illustrate this contention, let me suggest that, while most would agree that the existing material on the successes and failures of deinstitutionalization is contradictory and therefore open to various interpretations, this evidence is so ambiguous that almost any interpretation of success or failure is likely to be misleading.

In recent years, approximately 50 percent of all mentally ill persons released from state hospitals have been returned to those hospitals within the first year after release, and during the first three years following deinstitutionalization, 65 percent have been returned (Gottesfeld, 1977; Bassuk & Gerson, 1978). It has also been reported that substantial numbers of mentally retarded persons have been reinstitutionalized. Conroy (1977) reported that 34 percent of the mentally retarded persons released from public institutions in 1974 were reinstitutionalized, and indeed that readmissions have increased more rapidly than community placements. Other recent studies have reported lower return rates of 13 to 15 percent (Gollay, et al., 1978), but even this lower estimate is ample evidence that not everyone who is deinstitutionalized finds success in community living.

One of the guiding assumptions for deinstitutionalization, an assumption thought to be based on the best evidence, is that the majority of mildly retarded persons manage to achieve a successful adaptation to community life and many "disappear" into the community. As Cobb (1972, p. 145) has written: "The most consistent and outstanding finding of all follow-up studies is the high proportion of the adult retarded who achieve satisfactory adjustments, by whatever criteria are employed." And yet it is widely recognized that remarkably little is known about what constitutes "success" and "disappearance" or why some persons succeed while others do not. The variables that might be put forth as the "best" indices of success are so plentiful and so complex (Cobb, 1972) that most investigators have thrown up their hands and chosen a single "operational" criterion. Thus, success has often been defined as *remaining in the community;* failure, in turn, has become *return from the community to an institution,* either a public institution, or hospital, or a correctional institution (Windle, 1962; McCarver & Craig, 1974; Gollay, 1977). *Remaining in the community* and *being placed in an institution,* then, have become the operational criteria of success or failure in community adaptation.

There is a large corpus of research available that has utilized these simple criteria. Although this research indicates that the majority usually "succeed," this is not always the case. The percentage of success varies markedly from study to study and from one period of time to another. In one study 75.2 percent "failed" (Eagle, 1967); the mean failure rate for the period 1936–1953 was only 10 percent, but it was almost 50 percent in the period 1960–1970 (McCarver & Craig, 1974). How is one to interpret this pattern which seems to show that rather similar cohorts of mildly retarded adults have highly variable rates of success and failure?

As I have tried to indicate elsewhere (Edgerton, 1983), there is no clear-cut answer. As I noted, the evidence presented in *The Cloak of Competence* has usually been interpreted in generally positive terms. I did so myself. Others have reached a less positive conclusion (Heber & Dever, 1970). On reanalyzing the data myself, I have come to realize that these data are subject to various interpretations about success or failure. What is more, had this same cohort been released at another point in time, or in another state, their success/failure ratio might have been quite different.

This is not simply to say that things are always less determinate than most research, mine included, makes them out to be—although I think that this is true. There are some specific reasons why research on the assessment of success or failure in community adaptation is misleading. For example, I have described the deviance and criminality of another cohort of forty-eight mildly retarded adults who were studied quite intensively for a period of thirty months (Edgerton, 1981). The first problem has to do with when one chooses to assess success or failure. Perhaps eighteen of these forty-eight persons lived such exemplary lives that no one would reasonably argue that they were "failures." Surely they were not candidates for reinstitutionalization. But any one of the remaining thirty persons could well have been thought failures— and reinstitutionalized—depending on *when* during the thirty-month period an inquisitive social worker or police officer witnessed their behavior or received a complaint about it. Given the episodic nature of their crime and deviance, it mattered greatly when one sampled such behavior.

The dangers of sampling behavior at a few limited points in time rather than over an extended period are obvious, yet investigators continue to rely on data collected in just this way (Heal, Sigelman, & Switzky, 1978). The expense of relatively continuous, long-term data collection is undeniably high, but without such a continuous perspective on community adaptation any effort to assess "failure" or "success" must be illusory. That is so, because as I mentioned earlier, the lives of most of these forty-eight persons, like other mildly retarded adults, change frequently and dramatically. If someone had examined the behavior of this sample at a given point in time, some persons would have been found to be hospitalized for mental illness or suicidal behavior, others in jail, and still others involved in violent conflict with parents, friends, or employers. A month or even a week later, these same persons would probably have been out of hospital or jail and would have resolved their interpersonal conflicts. On the other hand, some persons who had seemed to be trouble-free at the first sampling point would have looked far more troubled only a short time later.

Problems in community adaptation should be construed as phases in a rapidly oscillating process, not as "outcomes" which should operationally define current success or failure. Neither should they be accepted as accurate predictors of future success or failure. For example, it cannot be assumed that the eighteen "model citizens" in this sample will maintain the trouble-free adaptation we recorded for thirty months. Indeed, we know that two of these eighteen people were in rather serious trouble in the years just prior to our research, and since our thirty-month period of intensive data collection was concluded, three others have encountered difficulties (one became severely depressed, two others developed bizarre behavior patterns) that could lead to rehospitalization.

It is not only *when* one looks, it is also *how*. If an investigator relies solely on records of reinstitutionalization to determine failure he will greatly underestimate the number of persons who would have been "failures" if their crime or psychosis had been reported. This is not just hypothetical. During the thirty months of this research, most of the persons who were in day-to-day contact with our sample members were remarkably tolerant of their behavior. Parents tolerated financial irresponsibility, workshop employers overlooked violence, coresidents of group homes tolerated sexual promiscuity, theft, and bizarre conduct of all kinds. Once in a while informal sanctions were brought to bear, but complaints to agents of social control such as regional center counselors, social workers, or the police were exceedingly uncommon. When complaints were made, they almost always came from persons outside the network of relatives, friends, coresidents, caretakers, employers, etc., that made up the face-to-face community for most of these retarded persons. These persons tolerated outrageous, bizarre, and even dangerous behavior. Persons outside it—neighbors, landlords, strangers in public places—were consistently less tolerant, but even when complaints were made, there were so many barriers to reinstitutionalization that even repeated and serious offenders avoided incarceration (Edgerton, 1981). But the opposite sometimes happens too. Individuals are "victimized" and find themselves in hospitals or jails without adequate justification.

For example, while offenders in Los Angeles usually go undetected or unpunished, in other states a highly disproportionate number of all incarcerated offenders have IQs below 70 (Brown & Courtless, 1968). To take one example of many, Fries and LaBelle (1969) found that 40 percent of all youthful offenders in South Carolina were mentally retarded.

All of this leads me to the point I want to make. If the simple, "objective" criteria of remaining in the community or returning to an institution are so powerfully affected by research methods and shifting socio-cultural circumstances that they yield both false negatives *and* false positives, then they are neither objective nor useful. And if we cannot utilize these criteria for community adaptation then what *will* serve as reliable and valid criteria? Community adaptation, like life itself, is too complex for such simple criteria. We need to heed Deutscher and recognize that our search for objectivity has emphasized simplicity to the detriment of accuracy. We need a new perspective. We need, as many including Scheerenberger (1976) have said, to learn how to assess the quality of life.

I recognize the intimidating conceptual and empirical problems that such assessment would entail. I frankly doubt that any acceptable measures will be generated, since concepts such as "well-being" or "quality of life" are even more inclusive and complex than "adaptive behavior," and even more relative to changing circumstances and personal preferences. But that is precisely why I believe that research on the topic would be so beneficial. It would not only help to lay to rest the notion that success or failure can be operationalized without being arbitrary, it would focus attention on life processes, complex and changing as they are, rather than on presumed traits like IQ or states like success or failure. And it would compel us to attend to the evaluations and preferences of the persons involved, to allow those persons whose lives are being judged to help determine what is to be thought valuable. Within reason, our citizens are free to choose their own styles of life. As I have argued before (Edgerton & Bercovici, 1976), we need to know much more about what mentally retarded persons choose and why they do so.

Instead of allowing mentally retarded persons to express their own values and preferences for "good living" or a better "quality of life," we, the experts, have attempted to define adequate adaptation for them. But since we have failed so conspicuously in our efforts to measure failure, we might be well-advised to take seriously the most basic premise of "normalization" and "least restriction" by allowing mentally retarded citizens the same freedom of choice in life-style as the rest of us. We could begin by listening to what they have to say to us, as Bogdan and Taylor (1976) have urged and as I tried to do when I first entered the field, and then we could take them seriously (Edgerton, 1982). Neither parents nor colonialists always know what is best for their children or their subject peoples. Research on deinstitutionalization has too often taken, or at least abetted, a parental or colonial perspective that is a disservice to all concerned.

I have been finding fault with some past approaches to research, but I hope not ungraciously, since I have not exonerated myself. I have also called for new perspectives, even though they may be impractical in these times of economic austerity. But since I have begun, I shall continue by suggesting a few other areas where I believe that we have made mistakes and need to adopt different approaches. The list of candidates for mention is imposing, to say the very least, but I would like to discuss the three that particularly catch my attention as a social scientist in this field. In doing so I shall try not to duplicate the priorities of other scholars, such as the work on handicap prejudice, conversion, and related issues so ably presented by various scholars at Syracuse University (e.g., Blatt, Bogdan, Biklen, and Taylor, 1977), or the social-ecological concerns of scholars at Vanderbilt (e.g., Haywood & Newbrough, 1981).

First, I would like to suggest that labeling and its consequences continue to be of central concern but that the study of these phenomena has achieved far less than it should have. The labeling, or "societal reaction," perspective is a controversial one (Sagarin, 1975; Gove, 1975), and its use in the field of mental retardation has not escaped criticism. The utility of the approach has been evaluated and debated (MacMillan, Jones, & Aloia, 1974; Hobbs, 1975), and specific applications of the perspective, as in Jane Mercer's significant work, have come under scrutiny (Gordon, 1975). These and other critical reviews of the literature on the effects of labeling on mentally retarded persons have led to a number of conclusions. There is general agreement that while the label "mentally retarded" is typically avoided because it is stigmatizing, the effects of this label on the social competence of labeled persons have not been clearly demonstrated (Guskin, 1978; Rowitz, 1981).

Most reviewers point out that research on the effects of labeling has greatly over-simplified what is a highly complex, nonlinear, interactive process. More specifically, this research has not adequately studied the experiences of the sample population that may have produced both low self-esteem and social incompetence before any label was imposed. Moreover, the possible presence and salience of more than one stigmatizing label and more than one labeler has been inadequately documented, especially in regard to setting-specific research such as that characteristically done in schools. The predicted effects of labeling usually have not been clearly specified, and the duration of the presumed effects has been as little studied as the mechanisms that are presumed to create and maintain them. It almost goes without saying that research which examines the effects of labeling in the totality of a person's life over a substantial period of time is altogether lacking.

Labeling can be shattering, as I mentioned earlier, yet our focus on labeling as an event followed by more or less inevitable consequences, all of them deleterious, has deflected attention away from the mechanisms that accompany it and actually bring about incompetence. It is the process of socialization that must be studied, not just a clinical or administrative event called labeling. The complex of expectations and practices that typifies socialization for incompetence begins with restrictions that deny mentally retarded children access to experiences that are commonplace for ordinary, nonretarded children. For the retarded child, certain experiences are "too dangerous" or "too difficult." Not all parents restrict experience in the same ways, but most parents *do* deny their mentally retarded children the opportunity to have experiences that they would allow, or even encourage, in their "normal" children. Subtle joking, teasing, and instructive interchanges based on nuances of language and shared knowledge are often replaced by direct didactic or corrective strategies in which the parent intervenes and completes problematic behavior for the retarded child. More overt restrictions may include efforts to shelter the child from risk and limit his or her participation in such matters as physical aggression, sports, bicycle riding, choice of playmates, caring for pets, or simply the use of tools, even kitchen knives.

The experiences of adolescents and young adults can be even more circumscribed than those of children. Now, sexuality must be restricted, along with smoking, drinking, and driving cars. For example, when the retarded son of well-educated and affluent parents first expressed an interest in alcohol, he was encouraged to drink as much as he possibly could so that the resulting extreme nausea and hangover would teach him never to drink again. It did. But when his nonretarded brother expressed a similar interest, he was closely instructed and supervised in his drinking by his father so that he could learn how much alcohol he could soberly tolerate (Koegel, 1978).

It can be hypothesized that these kinds of restrictions, arguably reasonable for more severely retarded children, cumulatively reduce the social competence of more mildly retarded children. Indeed, some parents come to understand that their socialization practices may have been unwise especially as their children become adults. One such mother, now a staff member of our research group, has learned to become an observer of her twenty-five-year-old daughter, Colette. Referring to her past restrictions on Colette's behavior and freedom and the conflicts that followed, she concluded (Kaufman, 1980, p. 22): "There are many kinds of success: The one that is most meaningful for her may turn out to be centered around all-night sessions with friends, a baby or two, and SSI for income. Ten months ago I would have shuddered at that scenario. Today I would be a good deal more accepting if it occurred."

When mildly retarded young adults leave their parents' home to live in group homes, their access to normal experience continues to be restricted. Certain behaviors are still seen as too dangerous or difficult, but in addition to these reasons for restrictions, group-home caretakers are usually under great pressure to manage and control several residents with limited time, energy, and expense. The result has been described often. The retarded person is isolated from nonretarded people and from ordinary experience. Residents are typically compelled to eat together, work together, and even have "recreation" together. As Bercovici (1981) has put it, they are "herded" with few opportunities to plan, make decisions, take risks, or make mistakes. Even time is planned and structured for them. Moreover, it is common for residents to be denied access to such everyday experiences as using a telephone, doing household chores, using money, making friends, or planning for tomorrow. Sheltered workshops sometimes provide greater autonomy or teach useful skills, but they, too, usually impose restrictions on normal experiences (Turner, 1983).

The regimentation and restricted autonomy of community residential and vocational settings is reinforced by the use of subtle practices such as requiring residents to call caretakers "Mom" or "Pop," while residents are openly referred to as "kids," continuing the familiar parent-child role of authority and dependency. More coercive tactics are also employed so that a rebellious resident may be subjected to threats including transfer to a large state hospital, loss of a desired job or friend, or the termination of "benefits" such as SSI. Mentally retarded persons are easily cowed by threats such as these since they overestimate the legal authority of caretakers to control their lives. But they also fear the caretakers' personal power, and that they do not overestimate. When other means of assuring compliance fail, some caretakers employ such practices as overmedicating residents with neuroleptic drugs, physical abuse, and "restriction" to a locked room. When, as is usually the case, there is no one in the outside world to whom the retarded person can appeal, compliance is the only alternative. Socialization for compliant dependency and incompetence, then, can continue throughout life.

Socialization is a two-way street, of course, and the experiences of many of the adults we have studied make it clear that there are benefits to be had in accepting dependency and restriction as a way of life. For example, there is no need to rise early each day, however ill or tired one might feel, to cope with the demands and tedium of the work-place, to solve anxiety-producing practical problems of money management, bill paying, and the like, or to save for tomorrow, groom oneself well, plan ahead, and defer to the needs and requirements of strangers in a complex and competitive world. For many people a set routine, few demands, television viewing, and fantasy, can become a preferred way of life, at least when the alternatives are so unpleasant and one's entire life has been spent in roles based on dependency and restricted freedom.

This portrait is hypothetical, of course, but if it is correct, then our research focus must be widened to include the "subcultures" within which mentally retarded persons are socialized. The event of labeling, including counteractive denial of the label or humiliating acceptance of it, is only a part of the process that we must learn to understand if we are ever to comprehend the etiology of social incompetence. Such research will not be easy, but the easy way is seldom right—it is only easy.

I would now like to turn to two final topics that concern me. I believe that social scientists interested in mental retardation—myself very much included —have contributed far too little to the study of these topics. In closing with a brief discussion of each, I am not just appealing to others to work on these topics; I am engaging in self-exhortation as well. First, we have neglected research on prevention. By *we* I mean social and behavioral scientists, and not those biomedical scientists whose research is primarily concerned with prevention. Past efforts to examine early learning such as Head Start or Follow-Through are exceptions, but the fact remains that social scientists have yet to devote themselves to effective research programs relevant to prevention.

We used to refer to "familial" retardation. Now the terms are psychocultural or sociocultural. The implications are the same. Most mentally retarded children come from low-income families in deteriorating neighborhoods; many also are reared with culturally different systems of belief, motivation, and communication. In a very general sense, then, research concerned with the prevention of mild mental retardation cannot avoid being social and cultural. This is not to suggest that malnutrition, disease, teenage pregnancy, ingestion of lead, poor maternal care, and the use of tobacco, alcohol, or other drugs are not important considerations, but only to point out that they all take place in a sociocultural context. The focus of research cannot be restricted to isolable factors that place a child at risk. It is essential that the interacting environment of the child—home, peer group, school—be studied holistically in search of relevant etiological factors. Moreover, the entire intergenerational life cycle must be examined.

In the halcyon days of the 1960s, poverty was clearly identified as an enemy, a *War on Poverty* ensued, and some good research was done. Rodger Hurley (1969) passionately and polemically pointed to the causal relationship between poverty and mental retardation, and Birch and Gussow (1970) contributed a good and compassionate book on disadvantaged children. Rena Gazaway (1969) movingly described the shocking intellectual and social incompetence of children and adults alike in an impoverished Appalachian hollow. More than a decade later, sociocultural mental retardation is not on the wane, and neither is poverty. The reports by Craig Ramey and his associates (Ramey et al., 1978) at North Carolina make the point as well as any. By showing that it is possible to identify children who will need special educational services before or during grade school through information available on birth certificates (mother's race and education, the month prenatal care began, survivorship of other siblings, and the child's legitimacy) the authors confront us with the chilling inevitability of the social and cultural creation of mentally retarded children. The children most at risk were male, black, and illegitimate. The answer lies somewhere in the poverty cycle. The search for the answer, or answers, has been hampered by the lack of close collaboration between social and biomedical scientists. The needed research will be hard, personally demanding, methodologically complex, and very expensive. But failure to carry out such research, and soon, will be tantamount to consenting to the continuation of human misery. That should be inspiration enough, but if it is not, we should be aware that the growing numbers of surplus people in our society cannot fail to create social hazards so grave that they can hardly be exaggerated.

Finally, I am convinced that our most fundamental mistake will prove to be our steadfast restriction of research to psychometrically defined mental retardation. The man with Down's syndrome of whom I spoke at the beginning of this essay is an important human being. His future and that of other people with Down's syndrome is important. Our research should never forget him and the others, no matter the form or severity of their handicaps. People who are psychometrically retarded are diverse and this heterogeneity involves every variable worth noting. I know the reasons, often defensible, why the concept, mental retardation, became a clinical entity, a type, a category, and a phenomenon. The motives were often goodhearted, as Sarbin (1969) noted for mental illness, but an administrative and metaphorical category, as Blatt (1976) has said, can also produce harmful consequences, however unanticipated. Mental retardation is such an omnibus category that one despairs of finding any scientifically sound reason for its existence. The sole criterion for "membership," as we have seen, is an IQ below 70. But why 70? What tells us that two standard deviations below the presumed mean is a useful cutoff point? Why not one standard deviation, now that jobs are scarce and computer skills so necessary? All of this is self-evident and tedious to recount. The category of mental retardation is arbitrarily defined by IQ and embraces such heterogeneity that it is meaningless in any scientific inquiry. So what?

Our efforts to understand so-called mentally retarded people who, as I have said, possess IQs between 50 and 70 have been thwarted all along by the arbitrariness of the concept. Why not IQs of 75, 80, 90 or more? I could extend and elaborate this line of argument much further, but the point should be obvious. What is intellectually acceptable to society is culturally relative. No doubt there is an irreducible minimum, but whether that lies at an IQ of 40, 30, or lower is not the issue here. The issue lies at the other end. Why have we confined the bulk of our social science research on mental retardation to persons with IQs of 70 or less? There are many answers, some good, some not so good. The result is a scientifically indefensible neglect of persons with IQs above 70 whose social and intellectual incompetence (for most practical purposes the two are indistinguishable) are not markedly different from persons with IQs close to, but under, 70. By ignoring persons of so-called borderline or dull-normal intelligence (psychometrically determined) we not only accede to the administrative fiction that mental retardation is existentially "real," we also deprive ourselves of the opportunity to learn something of value and to help people who need it.

Many people once labeled mentally retarded on the basis of an IQ below 70 are often subsequently found to test well above that mark. When they do, they often lose eligibility for services. They are no less in need, just less eligible for help. These so-called "borderline" people are the truly forgotten, the detritus of our social landscape. Not "psychotic," not "developmentally disabled," they are *not* a category of persons to be concerned about or helped. They have no advocates, no lawyers, no favorable court decisions.

That they are forgotten not only deprives them, it deprives those of us who hope to understand the plight of persons whose IQs are a few points lower. Their problems in community adaptation are not noticeably different, their role as surplus people no less conspicuous. It is bad science to confine our research to a category of people who share no etiology or behavioral repertoire. It is also bad science to ignore persons very much like those within our IQ-based purview simply because they have a few too many IQ points. That is so partly because they provide a revealing comparison population, not labeled as mentally retarded, yet incompetent in the same ways as those who are. They also provide a wider challenge because they form an underclass, perhaps an underculture, based on unhappiness, hopelessness, and social failure. The more we study mental retardation without consideration of all the other, even more numerous, people with similar problems, the less we shall learn and the greater will be our disservice to them and to all of us.

REFERENCES

Bassuk, E. L. & Gerson, S. (1978). Deinstitutionalization and mental health services. *Scientific American, 238,* 46–53.

Begab, M. J. (1978). From the foreword by Michael J. Begab to *Observing Behavior,* Vol. I, edited by Gene P. Sackett. Copyright © 1978 by University Park Press. Reprinted by permission.

Belknap, I. (1956). *Human problems of a state mental hospital.* New York: McGraw-Hill.

Bercovici, S. M. (1981). The deinstitutionalization of mentally retarded persons: Ethnographic research in community environments. In R. H. Bruininks, C. E. Meyers, B. B. Sigford, & K. C. Lakin (Eds.), *Deinstitutionalization and community adjustment of mentally retarded people* (pp. 133–144). (Monograph No. 4). Washington, DC: American Association on Mental Deficiency.

Bercovici, S. M. (1983). *Barriers to normalization: The restrictive management of retarded persons.* Baltimore: University Park Press.

Biklen, D. (1979). The case for deinstitutionalization. *Social Policy, 10,* 48–54.

Birch, H. G. & Gussow, J. D. (1970). *Disadvantaged children: Health, nutrition and school failure.* New York: Grune & Stratton.

Blatt, B. (1970). *Exodus from pandemonium: Human abuse and a reformation of public policy.* Boston: Allyn & Bacon.

Blatt, B. (1976). The executive. In R. B. Kugel & A. Shearer (Eds.), *Changing patterns in residential services for the mentally retarded* (Rev. ed.). (pp. 129–154). Washington, DC: President's Committee on Mental Retardation.

Blatt, B., Bogdan, R., Biklen, D., & Taylor, S. (1977). From institution to community: A conversion model. *Educational Programming for the Severely and Profoundly Handicapped.* Reston, VA: Council for Exceptional Children.

Bogdan, R., & Taylor, S. (1976). The judged not the judges: An insider's view of retardation. *American Psychologist, 31,* 47–52.

Bradley, V. J. (1978). *Deinstitutionalization of developmentally disabled persons.* Baltimore: University Park Press.

Brooks, P. H., & Braumeister, A. A. (1977). A plea for consideration of ecological validity in the experimental psychology of mental retardation: A guest editorial. *American Journal of Mental Deficiency, 81,* 407–416.

Brown, B. S., & Courtless, T. F. (1968). The mentally retarded in penal and correctional institutions. *American Journal of Psychiatry, 124,* 1164–1170.

Caudill, W. (1958). *The psychiatric hospital as a small society.* Cambridge, MA: Harvard University Press.

Clarke, A. D. B., & Clarke, A. M. (1977). Prospects for prevention and amelioration of mental retardation: A guest editorial. *American Journal of Mental Deficiency, 81,* 523–533.

Cobb, H. (1972). *The forecast of fulfillment: A review of research on predictive assessment of the adult retarded for social and vocational adjustment.* New York: Teacher's College Press.

Comptroller General. (1977, January 7). *Report to Congress—Returning the mentally disabled to the community: Government needs to do more* (HRD-76-152). Washington, DC: General Accounting Office.

Conroy, J. W. (1977). Trends in deinstitutionalization of the mentally retarded. *Mental Retardation, 15,* 44–46.

Deutscher, I. (1966). Words and deeds: Social science and social policy. *Social Problems, 13,* 235–254.

Dexter, L. A. (1964). *The tyranny of school: An inquiry into the problem of "stupidity."* New York: Basic Books.

Eagle, E. (1967). Prognosis and outcome of community placement of institutionalized retardates. *American Journal of Mental Deficiency, 72,* 232–243.

Edgerton, R. B. (1967). *The cloak of competence: Stigma in the lives of the mentally retarded.* Berkeley: University of California Press.

Edgerton, R. B. (1970). Mental retardation in non-Western societies: Toward a cross-cultural perspective on incompetence. In H. C. Haywood (Ed.), *Social-cultural aspects of mental retardation* (pp. 523–559). New York: Appleton-Century-Crofts.

Edgerton, R. B. (1971). *The individual in cultural adaptation: A study of four East African societies.* Berkeley: University of California Press.

Edgerton, R. B. (1975). Issues relating to the quality of life among mentally retarded persons. In M. J. Begab & S. A. Richardson (Eds.), *The mentally retarded and society: A social science perspective* (pp. 127–140). Baltimore: University Park Press.

Edgerton, R. B. (1979). *Mental retardation.* Cambridge, MA: Harvard University Press.

Edgerton, R. B. (1981). Crime, deviance and normalization: Reconsidered. In R. H. Bruininks et al. (Eds.), *Deinstitutionalization and community adjustment of mentally retarded people* (pp. 145–166). (Monograph No. 4). Washington, DC: American Association on Mental Deficiency.

Edgerton, R. B. (1982). Deinstitutionalizing the mentally retarded: An example of values in conflict. In A. Johnson, O. Grusky, & B. Raven (Eds.), *Contemporary health services: Social science perspectives* (pp. 221–235). Boston: Auburn House.

Edgerton, R. B. (1983). Failure in community adaptation: The relativity of assessment. In K. Kernan, M. Begab, & R. Edgerton (Eds.), *Environments and behavior: The adaptation of mentally retarded persons* (pp. 123–143). Baltimore: University Park Press.

Edgerton, R. B. & Bercovici, S. (1976). The cloak of competence—years later. *American Journal of Mental Deficiency, 80,* 485–497.

Edgerton, R. B. & Dingman, H. F. (1964). Good reasons for bad supervision: "Dating" in a hospital for the mentally retarded. *Psychiatric Quarterly Supplement, 38,* 221–233.

Edgerton, R. B. & Langness, L. L. (1974). *Methods and styles in the study of culture.* San Francisco: Chandler and Sharp.

Edgerton, R. B. & Langness, L. L. (1978). Observing mentally retarded persons in community settings: An anthropological perspective. In G. P. Sackett (Ed.), *Observing behavior, Vol. 1: Theory and applications in mental retardation* (pp. 335–348). Baltimore: University Park Press.

Edgerton, R. B. & Sabagh, G. (1962). From mortification to aggrandizement: Changing self-concepts in the careers of the mentally retarded. *Psychiatry, 25,* 263–272.

Farber, B. (1968). *Mental retardation: Its social context and social consequences.*
Boston: Houghton Mifflin Co.

Fries, W. & LaBelle, S. (1969). *A plan for the youthful mentally retarded offender*
(File Y:35–8–3.0). Charlestown, SC: South Carolina Department of Mental
Retardation.

Garcia, J. (1972, September). IQ: The conspiracy. *Psychology Today, 6,* 40–43, 92–93.

Gazaway, R. (1969). *The longest mile.* Garden City, NY: Doubleday.

Goffman, E. (1961). *Asylums: Essays on the social situation of mental patients and
other inmates.* New York: Anchor Books.

Goldstein, H. (1964). Social and occupational adjustment. In H. A. Stevens & R. Heber
(Eds.), *Mental retardation: A review of research* (pp. 214–258). Chicago:
University of Chicago Press.

Gollay, E. (1977). Deinstitutionalized mentally retarded people: A closer look.
Education and Training of the Mentally Retarded, 12, 137–144.

Gollay, E., Freedman, R., Wyngaarden, M., & Kurtz, N. R. (1978). *Coming back:
Community experiences of deinstitutionalized mentally retarded people.*
Cambridge: Abt Books.

Gordon, R. A. (1975). Examining labelling theory: The case of mental retardation.
In W. R. Gove (Ed.), *The labelling of deviance: Evaluating a perspective*
(pp. 83–146). New York: John Wiley & Sons, Inc.

Gottesfeld, H. (1977). *Alternatives to psychiatric hospitalization.* New York:
Gardner Press.

Gould, S. J. (1981). *The mismeasure of man.* New York: Norton.

Gove, W. R. (1975). *The labelling of deviance: Evaluating a perspective.* New York:
John Wiley & Sons, Inc.

Guskin, S. L. (1978). Theoretical and empirical strategies for the study of the labeling
of mentally retarded persons. In N. R. Ellis (Ed.), *International review of
research in mental retardation* (Vol. 9, pp. 127–158). New York: Academic Press.

Haywood, H. C. (1976). The ethics of doing research . . . and of not doing it.
American Journal of Mental Deficiency, 81, 311–317.

Haywood, H. C., Meyers, C. E., & Switzky, H. N. (1982). Mental retardation. *Annual
Review of Psychology, 33,* 309–342.

Haywood H. C., & Newbrough, J. R. (Eds.). (1981). *Living environments for
developmentally retarded persons.* Baltimore: University Park Press.

Heal, L. W., Sigelman, C. K., & Switzky, N. H. (1978). Research in community
residential alternatives for the mentally retarded. In N. R. Ellis (Ed.),
International review of research in mental retardation (Vol. 9, pp. 210–249).
New York: Academic Press.

Heber, R. F. & Dever, R. B. (1970). Research on education and habilitation of the
mentally retarded. In H. C. Haywood (Ed.), *Social-cultural aspects of mental
retardation* (pp. 395–427). New York: Appleton-Century-Crofts.
retarded. In H. C. Haywood (Ed.), *Social-cultural aspects of mental retardation*
(pp. 395–427). New York: Appleton-Century-Crofts.

Higham, J. (1955). *Strangers in the land.* New Brunswick, NJ: Rutgers University
Press.

Hobbs,N. (1975). *The futures of children.* San Francisco: Jossey-Bass.

Hurley, R. L. (1969). *Poverty and mental retardation: A causal relationship.*
New York: Vintage Press.

Kamin, L. J. (1974). *The science and politics of IQ.* New York: Halsted Press.

Kaufman, S. Z. (1980). A mentally retarded daughter educates her mother. *Exceptional Parent, 10*, 17-22.

Kernan, K., Begab, M., & Edgerton, R. B. (Eds.). (1983). *Environments and behavior: The adaptation of mentally retarded persons.* Baltimore: University Park Press.

Koegel, P. (1978). *The creation of incompetence: Socialization and mildly retarded persons* (Working Paper No. 6). Los Angeles: Socio-Behavioral Group, Mental Retardation Research Center, School of Medicine, University of California.

Koegel, P. (1981). Life history: A vehicle toward a holistic understanding of deviance. *Journal of Community Psychology, 9*, 162-176.

Koegel, P., & Edgerton, R. B. (1982). Labeling and the perception of handicap among Black mildly retarded adults. *American Journal of Mental Deficiency, 87*, 266-276.

Kolstoe, O. P. & Shafter, A. J. (1961). Employability prediction for mentally retarded adults: A methodological note. *American Journal of Mental Deficiency, 66*, 287-289.

Langness, L. L. (Ed.). (1983). *Coping, adapting and negotiating: Problems and strategies of the mentally retarded.* Unpublished manuscript.

MacAndrew, C. & Edgerton, R. B. (1964). The everyday life of instutionalized "idiots." *Human Organization, 23*, 312-318.

MacMillan, D. L. (1977). *Mental retardation in school and society.* Boston: Little, Brown & Co.

MacMillan, D. L., Jones, R. L., & Aloia, G. F. (1974). The mentally retarded label: A theoretical analysis and review of research. *American Journal of Mental Deficiency, 79*, 241-261.

Masland, R., Sarason, S., & Gladwin, T. (1958). *Mental subnormality.* New York: Basic Books.

McCarver, R. B. & Craig, E. M. (1974). Placement of the retarded in the community: Prognosis and outcome. In N. R. Ellis (Ed.), *International review of research in mental retardation* (Vol. 7, pp. 146-207). New York: Academic Press.

McKeon, R. M. (1946). Mentally retarded boys in war time. *Mental Hygiene, 30*, 47-55.

Mercer, J. R. (1973). *Labeling the mentally retarded.* Berkeley: University of California Press.

Ramey, C. T., Stedman, D. J., Borders-Patterson, A., & Mengel, W. (1978). Predicting school failure from information available at birth. *American Journal of Mental Deficiency, 82*, 525-534.

Richardson, S. A. (1978). Careers of mentally retarded young persons: Services, jobs, and interpersonal relations. *American Journal of Mental Deficiency, 82*, 349-358.

Rowitz, L. (1981). A sociological perspective on labeling in mental retardation. *Mental Retardation, 19*, 47-51.

Rubin, L. B. (1976). *Worlds of pain. Life in the working-class family.* New York: Basic Books.

Sagarin, E. (1975). *Deviants and deviance: An introduction to the study of disvalued people and behavior.* New York: Praeger.

Sarbin, T. R. (1969). The scientific status of the mental illness metaphor. In S. Plog & R. B. Edgerton (Eds.), *Changing perspectives in mental illness* (pp. 9-31). New York: Holt, Rinehart & Winston.

Scheerenberger, R. C. (1976), *Deinstitutionalization and institutional reform.* Springfield, IL: C. C. Thomas.

Schwartz, A. (1978). Social science potential for judicial formulation of educational policy. *Educational Research Quarterly, 3,* 3–11.

Scull, A. T. (1977). *Community treatment and the deviant—A radical view.* Englewood Cliffs, NJ: Prentice-Hall.

Soskin, R. M. (1977). The least restrictive alternative: In principle and in application. *Amicus, 2,* 28–32.

Tannenbaum, F. (1938). *Crime and community.* New York: Columbia University Press.

Throne, J. M. (1979). Deinstitutionalization: Too wide a swath. *Mental Retardation, 17,* 171–176.

Townsend, C. & Mattson, R. (1980). The interaction of law and special education: Observing the emperor's new clothes. *Analysis and Intervention in Developmental Disabilities, 1,* 1–25.

Turnbull, H. R. & Turnbull, A. P. (1975). Deinstitutionalization and the law. *Mental Retardation, 13,* 14–20.

Turner, J. L. (1983). Workshop society: Ethnographic observations in a work setting for retarded adults. In K. Kernan, M. Begab, & R. Edgerton (Eds.), *Environments and behavior: The adaptation of mentally retarded persons.* Baltimore: University Park Press.

Vitello, S. J. (1977). Beyond deinstitutionalization: What's happening to the people? *Amicus, 2,* 40–44.

Whittemore, R.D. (1983). Theodore V. Barrett: An account of adaptive competence. In L. L. Langness (Ed.), *Coping, adapting and negotiating: Problems and strategies of the mentally retarded.* Unpublished manuscript.

Windle, C. (1962). Prognosis of mental subnormals. *American Journal of Mental Deficiency, 66* (Monograph Supplement 5).

6

Explorations in
Prevention

Robert Guthrie

Robert Guthrie, born 1916 in Marionville, Missouri, earned his B.A. in Premedical Studies, B.S. in Medical Science, and B.M. in Medicine from the University of Minnesota (1941-44), his M.S. in Bacteriology and Biochemistry from the University of Maine (1942), and his M.D. and Ph.D. in Bacteriology and Biochemistry from the University of Minnesota (1945, 1946).

Dr. Guthrie is professor of microbiology (1970-) and professor of pediatrics and microbiology (1974-) at the State University of New York at Buffalo where he was research professor of pediatrics from 1971-74. Previously, Dr. Guthrie was research associate professor of pediatrics at the State University of New York at Buffalo (1958-71), principal cancer research scientist at Roswell Park Memorial Institute (1954-58), assistant in the Department of Chemotherapy at the Sloan-Kettering Institute (1951-54), professor and chairman of the Department of Bacteriology and Immunology at the University of Kansas (1949-50), and research scientist in the Division of Experimental Biology and Medicine at the National Institutes of Health.

Past chairman of the Prevention Committees of the American Association on Mental Deficiency and National Association for Retarded Citizens, Dr. Guthrie received the Kimble Methodology Award from the Association of State and Territorial Laboratory Directors (1965), a Science Award from the American Association on Mental Deficiency (1970), the Fifth Annual Career Research Scientist Award from the American Academy on Mental Retardation (1981), and the Distinguished Research Award from the Association for Retarded Citizens—USA (1983).

If I have made any significant contribution to science and human betterment, it was through my development of screening tests to detect rare metabolic conditions in infants, such as phenylketonuria (PKU) (Guthrie & Susi, 1963). "PKU is a well-known rare enzyme deficiency inherited as a recessive gene from healthy parents, that causes a marked elevation in the blood concentration of the essential amino acid, phenylalanine, shortly after birth, which is associated with severe mental retardation" (Tourian & Sidbury, 1983). Very few diseases in medicine can be specifically treated; PKU is one of these conditions. If the proper treatment is begun early enough, mental retardation can be avoided.

The development of the screening test for PKU in newborn infants was particularly important because it provided a stimulus for a change in attitude toward mental retardation. The worst thing a doctor can encounter is a patient with a disease for which he or she can do nothing. Doctors had felt negative about mental retardation because the medical profession had no treatment or prevention to offer. The hope of successfully preventing mental retardation produced a great interest in the possibility of detecting PKU and treating it in the early 1960s.

EARLY INTERESTS

I first became interested in microbiological research during the late 1930s as an undergraduate at the University of Minnesota. It was at this time, during the economic depression, that President Roosevelt set up work-study programs for students; my first work-study job put me out on a golf course with the maintenance crew. After two years of assorted jobs, I began working for a professor of microbiology, Dr. Arthur T. Henrici, taking care of his animal colony while in my first year of medical school. I still remember conversations with Dr. Henrici late at night when he came to check his guinea pigs while I fed them and cleaned their cages. I was very disappointed in medical school (too much memorization) and wanted to leave at the end of the first year. He helped me to get a teaching assistantship at the University of Maine in the Department of Bacteriology and Biochemistry, which was the beginning of my work as a microbiologist. I liked it much better than my experience as a medical student, even though I did return to finish medical school eventually.

It was at the University of Maine that I met a scientist from Poland, Dr. Stanislaus Snieszko, who had been head of the Microbiology Department at the University of Krakow. He had been in this country with his wife on a visit in 1939. When the Germans invaded Poland, he remained in the United States. We shared a laboratory, and I learned much from him about the practical aspects of laboratory work. Often we would share details of the work we were doing. He helped me gain confidence in myself and in my ability to work independently in a laboratory setting during the two years I needed to earn a Master of Science degree.

Another professor who had a great influence on me during my later work at the University of Minnesota toward my Ph.D. was H. O. Halvorson. He had been a chemical engineer before he went into microbiology and was one of the early pioneers who combined these two fields. He and others undoubtedly influenced me to take further training in organic, physical, and biochemistry, in addition to microbiology.

In 1946 I obtained my first permanent position at the National Institutes of Health (NIH) in Washington, where I was the only scientist working in biochemical genetics, a field which was quite new and very fascinating to me. There were other people, however, working in this area in other parts of the country. Three men in particular influenced the direction of my research during this period. I didn't actually work with them, but their research became the basis for my own. All three later won Nobel Prizes in the 1950s for work they had done ten years before.

The first two, George W. Beadle and Edward L. Tatum, received the Nobel Prize in 1959 for demonstrating that for each gene there is only one enzyme, the "one gene-one enzyme" hypothesis (Beadle, 1948). Initially, they did all their work with the mold, *Neurospora*. The other scientist, who received the Nobel Prize the same year, was Joshua Lederberg. He was much younger, and did his early work with Dr. Tatum (Lederberg & Tatum, 1946). Their publications, as well as personal contacts, fostered my interest in the idea of studying mutations in bacteria and the resulting biochemical changes. Dr. Tatum encouraged me in my research when I discussed it with him in a long-distance call and at a national microbiology meeting.

In 1951, while I was still involved in my research, I moved my family to Staten Island and began work at the Sloan-Kettering Institute for Cancer Research in New York City. I had become especially interested in childhood leukemia and its treatment by chemotherapy. In the early 1950s the first partial successes were achieved with amethopterin or methotrexate, which is an analog and antagonist of the action of the vitamin, folic acid. My own research involved antimetabolites of certain purine and pyrimidine molecules, and purine and pyrimidine metabolism.

MY INTEREST IN MENTAL RETARDATION

While we were living on Staten Island, my six-year-old son John was diagnosed as mentally retarded. My wife, Margaret, and I started attending meetings of a newly formed group for parents of retarded children. At one meeting, I suggested that this organization be called the Staten Island Aid for Mentally Retarded; it still bears the name thirty years later.

In 1954 I moved to Buffalo, New York, to join the staff of Roswell Park Memorial Institute (RPMI) and continue cancer research. By this time, microbial biochemical genetics had become a very active field of research. I felt that many of the same principles could be applied to human organisms, and that the study of human biochemical genetics had a bright future. The type of research I had been doing for several years, first at NIH, later at Sloan-Kettering, and finally at RPMI in Buffalo, was very important to my later work on the prevention of mental retardation through development of newborn screening tests, because it involved use of similar ideas and similar methods. I had used *Bacillus subtilis* as a bacterial "guinea pig" when I studied the mode of action of specific antimetabolitic inhibitors of bacterial growth; I hoped they would prove more toxic to cancer cells than to normal tissue. These were potential candidates for use in chemotherapy.

The first research of this type that I actually did on mental retardation was done at RPMI, as a result of a small grant, a few thousand dollars from the Sunshine League, a group of parents of mentally retarded children who were institutionalized in a state developmental center in western New York state. The Sunshine League had decided to join forces with the Erie County Association for Retarded Children (ARC), an organization Margaret and I had joined a year after we arrived in Buffalo. They still had some money in their treasury which they decided to use to help me start my research. It was their final contribution before they went out of existence. As a result, I hired Mrs. Ada Susi as a technician to work on this project with me at RPMI. Mrs. Susi was a very dedicated person who worked in the laboratory with me for twenty years. She and her husband were displaced persons from Estonia, a country overrun by the Russians in World War II. Because she had no records of her training as a nurse in Estonia (even though she had spent five years in Ohio as a chief surgical nurse), she found that in New York state she could not hold a job as a licensed nurse. Instead, she worked with me as a technician and her salary began with the grant of funds from the Sunshine League. Her husband, Karl, also worked in my laboratory until his death in 1981.

The project I began with this small grant involved the use of some of the same biochemical and genetic principles and microbial techniques I had been developing to select antimetabolite inhibitors for potential use in chemotherapy of childhood leukemia, except that now my aim was to search for new inherited chemical defects in children that might be one of the many causes of mental retardation. One such cause is phenylketonuria (PKU), an example of an "inborn error of metabolism," the term first used by Sir Archibald Garrod some eighty years ago (1902).

In 1957, I became acquainted with Dr. Robert Warner, the director of the new Rehabilitation Center of Buffalo Children's Hospital, through my role as vice-president and program chairman of the Erie County ARC. During one of our meetings, Dr. Warner spoke on the Rehabilitation Center as a diagnostic evaluation center for mental retardation. He had been introduced by the chairman of the Department of Pediatrics, Dr. Mitchell Rubin. After this meeting, the three of us got acquainted, and I discussed some of my ideas concerning the possible investigation of inherited metabolic diseases in children using some of my microbiological techniques. Dr. Warner contacted me later that year to tell me that he wanted to treat two young sisters who had PKU. He needed a method of measuring blood phenylalanine during treatment that would enable him to determine how successful he was in normalizing the high blood concentration of phenylalanine using a low-phenylalanine diet. I applied the same principles I was already using to quickly develop a bacterial test to measure blood phenylalanine quantitatively. This was done by combining *Bacillus subtilis* in a simple agar culture medium with a well-known available chemical antagonist of phenylalanine (beta-2-thienylalanine). I placed a measured amount of this inhibitor in the melted agar, poured it into a petri dish, and allowed it to harden. On the surface of the agar, I placed paper discs that had been punched from filter paper with an ordinary paper punch and impregnated with a measured amount of blood serum. Any phenylalanine in the blood would diffuse out of the disc into the agar. The agar would remain clear everywhere except for circles of growth surrounding discs containing phenylalanine, which prevented growth inhibition.

After incubating the petri dish overnight, I could estimate the amount of phenylalanine that was in the blood serum by comparing the diameter of the growth zones with the diameter of zones produced on the same agar plate from discs of blood serum to which I had added known quantities of phenylalanine (Guthrie & Tieckelmann, 1962). The test was easy to perform since it required only a tiny amount of blood from the child, which could be obtained by puncturing the skin with a lancet and drawing it into a capillary tube. This obviated the need for taking blood from a vein, a technique that is difficult to perform on a small child.

This method proved to be quite satisfactory for monitoring blood phenylalanine, as Dr. Warner continued his pioneering efforts to treat more and more children for PKU. Unfortunately, all of these children were already retarded because treatment was not started early enough. I became more and more interested in the problem of screening for PKU in infants so that treatment could start before damage had occurred. By this time, I had been attending national meetings of the NARC and had met people in positions of leadership, including Dr. Gunnar Dybwad, the executive director. I had already become acquainted with Dr. Richard Masland, who had been appointed as the director of the National Institute of Neurological Disease and Blindness (NINDB). Through a research fellowship from NARC, he had recently completed a survey of the state of research in the area of mental retardation. Dr. Grover Powers, then Professor Emeritus from Yale, had been highly influential in arousing the interest of American pediatricians in mental retardation. He was chairman of the NARC Research Advisory Committee. I first met him when he came to Buffalo Children's Hospital in 1957 to be the principal speaker at the dedication of a new building. It was partially due to his influence that I was able to become a member of the Department of Pediatrics at Children's Hospital.

This opportunity arose because Dr. Rubin had become interested in my ideas of using microbiology and biochemical genetic principles as an approach to studying the causes of mental retardation. He asked me if I would try to find someone who would join the staff of the Department of Pediatrics to carry out this type of research. I invited a young scientist friend of mine to visit the hospital to look into this possibility. As his guide, I took him through Children's Hospital and introduced him to different members of the staff. In the course of the tour, I myself became impressed with the hospital staff. It was impossible to create a position for this young man; however, within the year, I had left RPMI and made the transition myself. Through the influence of Dr. Powers the hospital obtained a joint grant from the NARC Research Advisory Committee and the Crippled Children's Foundation. As a result of the grants from these two organizations, Dr. Rubin was able to create a position that would pay my salary so that I could then apply to the National Institute of Neurological Diseases and Blindness for financial support. When I moved to the Department of Pediatrics, I carried over all my interests in microbial biochemical genetics and applied them to the human condition. I was primarily interested in looking for new inherited metabolic diseases in children similar to PKU that might be associated with mental retardation. I was not really interested in PKU itself yet, except as a model.

As a member of the Department of Pediatrics, I was successful in procuring a grant from the NINDB and also in being funded as part of the National Collaborative Study of Child Development initially coordinated by Dr. Masland. This was a large, grant-supported project at a number of children's centers in the United States, one of which was in Buffalo. An important part of my support came from an ancillary project to the child development study at Children's Hospital, headed by Dr. Donal Dunphy, a pediatrician, and Dr. Richard Baetz, an obstetrician.

I began an approach that used many different microbial inhibitors from among the hundreds which had been synthesized for use in cancer chemotherapy. Each of these could be used for an *inhibition assay* similar in principle to the one I was already using for measuring phenylalanine or phenylpyruvic acid in PKU. I hoped that I could use this approach to find new metabolic diseases in children. As subjects, we used mentally retarded children who had a sibling also known to be mentally retarded, but who had normal parents. This approach, using urine specimens, was similar to that used by the late Dr. Stanley Wright and others (Wright, Tarjan, & Eyer, 1959). It was inspired by Dr. Asborn Fölling's discovery of PKU in the early 1930s, when he was testing the urine of two young children who were severely retarded. Later, using the same test on the urine of patients of institutions for the retarded, he found many other cases of PKU which led to the statistical proof that PKU was inherited as a Mendelian recessive condition (Fölling, 1934).

SCREENING FOR PKU

After I had started my program in 1958, a rather amazing coincidence occurred. I learned that a baby born to my wife's sister, a thousand miles away in Minneapolis, had just been diagnosed as having PKU. Unfortunately, this child, who was named Margaret after my wife, was not diagnosed until she was fourteen months old and had already become severely retarded. The impact of this event convinced me to work on a screening test for PKU.

The simplest idea that had occurred to me was the possibility of applying the same test we were already using to monitor blood phenylalanine levels in Dr. Warner's handful of PKU patients, but to modify the procedure so it could be used to screen every baby born. The possibility occurred to me of simplifying blood specimen collection by using dried blood which had been collected from a puncture wound and spotted on filter paper. One could then use an ordinary paper punch to obtain a disc from this spot of blood for the test. The only change, therefore, was using this simple dried blood specimen instead of the liquid blood serum we had been using. Thus, the development of the screening test was actually a very simple step. Curiously enough, as far as I have been able to determine, no one in the entire history of medicine has used dried spots of blood on filter paper and a paper punch to obtain a quantitative sample for testing for any purpose! The quantitative aspect of this test is very important, otherwise the test would not be acceptable. As it turned out, the test was even better than I would have dared to dream. The amount of blood on each ¼-inch (7mm) disc punched with a paper punch from spots of blood-impregnated filter paper varies no more than about 3 to 5 percent (dry weight) from one disc to another. This meant that an adequately quantitative sample could easily be obtained, similar to liquid blood measured in a micropipette in the usual way.

It was important to try out this test on a pilot basis. The first and obvious step was detection of known cases in a high-risk population, namely an institution for the mentally retarded. The closest institution at that time was the Newark State School—under the direction of Dr. Henne—near Rochester, New York. My contacts with parents made it possible for me to arrange a trial at this institution. A Mrs. Antoinette Bergeron had a son who was diagnosed by Dr. Warner as having PKU when he was thirteen months old. His development at that time was so retarded that it could not be measured. When he was treated, however, the little boy showed an unexpected and unusual response. His measured IQ more than doubled within four years. An article appeared in a local newspaper with pictures and a description of the diet treatment. It also described Mrs. Bergeron's role in forming a group for PKU parents to assist others with PKU children. As a result of this publicity, a mother of four retarded children telephoned Mrs. Bergeron, who put her in touch with Dr. Warner. He determined that her four retarded children all had PKU. One of the children, who was three years old, was started on the diet. An older sister had been placed in the Newark State School at about the age of eleven. The medical staff at Newark had previously assured me that they were testing all their admissions and that they were familiar with all of their PKU cases. However, they did not know that this little girl had PKU. When this was pointed out to them, they decided to cooperate with me in screening the whole institution to see if we could find any other undiagnosed cases.

The pilot study was arranged during the summer of 1961. Two university students worked at the Newark State School to collect the dried spots of blood from approximately thirty-one hundred residents and mailed them to our laboratory. At the same time, they also performed urine tests with ferric chloride and kept their results secret from me. As a result of the screening, Ada and Karl Susi and I found twenty-three cases of PKU at Newark—four more than they had discovered by urine testing. Several of these cases had been previously undiagnosed.

It had been eight years since Professor Horst Bickel at Birmingham Children's Hospital had published the first dramatic results of a low-phenylalanine diet used on a two-year-old child with PKU who was very hyperactive. Dr. Bickel had prepared the diet himself, which meant that he had to hydrolize casein to make a mixture of free amino acids. He used a method that had first been described by Dr. Richard Block in 1939 to free the casein hydrolysate of phenylalanine by running it through a charcoal column. Dr. Block pointed out that his method could be the basis of a diet treatment for PKU, but no one responded to his suggestion. His process removed the aromatic amino acids: phenylalanine, tyrosine, and tryptophan. He then added the tryptophan and the tyrosine back to the casein hydrolysate, omitting the phenylalanine. The result was a phenylalanine-free mixture of all the amino acids necessary for growth. To this diet, which also included carbohydrates, fats, vitamins, and minerals, one could add the measured amount of phenylalanine needed by the child for development. This is the well-known low-phenylalanine diet for treating PKU. With the help of a biochemist, Dr. Beverley Gerrard, he carried out a microbiological assay to estimate the level of phenylalanine in the blood of the child. In this way, he was able to lower the blood phenylalanine until it was normal. Under these conditions, a marvelous change took place in the behavior of the child. Her bizarre behavior stopped; she began to smile at her mother and respond in a more normal way. After this transformation, Bickel did an important experiment that, to my knowledge, has never been repeated. He added pure phenylalanine to the diet without informing the mother and found that as the child's blood phenylalanine concentration rose again, the abnormal behavior returned. He then informed the mother of what he had done and normalized the child's phenylalanine again, restoring her more normal behavior. This was a dramatic demonstration in 1953 of the effect of increased phenylalanine on human behavior (Bickel, Gerrard, & Hickmans). There was, however, much skepticism in this country as to whether the diet could be effective in producing normal development, because so few cases were treated in early infancy.

It was also not known in 1961 just how quickly blood phenylalanine would rise in a newborn infant who had PKU. I wondered if a complete block in the ability to convert phenylalanine to tyrosine would cause the blood phenylalanine to rise fast enough, allowing one to detect the abnormal level in the first few days after birth. It had become obvious to me that the only practical time to get a dried blood specimen from a newborn baby was before it left the hospital. After this time, it would be difficult to collect a specimen. Many babies were discharged from the hospital before they were five days old, which might be too early for detection.

There was no way of obtaining this information except from those few people in the world who had followed a PKU child diagnosed soon after birth and had recorded blood phenylalanine levels in the first few days of life. From publications and private correspondence, I was able to obtain information from only six infants with PKU concerning their blood phenylalanine levels in the first few days of life. This data was encouraging. It seemed to indicate that phenylalanine did rise fast enough to be detected at this early stage. This left a big question: would the test that I developed using discs punched from dried spots of blood from newborn infants really detect most of the babies with PKU? The only way I could determine this was to somehow achieve the testing of many thousands of infants soon after birth.

At this time another coincidence occurred involving parents' groups. In 1961, the National Association for Retarded Children used for their poster in national publicity a picture showing two children—two siblings with PKU—instead of one child as was the usual case. The poster bore an inscription saying that there was hope for the mentally retarded because of new research. The picture showed Shiela, who was mentally retarded, and Kammy, her younger sister, who had been placed on the diet and was apparently developing normally. Of course, Kammy was diagnosed because of her older mentally retarded sister. In the absence of a good screening test for all infants, the only ones diagnosed and put on the dietary treatment shortly after birth were those like Kammy, who were suspected because a previously born sibling had already been diagnosed as having PKU because of mental retardation.

Because of this coincidence, Dr. Elizabeth Boggs, President of the NARC, pressed me to publish my screening test in a medical journal as soon as possible. My test could then be legitimately used for publicity with the message that an NARC grantee had produced a test for screening newborn infants for PKU. I prepared a short paper, and with Dr. Rubin's influence, it was published very promptly as a Letter to the Editor in the *Journal of the American Medical Association* in October, 1961 (Guthrie, 1961). That same month, the NARC at their annual meeting in San Francisco held a press conference to publicize my test. There, I posed with Kammy, the treated PKU child, for pictures to begin the NARC publicity campaign supporting the test.

Soon after this, *Life* magazine became interested and sent a reporter and photographer to interview me at Buffalo Children's Hospital. In January, 1962, *Life* published an article about a new screening test to detect PKU in newborn infants, a test that had at that time hardly been used for that purpose! Only a few specimens were being sent to me weekly by the staff of a small hospital in Jamestown, New York, who had become interested because of a lecture I had given in September to an ARC parents' group in Jamestown.

TRIAL OF THE SCREENING TEST

The national publicity undoubtedly influenced the federal government to fund a trial of the test. Dr. Arthur Lesser, Director of the US Children's Bureau, arranged to meet me in October of 1961 at the annual meeting of the American Public Health Association (APHA) in Detroit. Mr. and Mrs. Susi and I set up an exhibit of the test at this meeting. Dr. Lesser met me at our exhibit to ask questions about the test, including how many infants should be tested for a trial. If the results indicated that PKU occurred as frequently as 1 in 10,000 births, as I estimated, instead of 1 in 20,000 or 1 in 40,000, as was recorded in the literature, then 400,000 infants screened would reveal 40 cases; this should be sufficient for a trial. Dr. Lesser agreed to support my proposal and arranged to award a grant so that I could prepare all the materials and organize and administer a trial of the test in 400,000 infants. The Children's Bureau offered to pay the cost of sending personnel from every state health department in the country to Buffalo to be trained in the use of the test. Twenty-nine states agreed to participate.

With the funds from the Children's Bureau, we rented a house close to Children's Hospital and converted it into a miniature factory to prepare enough test kits so that all laboratories would have uniform materials. The test materials were prepared to fit into a small cardboard box. We arranged with a printer to prepare one million filter papers with serial numbers for distribution to the health departments. Since this preparation required collating and packaging, we suggested that the printer might arrange for this work to be done by a sheltered workshop for mentally retarded adults in Buffalo. A work force of about twenty-four people carried out the task. A little label from NARC was put on each package with the message "Retarded children can be helped." Also in each test kit was an NARC brochure with the picture of the two PKU children from the poster and a message about the test.

We prepared materials for one million tests. At first, we put together materials for one hundred tests per box; later, we were able to include materials for five hundred tests per box. Materials included the dried spores of *Bacillus subtilis*, dried culture medium, the inhibitor, mineral salts, and a strip of filter paper with spots of blood containing increasing concentrations of phenylalanine. The kit contained "instant" specimens, "instant" bacteria, as well as "instant" media, all of which could be prepared as easily as instant coffee. We set up quality control procedures to insure that the materials were uniform. The trial was very successful. Of the 400,000 babies who were screened by the twenty-nine state health departments, thirty-nine cases of PKU were detected, thus confirming the lucky guess I had made concerning its frequency.

I should also mention at this time others who played influential roles, particularly Dr. Robert A. MacCready, the state laboratory director at Massachusetts. Instead of sending a technician to the training program at our Buffalo laboratory, he came himself. Upon his return to Massachusetts, he was determined to test all the babies born in Massachusetts, not just the 10,000 that were allocated to him as his share of the 400,000. He was also very lucky because he discovered a case after the first 1,000 tests; three cases after the first 9,000; and nine cases after 54,000 babies (MacCready, 1962). Each time a case was found, he publicized it throughout the state to arouse interest. As a result, within six months after he started testing, every hospital in Massachusetts was sending in specimens, and by 1963, the Massachusetts legislature had passed a law requiring the test.

Another extremely important factor in the success of the trial of the test should be stressed: NARC's great interest and involvement. NARC influenced most of their state chapters to encourage state screening programs. Their Public Health and Prevention Committee, under the chairmanship of Dr. MacCready, after following the course of the test for a year or two, decided that the use of the test was simply not increasing fast enough. They recommended to NARC that they advise the state chapters to press for mandatory state laws, such as the one passed in Massachusetts. By 1967, about 35 states had passed laws requiring the test in the United States. Parents' groups for the retarded were helpful in other countries as well, but not in passing laws, because that wasn't necessary. In Germany, for example, the parents succeeded in persuading the government to pay for the cost of the diet treatment. In Canada, parents' groups encouraged the government to finance screening. It was only in the United States that laws were necessary because of the difficulty of getting screening started.

RESPONSES TO SCREENING

Perhaps I should add another chapter to the story of events in the US, which were so different from those in other countries. As I mentioned before, many of the doctors in the United States were not interested at all in the test. In fact, they were often very antagonistic to laws requiring the test. In all states except Massachusetts, state medical societies resisted the idea of a law if they acted on the issue at all. Much of their attitude is related to the way in which our health care is organized. Much of the controversy concerning PKU screening and treatment was stimulated by physicians' resentment against the fact that laws were passed.

Most European countries where no laws were necessary to carry out a large application of the test during this period had a form of socialized medicine. Pediatricians were usually leaders in establishing the screening programs. They often set up the laboratories themselves to screen a whole country, as was the case in Austria, Israel, the Republic of Ireland, the northern European countries, and some provinces in Germany. Professor Horst Bickel, the originator of the diet treatment, became extremely interested in the test, introduced it in West Germany, and was one of its leading advocates in Europe. His influence was important particularly after 1967 when he became professor and head of the Department of Pediatrics at the University of Heidelberg, a most prestigious position in European pediatrics.

In the United States, on the other hand, the screening programs were set up in public health departments under a state mandate. Doctors are not traditionally involved in public health; their role is usually in the private sector. Many doctors are in fact individual businessmen and have resisted government involvement in medicine. The laws requiring babies to be tested were considered by many doctors to be interference, an invasion by the government into a private medical matter. The rights of doctors seemed to be more important to them than the rights of infants to be protected from mental retardation. However, if the laws hadn't been passed, we would not have detected many children affected with PKU early enough for effective treatment. Because there was little leadership in the medical profession in the United States, there was no one to encourage doctors to use the results of the test and to treat for PKU. Of course there were many pediatricians who were interested and enthusiastic, but there were also many other physicians, including a few leading pediatricians, who were upset by the laws and skeptical about whether the dietary treatment would be effective. As a result of this situation, it became important to set up a study in our country to demonstrate that the diet was effective.

Dr. Richard Koch, at Los Angeles Children's Hospital, had been very interested in PKU for a number of years and had been president of the parents' group in California when the state law was passed. He was the leader in the fight to get the law passed against the active opposition of the California Medical Society. In 1964 Dr. Koch organized a national collaborative study on the dietary treatment of PKU. This is still continuing eighteen years later. With funds first from the Children's Bureau, then from the Maternal and Child Health Service, and also from the National Institute of Child Health and Human Development, he arranged with a dozen clinical centers, including Dr. Warner's in Buffalo, to follow all new infants diangosed as PKU through the screening programs and to compare their development with that of their non-PKU siblings (Williamson, Dobson, & Koch, 1977; Koch, Dobson, Blaskovics, et al., 1973). In this way 170 children were followed. It was eventually concluded that if the diet program was started within thirty days and adhered to carefully and if the phenylalanine was normalized and monitored, PKU children did have essentially the same development as their normal siblings. It was also discovered that if there was a delay beyond thirty days, there was some loss in development. This study finally settled the controversy in the United States that was associated with the screening test and with the dietary treatment of PKU.

RESULTS AND CHALLENGES

People in various countries around the world have encouraged me to continue developing new tests for prevention of mental retardation. There aren't many others who compete with me in this endeavor, and I would welcome it if there were. It's not a popular specialty, developing tests for babies using dried spots of blood. Dr. Jean Dussault, however, did develop a test for hypothyroidism that has aroused as much interest as the first PKU test.

In the promotion of newborn screening, several pediatricians in Japan have been very important (Naruse & Irie, 1983). They've developed the most highly organized, country-wide screening program in the world with federal support, whereas in the United States, federal support has recently decreased and parts of our country have serious deficiencies. Japan has also done some new things in newborn screening that have not been done in other countries. Japan is not ahead only in radios and cars! In many other countries (Sweden, Ireland, Israel, and Austria, for example) there have been people like Professor Bickel who have become my colleagues and friends. I have always been impressed with their efforts in starting programs. Usually, there is just one key person who makes all the difference. We continue our contacts and follow each other's progress as newborn screening gradually spreads around the world.

There has also been an important spinoff from newborn screening. Some of the conditions that have been detected were relatively unknown until the new tests began finding them in infants. Knowledge about these diseases, as well as PKU, has increased. Many infants might have died if their disease had not been diagnosed early. Many papers have been published, and much has been learned. For example, there is a controversy today over whether or not an infant should be treated for a condition called histidinemia, detected with one of our bacterial-inhibition screening tests. In this condition, the histidine blood levels, which rise slowly after birth, never get as high as the phenylalanine levels do with PKU. The very highest levels of histidine just approach the higher concentrations of phenylalanine in PKU. Histidinemia is being studied in ways that wouldn't have been possible before the screening tests, and as a result, we are beginning to learn more about histidinemia and its variations.

In the continuing work with PKU, there is recent concern for maternal PKU (Cartier, Clow, Lippman-Hand, et al., 1982; Levy, 1982). A woman who has PKU must normalize her blood phenylalanine level before she can have children; otherwise, she can damage her own infant before it is born. She must be careful during pregnancy to stay on the special diet. This serious new problem has been produced by solving the problem of PKU in infants.

There is continuing controversy about the need to maintain the diet after childhood. It is becoming accepted that the diet should not be discontinued during childhood (Koch, Azen, Friedman, et al., 1983). Further, each child is different in vulnerability. Probably some PKU patients should never stop treatment. PKU parents' groups have organized in many places to work with pediatricians and other professionals in dealing with these new problems that have resulted from the introduction of newborn screening.

I will continue to work in the same direction, as long as I receive federal funding. I am continuing to develop new tests and have a very good one at present which is being used in Japan. We have had difficulty getting it applied in the United States because the screening laboratories are losing federal support. Most are having their funds cut, in spite of the tremendous cost-benefits from prevention in infancy of nonlethal, severe handicap.

Some other developments in this area are significant. Dr. Sergio Piomelli and Dr. Davidow developed a test for lead poisoning using a dried spot of blood in 1973 (Davidow, Slavin, Piomelli, 1976). Dr. William Murphey, Mr. Adam Orfanos, and I improved that test somewhat in our laboratory (1977) and have become involved in screening preschool children for lead poisoning. Now, we are trying to convince the medical community and the public that *all* preschool children should be tested for lead poisoning, not just those living in the centers of large cities where the federal screening programs are located (Guthrie, 1982). With this program we are at the point where the PKU test program was twenty years ago, and, I believe, it has as great a potential. I foresee the development of regional periodic screening of preschool children to detect not only effects of lead, but numerous other environmental hazards as well.

There is a tremendous need to expand our knowledge to prevent mental retardation. There are many causes of severe mental retardation, and in possibly a third of the individuals affected we do not know the cause. We need much new information, but we also need to *apply* what we already know; this could help us prevent *half* of the incidence of mental retardation!

To meet the latter challenge, I have become more and more involved in organizing programs on a broad front to prevent mental retardation and developmental disabilities. I have found many others in parent and professional organizations at the local, state, and national level who are ready to act with me. I have worked with the National Association for Retarded Citizens (NARC), the American Association on Mental Deficiency (AAMD), and the President's Committee on Mental Retardation to organize many state, regional, and national conferences on prevention. As a result, the AAMD established its first prevention committee several years ago. In my own New York state, many are now organizing for prevention. The formula of combining the efforts of parents' groups and professionals will prove as

effective for prevention in the future as it has in the past in obtaining services
for the mentally retarded.

REFERENCES

Beadle, G. W. (1948, September). The genes of men and molds. *Scientific American.*
Bickel, H., Gerrard, J., & Hickmans, E. M. (1953). Influence of phenylalanine intake
 on phenylketonuria. *Lancet, 2,* 313.
Cartier, L., Clow, C. L., Lippman-Hand, A., Morissette, J., & Scriver, C. R. (1982).
 Prevention of mental retardation in offspring of hyperphenylalaninemic
 mothers. *American Journal of Public Health, 72,* 1386-1390.
Davidow, B., Slavin, G., & Piomelli, S. (1976). Measurement of free erythrocyte
 total protoporphyrin in blood collected on filter paper as a screening test to
 detect lead poisoning in children. *Annals of Clinical Laboratory Science, 6,*
 209-213.
Fölling, A. (1934). Uber ausschiedung von phenylabrenztraubensare in den harn als
 stoffweichselanomalie in verbindung mit imbezillitat. *Hoppe-Seylers Z. Physiol.
 Chem., 227,* 169.
Garrod, A. E. (1902). The incidence of alkaptonuria: A study in chemical individuality.
 Lancet, 2, 1616.
Guthrie, R. (1961). Blood screening for phenylketonuria. *Journal of the American
 Medical Association, 178,* 863.
Guthrie, R. (1982, November 22). Speaking out: All preschoolers should be screened
 for lead toxicity. *Medical World News, 94.*
Guthrie, R., & Susi, A. (1963). A simple phenylalanine method for detecting
 phenylketonuria in large populations of newborn infants. *Pediatrics, 32,* 338-343.
Guthrie, R., & Tieckelmann, H. (1962). The inhibition assay: Its use in screening
 urinary speciments for metabolic differences associated with mental retardation.
 In B. W. Richard (Ed.), *Proceedings of a London Conference on the Scientific
 Study of Mental Deficiency* (Vol. 2, p. 672). Dagenham, England: May
 and Baker Ltd.
Koch, R., Azen, C. G., Friedman, E. G., Williamson, M. L., O'Flynn, M., & Michals, K.
 (1983). Updated report on the effects of diet discontinuation in PKU.
 In H. Naruse & M. Irie (Eds.), *Neonatal screening: Proceedings of an International
 Symposium on Neonatal Screening for Inborn Errors of Metabolism*
 (pp. 213-218). Amsterdam: Excerpta Medica.
Koch, R., Dobson J. C., Blaskovics, M., et al. (1973). Collaborative study of children
 treated for phenylketonuria: A preliminary report. In J. W. T. Seakins,
 R. A. Saunders, and C. Toothill (Eds.), *Treatment of inborn errors of metabolism*
 (pp. 104-140). Edinburgh: Churchill Livingstone.
Lederberg, J., & Tatum, E. L. (1946). Novel genotypes in mixed cultures of
 biochemical mutants of bacteria. *Cold Spring Harbor Symposium on
 Quantitative Biology, 11,* 113-114.
Levy, H. L. (1982). Maternal PKU: Control of an emerging problem. *American
 Journal of Public Health, 72,* 1320.
MacCready, R. A. (1962). Editorial: Massachusetts Department of Health: Detection

of phenylketonuria in newborn infants. *New England Journal of Medicine,*
267, 1208–1209.

Naruse, H., & Irie, M. (Eds.). (1983). *Neonatal screening: Proceedings of an*
International Symposium on Neonatal Screening for Inborn Errors
of Metabolism, Tokyo, August 19–21, 1982. Amsterdam: Excerpta Medica.

Orfanos, A. P., Murphey, W. H., & Guthrie, R. (1977). A simple fluorometric
assay of free protoporphyrin in erythrocytes (FEP) as a screening test for lead
poisoning. *Journal of Laboratory and Clinical Medidine, 89,* 659–665.

Tourian, A., & Sidbury, J. B. (1983). Phenylketonuria and hyperphenylalaninemia.
In J. B. Stanbury, J. B. Wyngaardne, D. S. Fredrickson, J. L. Goldstein, &
M. S. Brown, (Eds.), *The metabolic basis of disease* (5th ed.) (pp. 270–286). New
York: McGraw-Hill.

Williamson, M., Dobson, J. C., & Koch, R. (1977). Collaborative study of children
treated for phenylketonuria: Study design. *Pediatrics, 60,* 815–821.

Wright, S. W., Tarjan, G., & Eyer, L. (1959). Investigation of families with two or more
mentally defective siblings. *A.M.A. American Journal of Diseases of*
Childhood, 94, 445.

7

A Developmental Theory on Mental Retardation

Edward Zigler

Edward Zigler, born 1930 in Kansas City, Missouri, received his B.A. in history from the University of Missouri at Kansas City (1954) and his Ph.D. in psychology from the University of Texas at Austin (1958).

Dr. Zigler is Sterling Professor of Psychology at Yale, where he also serves as director of the Bush Center in Child Development and Social Policy and as head of the psychology section of the Child Study Center (1959–   ). Previously, he was assistant professor of psychology at the University of Missouri, Columbia (1958–59).

Named by President Carter to chair the fifteenth anniversary Head Start Committee in 1980, Dr. Zigler was a member of the national planning and steering committee for Head Start and was appointed to Head Start's first national research council. He served the nation as the first director of the Office of Child Development and chief of the US Children's Bureau.

Dr. Zigler was the recipient of a special citation from the secretary of health, education, and welfare (1972), the Gunnar Dybwad Award from the National Association for Retarded Citizens (1964, 1969), the Career Research Award from the American Academy on Mental Retardation (1982), the G. Stanley Hall Award (1979) and the Award for Distinguished Contributions to Psychology in the Public Interest (1982), both from the American Psychological Association.

The field of mental retardation is nearly unrecognizable from the time I happened into it some twenty-five years ago. In those days anyone who worked with retarded persons usually had to travel to a large and remote state institution. Such an institution had several large hospital wards which housed victims of micro- and hydrocephaly, cretinism, PKU, prenatal exposure to rubella or X-rays, and other types of severe organically based retardation. In other areas, "garden-variety retardates" were being taught repetitive, monotonous tasks which capitalized on their assumed cognitive rigidity. On rare occasions, a retarded woman (typically sterilized) would leave the institution grounds for day work as a servant or waitress, or a man might work as a physical laborer for the state. Actually, we rarely called or even thought of these people as women and men. The most common label was "retardate," and "the retarded" was a collective noun. Today I sometimes shudder when I spot my own doctoral dissertation on the shelf, where the word "feebleminded" shines out from the gold-engraved title.

The past quarter century has brought about a near revolution in this scenario. The large central institution is being replaced by smaller, local facilities. Education takes place in special and even regular classrooms in public schools. Certainly the most awesome changes have occurred in the hospital wards. Progress in medical knowledge and technology has all but eliminated some types of gross organic disorder. (Excellent reviews of the status of prevention and treatment methods have been published by Begab in 1974, and by Clarke and Clarke in 1977.) Alleviation of mild, nonorganic retardation has not been as successful, but social prejudices and reluctance to provide help have softened somewhat. While there is still some stigma attached to the label *retarded,* there is growing acceptance of the fact that mildly retarded persons are much like everyone else in their feelings, trials, mundane abilities, and dreams. This can be seen in changes in public law— which is assumed to reflect public sentiment—where intellectual retardation is given equal status with other physical handicaps and victims are guaranteed the same rights enjoyed by all Americans. Words which connote mental subnormality are now descriptive adjectives rather than defining nouns.

I feel a special sense of pride at having been a part of these exciting and productive, if at times disputatious and chaotic, years in the development of the field. Yet, as I stated at the outset, I happened into the mental retardation area, and it is true that chance and circumstance were the primary instigators of this course of my career.

FIRST IMPRESSIONS AND OVERVIEW OF INFLUENCES

In my graduate school days at the University of Texas, my ill-defined interest concerned the learning process. I was greatly influenced then by Harold

This chapter is dedicated to the memory of David Balla. The Yale group has lost a valuable colleague, and the field of mental retardation has lost one of its most dedicated workers.

Stevenson, with whom I worked on a project to replicate with preschool children a learning effect that had been obtained with animals. This effect involved changing the amount of reinforcement at various points in a problem-solving situation to see how this would influence the child's learning. As is often the case in psychological research, the children we tested marched to the beat of some inner drum and appeared to be uninfluenced by our experimental manipulations. Although I kept trying, it became evident that I was quickly exhausting the entire nursery school population of Austin, Texas. Since Professor Stevenson and I were interested primarily in young (low mental age) children and were not particularly concerned about their intelligence levels, it dawned upon us that a sizeable population of low MA children was available at the Austin State Training School.

Interestingly, the retarded children I tested were just as impervious to our reinforcement changes as the nonretarded children. In fact, I was surprised by the similarity in the learning performance of the retarded and intellectually average groups. A striking difference, however, was that interaction with me appeared much more important for the retarded children than it had been for the preschoolers. This observation led to my initial theoretical theme that institutionalized retarded children are socially deprived and therefore more highly motivated to gain the attention and support of adults than are children who have not experienced such deprivation. Once I had experimentally confirmed this observation, I found myself explaining any and all behaviors of institutionalized retarded children on the basis of social deprivation.

Breaking away from this oversimplified view proved to be difficult, even when I began discovering empirical evidence to the contrary. What convinced me that I was far from having developed an adequate theoretical framework was the behavior of the retarded children I observed. I can still remember the retarded child I was trying to convince to play a harmless experimental game with me. After I raved about what a good time he was going to have, the child proclaimed that he knew I was going to hit him with a needle. My view, of course, was that I was dealing with a deprived child who hungered mightily for the social reinforcement that I could dispense. The child, however, was simply not buying it. For him the strange adults he encountered in the institution—especially those with the appellation "Doctor"—were sinister villains who might introduce tasks with sugary statements but would in due course create an unpleasant experience. This child's remarks were the impetus that enabled me to enlarge my theoretical approach. Specifically, whereas deprived children are motivated to seek positive reinforcement, the negative experiences which dominate their social histories make them wary of strange adults.

I learned a lesson at that time which continues to permeate my research, and one which I try to transmit to my students and encourage in my colleagues. I was clearly learning more from close observation of the retarded children I was testing than from those arbitrary measures which we were using for our investigation. When a study is essentially an egocentric activity in which the investigator determines the problem to present to the subjects, the reinforcers they will receive, and the specific behaviors to be analyzed, he or she often develops a considerable degree of tunnel vision, ignoring much else that is taking place. Thus the investigator loses the opportunity to appreciate other factors which could help illuminate the problem.

Following my final failure in the studies with retarded children, Stevenson and I held a postmortem analysis to determine what we might be doing wrong. This brought us the belated realization that we were naive in employing retarded children because we had overlooked a widely accepted dictum which set them apart from the nonretarded population. According to the work of Lewin and Kounin, retarded children of the type we had tested suffered from inherent cognitive rigidity: rigid cognitive processing prevented retarded children from grasping such things as logical sequence; instead, they had to learn and do everything by rote. Yet if this was the case, why was their performance on our learning task indistinguishable from that of the nonretarded children with similar MAs? The cognitive rigidity formulation and the empirical evidence I had to the contrary were what stimulated me to move deeper into the study of mental retardation.

Theoretical Beginnings

The Lewin-Kounin rigidity formulation had at the time great influence on ideas about mental retardation and on treatment and training practices. (For discussions of their work see Zigler, 1962 & 1969.) In this formulation one can see clearly the developmental as well as the difference positions which have continued to polarize the field. Kounin theorized that over the course of development the individual's cognitive system is characterized by an increasing degree of differentiation, i.e., the system acquires more zones or regions. This concept of differentiation is familiar to developmentalists and has been postulated as the underlying determinant of a broad range of cognitive phenomena (see Witkin, Dyk, Faterson, Goodenough, & Karp, 1962). In keeping with developmental thought, Kounin pointed out that degree of differentiation is not a function of chronological age but rather of the cognitive level attained, with the number of zones or regions increasing as one matured from lower to higher levels. For any particular cognitive level the number of regions would be the same for people with varying IQs; people with lower IQs, however, would take longer than those with higher IQs to achieve the same degree of differentiation.

In addition to the rate at which a particular level of cognitive differentiation was attained, both Lewin and Kounin felt a second factor was necessary to explain differences in retarded-nonretarded functioning. They called this factor *cognitive rigidity*, which referred not to rigid behaviors per se but to a formal feature of the cognitive structure itself. They reasoned that at the same level of differentiation, the boundaries between regions in the cognitive structure were less permeable in the retarded individual than in someone of normal intellect. Processes of cognition could not move as readily from zone to zone, which would inhibit intellectual "dexterity." Kounin conducted a classic series of studies in which he employed MA to equate retarded and nonretarded children on degree of differentiation. He did indeed find group differences on tasks thought to be sensitive to the postulated cognitive rigidity factor (see Zigler, 1962).

I present the Lewis-Kounin position in such detail because it is in the difference or defect camp which many have treated as the antithesis of my own developmental stance. Actually, Kounin's careful attention to certain features not only guided but became integral to the course of my own research. First, Kounin explicitly stated that his theoretical model did not apply to organically retarded persons, and he conscientiously limited his investigations to familial cases. Recognition of etiological differences became a cornerstone of my theory, and the topic of some lively professional disputes to be discussed later. Kounin also insisted that even if his groups were matched on MA, his experimental procedures would not provide an adequate test of the rigidity formulation if the groups differed in motivation. For this reason, he introduced procedures to equate groups in attitude and motivation, although these early attempts may have had the opposite effect. Still, Kounin impressed upon me the importance of controlling motivational factors if we are ever to answer the question of whether familial retarded persons have a cognitive deficiency over and above their slower rate of development.

Actually, attention to socio-emotional perspectives was coming of age by the 1950s and '60s. Several early workers in the field of mental retardation, such as Fernald and Potter, felt that the difference between social adequacy and inadequacy in borderline retarded persons was a matter of personality rather than intelligence, and a number of studies confirmed their viewpoint (see reviews by McCarver & Craig, 1974; Windle, 1962; Zigler & Harter, 1969). For example, Windle found that in most institutions for retarded persons, intelligence was presumed to be the critical factor in adjustment after release. However, the vast majority (over twenty) of the studies he reviewed reported no relation between intellectual level and postinstitutional adjustment. Rather, this literature showed that the factors associated with poor social adjustment included anxiety, jealousy, overdependency, poor self-evaluation, hostility, hyperactivity, and failure to follow orders even when requests were well within the range of intellectual competence. This school of literature, coupled with the recognition that two persons with the same IQ (be it high or low) can show quite varied degrees of adjustment, led me to focus more and more on motivational determinants of behavior.

Developmental Inclinations

Following graduate school I embarked on an internship in clinical psychology at Worcester State Hospital in Massachusetts. During these and later years I collaborated with Dr. Leslie Phillips in the construction of a general developmental approach to psychopathology. My thinking was enriched not only by my association with Dr. Phillips but also through interactions with the Clark group, especially Heinz Werner and Bernard Kaplan. Although I went to Worcester committed to the neo-Hullian approach then so popular, I left committed to what has always appeared the antithesis of American behaviorism, namely the cognitive-developmental approach exemplified by the work of Piaget and Werner. This approach has since characterized my work in self-concept, humor, and psychiatric symptomatology.

Though heavily immersed in research in psychopathology and in increasing my knowledge of developmental thought, I continued work with retarded children during the year at Worcester, conducting my dissertation research at the Fernald State School in Waverly. This work made me even more aware of just how complex are the determinants of behavior in retarded individuals; it also confirmed to me that any understanding of how institutionalization affects retarded children requires a consideration of their preinstitutional social histories. I continued to be amazed by the performance similarities between familial retarded and nonretarded children of the same MA. This observation did not come to theoretical fruition until Hirch's (1963) discussion of normalcy influenced my thinking about retardation. As a result, I came to view familial retarded persons as occupying the lower portion of the normal distribution of intelligence. These individuals progress through the same cognitive stages as persons of average or superior intelligence, but at a slower rate so that they never achieve the upper intellectual levels.

In 1959 I joined the faculty of the Psychology Department at Yale University and have remained at Yale to this day. My work at Yale has been greatly enriched through the years by numerous colleagues and students. Especially rewarding to me have been the relatively long-term collaborations with Earl Butterfield, Susan Harter, Victoria Seitz, and Regina Yando. My empirical and theoretical understanding of the effects of institutionalization was illuminated greatly by the efforts of the late David Balla (1939–1982), to whom this chapter is dedicated. David not only worked tirelessly on our research projects, but made sure that any findings were translated into practice to better the lives of retarded people.

Current Perspectives

After a quarter of a century in the field, I wish I could say that I have evolved a satisfactory theoretical framework for the understanding of mental retardation. However, at this stage the evolution of any such complete system seems less likely than it did so many years ago. Indeed, anything purporting to be a definitive theory of retarded functioning seems to me overstated, since it is my firm conviction that any truly satisfactory theory must await the explication of countless unresolved issues in the general area of developmental psychology. My involvement in many avenues of investigation has convinced me that mental retardation is not a separate subarea and cannot be understood through approaches and constructs narrower than or different from those which we employ to explain normal intellectual functioning.

This brings me to the current influences on my work. Maintaining an open mind is said to become more difficult with age, but the active pace and exciting developments in the mental retardation field would not allow even the most illustrious worker to rest on his or her laurels. The vigor and quality of current research is much superior to that of previous years, although the rate of improvement is jeopardized somewhat by funding cutbacks. We are hearing many new voices in the retardation discourse, including those in the fields of medicine, education, therapy, counseling, and prevention. These expanded interdisciplinary efforts are responsible for the basic understanding of mental retardation achieved today and are the hope of further enlightment in the years to come.

The thrust of our current research also owes much to scientists in countries other than the United States. For example, the impetus for a major branch of our research came from the Clarkes in England, who demonstrated that there is a relation between the amount of preinstitutional deprivation experienced by a child and changes in the child's IQ following institutional-ization. We are also indebted to another group of English workers—King, Raynes, and Tizard—whose care-practices inventory and basic approach to studying the effects of institutionalization played a central role in our own work here. The help of colleagues in a Scandinavian nation made it possible for us to conduct a cross-cultural study of institutionalization (McCormick, Balla, & Zigler, 1975).

The most recent and perhaps disquieting international influence came from my 1981 trip to Sweden with a group of American scientists headed by Dr. Robert Cooke. We were sent to examine reports that the incidence of mild mental retardation was markedly lower in Sweden than in the US and other industrialized nations. We discovered that Swedish attitudes and practices concerning mental retardation differ dramatically from our own. The consequences of these differences are reflected not so much in debatable incidence statistics but in the services provided to enable retarded persons to earn their living in society. I came to realize that the definition of mental retardation is not so much a semantic exercise as a troublesome practical question of great import. Balla and I therefore suggested that the entire basis for the definition and classification of mental retardation be changed (Zigler & Balla, 1982). We have advanced a new definitional and classification schema (discussed later), which now awaits reaction and counterreaction.

RESEARCH ON PERSONALITY FACTORS IN RETARDED FUNCTIONING

The course of my research, done in collaboration with many colleagues, illustrates the laborious process of adding knowledge rather than uncovering some definitive truth. The essence of my empirical work has been the systematic evaluation of experiential, motivational, and personality factors in the behavior of retarded persons. All of this began as a reaction to the common assumption that a cognitive deficiency was the sole determinant of retarded functioning. Mental retardation was believed to be a pervasive phenomenon that directed all behavior of low-IQ individuals and made them impervious to the influence of events known to affect the behavior of nonretarded persons. Things such as severe social deprivation, institutionalization, and a lifetime of failure and ridicule were ignored as determinants of poor performance, which was attributed only to impaired cognitive functioning.

This assumption can clearly be seen in the typical research paradigm used in studies of behavioral differences between retarded and nonretarded children. Often the groups compared are institutionalized retarded children, whose preinstitutional lives are frequently spent at the very bottom of the lowest socioeconomic status (SES), and middle-SES children who live at home. Such groups differ not only in the quality of their cognitive functioning as defined by the IQ, but they also differ greatly in their total life histories and the nature of their current social-psychological interactions. When a child of average intellect is subjected to the social deprivation associated with institutionalization or is a member of a particular SES, behavior theorists are extremely sensitive to how such life experiences give rise to particular goals, values, attitudes, motives, and roles, and to how these as well as formal cognitive variables influence the child's behavior. However, in the case of the retarded child, once we take note of the low IQ, we act as if we have nailed down all the variables that matter.

In defense of workers who use this paradigm, it could be argued that one need not be very concerned about motivational factors on tasks thought to be essentially cognitive in nature. In my opinion, such an argument is wrong, because performance on any task is not the direct and simple reflection of cognitive functioning, totally uninfluenced by emotional factors. Evidence in support of this point can be found not only in the fact that the search for a measure of pure intelligence continues, but in numerous studies showing that performance on "cognitive" tasks is related to things such as reinforcement, sex of examiner, and other situation-specific factors. For example, Zigler and Butterfield (1968) found that the Stanford-Binet IQ scores of preschool children increased by an average of ten points when the test was administered under an optimizing procedure designed to put them at ease. As I have reasoned in detail many times (e.g., Zigler & Trickett, 1978), performance on any task reflects formal cognitive factors, achievement factors (what one has learned or been exposed to), and the attitudes one brings to the testing situation. None of these elements can operate in isolation from the others.

The overly cognitive-deterministic approach to the behavior of retarded persons may stem from more than the narrow-mindedness the notion of low IQ produces. It is probably also the result of the lack of a sound and extensive body of empirical work on personality factors in the behavior of retarded persons (see Gardner, 1968; Heber, 1964). Had such a subarea developed over the years, it would unquestionably have moderated the overly cognitive approach. Today, of course, there is a growing body of literature (reviewed by Balla & Zigler, 1979; Zigler & Balla, 1982) which shows that due to atypical social histories, many retarded persons develop traits such as high needs for social reinforcement, strong social approach and avoidance tendencies, and vexing "I-can't-do-it" attitudes. Such motivational factors have a pervasive influence on behavior and can attenuate performance. Yet, this may be a classic case of too little too late. The cognitive emphasis in the study of mental retardation has been buttressed in recent years by the many advances in the field of cognitive psychology. Alas, although motivational factors are clearly operative, it remains the rare worker (e.g., Sternberg, 1981a, 1981b) who considers both cognitive processes and motivational variables when attempting to explain the behavior of retarded persons.

In an attempt to fill the empirical gap, my research and that of others has been directed at providing some hard evidence concerning the role of personality factors in the functioning of retarded persons. Over the years my colleagues and I have attempted to delineate a number of motivational variables—variables not unique to the performance of retarded children but ones particularly relevant to their behavior since they tend to encounter certain events much more than do middle-SES nonretarded children. We have been interested in discovering the specific experiences which give rise to particular motives, attitudes, and styles and how variation in these experiences leads to variation in the personality structure of individuals of both retarded and normal intellect. We have been especially interested in demonstrating that some performance of retarded children which has been commonly attributed to cognitive shortcomings is actually the product of particular motives. This does not mean that we have championed the importance of motivational over cognitive variables, since it is clear that these two classes of variables can, both independently and together, influence performance on any given task. We have also been aware that while it is conceptually feasible to draw a distinction between cognitive and motivational factors with respect to certain behaviors, this division is extremely difficult, if not totally artificial. Following are summaries of our work on those motivational factors which have been sufficiently delineated for us to demonstrate how each may affect retarded children's performance.

Social Deprivation

Our definition of preinstitutional deprivation includes events such as a lack of continuity of care by parents (or other caretakers), an excessive desire by the parents to institutionalize their child, impoverished economic circumstances, child abuse and/or neglect, and a family history of marital discord, mental illness, or social infractions. Each of these factors has been found to affect a wide variety of behavior. Perhaps the largest and most important body of research shows that social deprivation can result in a heightened desire to interact with a supportive adult—a greater responsiveness to social reinforcements (reviewed by Zigler & Balla, 1982). In these studies we have frequently used the marble-in-the-hole game to assess a child's responsiveness to social reinforcement. The child is instructed to drop marbles of one color into one hole of a large box and marbles of a second color into a second hole. He or she is allowed to persist at the task until satiated, at which time the correct holes for the colored marbles are reversed and the procedure repeated. The experimenter periodically praises the child's performance. The measure of responsiveness to social reinforcement is the total time that the child persists on both parts of the task.

According to our rationale, socially deprived children will be more responsive to the attention and support of the adult than a nondeprived child, and consequently will persist at the monotonous task longer. I obtained early support for this formulation by employing a clinical estimate of the extent of preinstitutional social deprivation (Zigler, 1961). I found that highly deprived institutionalized retarded persons persisted at the task significantly longer than less deprived individuals, a finding which has since been replicated many times with groups of institutionalized and noninstitutionalized retarded individuals rated on a more objective measure of social deprivation (Zigler et al., 1966). This heightened motivation to interact with a supportive adult which stems from a history of social deprivation is congruent with the common observation that retarded individuals actively seek attention and affection.

It should be noted that heightened motivation for social reinforcement has been used as an indicator of an important phenomenon discussed in the general child development literature, namely, dependency. Thus, with an almost imperceptible shift in terminology, we might conclude that a general consequence of social deprivation is overdependency. We cannot place enough emphasis on the role of such overdependency in the behavior of retarded persons. Given some minimal intellectual level, the shift from dependence to independence is perhaps the single most important factor which enables retarded persons to become self-sustaining members of society (e.g., Zigler & Harter, 1969).

Some indication of the pervasiveness of the dependency of institutionalized retarded persons may be found in a study by Zigler and Balla (1972). Intellectually-average and retarded children of three MA levels (7, 9, and 12) were compared in terms of their responsiveness to social reinforcement, as measured by the marble-in-the-hole task. In keeping with the general developmental progression from helplessness and dependence to autonomy and independence, children of higher MAs were found to be less motivated for social reinforcement than children of lower MAs. However, at each MA level the retarded children were more dependent than the nonretarded children. This disparity in dependent behavior was just as marked in the highest as in the lowest MA group. Indeed, the oldest retarded group persisted at the marble-in-the-hole task almost twice as long as the youngest nonretarded group.

The relation between preinstitutional deprivation and social reinforcement was strongest for the youngest retarded group, suggesting that the younger the child, the more his or her behavior depends on life experiences within the family context. Perhaps as children grow older and interact with a broader spectrum of socializing agents, their need for social reinforcement becomes less determined by the quality of social interaction within the confines of the family. Such a view is certainly consistent with the observation that with increasing age, a child's personality structure is more influenced by peers, teachers, and other nonfamily socializing agents. However, in this study we also found evidence that retarded children who maintained contact with their parents or parent surrogates were less dependent than children with more limited contact. Thus, it seems that excessively dependent behavior can be changed by increased contact with people important to the child.

Positive- and Negative-Reaction Tendencies

A phenomenon which appears to be at variance with retarded children's increased desire for social reinforcement is their wariness of adults. Experimental work to date has suggested that social deprivation results *both* in a heightened motivation to interact with supportive adults (positive-reaction tendency) and in a reluctance and wariness to do so (negative-reaction tendency).

The negative-reaction tendency construct has been employed to explain some of the performance differences between retarded and nonretarded individuals originally reported by Kounin (1941). Kounin employed a simple two-part task similar to marble-in-the-hole. A recurring finding in such studies (e.g., Kounin, 1941; Zigler, 1958, 1961) is that retarded individuals will frequently spend more time on the second part of the task than on the first. To explain this puzzling finding, I suggested that retarded children have a great desire for reinforcement from supportive adults but, as a consequence of their more frequent negative encounters with adults, are extremely wary of them (Zigler, 1958). The wary child apparently realizes during the first part of the task that the adult means no harm. Once this determination is made, he or she may become responsive to the social reinforcement and actually persist at the second part of the task longer than the first in order to obtain the desirable interaction.

In an early study (Shallenberger & Zigler, 1961), both intellectually average and institutionalized retarded children experienced either a positive or negative interaction with an adult prior to the marble-in-the-hole task. In the positive-interaction situation, all of the child's responses met with success and were praised, while in the negative condition all responses met with failure and disapproval. Regardless of intelligence level, both groups of children demonstrated greater wariness following the negative than following the positive situation. Yet, the retarded children were more strongly affected by the negative interaction than were the nonretarded children.

In other studies, a more direct measure of the negative-reaction tendency was used—how far children situated themselves from a stationary adult. Weaver (1966) found that noninstitutionalized retarded children who had experienced a negative interaction prior to the positioning task were more wary than those who experienced a positive interaction. Weaver, Balla, and Zigler (1971) replicated this finding with institutionalized children.

In several studies of the negative-reaction tendency, experimental preconditions were not employed. Harter and Zigler (1968) found that institutionalized retarded children seemed to have a generalized wariness of strangers whether they were adults or peers. Balla, Kossan, and Zigler (1980) found that after approximately eight years of institutional experience, retarded individuals with a history of severe preinstitutional social deprivation were still more wary than less deprived individuals. Thus, there is some evidence that socially depriving experiences can cause a wariness of adults that is quite longlasting. Balla, McCarthy, and Zigler (1971) found that retarded individuals institutionalized at a younger age were less wary than those institutionalized when older. Apparently, the institution used in that study made residents less wary of strange adults by increasing their exposure to them. Excessive wariness is thus not an inevitable consequence of institutionalization.

Expectancy of Failure

Another factor frequently mentioned as a deterrent in the performance of retarded persons is their high expectancy of failure. This has been viewed as a consequence of a history of frequent confrontations with tasks with which they are ill-equipped to deal. Investigation of the success-failure dimension has proceeded in two directions. The first has been an attempt to document the pervasiveness of these feelings of failure. The work of Cromwell (1963) and his colleagues has lent support to the general proposition that retarded individuals have a higher expectancy of failure than those of average intellect. In a related series of studies by MacMillan (1969; MacMillan & Keogh, 1971; MacMillan & Knopf, 1971), the experimenter prevented children from finishing several tasks and subsequently asked why they were not completed. The retarded children consistently blamed themselves, while nonretarded children did not assume the guilt so readily.

The second line of research has focused on how success and failure expectancies affect problem-solving behavior. The task typically employed in these studies is a three-choice discrimination problem in which one stimulus is partially reinforced and the other two stimuli are never reinforced. Children with low expectancies of success, as gauged by aspiration level or need-achievement measures, were more likely to display a maximizing strategy (persistent choice of the partially reinforced stimulus) on this task than children with high expectancies of success (Gruen, Ottinger, & Zigler, 1970;

Kier, Styfco, & Zigler, 1977; Ollendick & Gruen, 1971). Such findings are consistent with Goodnow's (1955) suggestion that greater maximizing behavior would be found when a person accepted less than 100 percent success as an acceptable outcome, while less maximizing would occur when someone expected 100 percent success, or a level of success greater than that allowed in the situation. Thus, on the three-choice probability task, children with higher expectancies of success would be expected to engage in strategies other than maximizing in the hope of achieving 100 percent reinforcement.

Consistent with the expectancy of success formulation, retarded children have been found to exhibit more maximizing behavior than children of average intelligence (Gruen & Zigler, 1968; Stevenson & Zigler, 1958). However, the tendency of retarded individuals to employ a maximizing strategy could also be interpreted in terms of the cognitive rigidity position of Lewin and Kounin. That is to say, the alleged inherent rigidity of retarded persons might lead them to persevere in the choice of one of the three stimuli, and not to abandon the choice even when it sometimes proves wrong. In an attempt to resolve this issue, Ollendick, Balla, and Zigler (1971) employed relatively long-term success and failure conditions and observed subsequent task behavior. They found that experiencing failure resulted in a low expectancy of success, while the reverse was true after experiencing success. From these data it seemed plausible to assume that the greater maximizing behavior observed in retarded individuals is related to motivation rather to cognitive rigidity.

Gruen, Ottinger, and Ollendick (1974) tried to determine whether the success-failure findings could be replicated in a more life like school setting. They found that retarded children in regular classes (presumably exposed to repeated failure) had higher expectancies of failure than retarded children in special classes (experiencing relatively higher levels of success). However, Caparulo and Zigler (in press) studied mildly retarded boys who were either partially or totally mainstreamed and did not find expectancy of success to be systematically affected by the intensity of the mainstreaming experience.

The Reinforcer Hierarchy

Due to factors in their experience, the retarded individual's motivation for incentives may differ from that of nonretarded individuals of the same MA. Stated somewhat differently, the position of various reinforcers in the reinforcer hierarchies may differ in retarded and nonretarded children. Much of the experimental work on the reinforcer hierarchy has focused on tangible and intangible reinforcement. It has been argued that certain factors in the histories of retarded children cause them to be less responsive to intangible reinforcement than are nonretarded children of equivalent MA (Zigler, 1962; Zigler & deLabry, 1962; Zigler & Unell, 1962). This work is of special importance, since intangible reinforcement (information that a response is correct) is the most immediate and frequently dispensed reinforcement in real-life situations. When such a reinforcer is employed in studies comparing groups of retarded and nonretarded individuals, any differences found may be attributable not to variations in intellectual capacity, but rather to the fact that the reinforcement motivated the two groups differently. The importance of the specific type of reinforcer used was highlighted by both Plenderleith (1956) and Stevenson and Zigler (1957), who found that when tangible reinforcers were given, institutionalized familial retarded individuals were no more rigid than nonretarded persons on a discrimination reversal-learning task.

Clearest support for the view that the retarded child is much less motivated to be correct for the sake of correctness than is the middle-SES child is contained in a study by Zigler and deLabry (1962). We tested MA-matched middle-SES, lower-SES, and retarded children on a concept-switching task (Kounin, 1941) using two kinds of reinforcement: (1) the information that the child was correct and (2) a toy of the child's choice if he or she switched from one concept to another. With the "correct" reinforcer, both the retarded and lower-SES groups were poorer in their concept switching than the middle-SES children. However, no differences were found among the three groups who received tangible reinforcers. Interestingly, both retarded and upper-SES children were found to switch concepts more readily in a tangible than in an intangible reinforcement condition (Zigler & Unell, 1962).

These studies highlight an assumption that has been noted as erroneous by many educators; namely, that lower-SES and retarded children are responsive to the same types of reinforcers as middle-SES children. However, although retarded children as a group may place a lower value on being correct than middle-SES children as a group, this may not hold true for any particular child. The crucial factor is not membership in a particular social class or intellectual retardation per se, but rather the child's socialization history. This point is aptly underlined in a study by Byck (1968), who examined the concept-switching performance of Down-syndrome and familial retarded individuals matched on MA, CA, IQ and length of institutionalization. The Down syndrome children showed better concept-switching when the reinforcement was intangible, whereas the familial groups did better with tangible reinforcers. This finding is consistent with the literature noted above if one remembers that familial retarded persons almost invariably come from a lower-SES background, whereas children with Down syndrome are more likely to come from middle-SES homes. It would appear that the social learning experiences acquired early in the child's life and prior to institutionalization are particularly influential in determining the potency of various reinforcers.

In later work, attention has shifted to the reinforcement intrinsic in being correct, regardless of whether or not an external agent dispenses a reinforcer. This shift in orientation owes much to White's (1959) formulation concerning the pervasive influence of the effectance or mastery motive. There can be little question that White's effectance concept is useful in understanding a variety of behaviors that appear very central in the individual's behavioral repertoire, e.g., the desire for optimal levels of sensory stimulation, manipulation, exploration, and curiosity. A series of studies (see Shultz & Zigler, 1970; Zigler, Levine, & Gould, 1967) has given some support to this view that using one's own cognitive resources to their fullest is intrinsically gratifying and thus motivating.

As with the case of intangible reinforcers, the strength of the effectance motive may be different for retarded and nonretarded individuals. Evidence on this point was provided by Harter and Zigler (1974), who constructed several measures of effectance motivation, including variation seeking, curiosity, mastery for the sake of competence, and preference for challenging tasks. On these measures, intellectually average children demonstrated more effectance motivation than retarded children. In keeping with the view that institutional life requires a degree of conformity, institutionalized retarded children displayed less curiosity than those who remained in the community. In summary, retarded children seem to be both less responsive to intangible reinforcers and less motivated by intrinsic effectance motives than children of average intellect.

Outerdirectedness

Findings that retarded children are more sensitive to cues provided by an adult than are nonretarded children of the same MA led us to the study of a general style of problem solving referred to as *outerdirectedness*. This style is defined as the degree to which the individual uses external cues to solve problems, rather than relying on his or her own cognitive resources. In the latest revision of this formulation (Balla et al., 1980), three factors are advanced as important in determining the child's degree of outerdirectedness: (1) general level of cognitive development, (2) the relative incidence of success the child has experienced when using his or her own abilities in problem-solving situations, and (3) the extent of the child's attachment to adults. Either too little or too much imitation of adults is viewed as a negative psychological indicator. Some intermediate level of imitation is viewed as a positive developmental phenomenon reflecting the child's healthy attachment to adults and responsiveness to cues from adults which can be useful in problem-solving efforts.

In general, the developmental aspect of the outerdirectedness formulation has received empirical support. With nonretarded children, outerdirectedness has been found to decrease as MA increases (MacMillan & Wright, 1974; Ruble & Nakamura, 1973; Yando & Zigler, 1971; Zigler & Yando, 1972). This developmental shift has also been found in institutionalized retarded persons (Turnure, 1970a, 1970b) and in noninstitutionalized mildly retarded groups (Balla, Styfco, & Zigler, 1971; Gordon & Maclean, 1977). The success/failure aspect of the outerdirectedness formulation has also been confirmed in several of the studies cited above. Presumably because of their histories of frequent failure, retarded persons are more outerdirected in their problem-solving behavior than nonretarded persons of the same MA, and both intellectual groups have been found to become more outerdirected following failure than success.

To this point, outerdirectedness has been discussed as if it were a unitary psychological dimension. Actually, at least two conceptually different measures have been employed, each representing a different realm of common experiences. Some studies used a learning measure where a cue extrinsic to the task could either help or hinder performance. There was clearly a right or wrong answer. It seems reasonable to expect that children living in an environment adjusted to their developmental level would be less imitative on this task than children living in an environment where they are confronted with their intellectual shortcomings and experience considerable failure. Indeed, Achenbach and Zigler (1968) found that noninstitutionalized retarded children were more reliant on external cues on this task than were those who resided in institutions. A second measure of imitation was a sticker game, in which an adult first makes a design and then asks the child to make any design he or she chooses. The child's designs are subsequently scored for extent of imitation of the model. While there are no right or wrong answers with this measure, it seems likely that greater imitation will occur in environments where a high degree of compliance has adaptive value (such as in institutions). In two studies (Lustman, Zigler, & Balla, 1979; Yando & Zigler, 1971), institutionalized retarded persons were found to be more imitative on this task than those who were not institutionalized.

Regarding attachment to adults, there is some evidence that individuals who have not formed a healthy attachment to adult caretakers will have an atypically low level of outerdirectedness (Balla et al., 1980). In this study we found that institutionalized retarded individuals whose caretakers had negative attitudes toward them were less outerdirected than those whose caretakers had more positive attitudes. Thus, individuals who have experienced negative responses may learn to ignore cues provided by adults, and thus become less imitative and lose available help and guidance.

Self-Concept

The self-concept construct has had a central role in general personality theory but has received relatively little attention in the mental retardation literature (Balla & Zigler, 1979). Traditionally, a person's self-concept has been viewed exclusively as a function of life experience. My colleagues and I (e.g., Achenbach & Zigler, 1963; Katz & Zigler, 1967) advanced an alternative developmental view of the self-image construct which identifies three aspects of the self-concept: (1) real self-image, which is the person's current self-concept; (2) ideal self-image, or the way the person would ideally like to be; and (3) self-image disparity, which is the difference between the real and ideal self. I have argued that the growth and development of an individual must invariably be accompanied by an increasing disparity between assessment of the real and ideal self. This thesis is based on the assumption that two determinants of the scores on typical self-image disparity measures are developmental in nature. The first determinant is an individual's capacity to experience guilt, a capacity that increases over the course of development with a growing ability to incorporate social demands, mores, and values (see Zigler & Child, 1969). Second is the phenomenon of increasing cognitive differentiation with development (e.g., Werner, 1948; Witkin, et al., 1962). In any cognitive act, a person at a higher developmental level would be able to employ a greater number of categories, or possible ways of thinking about things, and make finer distinctions within each category than an individual at a lower developmental level. The use of a larger number of categories should increase the probability of greater disparity between any two complex judgments—including those regarding real and ideal self-images. The developmental approach to self-concept has received empirical support in studies of psychiatrically disturbed and nondisturbed adults and children (see Achenbach & Zigler, 1963; Phillips & Zigler, 1980).

REFLECTIONS ON THE RESEARCH

My research over the years, combined with the total body of evidence concerning personality and the behavior of retarded persons, has led me to the following conclusion: *beyond any doubt, many of the reported differences between retarded and nonretarded persons of the same MA are a result of motivational and emotional differences that reflect variations in experiential histories.* This is not to say that I believe that the cause of mental retardation is motivational. The cognitive functioning of retarded persons unquestionably has a profound effect on their behavior. The crucial questions are, just how great is this influence and how does it differ across tasks with which retarded individuals are confronted? It has proven much more possible to alter aspects of personality than to change the cognitive structure itself (see Zigler & Seitz, 1982). Thus research into motivational influences on behavior carries the inspirational goal of improving motivation and enabling many retarded persons to apply their given abilities in the best ways possible.

Our research fits into this ultimate plan in only the most fundamental ways. That is, over the years we have questioned several relatively orthodox views and have tried to divest ourselves of those preconceived notions which stand in the way of increasing our knowledge of mental retardation. While we have attempted to broaden our thinking concerning the retarded child, we have certainly not replaced older views with any new orthodoxy. Indeed, we remain far from constructing any very satisfying network of interrelated personality and cognitive constructs which will provide the ultimate explanations for the behavior of retarded persons. Rather, we remain at the earliest stages of theory construction, namely, the isolation and mapping of those personality variables which we think are particularly germane to the functioning of various types of retarded children. For the time being this is the course we must continue to pursue.

While we have made some progress, certain notes of caution are in order. In our analyses we have often dealt with one personality factor at a time. While this may facilitate the presentation of the findings of a large number of studies, it may also suggest that, when a retarded individual is confronted with a task, only one factor is operative. This, of course, is not the case. The psychological processes and the motive states which I have been discussing operate in combination more often than in isolation. The behavior of the retarded child is a complex phenomenon determined by many factors.

Since so many of our studies also involve comparisons of retarded and nonretarded groups, it is also easy to conclude that we are searching for differences between the two. On the contrary, the bulk of our effort is directed at the discovery of how retarded persons are similar to more intelligent members of society. Once one accepts such a likelihood, we can turn attention away from personality traits thought to manifest themselves as an invariable consequence of intellectual retardation and toward those particular experiences in the socialization process which give rise to the relatively long-lasting emotional and motivational factors which constitute the personality. Once workers shift their orientation in this way, they can readily see that the personality of a retarded child will develop like that of a nonretarded individual in those instances where the two have had similar socialization histories. All of this means that once we think of retarded individuals as essentially rational human beings who respond to environmental events in much the same way as everyone else, we can allow our knowledge of normal personality development to give direction to our efforts.

This discussion has led me close to the topics of several debates I have entered in the field. I will digress for a moment to explain my role in these professional disputes, because much of what I have said has been misconstrued, perhaps because I have been vague or characteristically prolix. For the sake of those who may have been misled by a lack of clarity in my written presentations, let me unequivocally declare that I have never advanced a motivational theory of mental retardation, as several writers claimed (e.g., Milgram, 1969; Zeaman, 1968). While I have conducted much research on the role of motivational variables in the performance of retarded children, I have been specific in asserting that the essential problem in mental retardation is an intellectual or cognitive one. In respect to familial mental retardation, I have espoused a developmental theory which is essentially cognitive in nature, not motivational. The central controversy in which I am engaged is, therefore, between a developmental-cognitive theory and a collection of theories that I have referred to as difference or defect theories (see Zigler, 1969).

It is amusing that while some have criticized me for being too motivational and thus too experiential in my orientation, others have taken me to task for being too genetic (Wortis, 1967). The reason is that I have often proclaimed my belief that variation in cognitive development is determined in large part by polygenic factors. Rather than being like a different species, familial retarded persons represent the lower end of the normal distribution of intelligence. Again, this suggests similarities between retarded and non-retarded development which lead me to believe that we do not need a separate set of constructs beyond those used to explain normal behavior to illuminate retarded functioning.

THE TWO-GROUP APPROACH TO MENTAL RETARDATION

Perhaps the only other firm belief I hold based on my many years of work in the field is that there are two distinct groups of retarded persons, to whom different explanations might apply. The two-group approach is based on the assertion that genetic inheritance plays an important role in determining individual differences in intelligence. While some theorists (e.g., Kamin, 1974) have argued that there is absolutely no genetic component influencing variations in intelligence, I view such a position as untenable. I agree with Thiessen's (1972) conclusion that from 50 to 80 percent of the variation in IQ scores is due to genetic factors.

Given this genetic contribution, for the general population normal variation in intelligence is best conceptualized as a polygene phenomenon. That is, the genotype for intelligence is determined by the additive effects of several genes. Gottesman (1963) advanced a five-gene model which encompasses the variation in intelligence from IQs 50 to 150. Gottesman's polygenic model yields a distribution of intelligence approximating the normal curve, but the extreme limits are 50 and 150 rather than 0 and 200. Ignoring the problem of empirically-encountered IQ scores above 150 (see Jensen, 1969), we are left with the problem of how to explain the appearance of IQ scores in the 0 to 50 range.

If we accept the polygenic approach as a reasonably accurate explanation for the theoretical distribution of intelligence, we must postulate a second distribution for those whose scores are too low to be accounted for by polygene action. The majority of people fit into the larger distribution where the primary determinant of intelligence is polygenic inheritance. Individuals in the second group also begin life with polygenes for a given level of intelligence, but some major prenatal insult such as Down syndrome or irradiation, or postnatal encounters such as anoxia or lead poisoning, prevented the intended expression of these genes. These individuals are usually classified as *organically retarded*.

The majority of retarded persons have no known organic defects and are commonly referred to as *familial retarded* (or retarded due to psychosocial disadvantage, in the current terminology). Familial retarded persons typically are mildly retarded with IQs between 50 and 70 and at least one parent who is below average in intelligence. When mental retardation is defined simply as IQs below 70, approximately 75 percent of retarded persons are of the familial type.

There are at least four somewhat overlapping formulations concerning the etiology of the familial retarded group: (1) mild mental retardation is produced by psychosocial disadvantage; (2) mild retardation is due to some unspecified interaction between genetic and environmental factors; (3) individuals with mild retardation have suffered subclinical organic damage (Hagberg, Hagberg, Lewerth, & Lindberg, 1981; Kugel, 1967), but discovery of its exact nature awaits advances in medical technology; and (4) familial retardation represents the lower portion of the normal distribution of intelligence dictated by the gene pool of a population (Zigler, 1967), the position I have advanced. It is easy even for experts to forget that in any distribution there must necessarily be some who occupy the lower positions. Thus, while familial retarded persons may be less intelligent than other more typical manifestations of the gene pool, they are just as integral a part of the normal distribution as the three percent of the population who are intellectually superior, or the more numerous group of individuals considered to be average. Given the state of knowledge in the area, all four formulations are viable options at this point in time.

Diagnostic Correlates

Several influential workers (Bijou, 1966; Ellis, 1969; Ellis & Cavalier, 1982; Spitz, 1963) continue to support the position that all that differentiates retarded individuals are differences in IQs. Of course, it is true that organically retarded persons typically have lower IQ scores than those classified as familial, but this is not always the case. Further, considerable research (e.g., Weisz, Yeates, & Zigler, 1982; Zigler, 1969) has shown that there are important behavioral differences between those retarded because of organic causes as opposed to polygenic ones. Thus, David Balla and I proposed a classification system in which diagnosis is given the important status of a classificatory principle (Zigler & Balla, 1982). This proposal is presented in Figure 7.1.

The need to differentiate between organic and familial classes is dictated by the frequent finding of group differences when workers do bother to separate their retarded samples by diagnostic status (see Weisz, et al., 1982). On cognitive tasks, familial groups commonly outperform their IQ- and MA-matched organic peers. IQ alone cannot explain the difference. On the other hand, the model shown in Figure 7.1 suggests myriad causal elements. We could use the classificatory principle and base our explanation on the fact that one group has demonstrable organic difficulties which might affect those processes mediating the behavior under study. One could also use any or all of the correlates in the figure to inform the interpretation of organic-familial differences. For example, we might point to differences in SES level or in the severity of health problems. Not unimportant is the fact that organically retarded children tend to have siblings of normal intellect, whereas the familial group often have siblings with IQs below 100. From this we would expect that the organically impaired child might have a lower self-image ("I

Figure 7.1   A Three-Group Approach to the Classification of Retarded Persons

IQ	Organic 0–70	Familial 50–70	Undifferentiated 50–70
Classificatory Principle	Demonstrable organic etiology	No demonstrable organic etiology and parents having this same type of retardation	Cannot reliably be placed in either of the other two classes
Correlates	Found at all SES levels	More prevalent at lower SES levels	
	IQs most often below 50	IQs rarely below 50	
	Siblings usually of normal intelligence	Siblings often at lower levels of intelligence	
	Often accompanied by severe health problems	Health within normal range	
	Appearance often marred by physical stigmata	Normal appearance	
	Mortality rate higher (More likely to die at a younger age than the general population)	Normal mortality rate	
	Often dependent on care of others throughout life	With some support can lead an independent existence as adults	
	Unlikely to marry and often infertile	Likely to marry and produce children of low intelligence	
	Unlikely to experience neglect in their homes	More likely to experience neglect in their homes	
	High prevalence of other physical handicaps (e.g., Epilepsy, cerebral palsy)	Less likely to have other physical handicaps	

am not like those around me at home") than the familial retarded child. Thus, performance differences between the two retarded groups could be attributed in part to sibling configurations which result in quite different life experiences. We see in this possibility once again how motivational factors can influence performance even on tasks assumed to be cognitive in nature. While organic factors may affect such tasks directly, a poor self-image may also deter performance if it leads to a style of problem-solving characterized by learned helplessness (Weisz, 1982).

In our proposed system it would be preferable if inclusion in all classes were based on unequivocal knowledge about etiology. Yet, etiology is often the last aspect discovered about a pathological phenomenon (e.g., Zigler & Phillips, 1961), and classification cannot await such discoveries. Indeed, the greatest single problem in the field of mental retardation is that of the etiology of the majority of the retarded population that I call familial. IQ also cannot determine the classes, since the intelligence distributions of the organic and familial groups overlap to a considerable degree. We cannot know from an IQ score whether a retarded person should be assigned to the organic or familial group. Making such a distinction requires a diagnostician to use additional information such as neurological evaluations and assessments of the intellectual level of parents and siblings.

The difficulties in making assignments are illustrated in the example of a child with an IQ of 60 who has middle-SES parents of normal intelligence and no demonstrable organic signs. The child's retardation can be due either to a neurological impairment not detected by conventional screening procedures or to polygenic factors. The fact that the child's parents do not have IQs in the retarded range does not rule out the possibility that the child's retardation is due to polygenic processes. We must remember that there are relatively few individuals whose IQ scores are two *SDs* below the population mean. Thus, the numbers involved guarantee that the bulk of children having IQs between 50 and 70 will be produced by parents who are not intellectually retarded. On the other hand, even when one of the parents is in fact retarded, only 11 percent of the offspring will be retarded (Lubs & Maes, 1977).

Diagnosticians are actually not as helpless as this argument makes them appear. By using correlates in the figure it should be possible to construct an equation to help determine whether a retarded child labeled "unknown" is more likely to have an undiagnosed organic disorder or has a low IQ due to polygenic factors. The more correlates associated with the familial classification that a child has, the greater the likelihood that the child's intelligence is polygenically determined. A heavily weighted factor in this function is the sibling correlate. If the siblings have either very low (below 50) or relatively high (above 120) IQs, there is a high likelihood that the child's mental retardation is due to an undiagnosed organic defect (Lubs & Maes, 1977). If the child has siblings in the IQ range 50–90, polygenic factors are more probably implicated. The value of noting siblings' IQs can be seen in one estimation that the probability of a marriage with at least one retarded parent producing a retarded child is about 11 percent, but this probability jumps to 40–50 percent if both parents are retarded and have already produced a child with an IQ below 70 (Lubs & Maes, 1977). However, even with the application of our current knowledge concerning the correlates of the familial and organic classes, we still need an undifferentiated category.

Labeling

The two-group approach to the problem of mental retardation is neither new nor radical. Such a dichotomy has been employed either implicitly or explicitly for several decades. This can be seen in various terms that have been used to differentiate retarded individuals. Over the years the nomenclature has grown so large and confusing that the field has become a veritable Tower of Babel. The problem with many of our common terms is that they lack rigorous definition and are therefore confusing. To illustrate, consider the labels "trainable" and "educable." Where exactly does "training" end and "education" begin? In everyday usage, both terms are essentially synonymous. Actually, the trainable/educable distinction is more related to the assumed behavioral potential of the retarded groups. Those considered trainable are taught daily living skills (e.g., personal hygiene) and simple intellectual tasks (e.g., learning to direct attention). Educable individuals are taught more intellectually demanding tasks such as reading and mathematics—tasks which shade into what is taught to children who are slow learners but whose IQs are not in the retarded range. In using these labels we create a confusion between the classificatory principle employed to distinguish individuals and the behavioral correlates of the classes thus established.

When *trainable* is used as the classificatory principle, we have made assumptions about what people can learn and grouped them accordingly. Use of such a system becomes little more than a tautology, with attendant dangers of self-fulfilling prophecy. For example, we classify a person as trainable and then assert that he or she can only learn behaviors A, B, and C. How much any individual can learn is an empirical matter and not an assumptive or definitional one. Indeed, if we begin by defining an individual's limitations, these limitations become real because they may deter workers from searching for alternative methods of teaching or extending the curriculum.

When IQ is used as a classificatory principle, on the other hand, we make fewer assumptions about the individual so classified. What the child is actually capable of learning become the correlates of class membership rather than the basis of classification. Using IQ as a principle of classification, therefore, has the advantage of separating the classificatory principle and empirically discovered correlates of class membership.

The correlates of a sound classification system would involve not only what could be accomplished by individuals at given IQ levels, but also such details as what an individual in this category can learn when exposed to specified teaching methods. This type of study would do much more than expand the horizons of special educators. An assessment of what retarded individuals at different IQ and CA levels are capable of with and without educational programs would inform social policy. First, such catalogs of behavior might spur a change of attitude, inasmuch as recent intervention efforts have shown that retarded persons have much more potential than previously thought (Schroeder, Mulick, & Schroeder, 1979; Whitman & Scibak, 1979). The juxtaposition of catalogs of behavioral capabilities with and without intervention would also make clear just how much can be accomplished if our nation commits itself to available programs. Our society is reluctant to devote resources to human services. Such reluctance is more likely to be overcome if we can present a clear case for the value of such services rather than a continuing plea for more funds because it is the decent thing to do.

In addition to the confusion precipitated by the number of labels in use, some of these terms involve assumptions and predetermine complex issues which cannot be resolved by a simple naming process. Consider the category, *mental retardation due to psychosocial disadvantage.* This term emanates from a simplistic environmental approach to intelligence and makes it appear as if the perpetual nature-nurture debate has been decided in favor of nurture for this group of retarded persons.

While familial retardation is much more likely to affect individuals in the lower SES than those in higher classes, we do not know whether this is due to the impoverished environment or to poorer genetic potential in the lower SES population. Adoption studies suggest that both genetic and environmental factors are at work (Scarr-Salapatek, 1976; Scarr & Weinberg, 1979). Such evidence is less exciting than reports linking intellectual retardation with extremely depriving environments such as in the Appalachian hollows or on English canal boats. However, conditions in the typical working class environment are not nearly abysmal enough to produce marked differences in cognitive competence. Yet once the association between low SES and low IQ is made, it easily leads to the generalization that most members of the lower SES are of low intelligence. Nonetheless, the vast majority of children born into this SES level are not intellectually retarded. Indeed, the polygenic expectation is that more intellectually gifted individuals will come from the lower than from the higher SES group. The proportion of the intellectually gifted may be higher in the higher SES, but the greater size of the lower SES population guarantees that this group will contain a higher absolute number of gifted persons.

Not only lower SES, but a variety of cultural groups are demeaned if we insist on viewing variations in intelligence as the product of variations in upbringing. Children from minority cultures are more likely to be labeled retarded by the schools. At least three explanations for this phenomenon can be advanced. A simplistic environmental interpretation would be that different cultures produce children with different intellectual capacities. The second interpretation is that standard IQ tests are not valid measures of the "real" intelligence of minority-culture children, since these tests are biased in favor of the values and practices of the majority culture (Mercer, 1973). This likelihood probably influenced the AAMD to expand its definition of mental retardation to require a low IQ *plus* a deficit in social competence. A third interpretation is that there is a greater propensity to apply the label retarded to minority than to other children, even though there may be absolutely no difference in their intelligence levels. While Mercer's position is that too many minority children are labeled retarded, this possibility suggests that too few others are so labeled.

It is my position that whatever mental retardation is, it should be conceptualized as a stable characteristic of a person rather than a creation of social agents who apply descriptive terms to children. Labeling theorists argue that retardation is produced by the act of assigning this label to a child. If intellectual subnormality were nothing but such a creation, then the problem of mental retardation could be totally solved by deciding to drop that label. Such a decision would be correct only if: (1) no useful services ever accrued to persons as a consequence of being identified as retarded, and (2) knowledge about the prevention or amelioration of less than adequate functioning were in no way advanced by the use of the mentally retarded category. As I shall discuss below, I believe that such is not the case. We might be better off making the inclusion rules for the classification of mental retardation particularly demanding. The field did something of this sort by shifting the definition from one to two standard deviations below the population mean. Yet such practices do not influence the real occurrence of mental retardation if the condition is conceptualized in terms of actual cognitive functioning.

PREVALENCE OF MILD MENTAL RETARDATION IN THE US AND SWEDEN

These definitional issues became of major concern when scientists at the Kennedy Foundation took note of a report (Grunewald, 1979) that the prevalence of mild mental retardation in the US is seven to fifteen times greater than that reported in Sweden, even though the prevalence for severe retardation in the two countries is comparable. One intriguing hypothesis advanced to explain this difference (Kennedy Foundation, 1981) is that the many social programs mounted in Sweden have resulted in the prevention or amelioration of retardation in a large number of persons who in a different society would become mildly retarded. The nomenclature currently utilized in the mental retardation field makes such a hypothesis a plausible one. If mild mental retardation is in some part due to "psychosocial disadvantage," lower prevalence of mild mental retardation should be found in any society that mounts explicit programs to do away with those conditions that define such disadvantage. Sweden, a social welfare state, certainly appears to fit the definition of such a society. Thus, the possibility that the Swedish society has greatly reduced the prevalence of mild mental retardation must be entertained even by thinkers strongly committed to the view that this type of retardation is caused in large part by genetic elements.

A commitment to the importance of genetic factors does not deny the role of the environment in determining the actual expression of intelligence (i.e., the phenotype). The genes one inherits comprise the genotype for intelligence. The score achieved on an intelligence test reflects the phenotype for intelligence. Whatever an individual's genotype for intelligence might be, the phenotypic expression will be higher if the person experiences a good rather than a bad environment. Central to the argument between environmentalists and hereditarians is the issue of how large this reaction range is. Just as hereditarians view the heritability index for intelligence to be relatively large, environmentalists view the reaction range for the intelligence genotype to be relatively great. Rather conventional genetic thinking supposes that a good environment acting on all genotypes might result in the whole IQ curve being moved to higher levels. It would not take a particularly large increase in IQ phenotypes to produce the lowered prevalence rates for mild mental retardation reported by Grunewald. As Bereiter (1976) notes: "A 14 point gain in mean IQ for the population would reduce the number of people having IQs below 70 by a factor of more than 10" (p. 394).

The Swedish scientists were themselves divided in their interpretation of the Grunewald data. One point of view was that the entire intelligence distribution in Sweden had, in fact, been moved upward, resulting in a lower prevalence of mild mental retardation. Others felt that the prevalence of mild mental retardation in Sweden was the same as that in all industrialized nations, but that in Sweden there is a much larger number of individuals with IQs of 50 to 70 who are never identified. This latter position took on credibility in light of the ethos within which Sweden deals with retarded persons. Whereas Sweden and the US approach severe retardation in much the same way, American practices are more likely to identify mild retardation. America has many psychologists who administer tests both in and out of the schools. Sweden has very few psychologists and as a society has become particularly disenchanted with tests of all sorts, including intelligence tests. In America labels are routinely employed, whereas distinctions between individuals appear to be made only grudgingly in Sweden.

In addition, Sweden is more committed to the principle of normalization than is the US. It is taken for granted that all but the most severely retarded can successfully adapt to schools as children and to the society as adults providing they receive support through an array of social services (Gallagher, 1981; Kennedy Foundation, 1981). Thus, if a child does not do well in school, blame is more likely to be placed on the inadequacy of school services than on the intellectual shortcomings of the child.

The central question remains: For children with IQs of 50 to 70, is it better to label as few as possible "mentally retarded"? To the extent that being so labeled has deleterious consequences for the person, the label should be avoided. Discussion in our nation (Hobbs, 1975; Mercer, 1973) has emphasized the downside risks of labeling. Underemphasized is the fact that labeling may have advantageous consequences, such as worthwhile interventions and social services.

American workers learned quickly on the visit to Sweden about the dangers of not labeling children with low IQs as retarded. One Swedish educator pointed out that when a school child was labeled mentally retarded and placed in the Swedish registry with such a status, he or she immediately began receiving vocational training that would meet criteria for employment in the private section of the Swedish economy. On the other hand, mildly retarded individuals who were never labeled often found themselves un-employable after graduation from school—not unlike American students who receive "social" promotions. However, in Sweden these persons can request the status "mentally retarded" so they can avail themselves of the vocational education that will make employment possible.

The hypothesis that the attenuated prevalence of mild mental retardation was due to a large number of unidentified cases received striking confirmation in a study by Granat and Granat (1973). All nineteen-year-old males are given an intelligence test in Sweden on the occasion of their mandatory induction into the armed forces. Men previously listed in the Swedish registry as mentally retarded (.71 percent of the male population) are excused from military service and are not tested. Of the nineteen-year-old Swedish males never labeled retarded, 1.5 percent scored below the cutoff point for retardation on the IQ test. Adding this figure to that of those previously labeled, the overall prevalence of males in Sweden with IQs below 70 is 2.21 percent, an amount similar to that expected from the normal polygenic curve of intelligence.

In a follow-up study, Granat and Granat (1978) investigated the adjust-ment of nineteen-year-old men with low IQs who had never been labeled mentally retarded. Fifty percent were found to be well adjusted and 50 percent were found to be poorly adjusted. The investigators judged that half of these poorly adjusted individuals (25 percent of the unidentified retarded popula-tion) were likely to be officially labeled as retarded in the future. This study certainly provides some evidence concerning the dangers of not labeling mildly retarded individuals in the school years.

Influenced by the study of Baller, Charles, and Miller (1967), a view has developed that the postschool adult status of mildly retarded persons is not particularly bleak (Willerman, 1979). The extreme expression of this view is contained in the frequently repeated assertion that approximately half of mildly retarded persons blend into society in their postschool years. This assertion is based on the different reported prevalence of mental retardation between school and postschool ages (Gruenberg, 1964). The Granat and Granat (1978) follow-up study should lead us to be less sanguine about the adult adjustment of mildly retarded citizens. While it is reassuring to discover that 50 percent of mildly retarded young adults are well adjusted, it is disturbing that, even in a social welfare state like Sweden, the other half are having adjustment problems. It would not be surprising to discover that in a less supportive society such as the US, an even greater number of individuals in the 50 to 70 IQ range are having difficulty in social adaptation.

RESOLVING THE DEFINITIONAL PROBLEM

A clear and compelling definition of mental retardation would have two major goals: (1) to benefit those so classified in that it will be helpful to their clinicians and service providers, and (2) to bring order to the field, while directing workers to important issues in need of further study. As David Balla and I suggested (Zigler & Balla, 1982), the essence of mental retardation is a cognitive system in which cognitive processes are less effective than those found in an average person in society. A definition of mental retardation based on a measure of intelligence would, therefore, be sufficient.

There are currently two major approaches to the assessment of intelligence: (1) the psychometric approach, which relies on the use of standardized intelligence tests, and (2) the cognitive-developmental approach, based on the work of such theorists as Piaget, Vygotsky, and Bruner. Both approaches attempt to assess the same phenomena, namely, the formal cognitive structure and its information-processing characteristics. Thus, it is not surprising that scores on the two types of assessment are highly correlated. There has been some rapproachment between these two methods in attempts to construct instruments which apply standard psychometric procedures to the scaling of the cognitive processes emphasized by cognitive-developmentalists (see Zigler & Trickett, 1978). Refinement of this promising method of intellectual measurement is many years away, but the need for the definition and classification of mental retardation is pressing. Currently, we have no alternative but to utilize scores obtained on standard measures such as the Binet and Wechsler in the operational definition of mental retardation.

This reliance on IQ test performance runs counter to the current ethos in American psychology where it has become fashionable to bemoan the inadequacies of IQ scores (e.g., McClelland, 1973; Mercer, 1973). The truth is that the IQ is probably the most theoretically and practically important measure devised yet in psychology. The IQ score has more correlates than any other measure (Kohlberg & Zigler, 1967) and has predictive power across a wide array of situations (Mischel, 1968). While it is hardly a perfect measure of intelligence (nothing could be since we do not agree on what intelligence is), it is not all that bad either.

Given the nature of IQ tests, a definition of mental retardation based solely on IQ scores would not be problem-free. In view of the possibility of error in measurement, an individual should be tested at least twice before the label retarded is applied. The additional test(s) might be a cognitive-developmental measure or a different IQ test. If replicated, the IQ score would become the basis for classification. There would be no criterion for mental retardation other than the IQ score itself.

The only remaining issue is where on the IQ-score continuum we should draw the line to separate mentally retarded from nonretarded persons. Here we must keep in mind that such a cutoff is arbitrary. Given current conventions and the history of the field, it would appear best to adopt the two standard deviation cutoff and define as retarded any and all individuals who score below 70 on a standard individual test of intelligence. Most professionals are by now comfortable or at least familiar with this cutoff. A lower cutoff would deny services to mildly retarded persons who are in need of special services. A higher dividing line would create a retarded group with such heterogeneous needs they could not be met by standard educational practices. Thus, the two *SD* cutoff, while totally arbitrary, does appear to have some practical benefits.

The reliance on IQ scores to define mental retardation is in opposition to the definition of the AAMD and to the views of certain prominent workers in the field (e.g., Leland, 1969). The AAMD definition requires that, regardless of IQ, no individual can be labeled retarded unless he or she displays a deficit in adaptive behavior. A quarter of a century of our own work has convinced me that social competence should not be used as a definitional criterion for mental retardation. The construct of social adaptation is itself undefined and simply too vague to have much utility as a classificatory principle (Zigler, 1966; Zigler & Trickett, 1978).

An example should make this clear. Exactly what social expectations must be fulfilled before an individual can be considered socially competent? These expectations change with age and with the fluctuating nature of the social situation. Thus, a child with an IQ of 65 who fails in school would be seen as suffering a deficit in adaptive behavior and labeled retarded. Yet with some added services, perhaps as minimal as an understanding teacher, the child might succeed in school and no longer meet the definition of retardation. The child's cognitive processes would not have changed. All that would have changed is the response of others in his or her social environment. A similar situation can be seen in the case of low-IQ adults assessed against such a commonsense definition of social adaptation as being employed. The man with an IQ of 65 who holds a job is not retarded. Yet if he is laid off the job, on the day his employment terminates, he becomes retarded. Obviously social competence is not an enduring trait, and it leads to a classification system that allows individuals to flit from category to category.

The IQ-plus-social-competence definition of mental retardation also makes it impossible to determine the true prevalence of mental retardation in our society. As Silverstein (1973) pointed out, with the two-factor definition prevalence will be a function of (1) the correlation between the IQ measure and whatever measure of adaptive behavior is employed, and (2) the cutoff scores used on each measure to define mental retardation. Yet Silverstein correctly noted that even with a two *SD* cutoff on both indices, the nationwide prevalence for mental retardation can range from 104,000 to 4,550,000, depending on the correlation of the measures. The field of mental retardation cannot exist with a possible error factor of 45 in our prevalence rates. Excluding errors of measurement, the IQ-only definition of mental retardation produces a stable prevalence of 2.28% of the population. This stable statistic can at least provide a basis for planning the scope of programs and resources required to meet the needs of retarded Americans.

Dropping adaptive behavior from the definition of mental retardation does not imply that the concept is unimportant. On the contrary, the relationship between IQ level and adaptive behaviors in many situations is a crucial area of investigation for the behavioral sciences. What I propose here is that information on adaptation be used as a correlate of class membership rather than to define inclusion in the class. Making the IQ central to the definition of mental retardation is predicated only on our view that the behavioral sciences currently have no better measure to assess intellectual functioning.

In conclusion, then, we have espoused a classification system for mental retardation that has two axes. Along one axis individuals would be ordered on IQ scores. The other axis would consist of the organic, familial, and undifferentiated etiologies. Since there is no accepted theory of intelligence which underlies standard IQ tests, the IQ axis is empirically based. The etiological axis is theoretically derived inasmuch as it stems from a polygenic theory of variations in intelligence. Regardless of whether one espouses the polygenic model, or argues that there is no genetic component to intelligence, most workers have been able to use the three-group distinction in diagnostic practice.

While it is true that the label *retarded* carries some stigma, it is a label that conveys the need for special care or added help. We should not be so concerned with stigmatizing that we lose sight of the genuine needs of retarded individuals. Whatever else labels do, they can convey to laymen the depth and urgency of the assistance required by retarded persons and their families. Some years ago a small movement developed to substitute the term *exceptional* for the term *retarded*. Workers soon learned that Americans who were quite willing to pay for services for "retarded" children were not prone to give money to benefit children labeled "exceptional." We thus see that our classification systems and nomenclature have a forceful impact on the daily lives of individuals of low intelligence.

ADVOCACY

The publication of still another paper concerning mental retardation does not signify the end of our work. On the contrary, it may just be the beginning. I feel strongly that those of us who investigate mental retardation must also be advocates on behalf of those human beings we study. It is up to us to try to translate our research findings into concrete ways to improve the daily lives of retarded citizens. Like the research itself, this has proven to be an exceedingly difficult task. Yet those of us who are serious about advocacy can do no better than to follow the model of Elizabeth Boggs, our nation's truly outstanding advocate for retarded persons. I will quote from something she said some years ago, for her words are even more appropriate today: "This field is not suffering from lack of ideas but from failure to evaluate and assess both the old and the new, a failure to apply the scientific method to decision-making, and an over-optimism that almost anything new would be better than what we have."

Boggs's complaint can perhaps best be seen in the clinical counseling of parents confronted with the problem of whether or not to institutionalize their retarded child. This is one of the most heartrending decisions that any parent is ever called upon to make. I have not been very impressed with how our knowledge has been applied to help parents in making this very difficult decision. I have watched the literature over a good many years and have seen the tendency of workers to rely not on available knowledge about mental retardation but on personal values and contemporary attitudes.

To be more specific, until fairly recently when a family with a retarded child came and said, "We can't tolerate the stress of this," the inclination of many clinicians was to recommend quickly institutionalization of the child. At that time, of course, institutionalization was not considered to be all that bad. What has happened in the last fifteen years or so is that there has been a complete about-face. Our new slogans are normalization and deinstitutionalization; institutions are now seen as dehumanizing; the larger the facility, the more we condemn it. Counselors today rarely recommend institutionalization but instead seek ways to keep a retarded person at home and in the community. This is not to say that clinicians, knowledge gatherers, or even certain social policy makers deliberately impose their values on the families of retarded children. Rather, I think that today's anti-institution fanfare has had an impact on the minds of those to whom parents turn for help.

How then can the clinician or the knowledge gatherer better help parents who are struggling with a very painful decision? First, they should acknowledge that the current state of knowledge about institutionalization is far from conclusive. The most pressing job of the behavioral scientist is thus to discover the facts concerning the effects of institutionalization on retarded persons and to distribute these facts to parents. I believe it is safe to assume that we will find that some settings work best for certain individuals at certain times, while other persons fare better in a quite different milieu. And if this type of knowledge is to do anyone any good, these treatment alternatives must be made available to families of retarded children. By available I mean that the various settings must not only exist, but must also be described to parents. So, if we have to find some social policy principle for this issue, it is that we must be committed to the development of many alternatives, without championing one over another, so that parents can make an informed choice.

Another reason why this work is so important is that factual information concerning the effects of institutionalization is needed to guide the formation of social policy. Our society is currently spending a great deal of money for programs and services for retarded persons, in some cases up to $100,000 per person per year. I am troubled by the fact that we have little sense of how wisely these monies are being spent. Some of our policy decisions appear to have been made on the basis of rhetoric, vague values, and banners that have no empirical base. Much of our public policy is now committed to such concepts as deinstitutionalization and mainstreaming. I join many workers in the field who view these concepts as little more than slogans that are badly in need of support by scientific data. We do not yet know what is the best type of classroom environment for the retarded child nor what is the optimal institutional setting for those children who cannot remain with their families. Yet the nation is already doing away with special education classes and large central institutions and spending vast amounts on establishing alternative practices. We know so little about the effects of these practices that I believe it is legitimate to wonder if they will ultimately be shown to have deleterious consequences. The only antidote we have to moving from fad to fad is careful behavioral research to provide scientific underpinnings for programs designed to benefit mentally retarded persons. Only then can we be sure that our policies are both cost effective as well as humanly effective.

REFERENCES

Achenbach, T., & Zigler, E. (1963). Social competence and self-image disparity in psychiatric and nonpsychiatric patients. *Journal of Abnormal and Social Psychology, 67,* 197–205.

Achenbach, T., & Zigler, E. (1968). Cue-learning and problem-learning strategies in normal and retarded children. *Child Development, 39,* 827–848.

Balla, D., Kossan, N., & Zigler, E. (1980). *Effects of preinstitutional history and institutionalization on the behavior of the retarded.* Unpublished manuscript, Yale University.

Balla, D., McCarthy, E., & Zigler, E. (1971). Some correlates of negative reaction tendencies in institutionalized retarded children. *Journal of Psychology, 79,* 77–84.

Balla, D., Styfco, S. J., & Zigler, E. (1971). Use of the opposition concept and outerdirectedness in intellectually-average, familial retarded, and organically retarded children. *American Journal of Mental Deficiency, 75,* 663–680.

Balla, D., & Zigler, E. (1979). Personality development in retarded individuals. In N. R. Ellis (Ed.), *Handbook of mental deficiency* (2nd ed.). Hillsdale, NJ: Lawrence Erlbaum Associates.

Baller, W. R., Charles, D. C., & Miller, E. L. (1967). Midlife attainment of the mentally retarded: A longitudinal study. *Genetic Psychology Monographs, 75,* 235–329.

Begab, M. J. (1974). The major dilemma of mental retardation: Shall we prevent it? (Some social implications of research in mental retardation.) *American Journal of Mental Deficiency, 78,* 519–529.

Bereiter, C. (1976). Genetics and educability: Educational implications of the Jensen debate. In N. J. Block & G. Dworkin (Eds.), *The IQ controversy*. New York: Pantheon Books.

Bijou, S. W. (1966). A functional analysis of retarded development. In N. R. Ellis (Ed.), *Research in mental retardation* (Vol. 1). New York: Academic Press.

Byck, M. (1968). Cognitive differences among diagnostic groups of retardates. *American Journal of Mental Deficiency, 73*, 97–101.

Caparulo, B. K., & Zigler, E. (in press). The effects of mainstreaming on success expectancy and imitation in mildly retarded children. *Peabody Journal of Education*.

Clarke, A. D. B., & Clarke, A. M. (1977). Prospects for prevention and amelioration of mental retardation: A guest editorial. *American Journal of Mental Deficiency, 81*, 523–533.

Cromwell, R. L. (1963). A social learning approach to mental retardation. In N. R. Ellis (Ed.), *Handbook of mental deficiency*. New York: McGraw-Hill.

Ellis, N. R. (1969). A behavioral research strategy in mental retardation: Defense and critique. *American Journal of Mental Deficiency, 73*, 557–566.

Ellis, N. R., & Cavalier, A. R. (1982). Research perspectives in mental retardation. In E. Zigler & D. Balla (Eds.), *Mental retardation: The developmental-difference controversy*. Hillsdale, NJ: Lawrence Erlbaum Associates.

Gallagher, J. J. (1981). *Cross-cultural views of mild retardation: Sweden and United States*. Unpublished manuscript, University of North Carolina at Chapel Hill.

Gardner, W. I. (1968). Personality characteristics of the mentally retarded: Review and critique. In H. J. Prehm, L. A. Hamerlynck, & J. E. Crosson (Eds.), *Behavioral Research in Mental Retardation* (No. 1). Rehabilitation Research and Training Center in Mental Retardation. Eugene, Oregon: University of Oregon Press.

Goodnow, J. J. (1955). Determinants of choice distribution in two-choice situations. *American Journal of Psychology, 68*, 106–116.

Gordon, D. A., & MacLean, W. E. (1977). Developmental analysis of outerdirectedness in noninstitutionalized EMR children. *American Journal of Mental Deficiency, 81*, 508–511.

Gottesman, I. (1963). Genetic aspects of intelligent behavior. In N. R. Ellis (Ed.), *Handbook of mental deficiency*. New York: McGraw-Hill.

Granat, K., & Granat, S. (1973). Below-average intelligence and mental retardation. *American Journal of Mental Deficiency, 78*, 27–32.

Granat, K., & Granat, S. (1978). Adjustment of intellectually below-average men not identified as mentally retarded. *Scandinavian Journal of Psychology, 19*, 41–51.

Gruen, G., Ottinger, D., & Ollendick, T. (1974). Probability learning in retarded children with differing histories of success and failure in school. *American Journal of Mental Deficiency, 79*, 417–423.

Gruen, G., Ottinger, D., & Zigler, E. (1970). Level of aspiration and the probability learning of middle- and lower-class children. *Developmental Psychology, 3*, 133–142.

Gruen, G., & Zigler, E. (1968). Expectancy of success and the probability learning of middle-class, lower-class, and retarded children. *Journal of Abnormal Psychology, 73*, 343–352.

Gruenberg, E. (1964). Epidemiology. In H. A. Stevens & R. Heber (Eds.), *Mental retardation: A review of research*. Chicago: University of Chicago Press.

Grunewald, K. (1979). Mentally retarded children and young people in Sweden. *Acta Pediatrica Scandinavia Supplement, 275,* 75–84.

Hagberg, B., Hagberg, G., Lewerth, A., & Lindberg, U. (1981). Mild mental retardation in Swedish school children. *Acta Pediatrica Scandinavia, 70,* 1–8.

Harter, S., & Zigler, E. (1968). Effectiveness of adult and peer reinforcement on the performance of institutionalized and noninstitutionalized retardates. *Journal of Abnormal Psychology, 73,* 144–149.

Harter, S., & Zigler, E. (1974). The assessment of effectance motivation in normal and retarded children. *Developmental Psychology, 10,* 169–180.

Heber, R. F. (1964). Personality. In H. A. Stevens & R. Heber (Eds.), *Mental retardation: A review of research.* Chicago: University of Chicago Press.

Hirsch, J. (1963). Behavior genetics and individuality understood. *Science, 142,* 1436–1442.

Hobbs, N. (1975). *The futures of children.* San Francisco: Jossey-Bass.

Jensen, A. (1969). How much can we boost IQ and scholastic achievement? *Harvard Educational Review, 39,* 1–123.

Kamin, L. G. (1974). *The science and politics of IQ.* New York: Halsted Press.

Katz, P., & Zigler, E. (1967). Self-image disparity: A developmental approach. *Journal of Personality and Social Psychology, 5,* 186–195.

Kennedy Foundation. (1981). *Mild mental retardation: A comparative analysis of the US and Sweden.* Unpublished manuscript, Joseph P. Kennedy Foundation.

Kier, R. J., Styfco, S. J., & Zigler, E. (1977). Success expectancies and the probability learning of children of low and middle socio-economic status. *Developmental Psychology, 13,* 444–449.

King, R. D., Raynes, N. V., & Tizard, J. (1971). *Patterns of residential care: Sociological studies in institutions for handicapped children.* London: Routlege & Kegan Paul.

Kohlberg, L., & Zigler, E. (1967). The impact of cognitive maturity on the development of sex-role attitudes in the years four to eight. *Genetic Psychology Monographs, 75,* 89–165.

Kounin, J. (1941). Experimental studies of rigidity: I. The measurement of rigidity in normal and feeble-minded persons. *Character and Personality, 9,* 251–272.

Kugel, R. B. (1967). Familial mental retardation—fact or fancy? In J. Hellmuth (Ed.), *Disadvantaged child.* New York: Brunner/Mazel.

Leland, H. (1969). The relationship between "intelligence" and mental retardation. *American Journal of Mental Deficiency, 73,* 533–535.

Lubs, M.-L. E., & Maes, J. (1977). Recurrence risk in mental retardation. In P. Mittler (Ed.), *Research to practice in mental retardation* (Vol. 3). Baltimore: University Park Press.

Lustman, N. M., Zigler, E., & Balla, D. (1979). *Imitation in institutionalized and noninstitutionalized retarded children and in children of average intellect.* Unpublished manuscript, Yale University.

MacMillan, D. L. (1969). Motivational differences: Cultural-familial retardates vs. normal subjects on expectancy for failure. *American Journal of Mental Deficiency, 74,* 254–258.

MacMillan, D. L., & Keogh, B. K. (1971). Normal and retarded children's expectancy for failure. *Developmental Psychology, 4,* 343–348.

MacMillan, D. L., & Knopf, E. D. (1971). Effect of instructional set on perceptions of event outcomes by EMR and nonretarded children. *American Journal of Mental Deficiency, 76,* 185-189.

MacMillan, D. L., & Wright, D. L. (1974). Outerdirectedness in children of three ages as a function of experimentally induced success and failure. *Journal of Educational Psychology, 68,* 919-925.

McCarver, R. B., & Craig, E. M. (1974). Placement of the retarded in the community: Prognosis and outcome. *International Review of Research in Mental Retardation, 7,* 145-207.

McClelland, D. C. (1973). Testing for competence rather than for intelligence. *American Psychologist, 28,* 1-14.

McCormick, M., Balla, D., & Zigler, E. (1975). Resident care practices in institutions for retarded persons: A cross-institutional, cross-cultural study. *American Journal of Mental Deficiency, 80,* 1-17.

Mercer, J. (1973). *Labeling the mentally retarded.* Berkeley: University of California Press.

Milgram, N. A. (1969). The rational and irrational in Zigler's motivational approach to mental retardation. *American Journal of Mental Deficiency, 73,* 527-532.

Mischel, W. (1968). *Personality and assessment.* New York: John Wiley and Sons, Inc.

Ollendick, T., Balla, D., & Zigler, E. (1971). Expectancy of success and the probability learning of retarded children. *Journal of Abnormal Psychology, 77,* 275-281.

Ollendick, T., & Gruen, G. (1971). Level of n achievement and probability in children. *Developmental Psychology, 4,* 486.

Phillips, D. A., & Zigler, E. (1980). Children's self-image disparity: Effects of age, socioeconomic status, ethnicity, and gender. *Journal of Personality and Social Psychology, 39,* 689-700.

Plenderleith, M. (1956). Discrimination learning and discrimination reversal learning in normal and feebleminded children. *Journal of Genetic Psychology, 88,* 107-112.

Ruble, D. N., & Nakamura, C. (1973). Outer-directedness as a problem-solving approach in relation to developmental level and selected task variables. *Child Development, 44,* 519-528.

Scarr-Salapatek, S. (1976). Unknowns in the IQ equation. In N. J. Block & G. Dworkin (Eds.), *The IQ controversy.* New York: Pantheon Books.

Scarr, S., & Weinberg, R. (1979). Intellectual similarities in adoptive and biologically related families of adolescents. In L. Willerman & R. C. Turner (Eds.), *Readings about individual and group differences.* San Francisco: W. H. Freeman.

Schroeder, S., Mulick, J., & Schroeder, C. (1979). Management of severe behavior problems of the retarded. In N. R. Ellis (Ed.), *Handbook of mental deficiency* (2nd ed.). Hillsdale, NJ: Lawrence Erlbaum Associates.

Shallenberger, P., & Zigler, E. (1961). Rigidity, negative reaction tendencies, and cosatiation effects in normal and feebleminded children. *Journal of Abnormal and Social Psychology, 63,* 20-26.

Shultz, T., & Zigler, E. (1970). Emotional concomitants of visual mastery in infants: The effects of stimulus movement on smiling and vocalizing. *Journal of Experimental Child Psychology, 10,* 390-402.

Silverstein, A. (1973). Note on prevalence. *American Journal of Mental Deficiency, 77,* 380-382.

Spitz, H. (1963). Field theory in mental deficiency. In N. R. Ellis (Ed.), *Handbook* of mental deficiency. New York: McGraw-Hill.

Sternberg, R. (1981a). Cognitive-behavioral approaches to the training of intelligence in the retarded. *Journal of Special Education, 15,* 165–183.

Sternberg, R. (1981b). The nature of intelligence. *New York University Education Quarterly, 12,* 10–17.

Stevenson, H., & Zigler, E. (1957). Discrimination learning and rigidity in normal and feebleminded individuals. *Journal of Personality, 25,* 699–711.

Stevenson, H., & Zigler, E. (1958). Probability learning in children. *Journal of Experimental Psychology, 56,* 185–192.

Thiessen, D. (1972). *Gene organization and behavior.* New York: Random House.

Turnure, J. E. (1970a). Distractibility in the mentally retarded: Negative evidence for an orienting inadequacy. *Exceptional Children, 37,* 181–186.

Turnure, J. E. (1970b). Reactions to physical and social distractors by moderately retarded institutionalized children. *Journal of Special Education, 4,* 283–294.

Weaver, S. J. (1966). *The effects of motivation-hygiene orientation and interpersonal reaction tendencies in intellectually subnormal children.* Ann Arbor, MI: University Microfilms No. 67–3622.

Weaver, S. J., Balla, D., & Zigler, E. (1971). Social approach and avoidance tendencies of institutionalized retarded and noninstitutionalized retarded and normal children. *Journal of Experimental Research in Personality. 5,* 98–110.

Weisz, J. (1982). Learned helplessness and the retarded child. In E. Zigler & D. Balla (Eds.), *Mental retardation: The developmental-difference controversy.* Hillsdale, NJ: Lawrence Erlbaum Associates.

Weisz, J., Yeates, K., & Zigler, E., (1982). Piagetian evidence and the developmental-difference controversy. In E. Zigler & D. Balla (Eds.), *Mental retardation: The developmental-difference controversy.* Hillsdale, NJ: Lawrence Erlbaum Associates.

Werner, H. (1948). *Comparative psychology of mental development* (Rev. ed.). Chicago: Follett.

White, R. W. (1959). Motivation reconsidered: The concept of competence. *Psychological Review, 66,* 297–333.

Whitman, T., & Scibak, J. (1979). Behavior modification research with the severely and profoundly retarded. In N. R. Ellis (Ed.), *Handbook of mental deficiency* (2nd ed.). Hillsdale, NJ: Lawrence Erlbaum Associates.

Willerman, L. (1979). *The psychology of individual and group differences.* San Francisco: W. H. Freeman.

Windle, C. (1962). Prognosis of mental subnormals. *American Journal of Mental Deficiency, 66* (Monograph Supplement 5).

Witkin, H. A., Dyk, R. R., Faterson, H. F., Goodenough, D. R., & Karp, S. A. (1962). *Psychological differentiation: Studies of development.* New York: John Wiley and Sons, Inc.

Wortis, J. (1967). Mental retardation, *Science, 155,* 1442.

Yando, R., & Zigler, E. (1971). Outerdirectedness in the problem-solving of institutionalized and noninstitutionalized normal and retarded children. *Developmental Psychology, 4,* 277–288.

Zeaman, D. (1968). [Review of *International review of research in mental retardation* (Vol. 1.)] *Contemporary Psychology, 13,* 142–143.

Zigler, E. (1958). *The effect of preinstitutional social deprivation on the performance of feebleminded children.* Unpublished doctoral dissertation, University of Texas, Austin.

Zigler, E. (1961). Social deprivation and rigidity in the performance of feebleminded children. *Journal of Abnormal and Social Psychology, 62*, 413–421.

Zigler, E. (1962). Rigidity in the feebleminded. In E. Trapp & P. Himelstein (Eds.), *Readings on the exceptional child*. New York: Appleton-Century-Crofts.

Zigler, E. (1966). Mental retardation: Current issues and approaches. In L. W. Hoffman & M. L. Hoffman (Eds.), *Review of child development research* (Vol. 2). New York: Russell Sage.

Zigler, E. (1967). Familial mental retardation: A continuing dilemma. *Science, 155*, 292–298.

Zigler, E. (1969). Developmental versus difference theories of mental retardation and the problem of motivation. *American Journal of Mental Deficiency, 73*, 536–556.

Zigler, E., & Balla, D. (1972). The developmental course of responsiveness to social reinforcement in normal children and institutionalized retarded children. *Developmental Psychology, 6*, 66–73.

Zigler, E., & Balla, D. (1982). *On the definition and classification of mental retardation*. Unpublished manuscript, Yale University.

Zigler, E., & Balla, D. (1982). Motivational and personality factors in the performance of the retarded. In E. Zigler & D. Balla (Eds.), *Mental retardation: The developmental-difference controversy*. Hillsdale, NJ: Lawrence Erlbaum Associates.

Zigler, E., & Butterfield, E. C. (1968). Motivational aspects of changes in IQ test performance of culturally deprived nursery school children. *Child Development, 39*, 1–14.

Zigler, E., Butterfield, E., & Goff, G. (1966). A measure of preinstitutional social deprivation for institutionalized retardates. *American Journal of Mental Deficiency, 70*, 873–885.

Zigler, E., & Child, I. (1969). Socialization. In G. Lindzey & E. Aronson (Eds.), *The handbook of social psychology* (2nd ed.). Reading, MA: Addison-Wesley.

Zigler, E., & de Labry, J. (1962). Concept-switching in middle-class, lower-class, and retarded children. *Journal of Abnormal and Social Psychology, 65*, 267–273.

Zigler, E., & Harter, S. (1969). Socialization of the mentally retarded. In D. A. Goslin (Ed.), *Handbook of socialization theory and research*. New York: Rand McNally.

Zigler, E., Levine, J., & Gould, L. (1967). Cognitive challenge as a factor in children's humor appreciation. *Journal of Personality and Social Psychology, 6*, 332–336.

Zigler, E., & Phillips, L. (1961). Psychiatric diagnosis: A critique. *Journal of Abnormal and Social Psychology, 63*, 607–618.

Zigler, E., & Seitz, V. (1982). Social policy and intelligence. In R. Sternberg (Ed.), *Handbook of human intelligence*. New York: Cambridge University Press.

Zigler, E., & Trickett, P. (1968). IQ, social competence, and evaluation of early childhood intervention programs. *American Psychologist, 33*, 789–798.

Zigler, E., & Unell, E. (1962). Concept-switching in normal and feebleminded children as a function of reinforcement. *American Journal of Mental Deficiency, 66*, 651–657.

Zigler, E., & Yando, R. (1972). Outerdirectedness and imitative behavior of institutionalized and noninstitutionalized younger and older children. *Child Development, 43*, 413–425.

8

The Evolution of Special Education Concepts

James J. Gallagher

James J. Gallagher, born 1926 in Pittsburgh, earned his B.S. in psychology at the University of Pittsburgh and his M.S. and Ph.D. at Pennsylvania State University in child and clinical psychology.

Dr. Gallagher is director of the Frank Porter Graham Child Development Center and Kenan Professor of Education at the University of North Carolina at Chapel Hill (1970-   ), where he also serves as the director of the Bush Institute for Child and Family Policy, established in 1978. From 1967 to 1970 Dr. Gallagher was associate commissioner of education and the first chief of the Bureau for the Handicapped in the US Office of Education. He was assistant, associate, and full professor of Education at the University of Illinois, where he also worked as associate director of the Institute for Research on Exceptional Children (1954-68). Before that he served as assistant professor and assistant director of the Psychology Clinic at Michigan State University.

A former president of both The Association for the Gifted (1970) and the Council for Exceptional Children (1966), Dr. Gallagher is currently president of the World Council for Gifted and Talented Children, Inc. (1981-85). He has also held the position of chairman of the North Carolina Competency Test Commission (1977-80) and chairman of the Social Policy Committee, Society for Research in Child Development (1977-78). He is an advisor to the National/State Leadership Training Institute on the Gifted and the Talented and to the Research Program of Educational Testing Services.

In 1968 Dr. Gallagher was the recipient of the J. E. Wallace Wallin Award for Contributions to Special Education from the Council for Exceptional Children. He has also received the John Fogarty Award for Government Service (1972), the AAMD Education Award (1976), and the ACLD Learning Disabilities Award (1977).

The opportunity to talk about one's own life and career is irresistable. The problem of making that life interesting or professionally relevant to other people is much more difficult. It seems to me that there is one danger to which the reader should be alerted in this type of retrospective meandering. Historians, biographers, and autobiographers have in common a particular flaw: they are tempted to try to make sense after the fact where no sense exists. In order to create a logical and sensible story, they tend to weave divergent events together, to reinterpret what happened in ways that make a coherent pattern. It is only when we reflect on our own experiences that we realize that, while we can construct a pattern retrospectively, much of what happens to us in life is accidental, a matter of a particular conjunction of events or circumstances that we neither plan for nor necessarily appreciate at the time.

Nevertheless, certain themes have occurred and reoccurred throughout my career, which form a type of developmental progression: 1) children with special needs, 2) children who are gifted, 3) research for new ideas, and 4) public policy actions to bring forth better results to the families of these children. These themes will be identified as they appear and reappear in this manuscript.

EARLY INFLUENCES

After returning from the US Navy at the end of World War II, I faced a career decision. I wanted to go into some type of professional service. Medicine was clearly beyond my financial resources, but the new field of psychology seemed to be bubbling with energy and excitement. I finished my undergraduate work at the University of Pittsburgh in that field. As one example of those accidental events that cast long shadows in one's life, I was working as an assistant to Professor Larry Stolurow on a research project at Pittsburgh. College credits earned in the Navy made me a graduate in January instead of in June, as would be normal. I had nine months, therefore, to spend on some activity before entering graduate school. Larry had a good friend by the name of Milt Cotzin, who was a psychologist at Southbury Training School in Connecticut, and Larry recommended that I spend an internship with him at that institution. My prior knowledge of mental retardation was limited to hearing my mother tell about teaching mentally retarded children, but her ability to draw forth outstanding results from them was sufficient to convince me that I would be interested in such a setting. So I took off for Southbury, knowing little about institutions and less about the people I was to meet.

Children with Special Needs

It is sufficient to say that Southbury Training School changed my personal and professional lives in permanent ways. First of all, I met my future wife, who was a teacher there in the school program for young mentally retarded children. I also gained enough experience and interest in children with mental retardation to keep this an interest for the rest of my life. While I was at Southbury, Milt Cotzin introduced me to the joys of research and writing. We did a rather insignificant piece of research on short forms of the Wechsler Intelligence Scale that was nevertheless published, and I was exhilarated by the sight of my name in print and the thought that I was adding something, no matter how insignificant, to the sum of mankind's knowledge on the topic. Another major advantage of that experience was meeting Seymour Sarason, a consultant from Yale at Southbury Training School, who played a major role in convincing me that Pennsylvania State University would be a good place for a young psychologist interested in children and clinical work to take graduate training.

Research

Two disciplines to which I was introduced at Penn State had a great influence on me: 1) experimental design and learning theory, particularly the work of Clark Hull (1943), Kenneth Spence (1956), and others; and 2) the nondirective psychotherapy of Carl Rogers (1951), which was taught by William Snyder and presented quite a counterbalance to the laboratory-oriented sciences represented by learning theory professors like Bill Lepley and Joe Grosslight. The useful part of my graduate experience, apart from the actual knowledge and skills I gained, was the realization that learning theory and nondirective therapy did not fit together very well in describing human behavior. Each approach touched on a rather selective set of phenomena and convinced me that, while the ultimate answer may include each of these approaches, it certainly is not encompassed by either of them. It was at Penn State that I first discovered the work of Abraham Maslow, a humanistic scientist who combined the characteristics of the two areas, clinical psychology and learning theory, in a way more satisfying to me than any other that I had encountered until that time (Maslow, 1966). One additional experience at Penn State valuable to my future was taking a minor in "speech correction," as it was called then. This introduced me to the special problems of the cleft-palate child, the child who stutters, etc., and my familiarity with such problems probably contributed to my willingness to try the job of chief of the Bureau of Education for the Handicapped later on.

Children with Special Needs

I left Penn State with my doctorate under my arm, and spent about a year at the Hospital for Disturbed Children at Dayton, Ohio, working in a residential treatment center for emotionally disturbed children. It was there I had my first experience with autistic children. I was responsible for play therapy with a strange child who talked to trees in an incomprehensible language. He taught me that a Ph.D. was no substitute for wisdom or experience, a lesson I have learned many times since. We also had more severely disturbed youngsters than I had seen in a college guidance clinic, and I became a student of the more experienced psychiatrists there. It was at Dayton also that I had my first taste of how difficult and how valuable truly multidisciplinary interaction is, with social workers, psychiatrists, educators, and psychologists forming a treatment team to work with these children and their families on both a residential and an outpatient basis.

ILLINOIS

Children with Special Needs

When the opportunity came, however, to return to academic work, it was clear to me that this was what I really wanted and missed in this total treatment setting. I accepted an offer to join the staff in the Department of Psychology at Michigan State University that allowed me to teach and to work in the Psychology Clinic. My work in the clinic there added to my own range of experience in remedial work with children, but another of those accidents occurred that was to send my career in a very different direction. A professor from the University of Illinois was looking for a team of people to do some testing for a research project on mentally retarded children that he was working on in Michigan at that time. The name of that professor was Sam Kirk. We made contact and developed a friendship and mutual respect; he invited me to join him at the Institute for Research on Exceptional Children at the University of Illinois. This began my involvement with gifted and brain-injured children.

At one time, when I was a young professor at the University of Illinois, many special educators around the country would identify me as one of Sam Kirk's students. I used to be mildly irritated by such identification, saying, somewhat testily, that I had a perfectly appropriate professional education at Penn State and had had three years of experience beyond that, so I was hardly a student of Kirk's. In the larger sense, of course, anyone who has spent any time with Sam Kirk becomes one of his students, regardless of previous background. He is one of the truly strong pioneer leaders in the field of special education, and he taught me a great deal during the thirteen years I was at the University of Illinois.

Three major lessons that Sam Kirk taught profited me very substantially in my future experience. First, that it is possible to conduct a large research organization and still maintain the role of scholar and scientist. His directorship of the Institute for Research on Exceptional Children was something that I observed for thirteen years and really gave me the courage to try a similar role at the Frank Porter Graham Child Development Center at the University of North Carolina at Chapel Hill, where I still am.

The second major lesson he taught me was that it is possible to participate in political life and still maintain one's professional integrity and respect. His earlier willingness to head the Division of Exceptional Children in the US Office of Education in the early 1960s laid the groundwork for what eventually became the Bureau of Education for the Handicapped in the US Office of Education. He did that task with skill and without the loss of his own standards. This, in turn, encouraged me later to take the job of the chief of Bureau of Education for the Handicapped when it was formed, even though my own preferences were clearly not in that direction, but more with the academic life.

Finally, he taught me an important lesson about social policy—that it is necessary to have a clear sense of your goals and a determined persistence in pursuing them if you want a chance to succeed. His interest in the consequences of his research upon the larger society was something that also extended my understanding and interest in public policy.

The Institute for Research on Exceptional Children was remarkable for the variety of people who were brought together in that organization. There were people such as Bernie Farber, a sociologist who was interested in the family and made me regret my limited knowledge in that particular field; he convinced me of the value of thinking in sociological terms. Ernie Newland, official curmudgeon and master poker player, introduced me to the work of J. P. Guilford and encouraged me in my special interest in gifted children. A wide variety of people passed by during these years—Carl Bereiter, Oliver Kolstoe, Herb Goldstein, Len Blackman, Larry Stolurow (again!), and a raft of fine students, who all made their own contributions to the program. Every organization needs its official humorist, and Herb Goldstein filled that role with great distinction. A true wit and serious thinker, he created a climate of goodwill during his tenure there. There were also such permanent fixtures as Laura Jordan and Bob Henderson, who took on the important responsibility for the graduate training program. All of these people created an exciting mix of ideas that convinced me that blending together a combination of skills and backgrounds is likely to be a better strategy for understanding problems than sticking to a group of professionals who all come from the same discipline.

While at the Institute for Research on Exceptional Children at the University of Illinois, I followed two lines of research which have influenced my career ever since. The first was a project on the tutoring of brain-injured, mentally retarded children. For this project, we were able to gain the cooperation of one of the major state institutions for the mentally retarded in Illinois, Dixon State School. We hired a staff of tutors, directed by Paul Benoit, and followed a randomized experimental-control research design which evaluated the four-year tutorial program and demonstrated that tutoring could produce modest improvements in the developmental characteristics of eight- to twelve-year-old retarded youngsters within an institutional setting.

As in many research projects, what we learned on the side was more important than the basic results of the study itself. We embarked upon the project with a number of prior assumptions regarding brain-injured children that stemmed primarily from the work of Strauss (1955; 1947) and Cruick-shank (1961). These scholars had stressed a pattern of visual perception difficulties, hyperactivity, and distractibility in brain-injured youngsters; we were prepared to eliminate totally distracting stimuli, going so far as to paper over the windows and to remove all materials from sight except those that the tutor was using with the children. We soon found that such stimulus deprivation was not a necessary or desirable thing, as long as there was an adult in a tutorial one-on-one situation with the child. Furthermore, we found that visual perception was not really the fundamental problem for most of these youngsters, although some of them did show what is now referred to as the *Strauss syndrome,* a combination of visual perception problems, conceptual lability, and hyperactivity. The vast majority of these youngsters had basic problems in maintaining attention, plus a variety of behavior disabilities when compared with a similar group of familial (lacking obvious pathology) children (Gallagher, 1957).

Since that time, I have looked through the literature on brain-injured learning disabled children and have concluded that in many cases the ability to maintain attention rather than a specific visual perceptual problem is the key and that, therefore, extensive remedial exercises in visual perception are not needed. Furthermore, when such exercises work and the children improve, part of the improvement may come because the exercises force the youngsters to focus their *attention* on a particular stimulus. Another surprising finding was that one of the youngsters improved dramatically with IQ gains of over 20 points, well beyond the improvement of the others. When we reviewed this youngster's folder to see how his tutoring had gone, we were unable to detect any major reason why he should achieve more than the others.

However, we found out by discussions with the institution staff that this youngster had been taken off one of the large wards within the institution and been made a runner in one of the administrative departments. In this process he took messages back and forth to various staff members and was able to converse with them, vastly improving his opportunities for language practice in ways that had nothing whatsoever to do with the experimental treatment itself. It reminded us, if we needed any reminding, that there are many other dimensions influencing the behavior of children besides what we, as teachers, specifically try to do with them, and that sometimes these outside influences are even more powerful and more pertinent than the direct instruction that we try to provide (Gallagher, 1960).

Gifted Children

The second major project that I undertook at Illinois was the study of extremely gifted children (Binet IQs of 150 and over) and their adjustment within the regular classroom. During this period, it was of great instructive value to me to sit in on two or three case conferences on extremely gifted children in the morning and then fly in a university plane to Dixon State School in the afternoon to deal with the problems of brain-injured, mentally retarded children. If one wishes to see a full range of human diversity in cognitive performance, one could hardly do better than to have the experience I had. Most professionals and lay persons, in my judgment, do not have a full understanding of the extraordinary diversity of human potential within a given age range and thus are unable to deal with the educational issues and problems that such diversity creates.

Our first study of gifted children was an attempt to find out if the elementary school program could, once they found a youngster of extraordinary advanced development, adapt by changing the program or bringing additional resources to bear for the youngster. In pursuit of an answer, we did fifty-four case studies of children, all of whom scored over 150 on the Stanford Binet Intelligence Test (Gallagher, Greenman, Karnes, & King, 1960). This extraordinary number of gifted youngsters of elementary school age in Champaign and Urbana was undoubtedly a result of the presence of the University of Illinois since many (but not all) of the youngsters were sons and daughters of university professors.

The first message from that investigation, which I have never had any reason to doubt since, is that the schools, as they were and are structured, have relatively little chance of adapting to children of extraordinary ability. Many of these youngsters were performing three or four grades above their age level, were following extraordinary interests or hobbies of their own, and seemed to have little interest in school or felt that school could provide them with very little. Although we were able to make some meaningful difference in a handful of cases, most of the adjustments, such as providing the teacher with extra materials or bringing a psychologist in to provide additional counseling, did not seem to change dramatically the problems or the pattern of performance of the youngster. It was out of this experience that I concluded that something a good deal more special was needed in order to provide an appropriate education for gifted children.

Research: Sabbatical at Stanford

Most major universities provide a sabbatical leave after six or seven years of service, which allows professors to take a year off, travel, and refresh their intellects. While at the University of Illinois, I chose to take my sabbatical year at Stanford University to study mathematical models and statistics as a means of strengthening my research skills. I was fortunate enough to get a desk in Owen House, a research haven overseen by Bob and Pat Sears, who had collected together a distinguished group of social scientists and students; it provided a hospitable, warm, and stimulating setting for my experiences there.

My introduction to mathematical models, as taught by Pat Suppes, and the more standard statistical work done by Quinn McNemar left me impressed but not convinced. It seemed as though the mathematical models, as complicated as they were, were much too simple to capture the complex human behaviors that we were trying to describe in our classroom interaction research at Illinois. The statistical techniques, such as analysis of variance and covariance, were based upon earlier agricultural models and did not fit complex human behavior very well. The most useful conclusion I drew at that time was not to trust too much or accept at face value even the more sophisticated mathematical or statistical evidence without examining carefully its relevance to the phenomena being observed! The more one learns about the limitations of these tools (for that is all they are), the more realistic one can be in using them.

A second, and no less important, reason for going to California was to seek aid for one of our sons who had had severe bouts of asthma in Illinois. We were hoping that the California climate and California physicians could be of assistance. This was a much less successful part of the trip since our son became even more ill during that year.

Public Policy

At this time, I became interested in the development of a program to support the education of gifted children in the state of Illinois and became associated with two fine and competent persons responsible for the emergence of that program: Dave Jackson, then principal of University High School at the University of Illinois, agreed to take on the responsibility of state coordinator for the program and was highly instrumental in both designing and implementing the program, which still exists as a model in the country; Bill Rogge was an extraordinarily effective teacher/educator who designed and carried out inservice and special leadership training programs for would-be administrators of gifted programs. These training programs produced a cadre of competent and highly motivated administrators who provided the base of professional support for these programs in local school systems; they were the necessary complement to the political support obtained through the state education department and through outside forces drawn together by Dave Jackson. This state program provided demonstration centers for exemplary programs, reimbursement for each school district for special help, resources for training, and small amounts of money for research and for state consultants. My own role was to provide some scholarly backup to the educators on the firing line through reviews of what was known in the field and through research of my own in classroom analysis.

This peculiar combination of interests and talents seemed to work sufficiently to make Illinois one of the first states to provide a comprehensive program for gifted students, aided in no small measure by the Sputnik scare which gave a strong impetus to gifted education in the late 1950s and early 1960s.

Research:
My two earlier experiences in gifted education led me to embark on an eight-year adventure divising systems for analyzing classroom interaction for gifted students. I became convinced at the time that the answer to many of our questions lay in careful observation and analysis of what was actually happening in the classroom, particularly the cognitive interchanges between teacher and pupil. With this conviction and the support of grants from the US Office of Education, I began the attempt to put together an analytic system based upon the model of J. P. Guilford's *Structure of Intellect* (1967) that would enable a team of people to analyze what was happening in the classroom through a statement-by-statement study of student and teacher cognitive performance (Gallagher, Aschner, & Jenne, 1967). In the process of this study, we tape-recorded well over one hundred classroom sessions of an hour or more each, transcribing them at great pain to secretaries who used a primitive recording system to try to hear what the students and the teacher were saying. These tape scripts were then analyzed statement-by-statement; out of this a series of publications and monographs emerged which provided, in addition, the basis for much of what I was to say in a well-received book, *Teaching the Gifted Child* (Gallagher, 1975).

Many conclusions were drawn out of this complex research program. One of the major conclusions, which may seem trite now but was not at the time, was that the intellectual level of the discussion in the classroom and the particular style of thinking that is accepted depends almost entirely on the teacher. Teachers can, by the way in which they ask questions, modify and change the tone and level of the thinking processes of the students in the classroom. Such a finding led to a number of inservice training programs for teachers that focused on the way in which their questions could modify thinking operations of children (Gallagher, Nuthall, & Rosenshine, 1970).

A second major finding coming out of a special study done for the Biological Sciences Curriculum Study was that despite common training, common student level of performance, similar curriculum materials, and their teaching the same concepts, teachers still differed markedly from one another in their presentation of content and their style. The clear conclusion is that no curriculum package is "teacher-proof," and that how the material is presented will depend upon the personality and background of the particular teacher involved. Thus, one cannot settle the matter of educational reform by providing a competent set of curriculum materials, since these will always be filtered through the interests and preferences of individual instructors (Gallagher, 1967).

Another conclusion drawn from this research was that the link between divergent thinking and creative thinking, which was once considered to be quite strong, is a gross oversimplification. Creativity is more likely to be a product of a personality style than a particular set of cognitive skills. To be creative, one has to use all of the major dimensions of the Guilford system—memory, convergent thinking, divergent thinking, and evaluative thinking. Divergent thinking in the Guilford mode is useful in loosening the intellectual bonds that many students feel constrain them in the classroom and gives them the freedom to draw on all of their capabilities. But divergent thinking, in the absence of memory, evaluation, or convergent thinking, does not produce everything needed in the complex creative process.

One of my most significant experiences came through contact with various scientists at the University of Illinois who were engaged in the major curriculum reform movement of the 1960s. This curriculum reform movement, supported in large measure by the National Science Foundation, had its origin in the National Defense Education Act and similar legislation which revealed our nation's interest, if not panic, in regard to the Russian space initiative of the late 1950s. There was deep concern expressed throughout the country about the state of secondary education, particularly of talented students in the areas of science and mathematics.

The University of Illinois was one of the major centers of curriculum reform at that time. Major efforts toward curriculum changes at the secondary and elementary school level were being stimulated in almost every content field. The area of mathematics was represented by Max Beberman, who began the University of Illinois Committee on School Mathematics (UICSM) curriculum program in the 1960s. However, social studies, physical science, and elementary school science reforms were well represented by staff members at the university such as Mike Atkin and Ella Leppert. In addition, I became intrigued with the importance of the organization of the content in a curriculum. This was particularly true in gifted education. While many educators of gifted children had focused a strong effort on techniques for the stimulation of productive thinking and creative thinking, it became obvious to me through my contacts with the experts in content development that creativity means little without sophisticated content ideas and principles. Effective education of gifted students does depend upon a healthy marriage between the content fields (Bruner, 1960) and the effective use of thinking processes as represented by Bloom and Guilford (Guilford, 1972).

It also became clear to me that those people in the field of education of the gifted were extremely interested in the processes of thinking, in part, because that is what they knew best. Education is a process-oriented activity, and educators are extraordinarily interested in and intrigued by that process. It is only natural that the processes of thinking would become a major concern to many people whose primary field was education. However, content field specialists need to be included in any comprehensive program for gifted students. It was my contact with University High School, where many of these curriculum movements were being put into action, that allowed me to see the importance of the blend of content and process.

THE LESSONS OF WASHINGTON:
PUBLIC POLICY

One of the turning points of my career came with a telephone call from Washington while I was on leave from the University of Illinois at Duke University for one year in 1966. That telephone call suggested that I should be a candidate for the directorship of the Bureau of Education for the Handicapped that had just been established in the US Office of Education through congressional legislation. I was shortly to receive a series of other telephone calls from friends around the country, in a rather carefully orchestrated effort to convince me that this should be my job for the next few years of my life. I probably refused a total of six or seven times before accepting. The notion of going from a secure academic position to the unknown world of politics in Washington was not one that was inherently attractive to me.

However, the strong entreaties of my friends had a great influence on me. The key experience leading me to accept this job was probably a luncheon meeting in Washington, in which I was lobbied by six or seven people, some representing professional associations and others who were key congressional staff; all assured me that I would receive the strongest kind of support from Congress and from other sources to help me get the job done. Since these people represented powerful congressmen and senators from both the Democratic and Republican sides of the aisle, the offers of support seemed impressive to me. Combined with that congressional support was the presence within President Lyndon Johnson's administration of two people for whom I had the greatest respect. One was the commissioner of education, Harold "Doc" Howe, who was to be my immediate superior, and the other, Secretary of the Department of Health, Education, and Welfare John Gardner. I have always believed Gardner to be one of the most thoughtful and dedicated persons on the broad educational scene in the United States. This support convinced me that this job might be a worthwhile diversion from my academic career.

Later, I found out from someone whose job it was to recruit talent into the federal government that they often tell a job candidate he or she is the only person in the country who can do the particular job; such a statement is usually well received by the listener, who secretly believes it is true. At any rate, this argument certainly had an influence on me—for reasons the reader may guess.

Washington was a source of tremendous new information about the status of exceptional children in the world of politics. I became aware of three or four important concepts, each of which was to influence my future directions. The first was the extraordinary gap between the knowledge of the academic world and the world of political influence and power. I found little mutual understanding, and this began my current major interest in policy analysis, as one way of bringing the academic and political world closer together.

A second area of major discovery was the importance of the parents' movement in influencing legislation for the handicapped. Congress has long experience with various professional groups trying to influence legislation for their own interests. They tend to discount much of what the professional person has to say as being manifest self-interest. However, the parents' movement, which aroused private citizens to public action, was extraordinarily impressive to politicians who heard the voice of the people speaking when the parents requested, and at times demanded, more services for their handicapped children. It is unlikely that special education would have obtained nearly the resources it did, if it had not been for the strong continued efforts of individual parents of influence, and the collective influence of the parents' movement itself.

A third area of major interest in Washington was the early effort to develop the concept of program planning and budgeting. It became clear to many in the federal government that merely stumbling from one year to the next through the incremental budget process ("give me all I had last year and then some more"), with no relationship between programs, was a disastrous approach; something new was needed to systematize the budget process. The device that was utilized at that time emerged from the Department of Defense with Robert McNamara and his band of young intellectuals, who brought some order out of chaos in that department by insisting that each military service devise careful plans, statements of clear objectives, and cost figures to accompany those goals. These concepts were brought over into the Department of Health, Education, and Welfare and introduced to me, for the first time, in the area of planning. Fortunately, we adopted these ideas enthusiastically in the Bureau of Education for the Handicapped. It was this commitment to the planning process that gained the bureau the respect of the key managers in the Office of Education and reduced, in large measure, the inherent hostility of the office to the special education programs. The hostility to special education that was manifest when I entered the office had little to do with the basic nature of special education itself, but arose from the unusual act of Congress establishing a unit, the Bureau of Education for the Handicapped, within the executive branch of government. This was a most unusual move, and one that was deeply resented by many of the old line managers in the Department of Health, Education, and Welfare, who thought Congress was meddling in their business.

One of the significant elements in my first few weeks on the Washington scene was my introduction to a special educator by the name of Ed Martin, who had spent the last year or so as a staff member to the committee chaired by Congressman Hugh Carey. Carey, who had conducted a series of extremely important hearings on the education of handicapped children, continued his interest in handicapped children and eventually went on to be governor of New York. Ed Martin, with the congressional hearings over, was looking for a continuing position in Washington and agreed to become deputy bureau chief to the Bureau of Education for the Handicapped. His professional expertise and political knowledge gained over the months he had been working with the Congress allowed us to work as an effective team dealing with a range of issues that encompassed relationships with the professional fields, with Congress, with the administration, and with a variety of advocates, each of whom was convinced that their solutions to our problems were the only ones of importance.

In addition to fine leaders within the bureau like Ed Martin, Mike Marge, Jim Moss, Frank Withrow, and Len Lucito, we had the special advantage of an expanding budget which allowed us to provide more resources each year to people in the field of the handicapped. Many of the inevitable objections or concerns regarding individual policy decisions at the federal level were muted, to a large degree, by the fact that almost everyone in the local and state programs was getting more resources than he or she had the year before. In addition, we held seven public hearings around the country in which key leadership people were allowed to have their say about the directions in which they thought programs for the handicapped should go, what the major policy issues were, and how they should be solved. We paid very careful attention to the suggestions generated from the seven meetings, and they formed the fabric and framework of our policy over the next two to three years.

Our ability to respond positively to these suggestions from special educators in the field was in no small measure responsible for their enthusiastic support of our policies. We reaffirmed the basic lesson of government that if you wish to implement policy, you must give the people responsible for carrying out the implementation a fundamental say in what should be done and how it should be done. We became all too aware of how far Washington was, both geographically and symbolically, from the people who would have to execute the federal policies, and it was our willingness to listen and to try to shape our policies to meet the expressed needs of those on the firing line that helped keep our program in good favor, though we were, of course, aided by a continually expanding budget.

My final major lesson in Washington was a painful one. It is what happens when you possess political power and the power is withdrawn. When President Nixon came into office, his attitude toward education, while not directly positive, did not seem antagonistic either. He appointed as commissioner of education an experienced state commissioner, James Allen from the state of New York, who reorganized the Office of Education to become both commissioner and assistant secretary of education. He asked me to become deputy assistant secretary for planning, research, and evaluation. It was not something I had wished for myself, and I much preferred to stay as the bureau chief in charge of programs for the handicapped. However, when pressure was brought to bear, it became clear that I would either have to take the new job or leave. Mike Marge agreed to come with me as my deputy in the new job, and our next few months were filled with frustration and disappointment.

Allen revealed in the public press that he was really a Democrat (to the surprise of the Republican administration) and that he was dramatically and publicly opposed to the Cambodia campaign just undertaken by the administration. This outraged many of the key staff in the White House, who considered Allen disloyal, and the spigot was shut off for education in a number of areas.

Jim Allen refused to notice that he was being ignored. He was a moral man, and he had taken a moral stand. He ignored the hints and outright suggestions from the White House that he leave. After a few months of total frustration, I decided that my usefulness in the US Office of Education was at an end. Allen was summarily fired a month or so after I had officially resigned. But I left Washington with great respect for a large majority of the people who worked there—both legislators and executive office personnel. The top echelon of people that I met were both brighter and harder working than most of the people I knew in university work. For my own part, I have never worked as hard before or since. (My wife has commented that it was good that our marriage was reasonably stable going into Washington, or it would never have survived the pressures and tensions). The myth that people sit around in Washington and drink coffee and read newspapers at the office could not be less true. What is true is that they spend twelve to fourteen hours per day trying to make a complicated system of government, primarily designed to prevent things from happening, operate in some effective fashion.

It is very difficult to get a new law passed in Congress because there are so many barriers to its survival. There is such a dispersion of power (deliberately designed by our founding fathers) that it is hard to accomplish specific goals or, once having accomplished them, to implement them in a systematic fashion. We need to come to grips in this country with whether we wish the government to be effective in what it is supposed to do, or whether we are, in fact, happier with a federal government that is bumbling and ineffectual, even though we complain about it.

There is no denying that Washington was a town filled with a multitude of attractions. It is intoxicating to be invited to attend White House functions and to find oneself shaking hands with the president of the United States during bill-signing ceremonies. During the time I was in Washington, I also represented the US Office of Education at meetings in England and Italy, and thus had opportunities to interact with many others in the field of education and in general politics whom a college professor would not normally see. Nevertheless, Washington was filled with its own anxieties. Someone once remarked that the best definition of politics is "the art of allocating scarce resources." That is as appropriate a statement as any. Since resources are scarce and there are many people in pursuit of them, the struggle sometimes gets fierce. You find yourself fighting your own colleagues for the maximum of the budget in your own particular area. It is hard to form firm friendships with colleagues whom you suspect are after your budget, just as they look owlishly at you, obviously thinking the same thing.

Perhaps the set of experiences that produced the most anxiety was testimony before the Congressional Appropriations Committee. One of my responsibilities was to defend our budget request for programs for handi-capped children. As one veteran of the Washington wars once told me, "You have two possible outcomes from testifying before the Appropriations Committee, you can tie or you can lose." You never get any more money than you are requesting (winning), but if you do not adequately defend your budget request, you may get a good deal less. The realization that the resources of the special education community and exceptional children across the country depended, in some degree, upon the adequacy with which I, or later Ed Martin, defended the budget was enough to raise my anxiety level. The chairman of the House Appropriations Committee at that time was Congress-man Daniel Flood from Pennsylvania, a theatrical and dramatic chairman, complete with waxed mustache, flowing cape, and a fearsome reputation for hard questioning. He destroyed the career of more than one bureaucrat with his questioning. The Appropriations Committee members were not well-known and rarely got into print. They didn't have to! They were the ones who held power, that is, until a new budget committee procedure was adopted by the Congress. While other representatives and senators were out making speeches and giving newspaper interviews, the Appropriations Committee members were sitting quietly in a secluded room doing the bread-and-butter work of politics.

Of course, there is a tendency to overestimate what one experience or one contribution can do in the total complex of events. The budget hearings were only one piece of a whole mosaic, and probably not that critical to it. It is easy to be philosophical at a distance of fourteen years, but the dread of those moments when we entered the hearing room are not hard to recapture, even after all that time. The active professional and parent groups fighting hard for resources for handicapped children created a favorable environment, which made the bureau chief's job easier in the appropriations process. Nevertheless, the questions were difficult, and I was fortunate enough to be supported by a fine team of Martin, Lucito, Withrow, Moss, and Marge.

I also came to regard with great respect the work of the congressional staff members who provided their busy bosses with useful information and who also conveyed their basic position on issues to people in the executive branch. Their work goes largely unnoticed, and their satisfaction lies mainly in the role they play in making the government work and in sometimes getting legislation passed and programs supported. The basic message for special educators, or for any group hoping to catch some of these scarce resources, is that virtue is clearly not enough. One must have broad and vocal public support to gain the necessary leverage for success.

Perhaps the greatest danger to the activist movement in the field of special education has been an outbreak of "success." Success tends to weaken the resolve of people who feel that their goals have been attained. In addition, those who have been successful in obtaining resources face the temptation of fighting with each other over them. There is no greater mistake than to think that the battle once won is always won. We now see the first indications of court decisions being made against handicapped children and adults; questions are being raised regarding the appropriate level of support of programs for handicapped. I am convinced that these questions, while legitimate, emerge out of the growing silence of former activists who no longer think it is necessary to be vigorous or strident in the cause. Such an attitude in the long run, and perhaps even in the short run, can only lead to a transfer of those scarce resources to other groups whose needs are better and more vigorously articulated.

NORTH CAROLINA

Children with Special Needs

When I left Washington, my wife and I thought about where we would like to spend the rest of our lives and, weighing all considerations, decided upon North Carolina where there was a directorship of a research center on early childhood established by Hal Robinson. He and his wife, Nancy, with others, had the idea of testing the impact of early stimulation of young children, but they subsequently left North Carolina to accept positions at the University of Washington.

The early development of a staff and a program for the Frank Porter Graham Child Development Center was difficult because research in educational domains was not well supported at that time. (Not much has changed!) However, a program of research, development, and technical assistance gradually emerged, thanks to competent professionals like Dave Lillie, Craig Ramey, and Don Stedman, with Frank Loda and Al Collier providing leadership in the medical research program.

In the early 1970s, it was well-accepted that early childhood was a key force in the long-range development of the individual. That concept probably had its most extreme interpretation in the recent proposal of Klaus and Kennell (1970), which proposed that there exists a type of imprinting or bonding between the mother and child occurring early in infancy that is crucial and determined later affective relationships. There has been a reaction against such an extreme point of view, but few believe today that early childhood is not an important area, even if it can be modified by future experience.

Two opposing views existed side-by-side in the 1960s and 1970s. One is the significant determining force of genetics; the second is the importance of the environment and the ecology in which the individual operates in determining his or her behavior. Obviously, both of these cannot be totally correct. The likelihood is that each is partially correct in some fashion. Experiences in early childhood, no doubt, create many response patterns and attitudes that influence, if not determine, the child's later behavior. On the other hand, it is clear that modifying the environment can change the development of the child at later as well as earlier ages.

Public Policy

The area of public policy, which was stirred by my Washington experience, came back in a number of dimensions in North Carolina. First, the governor asked me to be chairman of the Competency Test Commission for the state of North Carolina. This was an offer that one does not refuse if one wishes to stay involved in public policy issues, and so began three years of turmoil and controversy. The commission decided early that we would stick with the measurement of basic skills in reading and mathematics and ran a trial test on all eleventh graders in North Carolina. The public's attention was captured by the fact that by any reasonable standard 30 to 40 percent of the eleventh-grade students would have failed and been refused a high school diploma. Thus began a great public interest and outcry about the tests themselves: Were they valid? Were they culturally biased? Were they unfair? Was this an attempt to blame the student for the failures of the educational system? Vigorous opposition came from some minority groups who felt that their students would be punished unfairly, from some handicapped parents who wondered what was going to happen to their children, and from an educational establishment that has never been very enthusiastic about revealing the products of their efforts to the public.

However, overwhelming public support for this program substantially drowned out the cries of the opposition. We went through elaborate efforts to cleanse the tests through a series of statistical procedures designed to eliminate cultural bias. Numerous adaptations of the tests were made for handicapped (e.g., it was translated into Braille). My own conviction that the competency testing could be an appropriate and useful tool for education was based on several factors, not the least of which was the governor's commitment to provide remediation money so that local school systems could hire additional personnel to help the youngsters who did not pass the test the first time.

Second, I remembered from my experience with handicapped children and young adults that we consistently underestimated their capabilities and potential and they have proven to us over and over that they can do a great deal more than we assume. This enabled me to brush aside the arguments that youngsters, once having failed the test, would either drop out or would not be able to pass the test again. As it turned out, of those youngsters who failed the competency test the first time, 50 percent passed it the next time, and there is only 2 to 3 percent failure rate at the time of graduation from high school. On the positive side, the competency testing has rekindled an interest in academic performance and has, by all accounts, reduced behavior and discipline problems within the schools dramatically. The program has now been in effect three years (1979–1982) and has become a routine part of the school administration, with the percentage of failures slowly dropping every year. It taught me once again that we can and should demand more of students and also that the educational establishment needs to have the clean and fresh air of public scrutiny blowing through its operations if we are to have high quality programs (Gallagher, 1979).

The development of the Bush Institute for Child and Family Policy became another part of the Frank Porter Graham Child Development Center. This is a training program supported by the Bush Foundation of St. Paul, Minnesota, which wished to do something to bring together the worlds of academia and public policy. This fit extremely well into my own interests, and North Carolina was successful in applying for funds to support graduate and mid-career fellows in a program that would introduce them to issues in public policy and allow them to carry out some policy research of their own during one or two years in the program. A wide variety of faculty members were invited to participate in the program. Faculty support came from political science, economics, maternal and child health, psychology, and other areas that joined in this multidisciplinary effort to find some means by which knowledge from the academic world could be translated more accurately and faithfully into long-range public policy. All the fellows carry out a policy problem, attend seminars and colloquia, and many serve internships during their tenure in the program. While many faculty members have contributed to this program, the driving energy of Associate Director Ronald Haskins clearly played a key role in its current success.

Gifted Children

My own interest in gifted children languished in the early 1970s, when most of my attention was captured by developing a research program in the FPG Center with funds that were earmarked for handicapped children. At a later stage, however, we were able to develop, through the cooperation of local school systems, a demonstration of a new model of teacher-scholar teams; these teams worked together to develop curriculum units combining the scholars' knowledge of sophisticated information with the teachers' skills in organizing and timing activities to put these ideas into practical form for gifted students. The reader may recognize this as a variation of the curriculum reform movement of the 1960s, but in this case we were dealing with a new pattern of delivering materials and services in special education through the resource room. We were trying to help these resource room gifted/talented teachers by devising a way of drawing content sophistication from the community into the school system.

During this time, Governor James Hunt expressed an interest in developing a school of mathematics and science for talented and gifted students which eventually came into being in Durham, North Carolina, as a residential school for over four hundred senior high school students. I became a member of the board of the North Carolina School of Science and Math and satisfied some of my continuing interests in gifted education.

UNINTENDED CONSEQUENCES

Individual Plans

Those who have sufficient years of service can think of ideas they have had or actions they have taken which took unusual and unexpected turns; I am no exception. One of the most unusual came from a presentation made at the Kennedy Foundation International Awards Seminar held in 1971. At that seminar, I called for a Special Education Contract between school and family which would state in detail what the special educator was proposing to accomplish with the individual exceptional child, together with a clear statement as to how these objectives would be evaluated; there would be a limited time span of no more than two years, after which the child would have to be returned to the regular classroom unless a special diagnostic team determined otherwise. The whole purpose of this contract would be to systematize what seemed to be a rather loose set of objectives for the child in special education and to prevent educators from shunting unwanted children into special education forever (Gallagher, 1972).

Some people have suggested that this was one of the seeds for the Individual Education Plan, which became a key section of Public Law 94–142. It was probably an idea whose time had come anyway, but I was somewhat appalled by the mandate that every exceptional child across the country should have an IEP developed before any attempt was made to field test this untried idea. The IEP is probably the single most unpopular aspect of that law, not only because it requires a great deal of work, but because the essence of the plan itself seems to have been lost in the mountains of paperwork. There certainly is little excuse for our claim to be specialists if we cannot say, in some detail, what special activities we have planned for the child and why. Unfortunately, the idea got bureaucratized before it could be refined into an effective tool.

Learning Disabilities

Another desire that I shared with many people was to eliminate the concept of *brain-injury* and to replace this neurological concept with an educational one, which eventually became *learning disabilities*. Having completed an intervention study on brain-injured children at Illinois, I concluded that the diversity of these youngsters and the total uncertainty of the neurological diagnoses seemed to call for a very different approach that should have its basis in educational remediation rather than in a suspect neurology. To my dismay and the dismay of many others, this concept of learning disabilities has ballooned into a grab bag of miscellaneous problems which have in common only that the child is not doing well in school. Far from being a fairly unique diagnostic portrait of youngsters with developmental imbalances, the concept has become a meaningless and grossly overpopulated category for problems that should not be handled through special education.

The Special Education Bureaucracy

One final issue that has caused some personal reflection is whether the long range interests of exceptional children have been served by building a powerful special education establishment. My concern is that by building a separate special education establishment, as was done through the mechanism of special legislation at the state and federal levels, we may develop a politically powerful self-interested group of professionals who might not easily accept the notion of integrating handicapped children into the regular education program. Since I was the first chief of the Bureau for Education of the Handicapped and in on the beginning of a decade of powerful federal contributions which *did* establish strong personnel and trained administrators devoted to special education, I have had to struggle with the question of whether this was in the long-range interest of education. On this point, I have few doubts or reservations. Those who can remember what happened to exceptional children before there were advocacy groups within the school know that they were often ignored or given a second-class education. The establishment of special education components within the educational system gave these youngsters a much better chance for quality education, though that chance was not realized in every instance. We still face the difficult issue of how to cooperate across the boundary line between special education and regular education to serve those many children who have mild problems which may not be sufficient to obtain full special education services but surely require something more than what regular education has traditionally provided in the way of auxiliary or supplementary services.

UNRESOLVED ISSUES

Each generation has a way of leaving a storehouse of unresolved issues and problems to be dealt with by the next generation, and the authors of this volume are no different. The current generation has brought about a multitude of changes, and these changes themselves have created new sets of problems. As long as there was no money and no resources, our problems were fairly simple: how can we find resources and trained personnel? When trained personnel do become available, the issues become the coordination and effective interaction with other professionals!

The Relationship of Regular and Special Education

Certainly the most chronic problem facing the special education community is its continuing and often abrasive relationship with the regular education program. On one hand, many people in the traditional education program look on special educators as outsiders. They are often seen as the physical manifestation of the inability of the regular educator to deal with certain problems. That no one individual, however competent, should be expected to deal with the range of problems with which exceptional children confront the school is not easily understood or accepted.

The second problem in the relationship lies in the fact that much of interaction between special education teachers and other professionals takes place at the peer level. Most other relationships in education are, in fact, on a hierarchical level! You are dealing with people who are either below you in status, such as the students, or above you in status, such as the administrators. There is a detailed set of rules as to who has the authority and who must follow directions. Those of us in education have had a multitude of practice in such interactions and so feel reasonably comfortable in one or the other of those roles. What turns out to be difficult is dealing with a person who is on a relatively equal status with you.

The special education teacher and the regular education teacher are peers. If there is a disagreement, then how does it get settled? If the special educator wants to make a suggestion about how to change a student's program, how can it be done without offense? Who takes the lead in discussions or planning for the student? There is a range of role uncertainties cluttering the landscape on such issues, and they make a difficult situation even more difficult. Suffice it to say, until we can establish a more effective working relationship at the peer level, there will continue to be much stress and tension in meetings, conferences, and other forms of professional interaction within the school building and the school system itself.

Who Belongs in Special Education?

A related issue is the problem of which children belong in special education. There is clearly a long continuum of various behavioral characteristics in children from social adaptation problems, to poor achievement, to misbehavior. Is the manifestation of any problem at any time an indication that the child should be sent to special education? Obviously not. However, how intense must the problem become before the major responsibility shifts from regular education to special education? Where is the dividing line on behavior problems, learning disabilities, mental retardation, or giftedness? It is difficult to find a clear-cut division point that would assign children to one category or another. In my own view, some form of special services organization within the school system should take the responsibility for the delivery of special services, whether under the authority of special education or not. It makes little sense to assign psychologists, speech pathologists, etc., only to those children who are eligible for special education and to ignore the other 15 to 20 percent of the pupils who need and could profit from the help of these specialists. For many of the youngsters near the borderline of this cutting point, some special services should be provided, whether officially supported by state and federal funds or not.

A LAST THOUGHT

Someone else will write the end of this story, but the play, of course, goes on. My own feelings about the human condition were best expressed by the naturalist Loren Eiseley (1957) some years ago:

> Down how many roads among the stars must man propel himself in search of the final secret? The journey is difficult, immense, at times impossible, yet that will not deter some of us from attempting it. We cannot know all that has happened in the past, or the reason for all of these events, any more than we can with surety discern what lies ahead. We have joined the caravan, you might say, at a certain point; we will travel as far as we can, but we cannot in one lifetime see all that we would like to see or learn all that we hunger to know. (p. 12)

REFERENCES

Bruner, J. (1960). *The process of education.* Cambridge, MA: Harvard University Press.

Cruickshank, W., Bentzen, F., Ratzeburg, F., & Tannhauser, M. (1961). *A teaching method for brain-injured and hyperactive children.* Syracuse, NY: Syracuse University Press.

Eiseley, L. (1957). *The immense journey.* New York: Random House.

Gallagher, J. (1957). A comparison of brain-injured and nonbrain-injured mentally retarded children on several psychological variables. *Society for Research in Child Development, 22,* 79.

Gallagher, J. (1960). *The tutoring of brain-injured mentally retarded children.* Springfield, IL: Charles C. Thomas.

Gallagher, J. (1967). Teacher variation in concept presentation in Biological Science Curriculum Study curriculum program. *Biological Science Curriculum Study Newsletter, 30,* 8-19.

Gallagher, J. (1972). The special education contract for mildly handicapped children. *Exceptional Children, 38,* 527-535.

Gallagher, J. (1975). *Teaching the gifted child* (2nd ed.). Boston: Allyn & Bacon.

Gallagher, J. (1979). Minimum competency: The setting of educational standards. *Educational Evaluation and Policy Analysis, 1,* 62-67.

Gallagher, J., Aschner, M., & Jenne, W. (1967). *Productive thinking of gifted children in classroom interaction* (CEC Research Monograph Series B5). Arlington, VA: Council for Exceptional Children.

Gallagher, J., Greenman, M., Karnes, M., & King, A. (1960). Individual classroom adjustments for gifted children in elementary schools. *Exceptional Children, 26,* 409-422, 432.

Gallagher, J., Nuthall, G., & Rosenshine, B. (1970). Classroom observation. *AERA monograph series on curriculum evaluation, 6.* Chicago: Rand McNally.

Guilford, J. (1967). Creativity: Yesterday, today, tomorrow. *Journal of Creative Behavior, 1,* 3-14.

Guilford, J. (1972). *The nature of human intelligence.* New York: McGraw Hill.

Hull, C. (1943). *Principles of behavior.* New York: Appleton-Century-Crofts.

Klaus, M., & Kennell, J. (1970). Mothers separated from their newborn infants. *Pediatric Clinics of North America, 17,* 1015–1037.

Maslow, A. (1966). *The psychology of science.* New York: Harper & Row.

Rogers, C. (1951). *Client-centered therapy.* Boston: Houghton Mifflin.

Spence, K. (1956). *Behavior theory and conditioning.* New Haven, CT: Yale University Press.

Strauss, A., & Kephart, N. (1955). *Psychopathology and education of the brain-injured child: Vol. 2. Progress in clinic and theory.* New York: Grune & Stratton.

Strauss, A., & Lehtinen, L. (1947). *Psychopathology and education of the brain-injured child.* New York: Grune & Stratton.

9

The Odyssey of a
Speech Clinician

Richard L. Schiefelbusch

Richard L. Schiefelbusch, born 1918 in Osawatomie, Kansas, holds a B.S. in social studies from Kansas State Teachers College (1940), an M.A. in speech pathology and psychology from the University of Kansas (1947), and a Ph.D. in speech pathology from Northwestern University (1951).

Dr. Schiefelbusch is a University Distinguished Professor of Speech and Language (1969–) and was previously assistant professor of speech pathology (1949–53) as well as director of the Speech and Hearing Clinic (1949–56) at the University of Kansas. He is also director of the Bureau of Child Research (1955–) and director of the Kansas Center for Mental Retardation and Human Development at the University of Kansas (1969–).

Former vice-president for education and scientific affairs of the American Speech and Hearing Association (1980–82), Dr. Schiefelbusch received Honors of the Association from the American Speech and Hearing Association in 1976 and a Special Award from the American Association on Mental Deficiency in 1975.

The period covered in this writing is approximately thirty-seven years—roughly the time since World War II. I have not integrated my undergraduate experiences (even though some of them were academically or professionally relevant) because the prewar period (1936–1940) was an era with a different mood and, for me, a different philosophy. Before the war, I was immersed in student politics, forensic contests, and theatre productions. In contrast, my return from military service was overlaid with a new philosophy—one more idealistic, humanistic, and service oriented.

INTRODUCTION TO THE CLINIC YEARS

My decision to become a member of a helping profession occurred while I was in a German prisoner of war camp during World War II. I was in the Luft-waffe Camp at Sagan, Germany, (Stalag Luft III) along with about two thousand other American Air Force officers. During much of the two years of forced confinement, I taught speech courses for fellow prisoners (Schiefelbusch, 1962). This effort was part of a plan ordered by our senior officers to improve camp morale. These group sessions drew a wide assortment of communicators. Many of the voluntary class members were gifted social leaders who had chosen the class as a means of enhancing their social skills for "civilian life." They were exciting, clever participants in the social exercises of the class.

Other participants seemed to have transaction problems. These problems were evident in their manner of speaking or communicating (voice quality, stuttering, or comprehensibility), in disordered thought functions (illogical sentences, word confusions, or disoriented meanings), and group-related fears and anxieties (stage fright).

I had a few common sense counseling skills derived in part from a social studies major in college, but my background was generally inadequate for helping my prisoner students. I soon realized that some of them were experiencing progressively more stress each month. I could find no professionally trained therapists in the camp to whom I could turn for advice. I continued to encourage and counsel as best I could while many of my students became noticeably less and less communicative. My desperate reaction to these experiences was to search for effective treatment procedures. I was aware, of course, that the stresses of a POW existence were extremely debilitating for many of the Kriegies.[1] Some of them seemed to be losing the struggle; others were showing signs of stress in limited, but socially apparent, ways. When I discussed my concerns with an American senior officer, he advised me not to assume responsibility for more than I could do. He also urged me to continue the classes because "the course provides a valuable experience for your fellow officers."

[1]From *Kriegsgefangener* (prisoner of war).

I accepted his advice with reservations. I was far more aware of the limitations than of the "valuable experience" features. I resolved then that I would one day acquire the professional skills that I lacked and the knowledge that I needed to be more effective in my teaching.

The search for that knowledge and those skills began when I returned to graduate school at the University of Kansas in the fall of 1945. I announced to my professors that I wanted to learn how to help people. It was rather remarkable, I think, that this declaration was not met with condescension when I enrolled in clinical psychology courses. In retrospect, I view my declared career intent as a natural expression of my experience, supported by the idealism of the postwar period. Many of the veterans and other college students of that time were similarly idealistic about their life objectives.

I soon learned that the skills and knowledge that I sought already had been given many different labels. Since the postwar years still others have been added: *psychotherapy, nondirective therapy, play therapy, group counseling, rehabilitation* (also *habilitation), sensitivity training, behavior therapy, language intervention, augmentation therapy,* etc. The styles of study and the techniques of application have changed greatly over the years, but then, as now, they were all embedded in helping professions.

One perceptive psychology professor arranged a reading course for me designed to explore the relevant strategies and designs for therapy that existed in hospitals, treatment centers, and institutions at that time (1946–1947). This perspective on therapeutic services included programs of remedial speech (now speech pathology) and remedial education (now special education). I decided on a graduate program in clinical psychology and speech pathology and eventually completed a doctorate at Northwestern University in 1951. During my five-year period of graduate education I made a practical transition to the real world of professional practice and its accompanying limitations. I also encountered a number of role models at the University of Kansas, at the University of Wisconsin, and at Northwestern University.

A role model to me was not someone to imitate but someone I could learn from and "level with" as I studied theoretical and philosophical systems of therapy. I soon learned that some practitioners were relatively effective and some were not. Effectiveness did not seem to be related primarily to the methods they employed. This did not upset me even in my idealistic frame of mind. However, what did bother me was that some seemingly bright and successful professionals were phonies. I perceived that the phonies were essentially unhappy about their lack of effectiveness, but that they did not know what to do about it. However, one prominent acquaintance from my student years did quit his profession. He left the field, I think, because he could not face a career of pretense. There simply were too many bright, skeptical students, probing parents, and observant critics, whose feedback he could not ignore.

In my early professional years I was bothered by the sales tactics used in some professional practices. For instance, I was appalled by the hype used then in raising money for cerebral palsied children. I was close to the team clinics in at least three prominent settings at that time, and I could not accept the extravagant therapeutic claims being made on radio and in the press (television came along later) in light of the limited number of lasting effects we were able to deliver.

My efforts to learn to help people during my graduate school years turned up two important reassuring facts. One was that even though there was only a modest amount of effective methodology available for the helping professions, some practitioners actually were effective. There obviously were some accomplished therapists, clinicians, teachers, counselors, and other human activators. To become such a person seemed a reasonable aspiration, if I could discover how.

The second reassurance was my own experience as a clinician. The reality of the clinical process became increasingly apparent to me during my graduate school years. *Empathy* was prominent in my lexicon of professional concepts. I seemed to have a facility for sharing in the experiences of my clients. I could sit with them and accept their condition, understand their struggles, and gain their trust. My war experiences had apparently prepared me for such clinical relationships. One experience seemed to occur again and again. On days when my own energies and creativity seemed to lag, I detected subtle but sustained efforts by my clients to work harder and more effectively. I assumed that they wished to improve their performance as a reassurance to me. In the process of clinical transaction they contributed more to compensate for my doing less. This was reassuring feedback for me, adding greatly to my early understanding of how social feedback influences human performances.

Two major academic benefits came from my master's level training at the University of Kansas. The first grew from courses and personal discussions with Dr. Beulah Morrison, Professor of Child Psychology at the university. She was a wise, gentle scholar, who could respond to the pretentions and intentions of students while guiding them to read and learn more about the interests that outcropped in their discussions. In my case, she led me to study service systems—why they existed, what their theoretical and methodological bases were, and what relationships they formed in service delivery arrangements. Later, as my interests in clinical speech became more pronounced, she influenced me to look at that field from the perspective of a developmental psychologist. Through her I learned of Dorothea McCarthy, Arnold Gesell, Arthur Jersild, M. M. Lewis, C. M. Louttit, Marian Monroe, and many others. She started me off as an interdisciplinary student with the admonition that each scholar has the responsibility to find the full extent of relevant knowledge, wherever it may be. The necessity to be competent, or at least fully knowledgeable, must be accepted by all professional workers in the helping disciplines.

A second long-term benefit came from Professor Margaret Anderson, who taught in the Department of Speech and Drama. Her courses were not especially memorable; but she had two passions, posture and writing, that she passed along to her students. The first of these did not greatly influence me, but the second haunted me for at least ten years. I suspect that the most important requisite of good writing, in addition to practice, is a sense of good standards. Even if one cannot write, but is given repeated examples of good writing and develops an eye for it, one is then not likely to be satisfied with poor writing. The trick is to learn to tell the difference and to work toward better clarity, order, and style. Margaret Anderson's influence extended far beyond my experience with her on my master's thesis. Other patient and competent helpers have contributed to this aspect of my career—Professor Lew Sarett and Dr. Harold Westlake at Northwestern University and Bob Hoyt, a journalist, who contributed greatly to the quality of my writing during the last fifteen years. I think, however, that the shaping one gets as a student has the greatest and most lasting impact on professional writing skills.

My research experiences during my graduate years did not add up to much. However, I should explain that I took a clinical degree, not a research degree. Speech pathology and clinical psychology in the '40s and '50s were not research fields. Nevertheless, I did acquire a philosophy of science. What I failed to learn about the rigor of methodological operations, I made up for in general applications of the scientific method, the logic of science, and a perspective on scientific activities. Because I have been a research administrator, not a bench scientist, this emphasis has not been a poor one, especially when coupled with a broad approach to knowledge systems. Nevertheless, I would urge all graduate students to gain experience with specific research projects during their graduate years. Science is a demanding vocation that cannot be practiced with half-learned skills.

My six quarters at Northwestern University were fast paced and complicated. During this brief, intensive time I learned about special education from Dr. Helmar Myklebust, about audition from Dr. Ray Carhart, and about people from Dr. Harold Westlake. Each of these strong men was a role model for a generation of graduate students who were to extend their influence across the land and into dozens of clinics, hospitals, and universities.

Myklebust was the humanist who could explain all dimensions of handicapping conditions as well as the strengths and weaknesses of humans, organizations, and disciplines. His understanding of parents was remarkable. I am not sure I was a superb graduate student at Northwestern, but I certainly became a better parent.

Ray Carhart was the most consistently enthusiastic and professionally involved professor I have ever known. His enthusiasm was infectious in his work, his causes, and his plans. Clinical audiology took off rapidly after World War II, and Ray Carhart was its flight leader. He formulated a style of clinical research that lasted twenty-five years and produced many of the diagnostic procedures and other practical audiological techniques developed during that time.

From Harold Westlake I learned how to initiate (actually how to undertake) new projects, new professional activities, and new clinical services. He never accepted the status quo; and because he was a bright, energetic man, he never assumed that he had to. He did not hesitate if he thought some new project should be undertaken. He would begin the new clinic in the new hospital as casually as he would eat his brown-bag lunch. The former would simply take longer.

THE CLINIC YEARS

My stay at Northwestern was unfortunately brief because I was on leave from the University of Kansas. I returned to Kansas in September, 1949, to start a speech and hearing clinic. The contrast between the Northwestern scene with its relationship to the large Chicago hospitals and the undeveloped scene in Kansas was unsettling. My new skills were not initially useful; and, of course, much of what I most needed in Kansas I had not learned at Northwestern. I soon learned that building a clinic and a graduate program must begin with oneself. The program cannot grow faster or better than the leader's knowledge or skills will allow. The realities of growing and knowing seem to emerge together. Consequently, most programs emerge slowly.

I was firmly identified with Kansas and wanted very much to develop a speech and hearing program there. Furthermore, I had an enduring belief that a clinical program could be built at KU. The Speech and Hearing Clinic and I literally grew up together. My own lack of professional experience was counterbalanced by the enthusiasm and the supportiveness of the students. Perhaps nowhere else has a program been so closely keyed *to* the interests of students or so literally designed *by* the students. They volunteered, supported, and worked overtime to make the program a reality. After graduation they extended this involvement into their clinical work in schools and hospitals and sought to validate the Kansas program through their efforts beyond the training years. I must humbly admit that not much is possible without the help of your friends, but if one has that help, one need not be quite so humble.

I directed the Speech and Hearing Clinic at the University of Kansas for seven years. Throughout this time I was aware that we lacked the methodologies and the strategies to do what our clinical responsibilities required. Thus, the seven years were devoted to a search for better procedures. The search extended into case conferences, seminars, staff meetings (with colleagues in psychology and education) and especially to clinic students and doctoral candidates from psychology minoring in speech pathology. One recurring problem related to the modes of clinical techniques used with speech-delayed children. Our efforts to shape specific patterns of speech required a direct, intensive style of training that was often not interesting or meaningful to the children. Our efforts to introduce playlike variations resulted in less focused, less intense, but more interesting activities. During my clinic years I never found a satisfactory way to combine the intensive and informal features of training. We adapted variations of play therapy, psychodrama, puppet theatre, and creative play activities. Children loved to come and parents spoke highly of the clinic, but we had not found optimal procedures for achieving our primary objectives. We even questioned these objectives, but in an academic training program one cannot readily transcend one's discipline. My largest problem was that I had limited data against which to judge success or failure in any aspect of the clinic.

So far as clinical research was concerned, the Gestalt (whole child) philosophy was an exciting way to think about speech and hearing problems, but was not a very good framework for defining operational issues. Orienting clinical systems such as psychotherapy, deep therapy, play therapy, and nondirective counseling have limited value for clinical investigations. Even the exciting field theory of Curt Lewin, for all its logical orientations, did not provide a data system to test assumptions and validate field diagrams. Somatopsychology, a system derived largely from field theory, seemed like a logical means for explaining certain problems of communicatively handi-capped persons, but it did not help stutterers or cleft-palate, motor-impaired, or hearing-impaired individuals. In our research efforts, all these approaches were regularly discussed and considered and then set aside to be considered again another day.

Another persistent deterrent to data-oriented research was the widely held assumption that speech disorders were really symptomatic of underlying problems that must be diagnosed and treated before the symptoms could be eliminated. Symptom reduction was regarded as a verification that the real problem had been treated. It was further assumed that, if we proceeded directly to treat the symptom, we might actually complicate the real problem and that all we could possibly accomplish would be the development of a different and possibly less observable symptom complex. A few intrepid leaders opposed this psychotherapeutic approach to speech and communication disorders. Charles Van Riper, for example, advocated a symptom approach to stuttering and articulation disorders. Wendell Johnson had a diagnosogenic theory of stuttering: he assumed that a child's dysrhythmic speech was likely to become worse after his speech was labeled as stuttering. He linked problem behavior to the feedback received by the child in social transactions.

At about this time I became puzzled by stutterers who sought admission to my clinic after prolonged periods of psychotherapy at the Menninger Foundation in Topeka, Kansas. They explained that they could now talk about their stuttering problem to friend and stranger alike; furthermore they now understood their problem fully—but unfortunately they still stuttered.

We made one heroic effort to understand the "underlying problems" of communication disorders. Our decision was fostered primarily by William Stephenson's *The Study of Behavior: Q-Technique and Its Methodology* (1953). Briefly, Stephenson's system enabled us to study self-referent aspects of personality. We were able to develop a method for ordering self-referent traits on a seven-point scale from *highly approving* to *disapproving*. We then planned to use a forced-choice strategy to induce each child to rate him or herself. We tried two different methods in setting up the categories of self-referents. One was to listen to children's self-referent comments: we intended to collect a large number of these sample responses from which we could create the self-referent categories. The most significant observation we made was that the children seldom made any self-referent responses. The second method was to choose arbitrary self-referent categories based on the literature about children's personalities. We were soon aware that we were introducing biases into the study that could not be reconciled with the objectivity we sought. So we still do not know what children think about themselves, but we did stumble onto one of the first approaches to designing a procedure for single-subject research, and we did discover a method for studying behavior—if we only had known what we wanted to study. Incidentally, Jersild (1952) did author a book based on a binary tactic of self-referent responding, asking children, "What do you like about yourself and what don't you like about yourself?" In his tabulations, the lists of *don'ts* were much longer.

During the seven clinical years, I helped start interdisciplinary teams for cleft plate and for cerebral palsied children at the Kansas University Medical Center (KUMC), and I helped write the provisions for a state program in speech pathology and audiology, including certification requirements for clinicians. For three years I supervised clinics all over Kansas under the auspices of the newly formed Division of Special Education in the Department of Public Instruction. For me, the most lasting effect of these efforts was that they somehow induced Chancellor Franklin Murphy to believe that I had potential as a director of research. He appointed me director of the Bureau of Child Research in 1955. Thus I began my middle years of professional work. I call the bureau beginnings my middle years because I quickly felt much older. At least this act made a fateful imprint on my career: it lead me to become a scientist.

THE BUREAU OF CHILD RESEARCH

The Early Years

The Bureau of Child Research is now a large, diversified program, but twenty-seven years ago it was a very small, nonacademic division in a university that had limited enthusiasm for federal grants. The entire annual outlay for the bureau was about $30,000 and that included half of my salary. The university, in effect, freed me from half of my teaching to develop a program which was to be monitored directly by the Chancellor's Office. I was provided with an associate director, Mr. Don Pilcher, who had a lively range of interests from his social-work background. Although our skills were comfortably complementary, we nevertheless had some difficulty in developing compatible, long-term plans. This planning snag derived more from our mutual inexperience than from any difference of opinion.

We were expected to coordinate the work pertaining to children at the university and at the medical center forty miles away. We cannot boast that we found a way to coordinate pediatrics, child psychiatry, child development (in the Home Economics Department), child psychology, speech and hearing, deaf education, social work, nursing, etc., since we lacked development money and space in which to undertake new projects. After a few meetings we dissolved our elaborate coordination committee plans, and the bureau undertook other activities. For approximately two years we published a series of public information booklets on topics selected by the Kansas Council for Children and Youth, an interdisciplinary, interagency council that acted as advocates for children in Kansas. The executive director of the council was located in the small bureau suite, and we were soon swept up in council causes. We collated the laws relating to minors and reported on children in the courts. We developed a chart book of demographic information and a directory of services for children. We also served as the coordinating office of an ad hoc special education committee constituted to recommend and support the new special education program in Kansas. I even undertook to direct a small research program on underachieving children in the Lawrence, Kansas, public schools.

Most of these projects were funded from small grants awarded by the University Research Committee. It was painfully apparent that any substantial growth or qualitative gains must come from outside funding. This was a most troubling realization for me, one that quickly produced a troubling course of action. I had no background for fund raising, grant writing, agency politicking, and little experience in research planning. Also, I saw that any step I might take in any of these strange areas would likely expose my ignorance. It is difficult to explain fully the aversive aspects of my first grant development efforts. It was a new and different experience.

I had two colleagues for short periods (but at different times) who helped me weather my early years in the bureau. Jack Michael in 1957 explained a heady new behavioral (operant) tactic that he was sure could be adapted to teaching children. He was a brilliant research designer and statistician who contributed to the research credibility of the bureau even though he was never officially a staff member. Unfortunately, he left Kansas for the University of Houston before we actually undertook collaborative research. The other colleague was Lee Myerson, an incisive psychologist who encouraged me to go to Washington, to meet agency people, and to learn how to secure federal grant support. His suggestions also led me to visit Parsons State Hospital and to consider the possibility of a grant project with them. He had a remarkably creative view of research with handicapped people. He also soon left for the University of Houston, where he teamed up with Jack Michael to form one of the early university training programs for operant psychologists.

So in 1957 I struck a fortunate agreement with Howard Bair, Superintendent at Parsons State Hospital that lasted until his retirement in 1979. The agreement eventually resulted in numerous joint projects and a long-range partnership between state and university to improve the quality of services to retarded citizens. Howard was a builder and developer during a period of questionable enlightenment in institutions for the retarded. He added force and credibility to the university-hospital partnership.

Funding for our first grant, A Language Program for Mentally Retarded Children, began on January 1, 1958. Our first task (larger than securing the grant) was to hire a staff for a project that had no real precedent in either the scientific or clinical literature. The recruiting took several months and resulted eventually in the appointments of Ross Copeland, Seymour Rosenberg, and Joseph Spradlin. Ross was a speech scientist with several years of experience with mentally retarded children. Seymour was a research psychologist who had finished several years of Air Force research. During his eighteen-month stay he was the project field director. Joe also was a research psychologist with previous experience in institutions for the mentally retarded. He became the field director after Rosenberg left. Jerry Siegel, a speech pathologist, joined the project during its second year and contributed greatly to a series of social assembly studies during the project's early years. This proved to be a productive assemblage of scientists. The Parsons Language Project became the first research project to study institutionalized severely retarded children using behavior analysis procedures. It was also the first effort to apply behavior analysis procedures to language studies.

The purpose of the project was "to develop an optimal language and communication program for mentally retarded children in an institutional setting." The subgoals were

1. The formulation of a set of experimental constructs relative to language and communication as features of social adequacy.
2. Diagnostic assessments of maladaptive patterns affecting language and communication.
3. The development of a battery of language and communication tests to assess verbal characteristics of institutional children and to determine gains made in the training program.
4. The development of specific clinical techniques for improving the verbal behavior of mentally retarded children.
5. The development of an environmental milieu for purposes of stimulating verbal development.

The last subgoal was an attempt to develop creative and motivational experiences in the child's daily activity.

In seeking ways to accomplish these extravagant objectives we discovered that the operant paradigm was effective with severely retarded children. Our approach was primarily stimulated by *Verbal Behavior* (Skinner, 1957). Other features in our theoretical frame of reference came from J. R. Kantor (1952), G. A. Miller (1951), and O. H. Mowrer (1952).

Our early work on language and communication was primarily a series of empirical studies in pilot form. Many of them were then replicated with alterations of format. The studies were intended to advance two major areas:

1. The definition and development of a representative sample of verbal behavior (a language battery).
2. The development of a set of applied manipulations to be used to promote verbal behavior.

By May, 1959, we had completed a series of studies which we presented in a panel at the AAMD meetings in Milwaukee. The feedback from the audience was enthusiastic. Their reaction told us more about the dearth of good work in the field of mental retardation and the hunger of its professional members for effective instructional tactics than it did about our work.

We had advocated a social frame of reference for teaching language to nonverbal children. Our data were encouraging, but limited. Nevertheless, our effort to adapt a reinforcement theory to retarded children was the start of applied behavior analysis in Kansas, although several years were to slip by before the procedures were so named.

In our early work, although social responding was promoted, spontaneous social behavior appeared to be a limited, almost nonexistent feature of the repertoire of retarded children. Consequently, we primed the children with tangible reinforcers to increase rates of verbalization. We soon published a number of nonlanguage studies related to eating, using the toilet, and self-help skills piloted during this period. These studies evolved into larger studies in collaboration with the staff of the hospital designed to alter the range of educational and social activities of the children.

In this exciting period we were enamored with the elegance and the power of the operant paradigm. There was a period of time (roughly the early 1960s) when we felt that we had a methodological answer to the needs of the helping professions. At least we were able to demonstrate learning in handicapped children whom educators and clinicians had previously avoided or excluded from instruction. This occupied much of our attention. We wanted to demonstrate the feasibility of training activities with children who had no previous history of educational success.

One is tempted to speculate about the bases of these beginnings of applied behavior analysis. Did we have these encouraging, albeit limited, successes because of the power of the system we had adapted or because of our spirited and strangely confident approach to proving that all children could be taught some useful new behavioral repertoire? There is no way to answer this question. Both answers seem plausible. In any event, the effects of the Parsons studies, in concert with similar studies at Southern Illinois, Arizona, Washington, and Boston universities, had great impact on programs for the handicapped because the procedural systems were observable, replicable, and feasible. They literally ushered in a new era of treatment and training for the severely and multiply handicapped. In a more limited way this early work at

Parsons helped define the problem of teaching useful language and other social skills to retarded children.

The power and elegance of applied behavior analysis was most apparent when the target of the effort was simple and clearly defined. We readily succeeded in teaching children to increase the number and rate of verbalizations, to respond to auditory feedback, to learn functional words, to walk with a better gait, and to listen to instructions.

Our achievements were less clearcut, however, in complex programming for which the targets and the program of training could not easily be specified. Nevertheless, our applied behavior analysis studies moved quickly from the simple designs of the early years to increasingly complex studies requiring explicit, but elaborate, responses. The project that most clearly demonstrated the elaboration of design was the Mimosa Project (Lent, 1968). This was an extensive effort begun in 1964 to train institutionalized, adolescent girls to assume roles in noninstitutionalized environments. It was a deinstitutional effort that occurred before the national emphasis on deinstitutionalization. The effort was based on the assumption that institutional environments could be altered to provide training for community living. It was the first of many comprehensive intervention programs that the Bureau of Child Research was to sponsor in the next few years.

The Middle Years

The first eight years of the Bureau's development (1955–1963) were my most difficult years. I was keenly aware of my personal limitations, including my limited research background. And I had difficulty accepting the administrative mantle. When I describe these as *growth years,* I am not simply using a cliché. In 1963 a remarkable event changed some of my views and gave me some much needed confidence.

In the early spring of 1963 we were scheduled for a site visit on the newly submitted three-campus program project, Language of the Mentally Retarded. This was a possible major expansion of our research program, and we all viewed it with excitement, apprehension, and awe. We prepared for the visit very carefully, working out beautiful audiovisual displays, rehearsing expositions of the work of each investigator, and carefully informing university and hospital officials about the grant plan. In short, we did all the things that a young, inexperienced research team could be expected to do under the circumstances—except one. We did not groom me to play the role of principal investigator. My preoccupation had been to get everyone else ready, but in the process I forgot myself.

When the magic moment arrived, we greeted the visitors and were poised to put on our audiovisuals, whereupon the chairman announced a slight change in the agenda. The panel requested a few minutes with the principal investigator, alone. The few minutes became an hour and a half. The first few minutes before the eight panel members were intense and harrowing for me;

but as we progressed and I detected evidence of support and agreement, the experience became easier and more enjoyable. When I returned to my team, I said, "We have just led with our Achilles' heel, but I think we have won." Somehow, during the hour and a half I became a research director, and I frequently refer to the experience as the end of my research apprenticeship.

The program project was funded for seven years and generated a phase of work that differed from previous efforts in the scope of research topics and the range of intercampus activities (Lawrence; KU, Kansas City; KUMC; and Parsons). The immediate advantages of the program project were a combining of resources for research, improved research training, and the maintenance of common themes for long-range research. This program was refunded several times, extending in a continuous line until 1980.

A number of prominent studies evolved directly from this program: studies by Hollis (1965) (1966); Waryas and Stremel-Campbell (1978); Spradlin (1963); Carrier and Peak (1975); McLean (1972); Rosenfeld (1972); Schiefelbusch, Copeland and Smith, (1967); Guess, Sailor and Baer (1974); Ruder and Smith (1974); and Butterfield and Belmont (1972).

The program included the study of basic behavioral processes considered to be important in the development of adequate social behavior and the application of research findings and approaches to the management, care and treatment of retarded children. This combination of basic and applied procedures contributed to the development of an application science that has since been extended to a range of important social problems. Another important effect was the establishment of interrelated settings that formed the locus for the research program of the Bureau of Child Research in Lawrence, Parsons, and Kansas City.

Many colleagues contributed significantly to the development of this range of work. At no time during these or subsequent years have I undertaken work that I regarded as entirely my own. The work was always group oriented, and the credits were always multiple. I had to struggle to achieve a set of new concepts about research administration.

Perhaps a tactical system for research administration has been refined and published. If so, I have not read it. Such a system was certainly not available in those days. It soon became apparent to me that I must help create and maintain research of better quality than I alone knew how to design. Investigators are motivated to follow interests to individual ends, but a program of research is more than a sum of its parts. I found that I could guide, encourage, and support the effort best by participating in all the work in some way rather than by pursuing my own interests intensively in one or more of the specific parts.

To fulfill such a strategy the administrator must identify with all of the work and take direct credit for none of it. Thus, the administrator is less the director and more the facilitator of research activities (Schiefelbusch, 1978).

One effect of the new program was that two years later we began planning the Kansas Center for Research in Mental Retardation. This effort stretched my perceptions and those of my staff beyond familiar models of research. The research center and the accompanying University Affiliated Facility (UAF) were approved in two stages in 1966–1967 and have solidified the format of multiple-campus research and training activities. The efforts of many diversely trained persons were blended into a long-term, comprehensive design for studying the important national problem of mental retardation. The research of the center includes a range of biological, developmental, behavioral, and educational research. Although the research of the center extends from, and maintains, the activities that were begun prior to its emergence, it is virtually impossible to trace the full impact of the earlier studies and to discuss the continuity of work up to the present.

The Kansas Center became the responsibility of the Bureau of Child Research, and the task of directing the center was added to my enlarged set of responsibilities. The management of the evolving program became an all-consuming effort for me. During the period of rapid growth from 1963 to 1972, I was the epicenter of a rapidly expanding research and training complex that included the construction of buildings on three campuses and the development of a research staff of approximately three hundred persons. The development of the Kansas Center would have been impossible without the special competencies and dedication of Ross Copeland. His fiscal and administrative services became indispensable in the research and training explosion that followed.

Another vital participant in the rapid expansion years was Joe Spradlin. Joe helped to prepare nearly all the grants developed in the bureau during the '60s. Together Joe and I planned, designed, wrote, or weathered any project that evolved.

During the early phases of the center development, Don Baer, Barbara Etzel, Vance Hall, Betty Hart, Todd Risley, Jim Sherman, and Mont Wolf joined the staff of the bureau after having worked together at the University of Washington. The amalgam combined the two most prominent behavioral analysis research teams active in the nation at that time. They soon joined with Frances Horowitz in developing the Department of Human Development and Family Life.

Another group came into the program as the result of new research space, new center grants, and other federally funded projects. New additions included Ogden Lindsley, Bob Fulton, Melissa Bowerman, Leija McReynolds, Henry Heffner, Jim Budde, Judy LeBlanc, John Wright, Don Bushell, Steve Warren, Ann Rogers-Warren and many others.

A number of additional projects soon added to the extensive research program that began with the Parsons Project. The most extensive of these developments was the Juniper Gardens Children's Project, a program of community-based research initially a supplement to the seven-year program project, Language of the Mentally Retarded. Fred Girardeau moved to Kansas City from Parsons to direct the new project during its transition period. After an initial three-year period, a new Juniper Gardens program project was developed in 1967 that has extended up to the present. Throughout this period the field director has been Vance Hall and co-directors have included Todd Risley, Mont Wolf, and Ed Christophersen.

This research program is located in a large, poor area in the northeast sector of Kansas City, Kansas. It was begun when idealism for a war on poverty was bursting on the nation and collaborations between the community and researchers were popular. A series of agreements with citizens of the district led to a neighborhood action group (NAG). The researchers and their NAG colleagues developed long-term plans for improving the educational and developmental experiences of neighborhood children and their families.

In 1964 the initial group of researchers made the following statement in a report to community planners:

> *Families living in deprived urban areas perpetuate a cycle of poor child rearing practices and inadequate school adjustment usually expressed in the form of academic failures and behavior problems which lead to early school dropouts, delinquent behavior, early pregnancies, and/or unstable marriages. These new families are soon added to the already staggering number of individuals supported by welfare programs, resulting in a further drain on the community and involving a poor prognosis for self-improvement. (Planning Document, Bureau of Child Research, July 17, 1964)*

This dramatic analysis led to plans, approved by NAG, for assessing problems and creating intervention designs and procedures. Eighteen years later these shared intentions are still in effect, and funding is currently projected for five more years. The research has resulted in scores of publications, reprints, replications, films, workshops, training materials, courses of study, and trainees. Over the years a community intervention research technology also has been created that now provides a range of validated data, procedures for program designs and replications, and research training.

The Juniper Gardens Children's Project (JGCP) is interesting for several reasons. First it shows the feasibility of a long-term collaboration between a university and a poor community which focuses its efforts upon problems chosen by representatives of that community. Second, it shows that social problems anchored in economic deprivation can be improved through carefully designed intervention research. Finally, it shows distinctive changes in the hypotheses about retarded performances in poor, urban areas.

The earliest hypothesis was that poor people have problems because they lack the skills required for effective participation in the majority society. Such a hypothesis leads to a deficit or a difference model and to the development of research strategies to evaluate and remediate the language, social, and academic skills of the poor. Much of the research of the '60s and early '70s was based on such a model. This research had a major impact on improving and increasing the technologies and teaching techniques available to schools and institutions. The intent was to teach those skills which were displayed by socially and academically successful children and youth.

A second hypothesis proposed that poor people have problems because they lack appropriate contexts in which to develop needed skills and behaviors. This hypothesis produces research strategies to evaluate and remediate the environments in which people live and learn. Research undertaken in accordance with this model has had an impact on the quality of environments in communities. This hypothesis was especially prominent in the Juniper Gardens Project from 1972–1980.

A third hypothesis proposes that the problems of the poor are neither solely a matter of skill deficits nor solely one of unaccommodating environments, but also a matter of how the behaviors of the poor interact with the majority culture's social institutions. Such a hypothesis leads to an interactional model and to research strategies for evaluating and remediating the interactions between the poor and the important social, academic, and health care contexts of their lives.

These hypotheses, of course, are not formulations limited to the Juniper Gardens setting, but they do explain the changing emphases that have evolved during the course of the project. The shift has been away from intensive, small-scale training programs toward larger, extended programs involving the homes and the community resources. The shift has extended the generalized effects of training. Also, research efforts focus on activity systems that can be managed and maintained by nonresearch personnel.

Current JGCP research focuses upon improved health care delivery systems, analyses of language (especially vocabulary development of young children), and the development of academic skills. Each research area is designed to determine causal links between the poor children's life circumstances and their reduced functioning. Conversely, the goal is to determine specific issues for effective and durable interventions.

The most elaborate outcome of both the Parsons and Juniper Gardens work has been the environmentally designed programs that were operationally defined and refined to the point where they can be replicated and disseminated as complete systems of intervention. The studies evolved a research and development technology that includes applied behavior analysis, systems analysis, behavioral ecology, and computer techniques.

A range of research and training projects have evolved in conjunction with this research technology. For instance, research training projects have been maintained since 1962. During these twenty-one years we have officially had 157 trainees, 45 of whom were postdoctoral. In addition, a large number of research assistants have received training. Much of the effectiveness of the research training activities was the contribution of Fred Girardeau.

The bureau has also maintained a multimedia system directed by Robert Hoyt that has produced more than fifty films and numerous videotapes, slide shows, books, monographs, and other media products. These productions have been effective in displaying both the scientific and the humanistic aspects of the bureau's research program.

The excitement of this early work was contagious. There was a striking increase in the range of severely and profoundly handicapped individuals included in new programs of treatment and training. The behavioral techniques were soon extended to additional contexts such as cottages, classrooms, recreation settings, and homes, along with technologies for designing, maintaining, and replicating programs.

The important issue for me in the work published under the auspices of the Kansas Center is that much of it indeed addressed basic and applied problems affecting the status of handicapped persons.

Present Influences

The present period began roughly in 1980. Of course, that is an arbitrary date. The *present* cannot be discussed as though it were an instant. So one must select a reasonably current time dimension. We might call it the *prescriptive* present, or the *strategic* present. It is the time frame in which we confront the future, including our own personal version of "future shock." Planning is done in the present.All decisions, analyses, and commitments are made in the present. We may string the present out a bit—perhaps that is the ultimate purpose of the "three year grant"—in order to confront the future in stages or by degrees, but ultimately we are forced to decide in the present.

I find that three influences dominate the present scene for the Bureau of Child Research. These influences are economic uncertainty, accountability, and research synthesis. These issues are not new, but they have reached a state of urgency in this decade.

Economic Uncertainty   The present is always a most difficult time but, it seems to me that the "current present" is more uncertain than most. Should we assume that the future for research settings will be much like the past, with only a small dip in the volume of activities? Or should we assume that we have come to the end of an era? The position I take is that the future is always a challenge. The risks may be different now, but so are the opportunities.

My university administrators disagree with me strongly about the present research scene. I am being counseled to engage in planned cutbacks so there will be funds to accommodate future reductions in grant support. This design for fiscal cutbacks may be sound from a money management perspective, but from the viewpoint of research development it is self-defeating. When one budgets for predicted recisions, one automatically reduces the potential for new developments. The reductions on the front end of a time frame automatically create reduced productivity at the far end.

This brief analysis highlights a current problem for research laboratories. Many seem to have lost confidence in the future of research programs bearing on human services. I find myself strongly resisting this mood. We literally do not know what funding conditions will be like in five years; but if we (the aggregate *we*) voluntarily reduce our staffing, our planning, our project submissions, and our research efforts, we can certainly predict that we soon will have a diminishing field.

Thus there is a dilemma in the present professional scene. If we move boldly ahead to start new research, we may find the funding inadequate to maintain the initiative. On the other hand, if we hold back, we make certain that the initiatives that have characterized our past twenty-five years will be erased or greatly reduced. This dilemma also confronts individual scientists, directors of service and training programs, and students who face the costs of several years of additional training. Each of these professional activities must be undertaken in the face of possible funding limitations.

Federal reductions in health, education, and welfare funds have produced a morale problem in both research and service programs. Our total support is reduced, and there is the anticipation of further cutbacks. The cost-of-living expectations, together with the uncertainty of overall funding, is eroding confidence at all levels of professional activity.

So the current scene is influenced by uncertainty. Each group or each individual scientist must make decisions about the course to follow. Older scientists recall periods of greater scarcity and lower expectations, but these relative perspectives are not popular topics of conversation. My guess is that the boldest and the most persistent scientists will emerge as the professional leaders in the future just as they did in the past.

Accountability   Our primary accountability is to special children and their families. It would be fortunate if our methods and procedures for training and care were optimal. Unfortunately, this is rarely true. Our methods are improving, but we are still in the uncomfortable position of being accountable for results that we cannot produce. There is an interesting and urgent sidelight to this problem: more is known about how to teach than many educators employ. We are somewhat like the farmer who canceled his subscription to his farm magazine because, "I don't farm as good as I know how to now."

Our accountability calls for us to teach as well as we know how to and to continue to learn more about how to. Care workers and other professionals in the helping professions have a career-long responsibility to be as competent as the state of knowledge and their own abilities permit. This responsibility may be too heavy for many professionals to accept. However, commitment and accountability is what special education is about.

One of the significant developments in special education during recent years has been the evaluation of *teacher responses.* This step literally improved the relevant data on methods studies and opened the way to new procedures of teaching. So long as we had only the data on children's responses and only general or cursory data about the teacher's "procedures," we could not develop a science of teaching. In other words, the teacher has assumed greater responsibility for the outcomes of instruction by putting his or her responses into the learning system. Where once the explanation for a child's poor achievement might be that he was "learning disabled," "retarded," "autistic," or "aphasic," we now question the instructional methods.

In addition to the "reality" of *retarded behavior* we may now acknowledge the presence of a *nonfunctional procedure*. The learning rates of children may clearly be the product of an appropriate (or inappropriate) instructional system. Accountability in this respect is the assumption of responsibility for making the instructional program effective and successful.

Research Synthesis In 1955 I changed roles, moving from the clinic to research administration. However, during the twenty-seven years since that time, I seem to have moved back toward the former role. Although the Bureau of Child Research currently maintains a combination of research and training activities, the thrust of most of these activities is service related. The bureau has become an extensive research and development center with a portfolio of studies and activities that extend into service settings often far beyond the physical confines of the campus.

This system provides a "real world" proving ground for many of the methods and the findings of the campus-based research staff. The qualities and the merits of this application of research are not widely accepted within the research community. However, it is clear that the procedural system cannot simply be designated as *applied* in contradistinction to *basic* research. The designs, the data codes, the specific research procedures, and the technologies used are often formulated to enable the researchers to study problems that cannot be undertaken in most basic science laboratories.

The research efforts we began at Parsons in 1958 were crude, idealistic efforts compared to the more aptly designed and scientifically validated studies of today. Yet they were basically similar in intent and in strategy. In both instances the researchers define an important, difficult problem and then design a way to study it. Simply stated, the scientists are often engaged in how-to-do-it exercises related to desired instructional outcomes, treatment goals, assessment objectives, and service delivery targets.

Science extends naturally to both laboratory and clinical contexts. It has been standard practice in psychology, special education, speech-language pathology, and human development to label the first the preserve of scientists and the other the preserve of clinicians, specialists, or teachers. It is my observation that this dichotomy should be discarded because it obscures to a great extent the true place of science in human service fields.

In the Bureau of Child Research there are a number of researchers engaged in basic science studies. Such research is rigorous, usually theory-related, and yields instrumental data which confirm or reject, validate or refine the process or structural properties under investigation. Such research often involves animal subjects and may yield results bearing on cognitive, sensory, bio-chemical, neuroanatomical, or neuroendocrinological theories. Research is usually considered to be *basic* if it adds to the knowledge base in important areas of science; it is considered to be *experimental* if it investigates a "what-if" question. Researchers test the effects of carefully prescribed modifications of single variables. A reliable knowledge base is built up from numerous scientific studies. A large part of the center's basic (experimental) science research is maintained at the KUMC under the auspices of Dr. Fred Samson.

However, there is at least one more basic science tactic in our program that also yields reliable knowledge. I refer to naturalistic process studies. Such studies are often identified with linguistics, ecological psychology, sociology, anthropology, and social psychology. There are many issues critical to the health, education, and welfare of human beings that must be observed and described in naturalistic contexts. Therefore, we must have a defined set of procedures for observing, recording, storing, analyzing, and utilizing data that are derived from "natural" setttings. Among the many examples of naturalistic process studies are mother-child studies, environmental impact studies, family-influence studies, and language-acquisition studies. Both experimental process and naturalistic process studies contribute to our basic knowledge about normal and handicapped children and adults. Both kinds of studies attempt to describe, analyze, or construct conditions that illuminate the realities of human problems.

Another kind of science, often described as applied research, seeks to *change* human behavior. This purpose introduced a set of procedures to alter environments or uses procedures to alter the status or skills of human beings. In effect these are educative, rehabilitative, or intervention sciences. They could also be described as "how-to" sciences. Applied behavior analysis (ABA) is primarily a "how-to" science. However, it also provides an effective technology for studying naturalistic process issues. Experimental analysis of behavior (EAB) continues to explore basic behavioral issues and usually conforms to the above descriptions of experimental process studies.

I identify two branches of the "how-to" science in the Bureau of Child Research. One includes *experimental clinical* studies. The word *clinical,* however, might be replaced with other terms, i.e., *educational, training, treatment,* or *intervention.* The important issue is that the research applies to selected, sought outcomes. The purpose of an experimental study is to design, implement, refine, and replicate procedures for changing human outcomes. Such studies involve an *environment* that serves the purposes of the study, such as an environment for teaching language; a set of *strategies,* either programs or procedures; and specific *operations,* e.g., assessment, programming, management, and evaluation. The experimental procedures are specified carefully so the activities are completely documented. This documentation can be used to refine the procedures and to replicate the experimental study at another time or place.

Examples of such studies are Achievement Place, Mimosa Cottage, Parent Co-op Preschool, Super School, and NonSLIP. These studies are all elaborate examples that evolved from years of development and eventual dissemination of materials designed to train others to replicate the studies. Other experimental studies might not be carried to such elaborate ends, but they nevertheless involve the creation of valid, refined procedures for improved training, treatment, or care.

A second kind of "how-to-do-it" research might be called *clinical intervention* studies. Here again the term *clinical* can be replaced with other adjectives such as *language, educational, reading.* The important element is that research is undertaken within a service system. The researcher does not select special experimental groups, a planned time frame, or an experimental format for programming, assessment, and evaluating. The research is applied to the service conditions. The research may also involve the adaptation of experimental procedures for clinical use. The most critical features of clinical research may be the assessment of client's performance levels before, during, and after training sequences. There are now practical and explicit ways of recording and interpreting such useful information. Clinics and classrooms are valuable sources of information about the effectiveness of all types of clinical or instructional procedures. The naturalistic and the experimental scientists must often depend upon the work of intervention investigators for the final application of their findings.

The practical applications indicated by this discussion are becoming more widespread. The technologies now available point to a future that is bright indeed. As our clinics and our instructional environments include more reliable procedures for assessment and evaluation, they are likely to improve the quality of education for special children.

RETROSPECTIVE THOUGHTS

My interests were captured in the late 1950s by a professional happening called the Parsons Project. I was unprepared professionally for the experiences that followed. I was also a little slow to interpret the implications of the operant movement that followed. I was aware, of course, during the next ten years that Kansas was becoming active in the applied behavior analysis movement. In 1972 *Psychology Today* announced that Kansas was the world center for applied behavior analysis. This identification with such a significant development had both favorable and unfavorable impacts on the Kansas setting.

The positive have far outweighed the negative effects. Nevertheless, both should be considered in retrospect. My part in the evaluation of behavior analysis at Kansas was not accidental nor incidental. From the beginning it was part of our basic planning. We evolved our approaches out of empirical necessity. We sought a procedure that would enable us to establish functional programs for teaching severely retarded children. We were unable to find such programs, and so we were forced to design our own.

Our excitement over this early work was based on our own perceptions of its effectiveness in teaching useful new behaviors to children with extremely minimal skills. For a wide range of projects involving self-help skills, daily living skills, grooming skills, and communication skills, our procedures achieved results that were strikingly better than the pessimistic literature of the time would lead one to expect.

From the beginning I had the enormous task of explaining our work to a surprised and often incredulous audience of professional peers during site visits, professional meetings, staff meetings, and consultation visits. Perhaps my most difficult audience was in the speech and hearing field. The American Speech and Hearing Association (ASHA) seemed almost oblivious to the possibilities of operant conditioning. Consequently, I found myself in "left field" with former colleagues.

Thus, I was one of the formulators and Kansas' chief public relations officer for the new movement. Much of my own understanding of the movement came from discussions with a vast array of doubters. From years of this duty I gained some expertise in creating "significance" and "rationale" statements. Also, I became a garden-variety behavior analyst who used positive "reinforcers" in establishing and maintaining an environment for studies of applied behavior analysis. There are many terms for the application of operant principles to human conditions. The most popular has been *behavior modification,* a term that eventually came under fire from a critical press. The more accurate and acceptable term of *applied behavior analysis* (ABA) is currently advocated by most of my colleagues.

Even though I continue to be active in the applied behavior analysis movement, there is an evolving philosophical gap between my published work and that of many ABA colleagues. In the administrative role I am an interpreter, accommodator, and (occasionally) a synthesizer of issues relating to, or confronting, the behavioral work.

However, my own publications are primarily related to language and communication. From time to time I have attempted to delineate the complex designs that language intervention work requires. The shaping of observable behavior is characteristic of most behavior change projects. But shaping has limitations when applied to language. The paradigm for language is a transactional one and must be schematically considered for two or more persons. Consequently, language influences involve social exchanges and differ greatly from an experimental operator ➜ subject manipulation system.

Also, language is a complex system of meaning events that are not easily programmed piece-by-piece in small increments. Language evolves in functional contexts and involves many cues, contingencies, and subtle events. The critical aspects of the language learning experience lie in social contexts and functional transactions. The amount of social influence in these transactions is not easily documented. The repertoires that a clinician or a teacher attempts to teach formally to a language-impaired child may not result in generalized communication skills. Although ABA technologies enable us to teach a range of language repertoires, they often do not produce effects which can be generalized to contexts other than those used in teaching.

Some ABA scientists have come to grips with this issue and have designed procedures to teach generalization (Stokes & Baer, 1977). Research by Warren and Rogers-Warren (1980) has provided a range of useful data about language in contexts. From such research we gather that generalized effects should not be taken for granted by educators because such effects are largely undocumented. That issue poses a major challenge for instruction scientists of all kinds. Generalization must not be limited to a minor role in educational and psychological laboratories, but must be analyzed in the ecological range of a child's life. This range is what determines the effectiveness of language instruction.

This discussion implies that ABA, though very useful in language instruction, has not created a full technology for such instruction. Cognitive, linguistic, and social principles are useful in combination with ABA. Site visitors and journal editors seem to be skeptical about the combining of cognitive-pragmatic-behavioral tactics for analyzing language. The problem is compounded when one attempts to blend the theories that support the different views.

My position is that one cannot formulate a theoretical approach to cover all the complex conditions, strategies, and operations that must be included in an experimental design for language intervention. Interesting changes take place in scientists (cognitive, social, and behavioral) in the process of promoting language for retarded children. Their ideologies are slowly turned into technologies. The price paid by such researchers is that they slowly turn their old prejudices in for a set of operationally effective procedures. By working together in behalf of handicapped persons and their families, scientists from different persuasions extract the best from each other. In the process they learn many of each other's research behaviors.

For a number of years I have judged this symbiosis of science to be absolutely essential to intervention research in language. Cognitivists alone, psycholinguists alone, and behaviorists alone cannot handle the full load, yet any of these positions can serve as a starting point for developing a functional design for studying language acquisition and intervention.

In retrospect I conclude that at Parsons we were forced by necessity to evolve a behavioral system for teaching severely retarded, institutionalized children. We found that our behavioral tactics, especially behavioral assessment and contingency management, applied to other groups of children and adults. Had we initially begun with gifted, cooperative children, we surely would have found other tactics to be initially more effective. As various professional groups transcend the parochialism of their beginnings, they often reach out for new procedures to add to their designs. As they do this, they add to the effectiveness of their research designs. I suspect that the next twenty years will show that all of us were at least partly right, but unfortunately simplistic. More advanced states of knowledge may also show that a number of important and enduring contributions were made by behavioral, cognitive, social, and linguistic scientists who had not yet learned to work together, but who, nevertheless, each in an important way, helped usher in an age of scientific synthesis.

The ABA paradigm has gone through major changes in accommodating itself to advances made in other systems. This accommodation has advanced

ABA and shaped it into a more useful system. We now have cognitive behaviorism, behavioral pediatrics, behavior therapy, and many other adaptations. It is in the field of language usage that ABA has been put to the greatest test. Language functions offer the richest and most elaborate set of variables for behavioral analysis. The complex set of influences that control language events may well be the most important challenge facing behavioral sciences.

REMAINING PUZZLES

This heading may have misleading implications. It might suggest that we have solved most of our problems in special education and that there are only a few remaining problems. This, of course, is not the case. There are so many remaining problems and there is so much left to do, that the heading might better be *Urgent Puzzles*. The truth is that we have only begun to develop a comprehensive educational system for handicapped individuals. In this section I intend to highlight only a few of our puzzles that have special significance from my perspective.

Puzzle Question I: How are we going to store, access, and use all of the information we are generating? Herold Pluimer, former National Aeronautic and Space Administration official, observes that the nation is in the midst of a knowledge revolution that will, in comparison, dwarf the agricultural and industrial revolution. As a result educators must prepare themselves for the shock of rapid change.

It took a century from 1800 to 1900 to double the amount of man's recorded knowledge, but it doubled again by 1936, and again by 1950. Today, man's recorded knowledge is doubling every six years. We create in this country about 30 billion original documents every year, and that is growing by 10 percent each year. Last year alone we added about 100 billion pages to the already overloaded files of this nation. We read only about half of the paper we receive each day. We throw the rest away, or file it. About 85 percent of what we file we never have reason to retrieve.

There must be a better way to handle information and to transmit the educational materials and communications we use in our work. We should not be deluged with information just because someone wants to send it to us. Nor should we be kept from information because of inefficient storage and retrieval systems. We should instead have a system that allows us to retrieve good, reliable information on any subject, and we should be able to retrieve what we need immediately and in whatever detail is required.

That means the dissemination systems should allow us to ask for and get immediate and useful information, so that we do not have to wait and hope that editors and publishers will give us something we want or need among all the other products they put out. What is needed is a state-of-the-art system that allows professionals to seek information effectively and quickly from any source. Perhaps there should be an information science—a sociology of informational systems, sources, and mediated formats. We should each become experts about our own informational fields and forms of access.

Puzzle Question II: How can we keep up with the rapidly advancing technology? A very few years ago Robert Hoyt and I coauthored an article in which we created an imaginary system called the National Educational Satellite Service Information Environment. The acronym was NESSIE. Our wondrous NESSIE could do almost anything, ranging from the diagnosis of learning needs to the complete design of a curriculum to overcome almost any learning problem in any child, and followed that up with computer-assisted instruction to support the learning environment of the child.

The response from the readers of that article (Schiefelbusch & Hoyt, 1980) was somewhat puzzling, even disturbing. Perhaps many of our readers did not realize that NESSIE was a fictitious system. Many probably thought it was just another federal project that had been funded to experiment with educational technology. Others thought it was too much like "Buck Rogers" or "Star Trek" and that we were only dreaming electronic dreams with no substance. And no doubt there were some who were intimidated by the prospect that technology might accomplish so many positive things and threaten their current modes of instruction. In any event, NESSIE never got off the ground, not even in the minds of our readers.

But here we are, hardly into the 1980s, and it is quite apparent now that the ten-year predictions made in that article have a possibility of coming true in a much shorter time than we predicted. If they do not become a reality, it will not be because the technology is not available—it will be because we are not prepared to use the technology.

There is no doubt that technology is ahead of us. Communications satellites can now reach all fifty states at once with live, interactive, and cost-effective video materials that are broadcast from earth stations and then relayed back from satellites in a geosynchronous orbit 22,000 miles out in space. If we began today to design materials and programs to apply through this new technology, we would have a difficult time keeping up with new developments being added to the capabilities of current technology. We are going to be hard pressed just to keep up with what is new and what is available.

There is already a video disc system on the market that can contain on a single disc the size of a phonograph record an amount of single-frame information equal to three hundred volumes, each 360 pages long. The system will give the user access to any single frame of the 108,000 frames on the disc in a matter of seconds. Think what such a device could do if coupled with a satellite relay system that could receive and transmit the information over half the world in a matter of seconds. What could such a device do for special education through research communications? And, certainly not least of all, think what that system might do in disseminating media materials to handicapped persons, particularly in remote areas.

It is true that current technology still requires large facilities, studios, transmitters, and receivers, along with relay stations that are less than compact and economical. But this is only the third year of the decade. Who can even guess what may happen during the next ten years in the areas of miniaturization and portability?

Puzzle Question III: How can we teach language to handicapped people so that they can communicate effectively in the real world? Perhaps the most practical learning experiences are those in which we learn and apply our learning in the same functional contexts. Skills are learned to be used. Skills that are learned in simulated or formal environments apart from usage contexts usually do not generalize well to those contexts. The widespread problem of generalization from classroom, clinic, and laboratory to the real world has received increasing attention during recent years.

Generalization is an especially critical issue in language instruction. The language repertoires may be taught effectively in a learning context and not used in a different context. Recent efforts to study the contextual nature of language has emphasized its social complexity. There are many causes for an utterance. Some of these causes directly affect its functionality; others shape the form. The most formal approaches to language instruction teach the form, but fail to instruct the child in skills of social usage. Consequently, the language usage is limited; generalization does not occur. One way to improve generalization is to teach the language in functional contexts so it is used where it is learned and learned where it is used.

The prospects for generalization also can be furthered by determining the variables that affect usage and by teaching the learner skills in relation to these variables. However, we do not yet have such a taxonomy nor have we yet designed an optimally functional environment.

Puzzle Question IV: How can cognitive and behavioral sciences be synthesized in creating a science of instruction? A field identified as instructional psychology has evolved from the combining of education and psychology (Glaser, 1982). The two dominant theoretical forces in instructional psychology are linked to cognitive and behavioral research. Although cognitive psychology may be the more dominant theoretically, most of the present applications in therapeutic situations, special education, and instructional settings at all levels of education rely on behavioristic approaches.

The work in applied behavior analysis has led to impressive accomplishments in many situations where easily defined and less complex aspects of human behavior are addressed. In addition, these results are providing evidence about the adequacies and inadequacies of the underlying scientific base. However, certain limitations of these applications are beginning to emerge: they do not lead to long-range generalizable effects and are relatively incomplete in shaping or programming the complex behavior involved in thinking, problem solving, and language usage.

Cognitive psychology, in contrast, is oriented toward the complexity of human performance. However, compared to behavioristic psychology, cognitive science is still a fledgling in the application of its findings and techniques to practical human endeavors.

Thus there is likely to be a rapprochement between two theories of psychology and between psychology and education in the formulation of a science of instruction. The advantages of a synthesis of application procedures and techniques is self-evident.

The "puzzles" just discussed will not be quickly solved. The puzzles, however, should not be judged by their ease of solution. Each puzzle statement poses a problem that all of us in some way must acknowledge. Acknowledgment often leads to concern and to efforts at solution. The overload of information, the rapid emergence of technology, the complexity of instruction and intervention, and finally, the confusion about generalization of learned and taught behaviors raise issues that must be considered on the way to more effective programs for handicapped persons. Only when we have solved most of these puzzles shall we be able to combine that knowledge into the creation of a true science of instruction.

THE LASTING PUZZLE

What has really happened during the past thirty plus years? What does it all mean? Have I ever found what I have been looking for? The answer to the last question is a qualified *yes*. However, in order to explain the qualified positives *I* must switch to the collective *we* in order to include numerous colleagues.

We have discovered effective research systems for designing and developing improved models of service. We have found that applied behavior analysis is an effective technology for activating, maintaining, and managing the learning efforts of handicapped children, especially if it is combined with other lines of technical progress. We have discovered that scientists from several disciplines can select an important target problem and work together in developing the necessary tools for mounting the investigation. We have learned that a service setting in an institution or a ghetto can be an exciting base for sustained research and that many important problems are best investigated under sustained natural conditions. We have learned that principles derived from basic research can be applied to the conditions of the real world, but they usually must be altered so drastically in the process as to be hardly recognizable. We have found that the dangers, risks, and hardships that attend researchers in service and community environments are readily neutralized by service or citizen colleagues who are willing to abide us and instruct us until we learn how to do research in the new and strange environs. These are a few of the bonuses we have perceived.

Perhaps, too, we have gained useful information about how to help plan meaningful—even significant—research, how to get it funded, and how to maintain the significant research activities. More importantly we have learned that behavioral science—if put to the test by scientists who are patient, cautious, and dedicated—can transform an environment of confused or apathetic persons into a functional group of confident and enthusiastic workers. Interventions undertaken by scientists hold great promise for society if the dialogue between academia and the service settings can be worked out appropriately and maintained in a design of shared functions. Working together in behalf of handicapped persons and their families, the clinicians and scientists can extract the best from each other. We may even have become wise enough to serve the purposes of the handicapped more directly than we do our own. If so, this may be the most important advance of all.

The *lasting puzzle* is about the future. It is true that we all draw from a broad field of advancing knowledge and we seldom get very far ahead of it. But the enduring possibility of making personal contributions to knowledge should always be a motivation. Each of us is unique, and we have the potential to make at least modest uses of existing knowledge and in turn contribute to the body of knowledge.

Because I have advanced to the age of the keynote speech and the autobiographical article, I am more interested in possible ways to synthesize and to adapt knowledge for human uses. For instance, I am currently motivated by a new plan for language intervention research. This research, of course, will be better than previous work (because we know more now than we did before). Now that our methodologies and our functional uses of knowledge have improved, I am beginning a textbook—one from which even I can teach. If my assumptions are correct and if I actually do these things, I may at last solve my own lasting puzzle—how finally to achieve a sense of competence. For one shining moment I should like to know that I have given back to others something like the best that I have received. That may be the best reality I can hope to attain. If so, I would not trade that experience for any other that I have enjoyed during my professional odyssey.

REFERENCES

Bushell, D., & Brigham, T. A. (1972). Classroom token systems as technology. *Educational Technology, 11*(4), 14–17.

Butterfield, E. C., & Belmont, J. M. (1972). The role of verbal processes in short-term memory. In R. L. Schiefelbusch (Ed.), *Language of the Mentally Retarded.* Baltimore: University Park Press.

Carrier, J. K., Jr., & Peak, T. J. (1975). *Non-SLIP: Non-Speech Language Initiation Program.* Lawrence, Kansas: H & H Enterprises.

Glaser, R. (1982, March). Instructional psychology; Past, present and future. *American Psychologist, 37.*

Guess, D., Sailor, W., & Baer, D. M. (1974). To teach language to retarded children. In R. L. Schiefelbusch and L. L. Lloyd (Eds.), *Language perspectives: Acquisition, retardation and intervention.* Baltimore: University Park Press.

Hall, R. V., Lund, D., & Jackson, D. (1968). Effects of teacher attention on study behavior. *Journal of Applied Behavior Analysis, 1*, 1-12.

Hollis, J. H. (1965). The effects of social and non-social stimuli on the behavior of profoundly retarded children, Part 1 and 2. *American Journal of Mental Deficiency, 69*, 755-789.

Hollis, J. H. (1966). Communication within dyads of severely retarded children. *American Journal of Mental Deficiency, 70*, 729-744.

Hopkins, B. L., & Conard, R. J. (1976). Putting it all together: Superschool. In N. Haring & R. L. Schiefelbusch (Eds.), *Teaching Special Children.* New York: McGraw-Hill.

Jersild, A. T. (1952). *In search of self.* New York: Teachers College, Columbia University Press.

Kantor, J. R. (1952). *An objective psychology of grammar.* Evanston, IL: Principia Press.

Lent, J. R. (1968, June). Mimosa cottage: Experiment in hope. *Psychology Today,* pp. 51-58.

McLean, J. E., Yoder, D. E., & Schiefelbusch, R. L. (1972). *Language intervention with the retarded: Developing strategies.* Baltimore: University Park Press.

Miller, G. A. (1951). *Language and communication.* New York: McGraw-Hill.

Mowrer, O. H. (1952). *Learning theory and behavior.* New York: John Wiley and Sons, Inc.

Risley, T. R. (1968). Jenny Lee: Learning and lollipops. *Psychology Today, 25,* 28-66.

Risley, T. R., & Hart, B. M. (1968). Developing correspondence between the nonverbal and verbal behavior of preschool children. *Journal of Applied Behavior Analysis, 1,* 267-281.

Risley, T. R., & Reynolds, N. J. (1968). Emphasis as a prompt for verbal imitation. *Journal of Applied Behavior Analysis, 1,* 267-281.

Rosenfeld, H. M. (1972). The experimental analysis of interpersonal influence processes. *Journal of Communication, 22,* 424-442.

Ruder, K., & Smith, M. (1974). Issues in Language Training. In R. L. Schiefelbusch and L. L. Lloyd (Eds.), *Language perspectives: Acquisition, retardation and intervention.* Baltimore: University Park Press.

Schiefelbusch, R. L. (1962). The Kriegies speak. *Todays Speech, 10,* 4-6.

Schiefelbusch, R. L. (1978). Administrative support systems for research. *The Behavior Therapist, 1*(2), 3-6.

Schiefelbusch, R. L., Copeland, R. H., & Smith, J. O. (Eds.) (1967). *Language and mental retardation: empirical and conceptual considerations.* New York: Holt, Rinehart & Winston.

Schiefelbusch, R. L., & Hoyt, R. (1980). The Decade of the satellite. *Journal of Special Education Technology, 3*(3), 1-4.

Skinner, B. F. (1957). *Science and human behavior.* New York: Appleton-Century-Crofts.

Spradlin, J. E. (1963). Language and communication of mental defectives. In N. Ellis (Ed.), *Handbook of mental deficiency.* New York: McGraw-Hill.

Stephenson, W. (1953). *The study of behavior: Q-Technique and its methodology,* University of Chicago Press.

Stokes, T. F., & Baer, D. M. (1977). An implicit technology of generalization. *Journal of Applied Behavior Analysis, 10,* 349-367.

Warren, S., & Rogers-Warren, A. (1980). Current perspectives in language remediation: A special monograph. *Education and Treatment of Children, 5,* 133–153.

Waryas, C., & Stremel-Campbell, K. (1978). Grammatical training for the language-delayed child. In R. L. Schiefelbusch (Ed.), *Language intervention strategies.* Baltimore: University Park Press.

Wolf, M. M., Phillips, E. L., & Fixsen, D. L. (1972). The teaching family: A new model for the treatment of deviant child behavior in the community. In S. W. Bijou & E. L. Ribes (Eds.), *First Symposium on Behavior Modification in Mexico* (pp. 51–62). New York: Academic Press.

10

Biography in Autobiography

Burton Blatt

Burton Blatt, born 1927 in New York City, holds a B.S. in education from New York University (1949), an M.A. in student personnel from Teachers College, Columbia University (1950), an Ed.D. in special education from Pennsylvania State University (1956), and an L.H.D. from Ithaca College (1974).

Dr. Blatt is dean of the School of Education at Syracuse University (1976-) where he served as director of the Division of Special Education and Rehabilitation from 1969-76, and in 1970 was named one of six Centennial Professors. In 1971, he founded the Center on Human Policy at Syracuse University. Previously, Dr. Blatt was professor and chairman of the Special Education Department at Boston University (1961-69) and associate professor, professor, and chairman of the Special Education Department at Southern Connecticut State College (1956-61).

Past president (1976-77) and a fellow of the American Association on Mental Deficiency, Dr. Blatt is also past president of the Teacher Education Division of the Council for Exceptional Children (1970-71), former book review editor and current associate editor of Exceptional Children, *and a former member of the Board of Directors of the Foundation for Exceptional Children.*

In 1965, Dr. Blatt was named an Outstanding Educator in the United States. He is the recipient of the Annual Award from the Massachusetts Psychological Association (1967), the Annual Award from the Massachusetts Association for Retarded Children (1968), the Annual Education Award from the Northeast Region of the American Association of Mental Deficiency (1973), the National Humanitarian Award from the American Association of Mental Deficiency (1974), the Newell C. Kephart Memorial Award from Purdue University (1974), and the award for Outstanding Contributions to the Field of Mental Retardation from the New York State Association of Teachers of the Handicapped (1976). A former consultant to the Joseph P. Kennedy, Jr.,

263

264 Biography in Autobiography

Foundation, he has also received several awards and citations from such governmental organizations and agencies as the President's Committee on Mental Retardation and the Department of Health, Education, and Welfare.

THE APOLOGY

Because I would find it unappealing (if not impossible) to do myself, I asked three generous students—Barbara Hawes, Helene DeSanto, and Jo-Ann Blaymore—to read as much of my work as they could bear in order to help me put this chapter together. Starting with New York and continuing in chronological fashion, the task they had was to collect my experiences as I've written about them as a public school teacher, and later while at Penn State, New Haven, Boston, and Syracuse. This mosaic of published papers that go back more than twenty-five years is an attempt to illuminate some of the events and significant people in my own professional life which I do not want to explain in the same manner I have often explained the works of colleagues in my capacity as reviewer and critic.[1] That is, most professors are too modest to personally publicize the positive critiques of their books and papers, even if they are all too willing to let you forget the negative ones. Hence the form of this chapter.

I dispense with quotation marks and the indentations normal with such material. Some updated or new connecting materials not previously published are added, and, where appropriate, in parentheses. Also, I changed or omitted a few repetitive phrases and corrected a few minor errors missed when these works were first prepared for journals and books. For reader convenience (I hope), italicized portions begin or end major sections, serving as dividers and transitions. All of these exceptions to conventional style are intended by me to enhance readability and, consequently, reader satisfaction. I apologize to any reader who is offended by the few repetitious or painfully remembered paragraphs he encounters here. This is a summary!

Like my earlier books and essays, what follows is another explanation of the self. In a sense, I've spent my entire adult life working on this chapter. If little else, it may suggest that I've been writing my history as I've tried to think through this life along the way of living it. This chapter especially follows in the tradition of my paper "Toward an Understanding of People with Special Needs" (1975b), quoted liberally here, and "How I became a Professor," recently published in my book, *In and Out of the University: Essays on Higher and Special Education* (Blatt, 1982), which depicted the very personal side of my life and, consequently, is not quoted in this more academic autobiography. Again, please forgive the bits of repetition here and there. All of my work deals essentially with people and, obviously, so does this chapter—the

---

[1]The reader interested in the more personal aspects of my life in mental retardation and the university can read, "How I Became a Professor," in my book, *In and Out of the University: Essays on Higher and Special Education*, Baltimore: University Park Press, 1982.

same people. Life repeats itself, is at times exhilarating, at times mundane and disappointing. One's life both surprises and bores. And, of course, the writer usually intends to excite, surprise, interest, and sometimes even exhilarate the reader. But, as in one's real life, a paper or book also provides its share of disappointments—to writer as well as to reader. That too is a lesson well worth learning.

ANOTHER EXPLANATION

New York

There was a beginning, and, like all beginnings, it was filled with innocence and with hope. (Blatt, 1975b, p. 394)

In 1949, I was teaching school, finishing a Master's degree at Columbia, trying to understand what teaching was all about, not yet able to comprehend what I was all about. The school had, among other features—including the basketball team, which I coached—a unit of several special classes for the mentally retarded. It was in this school where I met Horace Mann, now Professor in the Division of Exceptional Children Education at the State University College in Buffalo, New York. He was one of the school's special class teachers. His encouragement led me to this field and sustained me, especially during some difficult beginning years. He also led me to Dick Hungerford. Will I ever again meet a person with such dazzling brilliance and such zeal to do good for people as Dick Hungerford?

It had happened to others, now to me. I put aside what I had thought were primary goals. Instead, I became a special class teacher in the Coney Island section of Brooklyn, working with Dick, Horace, and others, each believing in our special mission and in the Occupational Education curriculum for the mentally retarded (Blatt, 1975b, p. 392).

I had a group of about 15 children from the ages of about 6 to about 17 or 18. The children stayed with me all the years of their schooling. So I knew some of those children six and seven years, and I knew their families. I used to visit the family, sit down around the kitchen table, and have wine with the mother and father. They were from a very stable, low-income neighborhood in the Bensonhurst section of Brooklyn, one of the ethnic neighborhoods that you read about. Most of them were children whom you would now call culturally deprived, and a few were what might be called minimally brain damaged. They were indistinguishable as soon as they left school (Connor, Kirk, & Blatt, 1977a, pp. 9–14).

Although there were other teachers before and after, I begin exactly where I should, with Richard Hungerford, who once thought my optimism refreshing and tested it to find me little more than merely optimistic. Without a direct word, Richard Hungerford taught me the difference between being happy and happiness, between honesty and honor, between what one should do for others and what one must do for himself, between ignorance and insensitivity, between untested innocence and innocence earned. He taught that goodness deprived of truth is more a liability than a virtue. I met that man on a winter's night in New York City, December, 1949. I was a teacher of English and social studies in a Brooklyn junior high school. He was the city's director of special education for the mentally retarded. I was twenty-two years old and thought him an old man (I wonder if my students now view me as an old man). We talked and talked, about many things, but mainly about me. I didn't understand all he said and, in retrospect, after we knew each other better, I hoped he didn't understand all that I said. He spoke about complex matters and, so it appeared to me, in ways that were almost deliberately evasive. A sentence begun wasn't finished with words but with a nod or a smile or just the faintest movement of a hand. And all the while I was supposed to hear what was said and understand what was intended. Surely, as if he knew it would happen, I did hear and did understand (Blatt, 1975b, p. 394).

The brilliant logic of his philosophy of occupational education and a close professional association with him and others in the New York City "Occupational Education Group"—Frank Borreca, Chris DeProspo, Irwin Goldstein, Horace Mann, Lou Rosenzweig, Leo Shainman, Ray Simches, and Nell White, my supervisor—convinced me of the need for the development of different, realistic curricula for the mentally retarded and, further, convinced me of the absolute superiority of the New York program over others with which I was acquainted. Involvement with this group of very bright and very dedicated special educators—as well as with two superb principals I served with, Lazarus Ross and Frederick Nislow—did a great deal to give me the confidence I needed to teach the mentally retarded, to improve and refine my teaching and, later, to seek advanced graduate training. Especially, the essays by Hungerford, "On Brotherhood" (1949), "On Locusts" (1950), and "Peace on Earth" (1946) greatly influenced my conceptions of the nature and needs of the mentally retarded. Today, I still consider them among the most provocative and beautifully written papers ever to appear in the fields of psychology and education (Blatt, 1967, p. 73).

Dick Hungerford taught me that any word has multiple meanings and that there isn't *truth* but many truths. He taught me that only the very young or the very insensitive deal with complex issues simply or believe that easy solutions to problems are as easy as they seem. He taught me about the law of the pendulum and that the only thing we learn from history is that we don't learn from history—that a person is doomed to repeat his acts and problems and their solutions uncountable times during his life. As I can't avoid the law of the pendulum, neither does the larger society—as I don't learn from experiences, neither do other people and groups.

Dick Hungerford taught me that, while truth is elusive and complex, it's the best that one can hope for in a human being, for while most people view honesty as a nuisance, for him it was no less important than his life. Yet I also learned from him that Don Quixote was a foolish loser, not because he fought windmills, but only because he didn't try to understand why others thought him the fool for the effort. He couldn't turn his battles to an advantage because he didn't "read" the minds of those with whom he needed to deal. He remained blissfully ignorant and, thus, his innocence was never put to the essential test of the mob.

Dick Hungerford instructed me as to the ways of the academy, which are to mistrust the abstract, the facile, the light, the generalist. He taught me why I should be wary of that of which academe is not wary, and why I must learn to appreciate and value that which is often disdained. He taught me that learning—discovering, changing—can be a moving experience for its own sake. It's wondrous because one finds that there is power in discovery and in gaining competency. It's especially grand as one learns about his own educability; the more one learns, the more one comprehends that he can learn more, and more, and more. Dick Hungerford helped me to believe again in my own educability. I learned from him that, when one is right, he doesn't need a miracle to win. In the end, the opposition needs the miracle to defeat him. He was the first of my great teachers and my indebtedness to him has been a lifelong affair, even though he is now gone (Blatt, 1975b, p. 395).

Pennsylvania

There was a time in my life when everything was marvelous because I didn't know enough. I had owned the earth, but now it owns me. I had innocence once. I thought that goodness was always rewarded and evil was always punished, that society needed only uncover injustice to rectify it. When I lost my innocence, I joined the mob who had lost theirs; yet amid their jaundice, I might someday recover it again. (Blatt, 1975, p. 394)

Suddenly, too quickly some thought, the time had come for me to continue graduate studies. Dick Hungerford advised me to seek out Margaret Neuber, Professor of Special Education at Penn State University. But was I ready for doctoral study? How will you know to answer that question if you don't seek informed and disinterested opinion? Why a doctorate? You are now capable of learning more elsewhere than you can here. And you need further graduate preparation to be ready for that time when you will be asked to assume greater responsibility. Why Penn State? Because Margaret Neuber is there. What is any place, any university, but its people? (Blatt, 1975, p. 395)

So, in 1950 I began doctoral study in special education under the tutelage of Professor Margaret Neuber. This experience, which was interrupted for four productive and fulfilling years when I returned to New York City to continue my special class teaching and to be married, caused me to change a great many of my preconceptions concerning the mentally retarded. Professor Neuber, a great teacher and a dedicated humanist, provided me with opportunities to test some of my cherished notions concerning the constitutional differences of all mentally retarded children (Blatt, 1967, pp. 7–8).

I became involved in innumerable stimulating debates with classmates concerning the relative merits of placing diagnosed mentally retarded children in special classes or regular classes. In my efforts to confront my opponents with irrefutable evidence of the absolute superiority of special classes for the mentally retarded (especially the logic and genius of New York City's Occupational Education program), evidence which I was certain existed in abundance—I proceeded to review, systematically, the relevant literature. To my surprise and chagrin, I was able to locate but two studies, both approximately twenty years old, that concerned themselves with analyses of the abilities of mentally retarded children in special classes as compared with retarded children attending regular classes. Unfortunately, at least from my point of view at that time, both studies presented data which could only lead to the conclusion that by placing retarded children in special classes, we in some ways interfere with their academic, personal, and physical development. Mentally retarded children appeared to profit more from regular class placement! Further analyses of these studies and review of criticisms of the research methodologies employed in executing them convinced me that a more rigorously designed study of the problem was long overdue; my research was the first of any kind in this area since 1936 (Blatt, 1967, pp. 7-8).

I began my first formal research experience in 1950, comparing the physical abilities of a selected group (nonrandom) of educable mentally retarded children with similarly selected typical children. Not only were no significant differences found between groups, but, in certain categories, the mentally retarded surpassed their typical schoolmates. A concurrent analysis of the literature disclosed that my findings were not particularly unusual. That study, plus my 1955-56 doctoral research (Blatt, 1956) added considerable ambiguity to what I considered both an unshakable philosophy and understanding of the etiologies of mental retardation and the consequences of them (Blatt, 1967, p. 74).

Numerous replications of my study conducted since 1956 have more or less substantiated my findings that, to date, special education, in and of itself, has no particular virtue. For some children, it appears that special classes are of benefit; for others, the benefits are dubious; for a third category, it doesn't appear to make too much difference whether they are placed in special or regular classes (Blatt, 1967, p. 7).

What I had learned from Dick Hungerford about my educability was widened by Margaret Neuber to encompass the educability of all people. I had matriculated, studied, and tried to understand things better. I even completed what was required of me. Yet, at least so I now believe, the victory was not in the degree but in earning Margaret Neuber's friendship and respect. Miss Neuber taught me about the correctness of things, order, values, and priorities. She helped me to comprehend the essentialness of judgment, the difference between one who has judgment and one who cannot make decisions because he has no values. I also learned to believe, because she so fervently believed, that the future for all people holds nothing but good. Yet she wasn't merely a fatalist, for she, more than anyone before or since, taught me that there would be times when I should take great risks, grasp the rod, or all that would remain would be the snake. I must not passively accept the world as it is, people as they are, or myself as I appear to be. I must try to change the world, and the beginning is always with oneself. I must change or nothing changes. I am at the center of the conflict, at its origin, and at the solution. Miss Neuber lived a life that taught anyone who would understand that innocence and goodness aren't rewarded. They are rewards, as honesty is the reward. Everything else is good fortune or bad fortune (Blatt, 1975b, pp. 395–396).

Connecticut

Now I teach . . . Once I was given everything; now I am supposed to give everything. The surprise of it all is that nothing has changed, and nothing will change. I remain the learner. (Blatt, 1975b, p. 397)

A degree was won and, in our culture, that signals the start of a different life. New Haven beckoned, not because I was special but more, I suppose, because someone special was needed and I was available. Why was I available? Not, in all honesty, because of New Haven's attractiveness at that time; more because no one else called or wrote. It was, as the saying goes, a marriage of convenience, and it turned out splendidly. There I met Seymour Sarason of Yale University, and the success of my first academic appointment and finding Seymour are not unrelated. I learned from that man. . . . I learned about the clinical ethos: Describe the observation. Separate it from your interpretation of its meaning and significance. What is the presenting problem? What did you do about it? What happened? If you had to do it over again, what would you now do differently?

I also learned about settings and how they are created, about community, in its psychological as well as physical sense. But, most importantly I believe, Seymour Sarason influenced my method and style in analyzing and attempting to solve problems. He taught me how to think better. . . . Seymour Sarason encouraged me to commit my thinking to paper; he caused me to want to become a writer (Blatt, 1975b, p. 396).

The Observational Seminar

In retrospect, it becomes increasingly clear that my tenure at Southern Connecticut State College was concerned with a search for understanding the discrepancy between the logic of Hungerford's nativism and the data I was beginning to accumulate through systematic evaluations of children.

Through Seymour Sarason, I became better acquainted with the works of Skeels and his Iowa associates, Spitz, Schaefer-Simmern, Clarke & Clarke, Ginzberg & Bray, and other more optimistic thinkers (Blatt, 1967, p. 74).

In 1957, Seymour Sarason and I—and several years later, with George Brabner, Frank Garfunkel, and Albert T. Murphy—began development of what we call an "observational seminar." It was created in order to narrow what we considered an overwhelming discrepancy between the experiences a teacher-education student has during his college preparations and the understandings, the skills, and the attitudes he is expected to display as a teacher once he assumes professional status. It was our further intention to utilize this seminar in a way that would give the college student experience in observing behavior, with methods to discriminate between what is observed and what is inferred, and with some notions concerning the nature of his prejudices and how he may better understand himself as both learner and teacher (Blatt, 1967, p. 190).

The most obvious difference between our approach and those currently employed resides in differing conceptions of supervision. The students were rarely *given* ideas or starting points; they had to subject *their* ideas, opinions, and suggestions to discussion; they were more or less forced to learn to give expression to and to depend upon *their* curiosity; they could express their puzzlements and ignorance without viewing them as signs of stupidity but as aids to productive learning; and they were enabled to see for themselves the complexity and selectivity of their own observational processes and their effects on action.

It is essential to our approach to expect that students will and must struggle, because learning to think independently is never easy, particularly when previous learning has been of the passive dependent variety (Blatt, 1963b, pp. 127–128).

What was obviously crucial to our approach was the opportunity for instructors and students together to observe a teacher and her class over a long period of time. One of the most important aspects of such an opportunity is the basis provided for the predictions made out of our observations. It is our impression that the observations of the students, which they would bring up for discussion, frequently involved three types of considerations: a description of the overt event, inferences about the internal or covert states of the children or teacher, and an implicit prediction about the consequences of whatever they observed.

An advantage of long-term observation is that we can count on being able to observe and discuss almost every kind of important problem a teacher encounters. In short, we deal not with an ideal situation, but with a representative one.

In the course of discussion of these and other problems, one principle was always emphasized: Once we have pinned a label on a child, our observations of him tend to pay more attention to what fits in with that label than what is discrepant with it. Consequently, we tend to "prove" our initial prediction when, in fact, contrary evidence has simply been overlooked.

The preparation of teachers, both for special classes and the regular grades, has not suffered from a lack of discussion. However, there has been a relative lack of effort to describe practices in a way which gives the feeling that one knows what is going on, how it is related to stated aims, and the problems one would encounter in scientifically testing the consequences of the preparation practices (Blatt, 1963b, pp. 128–131).

At this time, we have not sought evidence of the kind that can be labeled "research" to validate the efficacy of our approach. However, this experience ... has been a great learning adventure for our students and, in many ways especially, for us. We have rediscovered—but so much more clearly now—that teaching requires sustained intellectual discipline, continuous self-evaluation, control of one's prejudices, sheer undefinable artistry, and the humanism that we all must have. As one seminar student so sensitively put it, "We are wrestling here with our own retardation to cope, ultimately, with the retardation of others" (Blatt, 1963a, p. 94).

I am concerned about our inability to distinguish between the purposes and procedures of research and the responsibilities and tasks implicit in serving children. I am sensitive to the inefficiency and wastefulness of conventional student teaching models. There are problems that are amenable to solution or, at least, better understanding (Blatt, 1963a, p. 93).

Why research? For that matter, why education? Do the products of research or education make people smarter, more moral, more mentally healthy, more physically able? Is our president today, or the next one to be, more intelligent than Jefferson? Is this pope or chief rabbi more spiritual, a greater leader than the first pope or the first rabbi? Is there a connection between research results and practices? And if there is not, should we be disturbed about the matter?

Research and education are activities that cannot be separated from values and prejudices about people. Because of that, the one who conducts the research is most affected by it, as the one who engages in his education is most influenced by the experience. Research is valuable because of its effects on the people who engage in it. If it is helpful to the greater society, or disabled children, or the child you teach, all to the good. However, as unpopular as this may be to many, the history of research in the social sciences suggests that its primary value is for those who do it, and the payoff to the larger community results as those researchers and their various colleagues, and *their* colleagues, influence us (Blatt, 1975b, p. 409).

This [discussion] has been concerned primarily with the implications of the point of view that the teacher, far from being a technician or imparter of knowledge, is an applier of psychological principles in a particular kind of learning situation. One of the major implications of this point of view is that improvement of the quality of teaching is not likely to take place in any marked kind of way by merely increasing the amount and variety of information which teachers should have. Just as we must never confuse degree of education with degree of wisdom—the educated person is not necessarily "wise" in the sense that he can utilize or apply what he knows in appropriate, non-self-defeating ways—we must not confuse what a teacher knows with how she applies such knowledge (Sarason, Davidson, & Blatt, 1962, pp. 117–118).

The Institution

During my last year at Penn State (1955), I had made several visits to Laurelton State School, an institution for the mentally retarded located twenty or thirty miles from the University campus. I was struck by the beautiful grounds and bucolic setting of the school, but I did have some negative reactions. These were concerned mainly with the unavailability of schooling opportunities for the residents, many of whom were mildly retarded and, so it seemed to me then, some of whom appeared to be of normal intelligence. (Blatt, 1970a, p. 4)

It was not until I completed doctoral studies and began my college teaching career that I became a regular visitor to state institutions for the mentally retarded. After my appointment to . . . Southern Connecticut State College, I was responsible for the supervision of student teachers in Special Education, several of whom were assigned to the Southbury Training School and the Mansfield Training School, at the time the two state schools for the mentally retarded in Connecticut. Further, with Fred Finn, then the Director of Training at Southbury, I organized a workshop each summer for teachers of the trainable mentally retarded. These involvements caused me to become a very frequent visitor to the state schools. I attended staff conferences, child study committee meetings, and numerous other activities in these facilities. I visited all of the dormitories on innumerable occasions and, quite literally, became a kind of quasi-staff member, especially at the Southbury Training School.

In 1959, Governor Ribicoff appointed me to the first Connecticut Advisory Council on Mental Retardation. For the first time, I was now required to observe the institutions and to consider their needs from the viewpoint of someone who had responsibility for them and who pledged his commitment to serve them. However, during my years in Connecticut, including those on the Advisory Council, I had a general feeling about institutions that, although not completely positive, permitted me to sleep soundly and not worry about them or about their residents. Obviously, I had visited numerous back wards (although Connecticut did seem to have fewer of these than did other states and did seem to be doing more for its institutionalized retarded than other states) and attended innumerable etiological conferences. Even then, in my naive, less jaundiced stage of development, I was able to observe all of the obvious and many of the subtle barbarisms that seemed to be perpetrated daily in state institutions. I explained those observations to myself by using stock reasonings: "nature of things in institutions," "the invariant characteristics of the severely retarded," and "we are doing the best we can."

A glimmer of a more mature understanding of the things that are, and the things that need be, began to take hold during the last year of my service on the Governor's Advisory Council. Ernest Roselle, the first superintendent at Southbury Training School, articulated during the early 1950s a view of regionalization and community participation in programming that was brought to fruition a decade later by such individuals as Bert Schmickel and Fred Finn. Bert Schmickel, then Deputy Commissioner for Mental Retardation, and Fred Finn, then Superintendent of the Seaside Regional Center, with the approval and encouragement of the first Advisory Council, established a center that began to demonstrate the obsolescence of back wards, certainly, and the inappropriateness of large institutions, probably. We began to understand that the condition we termed "back ward life" is an invention of the nonretarded and a reflection of their character rather than a necessary concomitant to severe mental retardation. As we grew to appreciate the certainty that back wards could be eradicated, some of us learned with ever increasing anxiety and torment how truly evil these monuments to inhumanity were. While we could convince ourselves that back wards were necessary—were, in a way, providing the best care possible under intolerable circumstances—we were able to abide them. With the advent of clear alternatives, our defensive moat—"the nature of things"—crumbled. What was being demonstrated was that the architects of back wards, the progenitors of the feces-smearers, the culprits of this holocaust are normal men who create public policy. This realization did not come to me overnight and, in fact, I am still struggling with it (Blatt, 1970a, pp. 4-5).

> As this kind of biography of my teaching, clinical, and research activities unfolds, it may become clearer that my central—and abiding—preoccupation has been with testing the hypothesis that intelligence is educable. Further, to the degree to which this hypothesis obtains, it is certain that the hypothesis that intelligence is educable refers both to children and teachers; and to the extent we can influence the latter, we shall influence the former. Within this conviction lies the essential mandate for the teaching profession. (Blatt, 1967, p. 243)

Boston

> Who among us is untroubled and without regret for the things he might have done, for the chances gone, for the world that might have been?
> Who among us could have changed, but chose not to learn? (Blatt, 1973, p. 404)

In the fall of 1961 I assumed the chairmanship of the Special Education Department at Boston University. Among my responsibilities was the inauguration of a research program sponsored by the United States Office of Education and involving three- and four-year-old children from disadvantaged homes (Blatt, 1970a, p. 3).

Specifically, we were interested in the ways in which intervention into the preschool and early school lives of so-called disadvantaged children reduces the likelihood that such children will develop intellectual and academic defects so frequently found in youngsters from such backgrounds.

As I now leaf through the monograph that was one of the products of that study, I am almost surprised to learn again—one does forget so easily—how deeply and pervasively Binet influenced our thinking, in fact, led us to that work. For as a matter of fact, almost the entire preface dealt with Binet and his work, and the title of our monograph, *The Educability of Intelligence*, was taken directly from his book, *Les Idées Modernes Sur Les Enfants*. In fact, what we say in the very first sentence of that preface—"We are indebted to Alfred Binet as the progenitor of much of the inspiration for research reported in this volume"—might easily have been said by many during this century who have attempted to struggle with the puzzle of human intellect and its unfolding (Blatt, 1974b, p. 64).

It is ironic to note that the individual most blamed for the rigid and stereotyped manner in which educators and psychologists view the nature of intelligence and the probabilities for increasing it, Alfred Binet, decried the widespread prejudice he found against the proposition that intelligence is educable. I speculate that if Alfred Binet were witness to contemporary events, he would feel great concern over the continuance of programs and policies that lead to the intellectual disfranchisement of a great number of American youth and that result in impoverished learners denied their human and political rights to develop, a condition that will persist unless massive educational reforms are instituted (Blatt, 1967, p. 4).

First we thought him an environmentalist, then a nativist, again an environmentalist, and all the while he was simply Alfred Binet. Once he was blessed, later cursed; when he created that first scale with Simon, his contribution was the cure; at the end, it was the disease. Yet Binet changed only as a person changes; he learned. He grew, and reshaped some singular ideas. He grew; he learned.

But first—not "in the beginning" sense, but first "most importantly"— there was Alfred Binet who led a prudent, thoughtful, scholarly, and productive life. He learned, while society played games with what he learned. He changed, while the more we "changed" the more we froze, or the more we danced in meaningless circles (Blatt, 1974b, p. 63).

Binet was not the first scientist to propose the notion that intelligence is educable, i.e., it is modified by training and practice. There is a curious history of efforts to educate intelligence, of which the first record available is the early nineteenth century work of Jean-Marc-Gaspard Itard. The story of Victor, the wild boy of Aveyron, is a familiar one and need not be summarized here. However, Itard's principles of treatment are central to this discussion.

Itard was convinced that man left unattended is inferior to the domestic animal and, without human contact, cannot develop as well as an animal can. Further, man's imitative instinct is that force which educates his senses, and that instinct is most powerful during the early childhood years and decreases with age. Quite possibly, this is what John Donne meant when he said that man is not an island unto himself. We may go further; man may cease to resemble man as his relationships with others decline and there is a point beyond which there is little hope for return to a human style of thinking. This may have been Hungerford's meaning when he said "in an institution there is always tomorrow so that he who starts out a student ends up, by default, an inmate" (Blatt, 1967, pp. 128-129).

Our pre-school study has its roots in my inability in the 1950s to convince myself that there is some particular uniqueness or specialness in retarded children or in the interventions we impose on them in the public schools; the inability of prior investigators (Kirk and Fouracre) to locate pre-school mentally retarded children with intact central nervous systems; a developing climate of optimism in the scientific community as to possibilities for educating intelligence; and an intensive personal study of the prior research on this problem. A great many people contributed to this pre-school project, but the principals who joined me were Frank Garfunkel, Seymour Sarason, and George Brabner.

I became associated with Frank Garfunkel and Omar Moore just prior to leaving for Boston. At the time, Frank was Assistant Professor of Special Education at the University of Connecticut and Omar was Associate Professor of Sociology at Yale University. Through a series of interesting and unrelated circumstances, I began to study Moore's Responsive Environments and in the Spring of 1961, approximately three weeks after accepting the Boston University appointment, which was to commence the following September, I applied to the United States Office of Education, Cooperative Research Branch, for a grant to study the effects of Responsive Environments on the intellectual and social competencies of educable mentally retarded children (Project D-014, Contract 2-10-056). The proposal was approved and funded. I was designated as project director, Frank Garfunkel as design and statistical consultant, Seymour Sarason as psychological consultant, Omar Moore as consultant in Responsive Environments, and George Brabner—who joined us one year later—as associate project director. In September, 1963, Frank Garfunkel came to Boston University as Associate Professor of Special Education (Blatt, 1967, pp. 75-76).

Insofar as this study was concerned, we had neither significant nor convincing data to substantiate our research hypothesis that intelligence is educable, i.e., a function of practice and training. However, this study revealed that we still have a great deal to discover concerning the nature/nurture interaction, about the most efficient and sufficient period to begin interventions, and about the possible intervention models that may have the greatest desired effects. The information obtained in this study has encouraged us to continue the quest for processes and methodologies to educate intelligence and, for certain children, to prevent mental retardation (Blatt & Garfunkel, 1967, p. 601).

It was not until this project was nearly completed that I realized that one could spend a most fruitful research career investigating the hypothesis that intelligence is educable and that the overwhelming incidence of mental retardation derives from the intellectual disfranchisement of children variously called culturally deprived, sub-cultural, or poor. Two individuals are basically responsible for my involvement in the systematic testing of this hypothesis. I owe them each a deep debt of gratitude: Seymour Sarason, for nurturing this interest in me and providing me with a rich background of prior literature, and Frank Garfunkel, for possibly the first time making the scientific method clear to me and for encouraging me to develop and refine my scientific skills (Blatt, 1967, p. 76).

There are those among us who believe that given proper conditions, it can be demonstrated that intelligence is a function of practice and training. There are those among us who believe that this optimistic conception of human potential may be one of the greatest and most important ideas developed by modern man (Blatt, 1973, p. 98).

It is my conviction that intelligence is educable. By this statement I mean that there are procedures and conditions that intervene to bring out or elicit capabilities in an individual for changing, both in rate and complexity, his learning performance in school-related and other problem-solving tasks. Furthermore, it is my deep conviction that the essence of human rights requires that all individuals be afforded opportunities to develop skills to cope with our complex society. And, however these skills mature, each human being is entitled to an equal chance to prosper with the skill variable dominant to this possibility. It is my conviction that a large number of American children, variously called cultural-familial mental retardates, culturally deprived, school dropouts, or simply poor children, have not been given sufficient or even grossly equal opportunities to develop school-related skills and, further, those that have been able to survive and weather the school years have not been given equal opportunities to utilize their education in American competitive society (Blatt, 1967, p. 4).

What has again and again been brought to us so clearly is that the "educability" hypothesis has a pervasive fascination that sustains the researcher, for the concept includes all people and so many things that it can easily intrude into every nook and cranny of our time and energy; the hypothesis refers not only to children, not only to the mentally retarded, not only to those in the inner city or those in the institution; but, to the degree it has relevance for those groups, it has relevance for all of us—not only for children, but for their teachers, not only for their teachers, but for the teachers of their teachers. For a child to change, his teacher has to change. For my students to have changed, I had to (Blatt, 1975b, p. 415).

The Rhode Island Study

In 1962 and 1963, I was given the opportunity to investigate special-class conditions in the State of Rhode Island. (Blatt, 1967, p. 8)

It was the central purpose of this report to describe current programs for both educable and trainable mentally retarded children in the public schools in Rhode Island and, in so doing, to evaluate the degree to which the state has capitalized on more than a half-century of experience in this field.

This study did not make comparisons with competing types of regular-class programs. However, the Rhode Island study reinforced my conviction that the mere establishment of more special classes in the United States would not necessarily solve or mitigate the problems of the mentally retarded or the quandaries of those responsible for their education and care. It also greatly strengthened my prejudice against the casual manner in which I observed special classes to be developing.

The question to which Rhode Island must address itself is: To what extent are current programs for all eligible mentally retarded children concordant with those minimum educational opportunities that any civilized society assigns itself to provide for all of its children?

Three serious problems are raised here. In a great many instances, materials used in the special classes—and curriculum content as well—appear to be lower-keyed versions of curricula in the regular grades. In few instances did teachers prepare specialized materials for these children. In these classes, as well as in others, teachers are often more concerned with controlling discipline problems and reducing the amount of "noise" than in providing an environment where children can work cooperatively. Lastly, there appears to be no clear-cut notion of what comes next; certainly, many children and teachers in many of these classes appear to be confused as to what they are doing and, especially, why (Blatt, 1967, pp. 8, 27, 28, 47).

Christmas in Purgatory

In spite of some claims that it is darkest before the dawn, one may yet encounter terror at high noon; and one may thus conclude that man's days can be as black as his nights. (Blatt, 1975b, p. 421).

There is a hell. It is on earth. And, in America, we have our own special inferno. We were visitors there during the Christmas season, 1965.

During the early fall of that year, a United States Senator, Robert Kennedy, visited several of his state's institutions for the mentally retarded. His reactions to these visits were widely published in our various news media. These disclosures shocked millions of Americans as well as infuriated scores of public office holders and professional persons responsible for the care and treatment of the mentally retarded.

In the main, a segment of the general public was numbed because it is difficult for "uninvolved" people to believe that in our country in 1965, human beings were being treated less humanely, with less care, and under more deplorable conditions than were animals. A number of the "involved" citizenry—i.e. those who legislate and budget for institutions for the mentally retarded and those who administer them—were infuriated because the Senator reacted to only the worst of what he had seen, not to the worthwhile programs that he might have. Further, this latter group was severely critical of the Senator for taking "whirlwind" tours and, in the light of just a few hours of observations, damning entire institutions and philosophies.

During the time of these visits the senior author was a participant in a research project at the Seaside Regional Center. Fred Finn and he spent considerable time discussing the ongoing raging debate between Senator Kennedy and his Governor, Nelson Rockefeller. We concluded the following: It does not require too imaginative a mind or too sensitive a proboscis to realize that one has stumbled into a dung hill, regardless of how it is camouflaged. It is quite irrelevant how well the rest of an institution's program is being fulfilled if one is concerned about that part of it which is terrifying. No amount of rationalization can mitigate that which, to many of us, is cruel and inhuman treatment (Blatt & Kaplan, 1966, p. v).

After a good deal of thought, I decided to follow through on what then seemed, and what eventually became, a bizarre venture. One of my friends, Fred Kaplan, is a professional photographer. On Thanksgiving Day, 1965, I presented the following plan to him. We were to arrange to meet with each of several key administrative persons in a variety of public institutions for the mentally retarded. If we gained an individual's cooperation, we would be taken on a "tour" of the back wards and those parts of the institution that he was *most* ashamed of. On the "tour" Fred Kaplan would take pictures of what we observed, utilizing a hidden camera attached to his belt.

Through the efforts of courageous and humanitarian colleagues, including two superintendents who put their reputations and professional positions in jeopardy, we were able to visit the darkest corridors and vestibules that humanity provides for its journey to purgatory and, without being detected by ward personnel and professional staff, Fred Kaplan was able to take hundreds of photographs.

Had I known what I would actually be getting myself into and had I known what abnormal pressures would subsequently be exerted upon me as a result of this story and my efforts to bring it before the American people, I might have turned away from that first dormitory entrance as I was, finally, being admitted; and I might have fled to the shelter and protection of my academic "ivory tower" to ruminate on the injustices prevailing in society. As it was, I was in no way prepared for the degradation and despair I encountered.

I was soon to learn about decaying humanity. That story—my purgatory in black and white—which, ironically, was conceived of and written on the 700th anniversary of the birth of Dante, represents my composite impressions of what I consider to be the prevailing conditions of certain sectors of most institutions for the mentally retarded in this country. It is the hope of calling attention to the desperate needs of these institutions and, thereby, paving the way for upgrading all institutions for the mentally retarded in all dimensions of their responsibilities that this study was undertaken and this story written (Blatt, 1970a, pp. 12-13).

We distributed the first edition of *Christmas in Purgatory* in the early fall of 1966. One thousand copies were sent to a list of those individuals who we believed would be in the most advantageous positions to support a reform of institutions. The response to this publication was absolutely overwhelming. We received letters from the President of the United States, Mrs. Hubert Humphrey (several letters, requests for additional copies of the publication, and an eventual meeting), practically every United States Senator and practically every governor, and many, many commissioners of mental health and mental retardation, superintendents of state schools, professors of special education or fields allied to mental retardation, presidents of parent associations, and many hundreds of other people from all walks of life who had read the book.

At the time we were arranging for the publication of the book, I received a call from Charlie Mangel, senior editor of *Look*. . . . He had heard, through an unnamed source in "high governmental office," that we had completed a study of institutions for the mentally retarded and were having great difficulty in arranging for the publication of our report. After several meetings with him, I prepared an article and it was scheduled for publication in an issue planned for the coming fall. Actually, it was not published in *Look* until October 31, 1967, one year later (Blatt, 1970a, p. 7).

> *In humility and with knowledge that I am no better qualified as accuser than those to whom I speak, I seek redress for certain acts committed by and against mankind.*
>
> *I am a collector of injustices. Is there a profession as vilified, held more in contempt? (Blatt, 1973, p. 5)*

You see the children first. An anonymous boy, about six, squeezes his hand through the opening at the bottom of a locked door and begs, "Touch me. Play with me." A 13-year-old boy lies naked, on his own wastes, in a corner of a solitary-confinement cell. Children, one and two years old, lie silent in cribs all day, without contact with any adult, without playthings, without any apparent stimulation. The cribs are placed side by side and head to head to fill every available bit of space in the room.

The six-year-old who begged "Touch me," was one of 40 or more unkempt children of various ages crawling around a bare floor in a bare room. Their dormitory held about 100 children. It was connected to nine other dormitories containing 900 more.

In one dayroom, two male attendants stood by as half a dozen fights flared in different corners of the room. Three teen-agers were silently punching each other near a barred window. One young child, about five, was biting a second boy. Another resident, about 20, had backed a boy of about 10 into a far corner and was kicking him viciously, every now and then looking back at us. There were about 50 persons in the room. Their ages ranged from about 5 to 80.

Now I know what people mean when they say there is a hell on earth (Blatt & Mangel, 1967, p. 96).

AS HUMAN BEINGS, ALL PEOPLE ARE EQUALLY VALUABLE OR, IF NOT, THERE IS SOMETHING OF LESSER VALUE IN BEING HUMAN THAN WE HAD SUPPOSED (Blatt, 1975c, p. 8).

It does not have to be like this. We know better. We can do better—if we want to. A pleasant, estate-like home and school, the Seaside Regional Center in Waterford, Conn., has shown us how.

Seaside is a clear break with the past. Opened . . . as an experiment, it is a small, state-supported regional center designed to be a clearinghouse for all problems involving retardation within a two-county area. It was the nation's first. It was so successful that Connecticut approved 11 more like it.

Half of its programs are in the community. The center helps 850 non-resident retarded children or adults and their families. [By 1967, it operated] recreation programs in seven communities, day-care centers in five (for children able to live at home, but not eligible for school), two sheltered workshops and two day camps. There is no waiting list. No one is ignored.

"We have no magic," says Superintendent Fred Finn. "We just do not believe that because a child hasn't, means that he can't.

"Each of these children is entitled to the best and the most my child gets."

A special love exists at Seaside, a love capable of belief in the fulfillment of another human being. I am exasperated with institutional staffs that have offered me excuses, rationalizations and explanations for their behavior . . . their actions speak primarily of their character (Blatt & Mangel, 1967, pp. 96–103).

The public response pleased the editors. As for me, I became an instant, if short lived, minor celebrity (Blatt, 1974c, p. 525).

It is not possible to determine what sensitivities were most offended, what motivations were stirred, what it was that prompted each reaction. . . . Rather than being concerned with focal points of cause and effect, I prefer to react to the total impact of the article. It seems reassuring and encouraging to me that people did feel the need or desire to respond, and that emotions were aroused: anger, gratitude, dedication, sorrow. I was impressed with the variety of backgrounds of people reacting. While I have no reasonable estimate of how many people read the article and chose not to respond, I do feel that those who did represented enough of a cross-section to justify my encouragement with the article and its influence.

The article has long since been read, maybe not as easily digested by all. I feel that it "reached" some of the "right" people. Some of the effects were good. In predicting what the future holds for the retarded, I can only hope that, by such efforts, man's inhumanity to man might gradually be reformed into man's love and expectation of man, and that the small voice of the retarded and their advocates might eventually be heard more meaningfully than in the past. Someday, the mentally retarded will cease to exist as the least of the least (Blatt, 1970, p. 248).

The Connecticut Study

Why, in fact, do many colleagues predict better days ahead?

There have been some demonstrations that states will invest more resources for more humane rehabilitative centers on behalf of the mentally retarded. Experiences in Connecticut, Nebraska, Kansas, and other sections of our country have demonstrated that there are ways, procedures, and philosophies that obviate human mortification, that better guarantee for each man and woman a sense of dignity and relatedness. The author has been privileged to participate since its inception in a residential and community program that has returned human values to the concept of care and treatment for the mentally retarded—the Seaside Regional Center of Waterford, Connecticut. (Blatt, 1973, p. 93)

The following summarizes *Mental Retardation in Southeastern Connecticut*, December, 1970. The study was under the general direction of Fred Finn. James Feeney, former Director of Social Service at Seaside, was responsible for coordination of data collection activities. Frank Garfunkel, of Boston University, contributed greatly to the design of the study and data analysis. I participated in preparing the original study proposal, the organization of data collection teams, and in the writing of progress reports and most parts of the final report.

The purpose of this demographic survey of mental retardation in southeastern Connecticut was to illuminate the well-known discrepancies between psychometric estimates and known occurrences of mental retardation. Clinicians, planners, and scholars agree that a serious problem exists in the field of mental retardation, a problem that interferes with facility and program planning and one that most researchers have avoided examining. That problem is the identification of *known* mental retardation, as contrasted with the suspected or estimated prevalence (widespread existence) based on psychometric norms; e.g., 3 percent of the total population is mentally retarded, and therefore there are six million mentally retarded children and adults in the United States. For too many decades and for too much of our program and fiscal planning, estimates of the extent and degree of mental retardation have been predicated upon misleading extrapolations obtained from the study of normal probability curves, rather than from careful and systematic surveys of well-defined and controlled populations.

The striking and powerful results of this study illustrate the degree to which a regional center—one that began in the generally traditional mode of "enlightened institutional philosophy"—is able to extend its influence well beyond its geographic boundaries and historical authority. Analysis of these data demonstrates, rather forcefully, that a program dedicated to decentralized residential and community services can offer a full continuum of activities—and meet the needs of its area residents—with only a small portion of its total resources devoted to residential care. To state this another way, the Seaside

Regional Center, as reflected in these data, was able to guarantee to a region of more than three hundred thousand population almost immediate residential placement if needed, yet it was never required to place in residence more than approximately 260 people at any one time.

This demographic study . . . suggests the need to develop a newer concept—a movement away from the "center facility" to the "community-program orientation."

As noted earlier, Seaside Regional Center's overriding philosophy is to move as many clients as quickly as possible back into the mainstream of community life. Therefore, the Seaside is more than a center or a building, more than a geographically defined location. To understand the Seaside and the manner in which it functions in Southeastern Connecticut, one must appreciate the fact that it is a conglomerate located in many physical settings, held together by a common administration, mission, and public responsibility. Residential placement must be the last in a series of viable alternatives.

In addition to the information collected on programs and services available to the retarded, it is interesting to note that after six years of study we were able to locate only 2,587 persons known to be mentally retarded. This figure is somewhat less than one percent of the total population and significantly less than the number we had anticipated through extrapolated psychometric norms.

The Seaside Regional Center and, hopefully, other centers and programs, remain dissatisfied with the regional center concept—in spite of its obvious overwhelming superiority to traditional institutional models. The next phase must be to decentralize the regional center *completely*, to evolve a program where the "Center" will become a geographic area, where to visit the Seaside Regional Center will require one (or several) cars and a fair amount of gas, where the Seaside Regional Center will become the Seaside Regional Program. At least today, this appears to be our next step toward the unfolding of maximally humanizing environments for all human beings (Blatt, 1973, pp. 94-103).

The Department of Mental Health

The problem is not with officialdom's good intentions but with the limited vision of human potential and what the world may yet become. (Blatt, 1975b, p. 398)

In March of 1967, Dr. Milton Greenblatt was appointed Commissioner of Mental Health in the state of Massachusetts. Commissioner Greenblatt asked me to become the first non-medical director of the newly organized Division of Mental Retardation. I explained to him that I was not prepared to leave Boston University or university life. He explained to me that it was his understanding that I was scheduled for a sabbatical leave of absence for the coming spring semester. Why, he asked, couldn't I request a leave of absence, instead of a sabbatical? My first reaction was to refuse the director-ship. Probably the prime arguments for my later change of mind were the remarks made by several people in state government—remarks that I knew to be perfectly valid and to which I had no ready response. Essentially, I was reminded that men of good conscience cannot turn away in the face of their responsibilities to attempt to remediate those problems. I had articulated those problems and aroused a public storm. Here was my opportunity to do more than talk about them. How could I refuse it?

I began this new assignment with the Department of Mental Health on January 2, 1968, expecting to return to Boston University on September 1. Sometime during the late spring and early summer of 1968, after appropriate telephone calls from Governor Volpe and visits from Commissioner Green-blatt and myself to university officials, my leave was extended through the fall semester. In the late fall, a similar "attack" was mounted by various state officials and citizen groups, including Governor Volpe, but without Commis-sioner Greenblatt's or my participation (we had promised the University that I would return for the spring semester). I returned to the University in January, with a great many mixed feelings—excited and happy to be "back home," and, at the same time, regretting the friendships that must now be neglected, the "action" of the past, and the mission that must now be continued indirectly and without—to use a favorite term of Dr. Greenblatt's—govern-mental "clout."

This is where the "action" is. The Massachusetts Department of Mental Health, centered in 15 Ashburton Place, together with the State House, is a complex of authority, action and inaction, good deeds and bad deeds—but always power and influence. Life in this complex is always strange to the newly initiated, especially to one whose previous professional life was almost solely academic. The following is my attempt to bring some illumination to those who haven't experienced "government from the inside."

Admittedly, I take a very narrow view of things and have had very limited experience. To the degree that the reader finds me fair or unfair to certain kinds of individuals or operations, he will better understand that in a system such as I am describing it is not unusual to be both fair and unfair and to be treated both fairly and unfairly. Therefore, at the outset, I want to share my conviction that, in this particular system, decision making is a reflection of the System and its capacity to initiate good deeds or poor deeds, rather than of individuals and their attributes. It is my impression that the System does more to change individuals than individuals do toward changing the System.

A man can get along, quite adequately and for many years, on the elegance of his language and the passion and conviction of his speech. One would suppose that this is the hallmark of the university professor, and so it may be. However, I have observed sophistry and pedantries much more frequently in 15 Ashburton Place and its tentacles than in the halls of ivy. Very few people at 15 Ashburton Place *must* make decisions, if they do not wish to make them. The Commissioner of Mental Health must, as he is the Appointed Authority over all programs sponsored by the Department. The Business Office must, because they are responsible for both payrolls and hardware, items that are quickly missed if they are not delivered on time. Most other people—some high-ranking professionals included—do not have to make decisions, if they do not wish to. Obviously, many choose to make decisions, but they elect to decide and are not required to decide. For some, departmental activities are one grand round of debating, discussion, more debating, and more discussion. The payoff for sophistry is rather good, considering the investment. Men have been promoted on the passion of their verbal convictions, rarely having been required to influence the life of one child, but having persuasively proclaimed their regard for the lives of all children. Further, the System is such that one learns quickly of the peril of making certain decisions and the impossibility of making others. Rather than torment oneself with the uselessness of trying to "buck the System" (and one hears this time and time again), many men make their peace with it. They give expression to their good intentions, good training, and anger in activities that appear vigorous and dynamic but are empty repetitions, which are heard by no one of any importance or influence, but reassure the speaker that he is doing his job and that he is on the side of the "good" people (We should not discount the cathartic effect such activities provide the speaker.)

I permitted myself temporarily to head up an entire state program, not because I felt I had the answers and would right wrongs, but because I felt compelled to experience the problem in a position of responsibility. In a very basic sense I wanted to learn (Blatt, 1970a, pp. 8–9; 105–107, xi).

> *In spite of my great fortune in having enormous backing and strength derived from the faith people had in me and this work, it was—nevertheless—very painful to write* Exodus from Pandemonium. *However, I have no doubt that my pain would have been far greater had it not been written. (Blatt, 1970a, p. xix)*

In May I was invited to address a joint meeting of the Massachusetts House and Senate on the problems confronting our state schools for the mentally retarded. As matters were presented to me, it was one of the most delicate assignments with which I had ever been challenged. And I consider that address to the legislature, "The Dark Side of the Mirror," the most important I have ever given (Blatt, 1970a). Selected parts follow.

There is a dark side of every mirror, a side beyond inspection because it is without thought. And while the optimism and pride—the light—of our lives is for the gains made in civil rights, for our achievements in mental health, for the concept of the Declaration of Independence and the Constitution, surely a dark side in the evolution of our civilization in this mid-20th century must be reserved for the deep unremitting, unrewarding lives of drudgery and pain we inflict upon our institutionalized brothers who are called severely mentally retarded.

I have been to the depths, believing all the time that I would awaken, as I always had before, from this most terrifying of all nightmares. And, as I always had before, I did awaken—to the mawkish horror and degradation of N and W Buildings. I have walked beside their soiled waters where, floating gently by their dayroom shores, were the human flotsam and jetsam, the wasted and unfulfilled programs, hopes and plans of countless generations of discouraged failures who were once known in these buildings as patients, attendants, and professional staff. I have filled my nostrils and inflated my lungs in N Building until every pore of my body felt the nauseating zing of 70 years of cankered rot that will continue to generate *ad infinitum* until the seams of N's construction burst at the top and at the bottom and at its sides, until its cup of human refuse and despair runs over and drowns us all or causes us to realize, in time, what grief we perpetrate there. I have sat in its dayroom, surrounded by desperately lonely patients huddled together in their nakedness of body and spirit, defenseless against the elements, defenseless against assaults to their persons, to their souls, and to their consciousness. I have seen a hand reach out for human contact—if not for ennobling friendship—only to see it struck down by the fear and confusion of its intended recipient, as he was struck down by the fear and confusion of another recipient, as he was struck down, as he was struck down—*ad nauseam*.

If these remarks this day communicate any of my deepest thoughts and hopes, it should become very clear that I do not believe we can correct the blight of an N Building and the plight of its residents with a new set of curtains, or a new paint job, or modern plumbing, or increased attendant staff there, or new words and slogans. In the past, to one degree or another, all of these shibboleths and gestures were implemented and found wanting. All were enveloped by the mire of that totally oppressive environment. We do not suffer so much the lack of structural architects and interior designers as we do the absence of ideational architects and moral interventionists.

I have irrefutable evidence, from 18 years of clinical experience in the field of mental retardation, that NO RESIDENT needs to live in a denuded state, needs to be a head banger, or needs to be locked in solitary confinement. I have irrefutable evidence that practically every resident can be taught to eat meals independently, can be taught to live among his fellows without being of danger to himself or others and without the use of physical restraints. I have irrefutable evidence that *all* building odors can be eliminated without the need for even more powerfully repugnant chemical treatments or electronic gadgetry that masks the sources of these odors but does not eliminate the causes: filth and neglect. I have very substantive evidence that intelligence is educable, that is, people can change—learn—and that this concept applies both to the retarded and those who minister to their needs. It applies to us too. We can change in our conception of human potential and, thus, we can promote change in others. The lives of Anne Sullivan and Helen Keller speak volumes about this concept, as do the lives of Jean Itard and Victor, the Wild Boy of Aveyron.

Believe that you are more than your brother's keeper. Believe that, while on this earth, you are his savior and he is yours (Blatt, 1970a, 255-259).

> *To me, governmental utopia would provide a System that is stable—i.e., a System that is reliable and tested, one that can be counted upon to deliver goods and services—while it would always have at its command options to change parts of the System radically or the entire structure of the System evolutionarily. For me, governmental utopia means stability and comfort and reliance, on the one hand, and options and dynamism, on the other hand. While it is quite understandable that we have not achieved utopia, it is regrettable, to the extreme, that we are barely on the right road. Our optimism must lie in the knowledge that now, at least, we may have stumbled onto that road. I believe we have, or people such as myself would never have been permitted to study the things we have studied and say the things we are saying. (Blatt, 1970a, p. 118)*

For me to change and thus for the world to change, I must believe in a design of things, and that the design for all of us holds nothing but good. I must become a new man (Blatt, 1975b, p. 421).

Syracuse

> *Yet, as I observe the chaos enveloping each of us, there is reason to have hope, if not to be optimistic. For I have also observed that the evil man needs no rules to do good while the good man must be taught if you would use him for evil ends. There is hope that if society could be but shown more clearly what madness it has created, it would find ways to do better for mankind. (Blatt, 1973, p. 53)*

Syracuse University

> *I am in my [thirty-fifth] year of teaching, the last [15] at Syracuse University. I have interacted with many groups of students; I have known some of those people as well as most teachers know their students; I think I have influenced my share, and they have influenced me. The truth of the matter is that I'm proud of my students and of my teaching. But what is truth?*
>
> *And what is self-justification? Why does it appear as if immodesty usually follows "truth"? I hope that you are not offended by the immodesty. I didn't find a better way to prepare you for what I want to communicate. I was unable to summarize the antecedents without, I'm fearful, giving the impression that my friends and anyone I admire are the best and the most talented. If these words appear that way to you, forgive me and please understand that it is no more possible to be objective about one's work than about one's values. (Blatt, 1975b, p. 393)*

Across America, from megalopolis to small hamlets, there are children who live in precarious circumstances, constantly on the fringe of normal society and on the verge of being excluded from it. These children represent a focal point for troubled families who exist on the brink of disaster. These children are, in the truest sense, "clinically homeless"; that is, they are unable to gain admission to educational, recreational, training, therapeutic, or other programs designed to enhance human growth and development—programs that should be available to *all* children. The "clinically homeless" are not only denied admission to special programs, but are virtually denied access to *all* programs. For most of these children, institutionalization is not an alternative but the *only* available, albeit poor, resource. That is, there is either the institution or the "nothingness" of a desperate home, burdened by an indescribable problem and with no prospect for community help or, even, concern.

Our essential problem is to develop new and enlarged community commitments on behalf of *all* children and, thus, on behalf of children with extraordinary needs, the "clinically homeless." We propose, through a community-based child advocacy program, to improve and extend existing service networks for children and, consequently, to foster an atmosphere of "normalization" for all children. Our purpose is to so infuse the greater Syracuse area with service and program alternatives, and so foster the development of new commitments and missions, that the extraordinary child may have better opportunities for "normalization" than in the past. The pervasive problem to which we have devoted ourselves is the development of humane and enriching environments for all people.

The central objective of this effort is to develop a community-based advocacy program on behalf of the target group. With the improvement of both quality and availability of community services for all children—and the creation of highly specialized services for children with extraordinary needs—it is expected that (a) a significant number of the "clinically homeless" will not require referral and placement in residential hospitals and training schools, and (b) another substantial group will be returned from institutions to their homes or other community residential settings such as foster homes, group-care homes, halfway homes, and hostels. In short, this work aims to obviate the need for institutional care by creating community alternatives such as group homes and recreational and educational programs.

It is our further objective to contribute to the improvement of legal-social protection and guarantees for *all* children to receive access to human resources needed to facilitate their optimal development.

The term *advocacy* has been assigned many meanings over the past few years. Perhaps because of its overuse, it is a term which invites misunderstandings. When we speak of advocacy, we must answer the questions "advocacy for what?" and "advocacy for whom?" Our own understanding of the word derives from the problem we have just described. By *advocacy* we mean a system of change that will alter the current patterns of services to children. We mean specific strategies whereby the people who suffer or endure the injustices and inadequacies of social services can begin to formulate solutions to their own problems. We envision a system where agencies will work *with* clients rather than *for* clients.

It is our mission to create a new atmosphere of community service in which all children can find adequate and appropriate services in normalized settings and where no one is either completely ignored or shunted off to inappropriate or inferior settings. Part of the problem we seek to solve stems from well intentioned, albeit inappropriate, efforts in the past to serve a particular group or type of children (unpublished proposal for Child Advocacy Program, February, 1971, pp. 1-2; 6; 15-16).

We were about to begin a new phase in our efforts to help to "normalize" society. For two years, we sponsored workshops on human abuse, protection, and public policy. We studied state programs as well as regional and local programs designed to deliver services to children and adults with special needs. On modest levels, we even designed and implemented services that we maintained responsibility for, e.g., the halfway house for ex-residents of the Syracuse Developmental Center, staffed by our students and faculty.

These activities—research, training and, especially, service—had led in 1971 to the creation of a Center on Human Policy, devoted to the study and promotion of open settings. This Center remains today a reality. It had been supported by the United States Department of Health, Education and Welfare, the New York State Departments of Education and Mental Hygiene, and voluntary and public agencies in the Greater Syracuse area and Syracuse University. Today, a group of university students and professors, as well as a network of community consumer and professional participants, continue to engage in service programs, training activities, and research on behalf of those who are now considered "high risks" for institutionalization or other types of segregated placements. [Of course, outside fiscal sponsorship continues, but the agencies involved have changed from time to time.]

It is our earnest hope that a subsequent book will be able to claim . . . that Man can change, that capability is educable, that institutions are reflections of society's stupidity, not of a man's mental retardation, that if the world is to change—if our thinking is to improve—then I must change.

I contribute to whatever Mankind is (Blatt, 1973, p. 453).

Massachusetts Study

On January 1, 1970, a team appointed by the Massachusetts Advisory Council on Education embarked upon a study of handicapped and disadvantaged children in the Commonwealth. This study—one that has taxed our intellectual resources and ingenuity—embraced three major foci: (1) the identification and description of those children who are known to have special needs, but are not being served by "official" agencies, (2) descriptions of life in classrooms, institutions, and other special settings for the handicapped, and (3) the development of programs, recommendations and legislative proposals leading to a preliminary master plan designed to bring into more workable and useful juxtaposition our current capability for delivering services and the need for the modification, improvement, and extension of such services.

Well meaning, concerned, humanistic people may be tempted to turn away from the challenge presented by the data and conclusions of this report. The temptation is to view each difficulty, each layer of ambiguity and confusion heaped upon the years of neglect and unconcern as evidence that little has been accomplished and that the past is a reflection of the future. On behalf of those who have no opportunity to advocate for themselves, we must move ahead in a meaningful and effective manner.

When one is forced to review the data in this report, can he deny that we have shamefully labeled and stigmatized children (and their families)? Ironically, and to our despair, the labels have each led to the embodiment of prejudice rather than better programs. We have learned that labeling "for no purpose" does little more than manufacture outcasts. Now, we must learn how to delabel, how to remove from statutes the stigma of once moral and humanistic, but now pejorative and harmful, terms. We must learn how to guarantee fair and comparable programs and service for *all* children, including those with special needs! We must develop more uniform funding principles, more viable incentives for accomplishing humanistic objectives, and firmer guarantees. Those who are least able to support programs for children with special needs must be recognized and considered by authors of legislative programs and by those who make decisions for implementation. We must find ways for children to remain at home with their families rather than being placed in institutional settings, and for *all* children, regardless of age or economic circumstance, to be guaranteed the education, training, and/or treatment that each requires to realize his potential. We must discover systems of interagency communication, for coordination of services on behalf of all children, and for effectively utilizing the scarce resources available in the Commonwealth. Possibly, for the first time in the history of this, or any other, society we have an opportunity to design an administrative, programmatic and humanistic system that will guarantee each child (and his family): (1) an adequate and helpful assessment of his needs, (2) an assessment based on potential rather than on deviancy and pathology, and (3) procedures for "due process" that are embedded not only in law, but in the moral convictions of those who uphold the law. We must recognize that public servants and agencies *must* be held accountable. We must guarantee to each citizen the eventual creation and support of an agency to serve all children with special needs (Blatt, 1971a, pp. 1; 41–42).

> *What was the "promise" that special education was to keep? It was to demonstrate to all people, and especially to those of us most intimately involved, that each person can contribute to the larger society; that all people are equally valuable; that a human being is entitled to developmental opportunities; and that development is plastic. We have been faithful; we have supported humanistic precepts and philosophies, and we have believed*

*that there is "enrichment through difference." Thus the promise of special
education has always been, and remains today, not a special curriculum, or
special methods, or even special teachers. The gifts that this movement was to
endow us with were the gifts of optimism and belief in the human ethos;
charity and love for our brothers; and the conviction that our work is not to
judge who can or cannot change but rather to fulfill the prophecy that all
people can change; each person can learn. For the promise to be kept, for
these things to occur beyond wish or fantasy, one must begin with oneself.
Before I ask the world to change, I must change. I am the beginning step.
(Blatt, 1975b, p. 399)*

Confrontation and Inspiration

One summer day in 1971, I took a telephone call from a Philadelphia lawyer, Tom Gilhool. I had heard about the Pennsylvania Association for Retarded Citizens (PARC) litigation but, frankly, knew very little of its substance, except that Gunnar Dybwad was involved and, if for no other reason, that made it interesting to me. Exactly one month later, several things impressed me: the impenetrableness of the team of judges, the intimidating nature of the courtroom itself, and the imperturbability of "my" attorney, Gilhool. I think I would have made a complete shambles of my testimony had it not been for an encouraging and receptive face in the courtroom, that of Ignacy Goldberg, a distinguished educator now retired from Teachers College, Columbia University. Knowing he was there, having the support of Gunnar Dybwad, and seeing some other friendly faces permitted me to think a bit more clearly about the questions and, possibly, a bit more thoughtfully about my responses; and then it was over (Blatt, 1975c, p. 470).

*Man spends his lifetime in thinking, speaking, and doing—the singular
objective of which is self-justification. (Blatt, 1973, p. 4, reflecting on the
philosophy of Cesare Parese, who once wrote that man's great work in life is
to justify himself.)*

In the state school, death is the final recourse and solution. In the finest tradition of the social scientist—and with interests similar to those of John Carver, Edgerton, Goffman, and Vail—the authors, Benjamin and Dorothy Braginsky, enter into the controversy between general developmental theorists and defect theorists and they conclude that the mildly mentally retarded are, essentially, normal unwanted people. Brilliantly, they examine the metaphor "mental retardation" in a way that will gladden Tom Szasz (although, unfortunately, their conclusions may cause him to be very sad indeed). The Braginskys discuss the mentally retarded as an administratively designated subset of people who function at an arbitrarily determined subnormal level. That is, they question the integrity of the concept "mental retardation," the assumption that the symptom of a low intelligence quotient categorically denotes an underlying condition of mental retardation. They will cause the reader to ask whether "mental retardation" is little more than an administrative label, whether it has any scientific integrity, whether "mental retardation" is not only an invention of Man's, but a creation of his fantasy and political, rather than his scientific self (Blatt, 1972a, p. 246).

Tom Szasz once said to me that, if I want to learn about psychiatry, I should not read Freud but rather Mark Twain and Dostoevsky. For whatever reason one has, read Szasz. In a way, and playing on one of Szasz's chapter titles, he is psychiatry's hope, *just because he is the internal enemy*, and because psychiatry is its own enemy and, apparently, only Szasz truly understands this (Blatt, 1972b, p. 75).

Tom Szasz disputes the wisdom of Rousseau's famous aphorism, "Man is born free, and everywhere he is in chains." Szasz concludes "if freedom is the ability to make uncoerced choices, then man is born in chains. And the challenge of his life is liberation" (*Ideology and Insanity*, New York: Anchor Books, 1970, p. 1).

I stand with Rousseau, while in sympathy with Szasz. Man is never so free spiritually, and so enchained physically, as during prenatal life and infancy. Even before its severing, the umbilical cord represents both physical dependency and the most intimate interrelatedness. It is not possible for the expectant mother to deprive her unborn child. It is not possible for the totality of that unborn child's universe to ignore or coerce him. He is enchained; yet, he is free. Although with ease he can be destroyed, his spirit will not be contained.

Man is born a human and free spirit. As he lives, and as life overwhelms and envelops him, basic anxiety accrues. Neuroticisms beget neuroticisms, and these beget disabilities, and these beget handicaps.

If freedom is in the mind and in the soul, then a man in fetters may be as free as he whose castle is his prison (Blatt, 1973, p. 405).

The American Association on Mental Deficiency

What is the promise for people? What are we, and what must we become? We have seen the views of monoliths from behind windows to nothing and we are not pleased. Therefore, we wonder what our people have become—and what we must now do. The answer is as plain as it is complicated, clear as it is opaque.

We must create an organization that earlier reformers, were they here today, would join. We must unite, not about specific task orientations but about powerful ideologies, not about special means but about a consensus of humanistic ends, not about silly slogans thoughtlessly chanted but about the infinite perspectives of a complex dilemma. We must describe and understand the subtle as well as the flagrant, ennui as well as flailing arms and diffuse excrement, and pandemonium as an extension of the best-managed "model" institution. We must act as if Itard, Howe, Dorothea Dix, Helen Keller, and Emil Kraepelin are our judges. (Blatt, 1975b, p. 420)

In June, 1976, I began a year as the president of the American Association on Mental Deficiency. I did what most AAMD presidents do: participate on several regional and state programs, answer and make many telephone calls, write lots of letters, and attend meetings. Out of that came some good, hopefully, and some bad, probably, the latter to be left to your knowledge or imagination.

Certain events during this past year have convinced me that a major socially incorruptable and politically unimpeachable voice is needed in our field. The American Association on Mental Deficiency can be that voice. I truly believe that AAMD could do no greater good for society than to choose that sometimes unappreciated role. More than ever before, there must be a group around who can be counted on to try to tell the truth, not to always be right but to be always honest. There must be a group around that is smart enough to know that believing in anything in this ambiguous world is dangerous and can be foolish, while it has character enough to nevertheless hold principles that it lives by.

AAMD should be the voice that can be trusted. But if we accept that role, we must earn that lofty but burdensome position (Unpublished abridged report to the Council, AAMD, May 1977).

The burden of that honesty was mine when I presented my presidential address to AAMD in May, 1977. The address which follows also included a slide show—a family album created with Andrejs Ozolins and Joe McNally approximately a decade after *Christmas in Purgatory.*

This presentation is an indiscretion, and there are many who will be angry with us for committing it because no family likes its sordid side brought into public view. The sordid side of ordinary families can remain hidden—to reveal it is often even more sordid. But there are other kinds of family— families like The Pentagon or the Nixon-White House. To reveal their secrets can sometimes become not just permissible, but necessary. A family of this latter kind is the large group of men and women who have by self-deception succeeded in preventing thousands of mentally retarded people from participating in the entitlements of their citizenship.

The Family knows things that we haven't been telling the world about. Important things, more important than the Pentagon Papers, which were about senseless war and unnatural deaths.

And, who is this Family? It is all of those who work, or say they work, with the problems of retarded people in institutionalized settings. It is the supervisors and superintendents and commissioners. It is the professional societies such as the American Association on Mental Deficiency and the Council for Exceptional Children. The Family includes government agencies such as the National Institute on Mental Health and the Office of Education, even groups like the Associations for Retarded Citizens. From the attendants who show up for an impossible job every day, to prestigious professionals who often don't show up at all, the family consists of everyone who should know better than to permit that hidden world to continue. And the academic community, which legitimates it all by issuing so-called credentials and generating so-called expertise is also part of the Family. Many of you, our audience, are probably members, as are two of the three of us who worked on this study.

In spite of professed intentions, and ideals, and commitments to reform, The Family has acted to preserve the most abhorrent abuse of human beings. To some extent this has been done through concealment and secrecy. Ten years ago, one could visit institutions only by stealth or arm-twisting or string-pulling; ten years ago the only photographs we could get had to be taken with a concealed camera. The barricades of rules and restrictions are less formidable today, but they still exist. Institutions are still hard to get into, and taking photographs is still very difficult for anyone and next to impossible for most people. And, the Family does not want to see publicized pictures finally obtained.

But more impenetrable and sinister than overt secrecy is the misleading publicity with which the Family defends its dominions. The hypnotic language of humanitarian concern encapsulates the victims of institutionalization and seals their world off from examination or understanding or hope. We are used to condemning this kind of practice when we discover it somewhere else: If the Soviet Union locks up political dissidents in psychiatric hospitals on the pretext of looking after their mental health, we are quick enough to protest. Yet, in our own institutions for retarded people, thousands of Americans continue to be locked up on the pretext of receiving care, training and education, and we continue to speak as though the pretext were reality; we call for more money and resources to implement the pretext rather than confess it was all a terrible mistake.

If there is hope in what we have learned in our examination of institutionalization, it is not in any improvement of institutional life—imprisonment and segregation can be made more comfortable, but they can never be made into freedom or participation. The only hopeful sign is that, while ten years ago and for generations before, those institutions were run by one happy family; today they are run by one unhappy family. If it must become unhappier still before it changes its ways, then we are willing to contribute to The Family's unhappiness with our report.

As we did 10 years ago, we have revealed some of America's papers, a Family's papers. We feel no guilt, because we show you papers from the guardians of a closed society which professes that any decent society should be open. As you will see, everything has changed during the decade between Purgatory and today. As you will see, nothing is changed (Blatt, 1977c, pp 3-4).

Head Start Study

What are the consequences of unitary approaches to complex problems? What results from a system that has forgotten the difference between special education and special class? What is the price society must pay for a contemporary system that has too little vision and a fragile optimism, where the only hope is to expect a future that is little more than a larger mass of the past? (Blatt, 1975b, p. 398)

In an age of national criticism it would be easy to lose sight of significant gains registered by public education over the past decade. Two of the advances recorded—the trend toward preschool programs and the right to education for all children—have found meaningful convergence in the 1972 Amendments to the Economic Opportunity Act. This mandate required that not less than 10% of the Head Start enrollment opportunities nationwide be made available to handicapped children (Public Law 94–424, 1972).

Since the inception of Head Start, the Office of Economic Opportunity (OEO) and the Office of Child Development (OCD) have sought to serve a heterogeneous population of children, principally drawn from the socio-economic "have nots" of American society. Deliberate efforts have been made to meet the developmental needs of disadvantaged children irrespective of intelligence, physical condition, emotional stability, or language development. In the face of such conviction, it is puzzling that Head Start has, to a large degree, neglected the seriously disabled child (Ensher, Blatt, & Winschel, 1977, p. 202).

Based on our research, we made the following recommendations for change in policy:

1. The requirement that not less than 10% of the enrollment opportunities in Head Start be made available to handicapped children should be reevaluated. This portion of the mandate has resulted in the labeling of some youngsters with minimal deficits, while others with more serious impairments have remained unserved. Whether the legislation was intended for all degrees of handicapping conditions (mild, moderate, and severe) or specifically intended to bring services to the severely involved is a matter requiring clarification. Regardless, it should remain the goal of OCD and its agencies to significantly increase the participation of moderately and severely handicapped children in regular Head Start programs.

2. Head Start programs should emphasize the identification and recruitment of severely and multiply handicapped children. A percentage requirement, if maintained, may be most appropriate to this group. National consultants to this investigation suggested a figure between 3% and 5%. Head Start must take an unequivocal stand against the exclusion of children as justified by the severity of their handicaps.

3. The organization of segregated settings is anathema to the long-term interests of handicapped children and must be prohibited. Even short-term exceptions should be viewed as preludes to permanent segregation.

4. To promote greater inclusion of severely impaired children in Head Start programs, major strategies should be developed for collaboration with related community agencies and public schools. Intercommunity cooperation is the cornerstone of responsible recruitment, treatment and the continuity of services once begun.

5. Parents must be involved in policy development and implementation as full partners in the decision making process. It is not that parents are more worldly, or wise, or trustworthy than professionals, but rather that parents have different agendas and different needs and therefore must be heard.

6. Additional staff and resources should be made available to those programs serving appreciable numbers of the moderately and severely handicapped. Personnel specifically trained to work with these children should do so within integrated settings. Teachers with special abilities—like children with special problems—are in need of the normalcy of typical teaching-learning environments.

7. Teachers with strong backgrounds in child development and clinical teaching may best serve the young handicapped child. Inservice training should emphasize the normalizing aspects of early childhood programs and minimize both the pathologies of handicapped children and the general deficit orientation of typical special education approaches.

8. Local Head Start programs should receive more technical assistance and professional consultation related to services for the handicapped. The professed inadequacy of training and assistance was a recurring theme throughout this investigation.

9. To provide data on the costs of services to handicapped children, a cost accounting procedure should be designed and implemented with a representative sample of Head Start programs. The results of such study should be incorporated into OCD guidelines covering permissible services and the range of expected costs. These guidelines would better enable local units to draw funds, deliver services, and document expenditures in a fiscally responsible manner.

10. With leadership from OCD and the Bureau for Education of the Handicapped (BEH), a national plan should be developed to infuse the public with the concept of child variance as a natural aspect of the human condition and seldom indicative of the need to separate, segregate, or exclude.

The Head Start movement is a promising force in the continued struggle against the segregation of the weak, the disadvantaged, and the handicapped. Unfortunately, its potential for serving handicapped children has not yet been sufficiently challenged (Ensher, Blatt, & Winschel, 1977, p. 209).

MORE EXPLANATION

I don't seem to tire of explaining myself. Even while I fight the continuous battle with those three universal human traits—self-justification, a sense of embarrassment, and a need for privacy—I set down on paper these recollections and thoughts about my life. (Blatt, 1975b, p. 391)

On March 31, 1969, I saw, finally, the film *Titicut Follies*. I was in New York City for a meeting of the American Orthopsychiatric Association.

Through the kindness of several people who had access to the film and were responsible for its showing to the Association membership, I was privileged to see it at a private screening held for two or three people who were preparing for public discussion of the film to be held two or three days later. I wish to state publicly—for whatever it may be worth—that I believe that Frederick Wiseman is a cinematic genius[2] and that this film, *Titicut Follies,* will live in history alongside such documents as Dorothea Dix's Address to the Massachusetts Legislature, the original work of Clifford Beers, and the contributions of such men as Albert Deutsch, Emil Kraepelin, and Upton Sinclair.

The important judgment about that film, the important morality that should be discussed and debated, the important issues that have been set before us, the important human needs and values that the film illustrates are related to the things that are happening (and why they are happening) at Bridgewater State Hospital and not to the idiosyncratic world of Frederick Wiseman— however beautiful or mendacious his life and world are.

I don't give a damn about Frederick Wiseman or his manners and morals. If his film is an accurate portrayal of life at Bridgewater—which I have every reason to believe it is—then our energies and efforts should be dedicated to the reformation of Bridgewater, not Mr. Wiseman. If his soul is damaged or defective, I am certain that civilization can entrust its repair to whatever resources Mr. Wiseman can bring to this need. There is still a home, a church, a self to deal with one's moral and spiritual character. Organized civilization must concern itself with the issues in the film, not with the mind or the heart of the film maker. Kurt Vonnegut once said that people are exactly what they pretend to be. Therefore, each of us must be terribly careful about what we pretend to be. Wiseman is a remarkable man and it is hoped that others have learned with us why and how such people become remarkable (Blatt, 1970a, pp. 249-251).

Our large, traditional institutions should be evacuated as speedily as possible. They neither help people, nor are they necessary; they persist only because they serve magnificently that portion of our society who are responsible for the creation and maintenance of human slot fillers, wherever they are and for whomever they are (Blatt, 1975b, pp. 416-417).

There is an urge that we seem to have to segregate while we engage ourselves in a constant flirtation between order and disaster, humanism and barbarism, love and hate. Little wonder that we have lost sight of the distinction between human privileges and human rights (Blatt, 1975b, p. 419).

Why this discrepancy between what we know and what we do? Why the back wards of state institutions? Why have we moved so grudgingly from Dorothea Dix to the twentieth century? Why do we, in the United States, know more about and do less for disabled people than other Western cultures? Are

---

[2]As I complete the final editing of this work, word is received that indeed, Wiseman has been "officially" designated as "genius"—one of nineteen announced on July 14, 1982, to receive the John D. and Catherine MacArthur Foundation Award to "exceptionally talented" people.

we, in fact, a nation devoted to our young and our vulnerable? We speak as if we are; our proclamations are frequent and strident.

We must think seriously about the notion that we are not a "child-centered society," that we use this term in an unexamined way. On the evidence of too many reports, I am forced to consider the possibility that we never had a child-centered society. We are for children to the degree that children are for us; but first, and sometimes only, in this adult-centered society, each person is for himself. At least, one would be hard put to find sufficient evidence to reject this characterization of us—not of "them" or even of "you," but of *us*.

While I wait for a better world, I reflect on those days of our youth and callowness when we thought that, if people only would "understand," mental retardation would be prevented. But while I wait, I must change. While I wait for the millenium, I painfully record our human frailties, our inabilities to face life for whatever it is and for whatever it had to offer, and I must, in spite of its vicissitudes and the unfairness of it all, respect living as the one thing we have in common; for better or worse, it is all we have to stay alive. And, if your retarded child is all you have, that child is part of the reality of your life. That human being is part of the enrichment of your life. Without her, your life would be less full, and you would have fewer opportunities to learn, and contribute, and love. She owns part of your world, as you must own part of hers.

And I, too, own a part of my family, a part of the university, a part of society, a part of the total "action." I, too, must think and do, not only for others, but for myself. But what I must do most urgently is change. For the world to change, I must change. If I blame an evil world, a stupid system, ineffective leaders, or man's obvious imperfections, I may be right. But if it means that I do not have to change, I contribute to the evil. Before we can change humanity, we must change ourselves. Before I attempt to solve the human puzzle, I must solve the riddle "I" (Blatt, 1975b, p. 419).

Segregation is *always* more expensive than integration, both in terms of real dollars and for the preservation and enhancement of human resources. It is also a fact that most people want to live with their families and friends in ordinary communities. Simply, those are the facts about the dollars and the politics of people.

And yet, we continue to construct enormously expensive institutions and schools for which some of us are willing to pay a high price to separate one brother from another. How far will we permit those with vested interests, unreasonable interests, not only to rob our pockets but also to erode our values and convictions concerning human beings, their capabilities, and our inter-relatedness?

And, what of politics? The politics are the people, and the will of the people should be felt, for then good may eventually be obtained. The people know of what the world is made and what a human life needs (Blatt, 1975a, p. 14).

The handicapped have always been a paradox to Americans. And in America, in this Land of Opportunity, they seem unable to seize opportunities. In the Land of the Free, they are enchained. In the Land of Plenty, they are in need. In America the Bountiful, they are treated meanly (Blatt, 1977a, p. 2).

There is nothing inherent in disability to produce handicap, i.e., a belief in one's incompetency. Further, it is not the primary responsibility of the behavioral sciences to determine the validity of the aforementioned statement, but to make it valid. We have supported far too many studies purporting to demonstrate differences between groups or the disorders of one child in contrast with another. All these years, we should have promoted and encouraged research that sought to make it come true that a child would learn after participation in a special program or curriculum (Blatt, 1977b, p. 24).

Basically, there is never a difference between people. That is, we will eventually understand that, as human beings, people are just people; and our shared heritage cuts through a veneer of potentially enriching variability which, although thin, causes us too much grief as one excludes the other from his "turf" and consciousness (Blatt, 1975b, p. 418).

Can a man, truly, have an equal chance for life and happiness if he is not guaranteed *some* equal results? Isn't *this* equal chance dependent upon *that* equal result? Can a man be said to have an equal chance to develop if you offer him a schoolhouse but no home, if you permit him to vote but guarantee him no means to learn, if you keep his body alive but overwhelm and destroy his spirit?

I believe that if, after countless millennia, mankind is unwilling to guarantee equal results, it is affirming its sufferance with equal chances. If this is the road man has taken and if this is the progress he has made, this faithless journey was not worthwhile (Blatt, 1970b, p. 10).

The process of teaching requires a kind of pedagogical artistry that may be stifled by the drudgery of too many thoughtless courses, mindless activities, and boring experiences. Therefore, while teachers should be given opportunities to explore and evaluate the basic pedagogical premises, theories, methodologies, and techniques that the literature and clinical experiences make available, equal attention should be directed to the creative needs teachers have for self-expression and the development of original teaching styles. As mentioned earlier, teachers in training should be given sufficient opportunities to struggle to understand *themselves* as learners. They should be given encouragement to develop their own—not imitative—styles of teaching and interacting. They should be given opportunities to become creators, not merely implementors, of educational environments. Insofar as the university is concerned, their major interests in teacher preparation should be the degree to which teacher creativity (not merely technical competency) is developed and enhanced.

Lastly, basic to this preparation should be a process of clinical involvement which permits the teacher to develop skills as an observer and interpreter of human behavior. Rather than a continuation of lifeless lecture courses or trivial and unrelated discussion groups, a significant portion of a university student's program might involve one in a psycho-educational experience which prepares a person to observe, to discover that what one sees and what one infers must be held separate or an already complex task becomes unmanageable. This clinical training may help to remedy the kind of "slot machine" education—normative teaching—that practically all children are continually exposed to and practically all teachers universally support.

We must engage in more deliberate efforts to promote scholarship for the sake of scholarship, and scholars for the sake of the university.

If it is going to satisfy us, the future for teacher education in the university is one *we in the university* must deal with, one that should not be left to the state department of education or those who prophesy economic or political pulls and fortunes. And, our future will unfold not only from what we do, but from how we think differently about the creation of environments that permit maximum freedom yet demand unusual responsibility (Blatt, 1974a, pp. 5-15).

Consequently, there is an apparent—and in a sense, real—flexibility and innovation to be found in our schools! We advertise segregated schools, open schools, free schools, and ungraded schools in the education supermarket for the same reasons others advertise Chevrolets, Keds, and Popsicles; we believe we have the best products or, at the very least, we wish to convince the consumer that our products offer the most value. As a result, our schools virtually have become franchised—duplicative in the same way General Motors and Howard Johnson's are duplicative—strengthened by our teacher's colleges, which have been educational supermarkets: "You don't have to (we know you can't) think independently; see all the goodies we offer, choose within this wide array, and consume to your satiation level, beyond if you wish; buy, but do not create, do not struggle to understand the process from the product, do not go beyond the boundaries of the marketplace; be different but do not be different from any of the rest of us, be a part of this wonderful educational slot-machine world."

What we need more of are child and teacher independence (thus, fostering their interdependence); learning towards greater generalizations, inductive models, options, and the maximization of heterogeneous groupings of people. What we need less of are mandated curricula, lonely teachers and children, segregated classes and schools—for whatever the reasons—consumerism to the discouragement of creativeness, and program consolidation.

In education, as we have indicated, the monolith is not the teacher's college, or the segregated class, or even the pedantic curriculum. The monolith is created and held together from the rubble of destroyed options, from the absence of not so much the bricks and structures of alternative educational designs (for these, too, have been known to victimize those who hold minority views), but from the absence of alternative thinking and values.

The franchised school and the educational supermarket—the fulcrum of the monolith—are the enemies of those who would seek an education for themselves, enemies not because of any deliberate wickedness but because they represent a limited view of human potential, of what the world can become, that the world is each person, not multiplied but singular, unique and valuable, and that each person can create to help himself and, possibly, to help others (Blatt, 1975b, pp. 411-412).

The question we have in special education is not: How are we going to get those "rotten teachers" to teach? What we have to ask is: How can people who have enjoyed the benefits of this country and have had education, who have done so many wonderful things—how can they turn away from including all children in their schools? How do we make the schools work? When the parents are told the truth, when the parents of the ordinary child learn the truth about the handicapped, they are going to open up the schools to these children. But you have got to go to those people, and you have got to talk with them—you have got to show them (Connor, Kirk, & Blatt, 1977a, p. 13).

The one thing about this Public Law 94-142 which makes it as important as any education law that has been passed in this country, is that the country has articulated what people deserve. We are no longer talking about institutions as the one option (which is no option). We are no longer talking about segregated programs as *the* program for the handicapped. We are talking about consumerism, about zero rejects, about least restrictive environments. That is the language of the day. It is only a matter of time before new programs, with their personnel and ideologies, are going to be the functional law of the land. There is no way we can stop until we complete this reform. Period. There is absolutely no way (Connor, Kirk, & Blatt, 1977b, p. 21).

Is mainstreaming a valid educational issue? I conclude that it is not! The program, the curriculum, the label, the organization—the most obvious components of education—are strangely irrelevant to the relationships we seek to understand. Those educational components which do matter—largely ignored in our research—are the teacher as a human being who teaches and learns, children as learners with potentials and rights, and the environment—rich, flexible and thoughtfully created. (At the same time, one senses the futility of segregation. The environments people need are more often obtainable and more easily created in the heterogeneous "normal world." But that is another debate.)

How far have we come in our ability to educate the child with special needs, the different individual? Would mainstreaming help our cause or harm it, or make no difference? With the wisdom and technology of our age, could we teach Helen Keller as Anne Sullivan did or instruct Victor as Jean Itard once taught that "wild savage"? And if we could, would we not also be marked in history as noble people, kin to those who have glorified human potential and honored the human traits of compassion and decency?

There was a uniqueness that marked the education of Helen Keller, Victor, and the innumerable others who dot the history of the special education profession. Was it a segregated program, the mainstream, a curriculum, "a something" codified and lawful that caused those people to learn and to change? It was not! There was a human spirit who sought an understanding with itself and with the finite world. And there was a great teacher. Inevitably, there was the interaction. That's what mattered (Winschel, Ensher & Blatt, 1976, p. 12).

We, in this culture, do not love all children. Some do not even love their own children. Merely, we have deluded ourselves in another love affair, a love of the idea that we should cherish the weak, the young, the feeble, the different. We must create ways to begin to understand and deal with what both misadventure and we have created (Blatt, 1974, p. 527).

YET MORE HISTORY, MORE EXPLANATION

During the past few years, I've written and talked so much about the most and least important aspects of the Syracuse University School of Education that I must work hard to neither parrot myself nor strain to say something different and distort what I believe. Now that I've confessed those worries, I'll add this confession that is sure to please some and annoy others: The most important aspects of our school are connected with the cultivation of research and scholarship in education. That's the concern, but why we engage in one area of investigation rather than another or why a professor writes a certain book rather than another has to do with the sense of urgency and concern felt here about the fate of this world. Therefore, perhaps I should say something about some of the ways in which the School of Education is responding within the academic tradition to contemporary challenges. We sponsor a number of important clinic and school programs in the larger community, some of these serving as primary community resources and a few so uniquely conceived and developed as to attract national interest. Current and past examples of such involvements include: an open integrated school for typical children as well as those with special needs; a public school on campus sponsored by our university and Syracuse City Schools, serving children whose needs are such that they require intensive individualized programs in a carefully designed special school environment, with the goal being to eventually return them to regular classes; a multi-disciplinary community program which includes a communicative disorders clinic, psycho-educational clinic, and a setting for infants with special needs (Blatt, 1977d, p. 3).

I came to Syracuse University in 1969 to succeed William Cruickshank as director of the Division of Special Education and Rehabilitation. As always seems to be the case in the eyes of the newcomer, there was a lot of rebuilding needed in special education and rehabilitation when I appeared on the scene. Not only had Cruickshank, one of the pioneers of our field, left to direct a research and training center at his alma mater, but several other distinguished professors in the division had either retired or resigned to pursue opportunities elsewhere. You may remember that the 1960s were a time when universities were growing faster than the capabilities of graduate schools to produce new professors and, consequently, if any decade could be labeled meaningfully, *that* period might have been characterized as the era of the "Academic Gypsy." With a lot of good luck and, possibly, a small amount of wisdom, within a few years we had recruited several outstanding professors and, furthermore, created in Special Education a Psycho-Education Clinic, an institute to train advocates, and the Center on Human Policy, a facility now nationally known for its work in organizing consumer groups and shaping policy on behalf of the handicapped.

During the same period, under the leadership of Dean David Krathwohl, the School of Education established several of the first and most effective teaching center programs in the United States, programs which, I'm pleased to report, continue to thrive. Also during the early 1970s, our program in Instructional Technology achieved its "emancipation" from the traditional concept of "audiovisual aids" and developed a much broader and scholarly graduate program in what we today call Instructional Design, Development and Evaluation.

I was invited to become dean of this School in 1976 and, while I can't speak for those I serve in this position, I never for a moment regret having accepted the opportunity that was handed me. Here again, the newcomer concluded that a great deal needed to be accomplished if this school was to survive the severe enrollment and budgetary problems which virtually every major graduate school of education in America has been suffering since the halcyon days of the 1960s. Of course, one of the things I felt was needed immediately was a reorganization of the school and the development of a clear statement of the school's mission. (Doesn't every new dean feel the need to reorganize the environment and clarify its goals?)

Well, we accomplished those tasks, and in the process we also were able to decentralize the school's operating budget, thus giving program directors greater responsibility in assigning and accounting for the scarce dollars available. Possibly because of the decentralization, which surely highlighted the direct link between resources and expenditures, but even more because of the cooperativeness and capabilities of our faculty, we made it our business to find external resources to keep our faculty up to full strength at a time when most schools of education were terminating significant numbers of their faculty and when more than a few schools of education were terminating all but their tenured faculty. With the support of our central administration and our success in quadrupling external funds for research and training, we have virtually as many faculty members in this School of Education as we had ten and fifteen years ago.

Has it all made a difference? How does one judge the excellence of a college? There are indicators: the quality of its students, the publications of its faculty members, the skills of its teachers, the school's attractiveness to external funding agencies, the size and quality of its research library, its reputation among similar schools. Today, our School of Education enjoys an excellent international reputation. Its one hundred faculty members have prepared themselves at the leading research universities here and abroad. Its 1,500 students come from virtually every state and most foreign nations. And many of its 9,000 graduate alumni and 5,000 undergraduate alumni are distinguished leaders in education and related fields. National surveys rank us among the outstanding graduate schools of education in the United States. And studies based on reputation reveal that at least a half dozen of our programs are regarded nationally as truly distinguished, and several others are ranked among the better ones in the country.

In surveying the past ten years, there are only three things that seem clear: we survived (the challenges); we prospered (by adapting); we will have to change again (through some synthesis).

We did survive, and that in itself is quite an achievement since some other schools of education didn't survive. What we survived was two waves of challenges. The first, spilling over from the 1960s, was a challenge to the way we viewed our world. From our serene, academic detachment, we were suddenly in the thick of social action. We had to learn, and learn quickly, how to work in the "real world," to have our priorities defined for us rather than by us, to confront teacher failures where we once saw pupil failures, to meet the charge of "irrelevance" by becoming involved in every aspect of our society.

The second challenge came a little later—the market dried up and our enrollment decreased. From a period when the only limit on our enrollment was our willingness to expand, we found ourselves unable to prevent a significant and steady attrition rate. Of course, as academic people, we like to think our attention should be on loftier things than money. But it became clear that unless we thought very seriously about the resources available to us, the lofty purposes would soon be thwarted.

Most of us are aware of the seriousness of this latter challenge to the vitality of the School of Education—especially because of the still darkening clouds in Washington. However, we should also appreciate, in a historical view, that the challenge of the 1960s too was dangerous in its way. We tend to identify that period of social involvement as one of affluence since we got plenty of tuition-bearing students and government at all levels was as generous as it was eager for our help. The problems which we had to address were serious and the risks in attempting solutions were far from purely "academic." But, we survived. And we survived both challenges in similar ways, by somehow making the right moves. To the social challenge, we not only adapted but took a lead in responsive educational innovation. The Teaching Centers, Center on Human Policy, clinics and practica were, especially in retrospect, the right answers at the time. Today, those responses seem almost "obvious," inevitable. But they weren't obvious, and our ability to hit upon them was evidence of a school with a thoughtful, scholarly faculty. And this same excellence came to bear on the challenge of enrollment declines. The faculty that had created the programs became one which could draw "soft money" to study those and other problems when money elsewhere was all but unobtainable. We adapted by becoming a much more predominantly graduate and research-oriented institution.

It should be clear that the story of this decade hasn't ended. We have not stopped the sort of imaginative and risky innovation with which we began to build our current reputation a decade ago. And we can't very well go on forever studying the processes and machinery of education without once again stepping out to test our conclusions in the real world. I don't know how well we have learned it, but surely the central lesson of this decade has been to expect change. What changes we will make, though, remains a question. "Will we make changes?" is even a question. I think we will—we always have—but . . . (Blatt, 1981, pp. 2-3).

AND ANOTHER APOLOGY

I write what I believe needs to be written and what I need to write; for better or worse, words are my therapy.

But I don't want my words to be wispy feathers, with wings of wind and fantasy.

I wanted this work to create rocks, strong matter that will build and be sustained.

I have a "mind's eye" picture of works that are peculiar to my métier and to my mission and to my listeners.

I hear words and rhythm that intrude into life, that have life because they try to be honest and plain.

No one should speak of this graceless prose, for they would not speak to my vision.

For my vision is not involvement in a prissy race to tell or to write, but to engage oneself—truly—in man's ideas.

My vision is to examine the soul, and the body, and the flesh, and our oneness.

I write for any reader who will chance it but, especially, I hope for a Wolfensberger now and then who has the kindness to judge a writer by his "best" words. I am grateful to Wolf Wolfensberger who understands so precisely that the end of my book did not end the horror, that the book's conclusion is nothing more than a technical break, that the madness will endure. Lastly, I am grateful that the reviewer saw through my apparent pessimism and found that, although some of my words are plotless,

Living itself is plotless,

While all lives are part of a Grand Design (Blatt, 1971b, p. 612).

Each of us was conceived less in reality than in hope. For each there must be a life more ambiguous than living. Yet, all know that the end will be less certain than was the beginning. Or this improbable journey. (Blatt, 1973, p. 249)

Piecing shards together can't result in a finished and smooth work. But isn't it true that not only potters but people too repeat themselves? And so much so that, from the rubble of a dig, something whole can be fashioned. People too are so consistent that, among dozens and dozens of seemingly discrete papers and books, a coherent story can emerge. One's life is a puzzle, but not because it can't be put together; more so because it can be put together in so many interesting and logical ways. And however different, each way— each story—can be true. To me, the puzzle is not in knowing what to do with the extra pieces. What puzzles me is that everything can make sense, every act has an antecedent, every occurrence a reason. How my students put together the first draft of these shards might have differed from how I would have done this job. But when it comes to figuring out what happened, while their guesses might not be the same as mine, I think their story is as good. After all, although I had the advantage of the firsthand experience, they enjoyed the luxury of taking distance. I believe there's is an honest reconstruction of what I've said about my more than thirty-five years in this calling. And I am exceedingly grateful to them for the time they took to examine what I had written for publication, and then reduce that mountain of verbiage to something more or less representative and readable. Speak about human abuse!

REFERENCES

Blatt, B. (1956). *The physical, personality, and academic status of children who are mentally retarded attending special classes as compared with children who are mentally retarded attending regular classes.* Ann Arbor, MI: University Microfilms.

Blatt, B. (1958). Physical, personality and academic status of children who are mentally retarded attending special classes as compared with children who are mentally retarded attending regular classes. *American Journal of Mental Deficiency, 62,* 810-815.

Blatt, B. (1963a). Hail the conquering dolphin: Reflections on the pre-service preparation of special class teachers. In *Perspectives in theory and practice.* Reston, VA: Council for Exceptional Children, NEA. [Also published in B. Blatt (Ed.). (1974). Mental retardation: Its consequence and treatment. *Journal of Education,* pp. 84-94.]

Blatt, B. (1963b). Some observations and questions concerning an unstudied problem in special education. *Training School Bulletin, 59,* 121-131.

Blatt, B. (1967). *The intellectually disfranchised: Impoverished learners and their teachers.* Boston, MA: Massachusetts Department of Mental Health, Community Mental Health Monograph Series.

Blatt, B. (1970a). *Exodus from pandemonium: Human abuse and a reformation of public policy.* Boston: Allyn & Bacon.

Blatt, B. (1970b). On the educability of intelligence. *Syracuse Scanner, 15,* 7; 10.

Blatt, B. (Project Director). (1971a, January). *Massachusetts study of educational*

opportunities for handicapped and disadvantaged children. Boston:
Massachusetts Advisory Council on Education.

Blatt, B. (1971b). [Response to review of *Exodus from Pandemonium: Human Abuse and a Reformation of Public Policy*]. *Exceptional Children, 37,* 612.

Blatt, B. (1972a). [Review of *Hansels and Gretels: Studies of children in institutions for the mentally retarded,* by Braginsky & Braginsky]. *American Journal of Mental Deficiency, 77,* 245–247.

Blatt, B. (1972b). [Review of *The manufacture of madness,* by T. Szasz.] *Exceptional Children, 39,* 72–75.

Blatt, B. (1973). *Souls in extremis: An anthology on victims and victimizers.* Boston: Allyn & Bacon.

Blatt, B. (1974a). Public education and the university. *Journal of Education, 156,* 5–15. (Also published in *Family Involvement,* 1975, *8,* 19–25.)

Blatt, B. (1974b). [Review of *Alfred Binet* by Wolf] *Exceptional Children, 41,* 63–65.

Blatt, B. (1974c). [Review of *Something's wrong with my child* by Brutten, Richardson & Mangel] *Exceptional Children, 40,* 525–527.

Blatt, B. (1975a). The integration-segregation issue: Some questions, assumptions, and facts. *Family Involvement, 8,* 10–14.

Blatt, B. (1975b). Toward an understanding of people with special needs. In J. M. Kauffman & J. S. Payne (Eds.), *Mental retardation: Introduction and personal perspectives.* Columbus, OH: Charles E. Merrill.

Blatt, B. (1975c). [Review of *Right to education,* by L. Lippman & I. Goldberg] *American Journal of Mental Deficiency, 79,* 470–471.

Blatt, B. (1975d). The nine pillars of mental retardation. *Family Involvement, 8,* 2–10. (Also published in J. P. Collins & J. Mercurio (Eds.), *Meeting the special needs of students in regular classrooms.* Syracuse, NY: National Consortium of Competency-Based Education Centers, 1977.)

Blatt, B. (1977a). On the Bill of Rights and related matters. In R. Heinich & S. C. Ashcroft (Eds.), *Instructional technology and P.L. 94-142.* Columbus, OH: National Center on Educational Media and Materials for the Handicapped, Ohio State University.

Blatt, B. (1977b). Curriculum and methods research in special education. *Family Involvement, 9,* 19–25.

Blatt, B. (1977c, October). The family album (Summary of AAMD Presidential Address). *Mental Retardation, 15* (5), 3–4. (Also published in *Arise,* March 1978, pp. 13–14; and *The MARC,* Maryland Association for Retarded Citizens, Spring 1978, pp. 4–5.)

Blatt, B. (1977d, November 2). Tradition and the contemporary challenge. Syracuse University *Daily Orange,* November 2, 1977, p. 3.

Blatt, B. (1981, November). On the recent history of the School of Education. *Education Exchange,* Syracuse University School of Education, pp. 2–3.

Blatt, B. (1982). *In and out of the university: Essays on higher and special education.* Baltimore: University Park Press.

Blatt, B., & Garfunkel, F. (1967). Educating intelligence: Determinants of school behavior of disadvantaged children. *Exceptional Children, 33,* 601–608. [Also published in F. Warner & R. Thrapp (Eds.). (1971). *Reading in controversial issues in education of the mentally retarded.* New York: MSS Educational Publishing.]

Blatt, B., & Kaplan, F. (1966). *Christmas in purgatory: A photographic essay on mental retardation* (2nd ed.). Boston: Allyn & Bacon. (Also published in Syracuse, NY: Human Policy Press, 1974, 3rd ed.)

Blatt, B. with Mangel C. (1967). The tragedy and hope of retarded children. *Look, 31*, 96-103. [Also published in S. S. Brown (Ed.). (1970). *Topics in child psychology.* MSS Educational Publishing Co. in F. Warner & R. Thrapp (Eds.). (1971). *Readings in controversial issues in education of the mentally retarded.* MSS Educational Publishing Co.; and in S. Brown (Ed.). (1976). *Exercises in child and adolescent psychology.* Dubuque, IA: Kendall Hunt.]

Blatt, B., Ozolins, A., & McNally, J. (1978). *The family album: Views of residential settings for mentally retarded people.* [Slides-tape] Syracuse, NY: Human Policy Press.

Blatt, B., et al. (1971, February). *A proposal for a child advocacy program.* Unpublished manuscript, Syracuse University, School of Education, Syracuse, NY.

Connor, F., Kirk, S., & Blatt, B. (1977a, August). Special education yesterday, today and tomorrow. *Exceptional Parent, 7,* 9-14.

Connor, F., Kirk, S., & Blatt, B. (1977b, October). Special education yesterday, today and tomorrow: Part two. *Exceptional Parent, 7,* 16-21.

Ensher, G., Blatt, B., & Winschel, J. (1977c). Head start for the handicapped: Congressional mandate audit. *Exceptional Children, 43,* 202-210.

Hungerford, R. H. (1946). Peace on earth. *Occupational Education, 4*(3), 49-51.

Hungerford, R. H. (1949). On Brotherhood. *Occupational Education 6*(6), 125-130.

Hungerford, R. H. (1950). On locusts. *American Journal of Mental Deficiency, 54*(4), 415-418.

Sarason, S. B., Davidson, K., & Blatt, B. (1962). *The preparation of teachers: An unstudied problem in education.* New York: John Wiley and Sons.

Szasz, T. (1970). *Ideology and Insanity.* New York: Anchor Books.

Winschel, J., Ensher, G., & Blatt, B. (1976). Mainstreaming for the mildly retarded: Three views. *The Exceptional Parent, 6,* 6-12. Section B. Blatt also published as "Mainstreaming: Does it matter," in J. W. Schifani (Ed.). (1977). *Perspectives and resources for mainstreaming exceptional persons.* Dubuque, IA: Kendall Hunt.

About The Editors

Burton Blatt is Dean of the School of Education at Syracuse University, where he previously served as director of the Division of Special Education and Rehabilitation. In 1970 he was named as one of six Centennial Professors at Syracuse University. The recipient of many awards and honors, Dr. Blatt has served as a consultant for federal and state agencies, has lectured frequently throughout the United States, and has written and edited numerous books, reports, and articles in the field of special education.

Richard J. Morris is Professor of Educational Psychology and Director of the Children's Psychoeducational Services Clinic, College of Education, at the University of Arizona. His most recent authored and co-edited books are: *Treating Children's Fears and Phobias: A Behavioral Approach,* and *The Practice of Child Therapy,* co-authored and co-edited, respectively with Thomas R. Kratochwill. He is also the author of other books on intervention strategies with handicapped children.

Index